Motorcycle Workshop Practice Techbook

by John Fidell and Pete Shoemark

(3470-224-4Z1)

© Haynes Publishing 2000

A book in the **Haynes Techbook Series**

ISBN 978 1 78521 376 2

British Library Cataloguing in Publication Data
A catalogue record for this book is available from the British Library

Library of Congress Catalog Card Number 98-70328

Printed in Malaysia

Haynes Publishing
Sparkford, Nr Yeovil, Somerset, BA22 7JJ, England

Haynes North America, Inc
859 Lawrence Drive, Newbury Park, California 91320, USA

Printed using NORBRITE BOOK 48.8gsm (CODE: 40N6533) from NORPAC; procurement system certified under Sustainable Forestry Initiative standard. Paper produced is certified to the SFI Certified Fiber Sourcing Standard (CERT - 0094271)

0•2 Contents

Intended more as a reference book rather than one to read from beginning to end, this manual is intended to cover all equipment needed and tasks likely to be undertaken by the DIY motorcycle mechanic. With the experience and confidence gained by servicing and repairing their own machines, most motorcyclists will venture on to more complicated repair and overhaul operations, requiring advice on the different repair methods and techniques available. Note that this manual does not take the place of a model-specific workshop manual, which is still needed for specifications and procedures relating to your particular make and model of motorcycle.

Much of this manual is devoted to common and specialist tools likely to be needed by the motorcyclist. Tool selection and usage is fully covered and advice given on building up a comprehensive tool kit which will deal with most jobs. In addition to those items which may be bought from a tool supplier, the manual also covers the use of improvised and home-made tools.

Materials used in manufacture and repair are discussed at length and details given of their applications and properties. Equally the manual covers the wide range of chemical compounds which are used as thread retainers, sealants, adhesives and solvents. Fuels and lubricant types and applications are also explained in detail.

The inclusion of a chapter on powered and machine tools reflects the increased availability of this type of equipment. Instruction on the use of the equipment is not within the scope of this manual, however examples are given to show the range of work which may be undertaken. Machine tools are particularly useful if you are restoring a classic motorcycle or making parts for a custom bike.

One important point for any mechanic is when to ask for help and professional assistance. This manual should help in understanding what is required when seeking professional advice and contracting for the supply of parts or materials.

Throughout this manual, the importance of working safely is impressed upon you.

This is especially true when using powered tools and certain chemicals. Note that workshop safety applies not just to yourself, but also any visitors to your workshop. Safe working practice is sound workshop practice and both will enable you to get pleasure from carrying out jobs and improve your skills.

Never be afraid to ask for professional help if you are limited by lack of workshop equipment or knowledge. Even if you have to contract out a particular job, there will be some saving by doing much of the preparation yourself and providing exact details of specification.

Note that the text in each chapter is arranged in numbered section order and will correspond with the contents list at the beginning of each chapter. If a section in another chapter is referred to, a typical instruction 'see Chapter 4, Section 8' will be found. All illustrations, are keyed into the text with their section number and paragraph number, eg 3.2 refers to section three paragraph 2 in that Chapter.

Acknowledgements

Our thanks are due to all who have given assistance in the origination of this manual, particularly Bearing Services Ltd of Bath for bearing and seal information, Cooper-Avon Tyres Ltd for tyre information, the Cross Manufacturing Company (1938) Ltd for wire thread insert information, Duckhams Oils for advice on lubricants, European Industrial Services who supplied fastener information, Lumiweld UK who supplied the Lumiweld kit, John Morgan who supplied information on carburettor tuning equipment, Laser Devon for compressed gas information, Lucas Aftermarket Operations for brake fluid information, M & P Motorcycle Accessories and MPS Motorcycle Accessories for product information, Machine Mart provided information on workshop tools, Motad supplied information on aftermarket exhaust systems, NGK Spark Plugs Ltd provided spark plug information, Sealey Power Products supplied tool information and gave permission to reproduce certain illustrations, Shell UK Ltd supplied fuel and oil information, Tran Am Ltd provided chain information, and Yuasa supplied information on batteries

Thanks are also due to Tony Foot of TF Engineering Motorcycles and Nigel Carpenter of Carpenters Engineering Services for allowing us access to their workshops, and Paul Branson Motorcycles for providing some of the components featured in the photographs. Tony Tranter kindly allowed us to reproduce illustrations from his book, the *Motorcycle Electrical Manual* published by Haynes.

We are also grateful to Kawasaki Motors (UK) Ltd and Mitsui Machinery Sales (UK) Ltd for permission to reproduce their line drawings.

Professional mechanics are trained in safe working procedures. However enthusiastic you may be about getting on with the job at hand, take the time to ensure that your safety is not put at risk. A moment's lack of attention can result in an accident, as can failure to observe simple precautions.

There will always be new ways of having accidents, and the following is not a comprehensive list of all dangers; it is intended rather to make you aware of the risks and to encourage a safe approach to all work you carry out on your bike.

Asbestos

● Certain friction, insulating, sealing and other products - such as brake pads, clutch linings, gaskets, etc. - contain asbestos. Extreme care must be taken to avoid inhalation of dust from such products since it is hazardous to health. If in doubt, assume that they do contain asbestos.

Fire

● Remember at all times that petrol is highly flammable. Never smoke or have any kind of naked flame around, when working on the vehicle. But the risk does not end there - a spark caused by an electrical short-circuit, by two metal surfaces contacting each other, by careless use of tools, or even by static electricity built up in your body under certain conditions, can ignite petrol vapour, which in a confined space is highly explosive. Never use petrol as a cleaning solvent. Use an approved safety solvent.

● Always disconnect the battery earth terminal before working on any part of the fuel or electrical system, and never risk spilling fuel on to a hot engine or exhaust.

● It is recommended that a fire extinguisher of a type suitable for fuel and electrical fires is kept handy in the garage or workplace at all times. Never try to extinguish a fuel or electrical fire with water.

Fumes

● Certain fumes are highly toxic and can quickly cause unconsciousness and even death if inhaled to any extent. Petrol vapour comes into this category, as do the vapours from certain solvents such as trichloro-ethylene. Any draining or pouring of such volatile fluids should be done in a well ventilated area.

● When using cleaning fluids and solvents, read the instructions carefully. Never use materials from unmarked containers - they may give off poisonous vapours.

● Never run the engine of a motor vehicle in an enclosed space such as a garage. Exhaust fumes contain carbon monoxide which is extremely poisonous; if you need to run the engine, always do so in the open air or at least have the rear of the vehicle outside the workplace.

The battery

● Never cause a spark, or allow a naked light near the vehicle's battery. It will normally be giving off a certain amount of hydrogen gas, which is highly explosive.

● Always disconnect the battery ground (earth) terminal before working on the fuel or electrical systems (except where noted).

● If possible, loosen the filler plugs or cover when charging the battery from an external source. Do not charge at an excessive rate or the battery may burst.

● Take care when topping up, cleaning or carrying the battery. The acid electrolyte, evenwhen diluted, is very corrosive and should not be allowed to contact the eyes or skin. Always wear rubber gloves and goggles or a face shield. If you ever need to prepare electrolyte yourself, always add the acid slowly to the water; never add the water to the acid.

Electricity

● When using an electric power tool, inspection light etc., always ensure that the appliance is correctly connected to its plug and that, where necessary, it is properly grounded (earthed). Do not use such appliances in damp conditions and, again, beware of creating a spark or applying excessive heat in the vicinity of fuel or fuel vapour. Also ensure that the appliances meet national safety standards.

● A severe electric shock can result from touching certain parts of the electrical system, such as the spark plug wires (HT leads), when the engine is running or being cranked, particularly if components are damp or the insulation is defective. Where an electronic ignition system is used, the secondary (HT) voltage is much higher and could prove fatal.

Remember...

✗ **Don't** start the engine without first ascertaining that the transmission is in neutral.

✗ **Don't** suddenly remove the pressure cap from a hot cooling system - cover it with a cloth and release the pressure gradually first, or you may get scalded by escaping coolant.

✗ **Don't** attempt to drain oil until you are sure it has cooled sufficiently to avoid scalding you.

✗ **Don't** grasp any part of the engine or exhaust system without first ascertaining that it is cool enough not to burn you.

✗ **Don't** allow brake fluid or antifreeze to contact the machine's paintwork or plastic components.

✗ **Don't** siphon toxic liquids such as fuel, hydraulic fluid or antifreeze by mouth, or allow them to remain on your skin.

✗ **Don't** inhale dust - it may be injurious to health (see Asbestos heading).

✗ **Don't** allow any spilled oil or grease to remain on the floor - wipe it up right away, before someone slips on it.

✗ **Don't** use ill-fitting spanners or other tools which may slip and cause injury.

✗ **Don't** lift a heavy component which may be beyond your capability - get assistance.

✗ **Don't** rush to finish a job or take unverified short cuts.

✗ **Don't** allow children or animals in or around an unattended vehicle.

✗ **Don't** inflate a tyre above the recommended pressure. Apart from overstressing the carcass, in extreme cases the tyre may blow off forcibly.

✔ **Do** ensure that the machine is supported securely at all times. This is especially important when the machine is blocked up to aid wheel or fork removal.

✔ **Do** take care when attempting to loosen a stubborn nut or bolt. It is generally better to pull on a spanner, rather than push, so that if you slip, you fall away from the machine rather than onto it.

✔ **Do** wear eye protection when using power tools such as drill, sander, bench grinder etc.

✔ **Do** use a barrier cream on your hands prior to undertaking dirty jobs - it will protect your skin from infection as well as making the dirt easier to remove afterwards; but make sure your hands aren't left slippery. Note that long-term contact with used engine oil can be a health hazard.

✔ **Do** keep loose clothing (cuffs, ties etc. and long hair) well out of the way of moving mechanical parts.

✔ **Do** remove rings, wristwatch etc., before working on the vehicle - especially the electrical system.

✔ **Do** keep your work area tidy - it is only too easy to fall over articles left lying around.

✔ **Do** exercise caution when compressing springs for removal or installation. Ensure that the tension is applied and released in a controlled manner, using suitable tools which preclude the possibility of the spring escaping violently.

✔ **Do** ensure that any lifting tackle used has a safe working load rating adequate for the job.

✔ **Do** get someone to check periodically that all is well, when working alone on the vehicle.

✔ **Do** carry out work in a logical sequence and check that everything is correctly assembled and tightened afterwards.

✔ **Do** remember that your vehicle's safety affects that of yourself and others. If in doubt on any point, get professional advice.

● If in spite of following these precautions, you are unfortunate enough to injure yourself, seek medical attention as soon as possible.

Chapter 1
The Workshop

Contents

1 Introduction

Every mechanic wants a workshop which fulfils certain basic requirements: it must be dry and warm, and provide a safe and secure place to work and leave tools and the bike.

Additionally it must have adequate space, lighting, and power. Ideally it would accommodate all the power tools, and storage we could ever need, and be a place which is not shared for any other purpose. The best readily-available building would be a normal car-sized garage. This provides ample working and storage space and room for a large workbench. That said, I know of enthusiasts who have completed full restoration jobs on vintage machines within the confines of a small timber shed. In the end you will have to make do with whatever shelter you can find, and adapt your workshop and working methods to this.

Whatever the limitations of your own proposed or existing workshop area, it is well worth spending a little time considering its layout. Even a well-established workshop will benefit from occasional reorganisation. Most users of home workshops find that lack of space causes problems, and this can be overcome to a great extent by giving careful consideration to the layout of benches and storage facilities.

2 The workshop

1 A solid concrete floor is probably the best prospect for any workshop area. The surface should be as even as possible, and must be dry. The surface can be improved further by applying a coating of paint or sealer suitable for concrete surfaces. This will make oil spillage and general dirt easier to remove and will lay the dust, always a problem with concrete.

2 A wooden floor is less desirable and may be damaged by the localised weight of a motorcycle centre stand. It can be reinforced by laying sheets of thick plywood or chipboard over the existing surface. A dirt floor should be avoided.

3 The floor can be covered with carpet although this presents cleaning problems. Rubber matting, old car foot mats, or even a wooden board will help to keep your feet off a cold concrete floor.

4 Walls and ceilings should be as clean as conditions allow. It is a good idea to clean down the walls and, if possible, to apply a couple of coats of pale pastel or off-white paint. The ceiling can be painted white. The paint will minimise dust and reflect light inside the workshop.

5 The more natural light there is the better, although it is desirable to have diffused light rather than direct sunlight which will cause shadows and heat build-up. Careful consideration should be given to lighting the workshop. As a general rule, fluorescent lamps are the best choice, giving even and shadow-free illumination. Position ceiling-hung lights to create an evenly distributed level of illumination in all the working areas. Lighting in particular areas can then be supplemented by low voltage lead lights and lamps on flexible stalks above bench and machinery. Fix the lamp at right-angles to the machine, or fit one lamp slightly to each side of the area to give even illumination.

6 A normal domestic doorway is just wide enough to allow all but the biggest machines through, but not wide enough to allow it through easily. If possible, a full-size garage door is preferable. The normal up-and-over door will need some attention to prevent draughts around all four edges, and the steel panel can be insulated with polystyrene foam material, the sort used as cavity insulation in house walls, to prevent heat loss.

7 Steps, even one of them, are difficult to negotiate with the dead weight of most machines; make up a ramp to allow easier entry if the step cannot be removed or replaced by a permanent concrete ramp.

8 Heating is best provided by electric space heating. If your workshop is next to, or integral with the house you could tap into the domestic central heating system. A solid fuel stove requires a separate chimney and

creates dust whilst any type of heating which involves naked flames is a safety hazard.

9 Make sure that there is adequate ventilation in the building, particularly during winter. This is essential to prevent condensation problems. Try and keep the temperature constant because temperature fluctuation and poor ventilation provide excellent conditions for the formation of rust. Good ventilation is also a vital safety consideration where solvents and volatile liquids are likely to be used. It should be possible to open one or more of the windows for this purpose, and in addition, opening vents in the walls or roof are a desirable feature.

10 A good approach to designing the workshop is to look at how others do it. Try approaching a respected local dealer and asking to see his professional workshop; take note of how working areas, storage and lighting are arranged, and then try to scale this down to suit your own workshop area, finances and needs **(see illustration)**.

11 A sketch plan drawn to scale will help plan the position of lighting and power sockets and allow you to check that there is adequate and safe working areas around the bench, any machine tools, and a lift or area for the motorcycle **(see illustration)**.

> **HAYNES HiNT** *One important point not to be overlooked is security, not just that of the equipment contained in the building, but also the motorcycle, especially if it will be stored in the building when not in use. It is strongly advised that you cement a floor anchor into the workshop floor and invest in a security chain to shackle the bike when it is not being used.*

2.10 A professional's well equipped workshop. Note the cleanliness and tidiness, even though this is a busy place

3 Electrical supply

1 Of all the facilities useful in the workshop, a supply of mains electricity is by far the most essential. This is relatively easy to arrange where the building is near to or part of the house, but can be difficult and expensive if it is some distance away.

> ⚠ *Warning: It must be stressed that safety is of prime importance when working on mains electrics, and unless you have a very good working knowledge of electrical installations, the work should be left to an electrician.*

Remember that installing a power supply may mean complying with local bylaws. The notes below are intended to help you in considering any proposed electrical installation, but are by no means definitive; a skilled electrician will be able to advise on the best choice of equipment and materials for a given installation, and will be able to carry out the work safely. Note that in areas outside the UK, legal requirements and working methods may vary from those mentioned here.

2 You will need to consider the total electrical requirements of the workshop, making due allowance for later additions of equipment. The power cable can be run from a separate fused connection from the house supply. The cable should preferably be run underground, in which case special armoured cable will be needed. Short overhead runs can be made using conventional PVC insulated cable of the appropriate size, supported by a catenary wire; a steel cable fixed across the area to be spanned, allowing the electrical cable to be suspended from it to prevent damage through stretching.

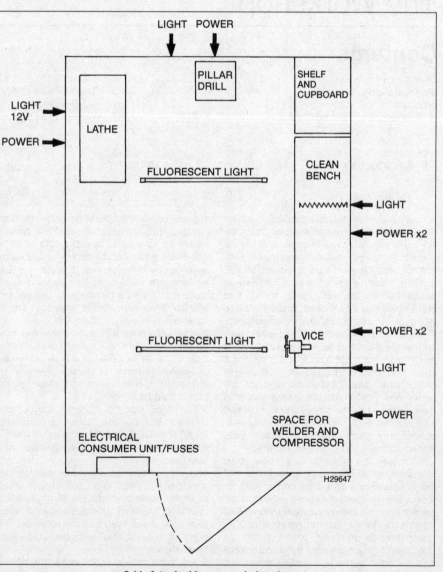

2.11 A typical home workshop layout

3.3a The consumer unit containing fuses showing ratings for power and light supplies. It may be convenient to separate the supply for machine tools even though they can be supplied through a normal power socket

3.3b A residual trip switch which will isolate the supply on detecting a fault

3 Inside the workshop, the incoming power cable should be connected to an approved consumer unit (fuse box) from which the lighting and power circuits can be run. It is strongly recommended that in addition to the normal fuse, the power circuit is protected by residual current circuit breakers. These devices have the great advantage that they will break the supply very rapidly in the event of a short circuit, a feature which could save your life if something goes wrong **(see illustrations)**.

4 Power sockets should be positioned well away from areas where they are likely to be damaged while working, and should be of a good quality industrial type housed in surface-mounted metal boxes. The wiring connections should be made using armoured cable, or by running PVC cable through metal conduit **(see illustrations)**.

5 Lead lights and lights used over machine tools can be 12 volt. This supply can be provided from a transformer, or by making use of a spare battery.

6 The mains plugs used in the workshop should always be of the moulded rubber or nylon type; *never* hard plastic which can break if dropped **(see illustration)**.

7 Where extension leads have to be used, be aware of any load limitations applicable to them. Most recently-produced extension leads are marked to indicate the maximum rating, both fully extended and when coiled around the reel. In the latter case, the rating is significantly reduced. This is because when coiled, inductance in the lead allows heat to build up. Even though most portable power tools do not draw a great deal of current, it is preferable to uncoil any unmarked extension lead fully to avoid this risk. Equipment such as arc welders draw a much heavier current, and with these it is best not to use an extension lead at all. If it is unavoidable, check that the lead is as short as possible, and that it is sufficiently heavy to cope with the demands on it.

8 Any electrical equipment used in the workshop poses a fire risk when the inevitable solvents and fuel present are considered. If fuel vapour is present, the slight arcing from a power tool can be enough to ignite it. Bear this in mind before using power tools, and minimise the risk of a build-up of flammable vapour by storing solvents and fuel safely, preferably outside the main workshop area, and ensuring adequate ventilation.

9 Note that where solvents or flammable liquids are likely to be used, flameproof fittings should be employed to minimise the fire risk.

4 Workshop fittings

1 The traditional workshop has a place for everything, however when the garage or workshop has to be shared with the family car and fill the role of a general repair shop in addition to any motorcycle needs it may be worth while considering adopting a more

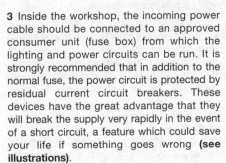
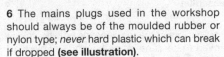

3.4a This socket, which contains its own trip switch, is hard wired for safety

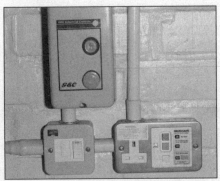

3.4b Industrial type fittings offer the best protection. The large switch above is a remote starter/isolator for a machine tool

3.6 Equipment leads should be fitted with unbreakable plugs and moulded-in connections

4.2a A strong and rigid bench is essential

4.2b A mobile bench and storage

flexible approach. Mobile tool storage, lifts on rollers, even a mobile bench may provide a more efficient working environment. A more flexible layout will require more careful thought about the layout and type of power outlets and lighting.

The workbench

2 This should be of robust construction with welded angle iron or timber frame. The top can be of flooring grade chipboard, block board, or 50 mm thick timber planks. The use of a slotted angle construction allows a bench to be built to suit the available space quickly and easily, however this type of angle is usually of lighter gauge and will need solid bracing. If the bench is placed next to a wall it can be bolted to it for additional rigidity **(see illustrations)**.

3 Wooden tops are absorbent and likely to soak up oil spillage. It is a good idea to cover all or part of the top with a steel or aluminium sheet. A spare piece of light coloured vynolay can be used as a mat for clean operations.

4 The area of the top depends on what things need to be done at the bench. You need an area sufficiently large for working, plus an area for your vice. Having got a solid frame it may be convenient to mount a pillar drill, or other fixed tools at one end, or have an area which is kept clean for measuring and marking out.

5 The height of the bench depends on the stature of the user and the size of vice. The vice should be mounted toward one end of the bench; which side depends on user preference. As a guide, the top of the vice jaws should be approximately at the height of the user's elbow so that when operations like filing and sawing are done the fore arm is moving horizontally.

6 Fixed shelving below the bench surface will make the construction more rigid and will provide useful storage space.

The vice

7 A bench vice is a work centre on its own. A vice having a jaw width of 100 mm and a maximum opening of 150 mm will cope with most jobs **(see illustration)**.

8 The vice should have replaceable hardened steel jaws. Alternative jaws, or inserts which fit over the jaws, of soft material, fibre or plastic, are useful for holding soft materials. Jaws are available with notches for holding round material. Home-made jaw protectors can be made from aluminium or wood **(see illustration)**.

9 The vice should be mounted toward one end of the bench; which end is a decision for the user. Position the vice so that the fixed jaw is in line the edge of the bench to allow long pieces of work to be held vertically. Fix the vice using bolts and use large washers or a steel plate under the holding nuts. Without the washers the nuts will crush into the bench top, and make firm fixing difficult.

Motorcycle lifts (ramps)

10 If funds and space allow, some form of lift is a very useful refinement in the motorcycle workshop. Working on a machine without having to bend or kneel is much more convenient and less tiring **(see illustration)**.

4.7 A typical engineer's vice. This one has an optional swivel base

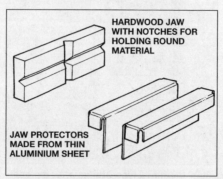

4.8 Sketches of vice jaw protectors which you can make at home

HARDWOOD JAW WITH NOTCHES FOR HOLDING ROUND MATERIAL

JAW PROTECTORS MADE FROM THIN ALUMINIUM SHEET

4.10 A typical bike lift (ramp)

4.11 On this type of lift, the front wheel is clamped and the rear section can be removed

4.12 The bike is fixed with tie-downs to prevent the risk of toppling

4.13 Always use a softwood block between the engine and the jack head when lifting in this way

11 Most professional lifts are operated by hydraulic or pneumatic rams. The machine is wheeled onto the lift which is then raised until it is at a convenient working height. Less expensive versions are available which raise the working platform mechanically. Once at the correct height, a safety bar is inserted into the lift to prevent it collapsing should the operating mechanism fail. For safe working the bike must be supported when the lift is raised. Most lifts are fitted with a device for clamping the front wheel and have a section of the platform which can be withdrawn to ease the removal of the rear wheel **(see illustration)**. Take care when tightening the clamp not to damage the front wheel – use softwood blocks on each side to prevent this.

12 Secure the bike to the lift platform using tie-downs, such as the type used by off-road riders for securing their bikes to a trailer for transportation **(see illustration)**.

13 A bike resting on its centre stand can be supported under the crankcase to prevent it toppling when either wheel is removed. This support is best provided by axle stands or

wooden blocks. Trolley jacks should only be regarded as a temporary support **(see illustration)**.

14 If the bike has only a side stand, support the bike on an auxiliary/paddock stand **(see illustration)**.

15 Special scissor lifts are available for use on the floor or on the bike lift, however they are expensive **(see illustration)**.

16 Cheapest of all is a home-made equivalent consisting of a stout low bench about 600 mm high, and with a platform measuring about 2 M by 600 mm. The machine can be wheeled onto the platform using a strong plank. Although this arrangement is less convenient than the professionally made equivalents, it will prove adequate for occasional home use.

 Warning: Motorcycles are heavy – you will need several pairs of hands to manoeuvre a large machine onto the platform safely.

17 A home-made bench with a platform 600 x 600 mm is a useful size when building a bike up from scratch. Both wheels hang in the air

and the machine is safely supported on the bottom frame rails or the crankcase **(see illustration)**. For safety you will need assistance to lift the machine to the floor, and the machine can be held with straps as it gets heavier nearing completion.

18 An hydraulic lift which can raise the bike from one side with both wheels free is also available at a reasonable cost. This type takes up less space than the conventional lift.

Bike stands

19 Often referred to as a paddock stand, this device allows either the front or rear of the bike to be lifted clear of the ground so that a wheel can be removed.

20 The stand fixes around either the rear wheel axle or the swingarm pivot. As leverage is applied, the bike rolls over the centre of the stand to a stable position.

21 Although designed for use in the paddock, they can be effective in workshops with limited space. Where a centre stand is not fitted to the machine, an auxiliary stand is a must.

4.14 This auxiliary or paddock stand attaches to the swingarm pivot or wheel axle

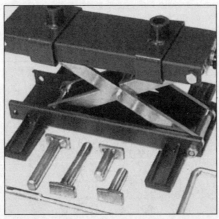

4.15 Perhaps for professional use only, this scissor stand can be used on the floor or on a lift

4.17 A home-made bench put to good use

4.22 A simple wooden cradle will act as a good engine support for use on your bench

Engine stands

22 Many manufacturers recommend the use of a special fixture to hold the engine during dismantling and reassembly. In practice, most owners will have to make do with a selection of wooden blocks which can be used to prop the engine unit on the bench. These can be arranged as required so that the engine is supported in almost any position **(see illustration)**. It is very helpful when using this approach to have an extra pair of hands to assist in steadying the unit while fasteners are removed or tightened. In some situations, the unit can be held by one of the mounting bosses clamped in a vice, but care must be taken to avoid damage to the castings.

23 The popular portable adjustable workbench can be very useful for holding engine/gearbox units in position during an overhaul. Note that a large engine may be too heavy for the lightweight versions, however, and it is important to check that the unit's weight does not exceed the rated capacity of the bench.

Storage and shelving

24 A motorcycle will occupy a great deal of space when dismantled, and adequate storage space is essential if parts are not to be mislaid. In addition, storage space for oils, greases and assorted consumables will be required, as well as for tools and equipment.

25 Keep tools, nuts and bolts, cleaning materials, bike body parts, bike engine parts etc separate on the shelving. To save space, build your storage in a range of sizes; large shelves for tanks, fairing panels and seats, and smaller spaces for engine parts.

26 If space permits, fit slotted angle racking around the walls, making sure that the racking is bolted firmly to them. Arrange the shelves so that they are widely spaced near the bottom to take heavy or bulky items, with closer spacing towards the top to take smaller and lighter items. Slotted angle systems are expensive to buy, but make the best use of available space. An added advantage is that the shelf positions are not fixed permanently and can thus be altered as and when necessary.

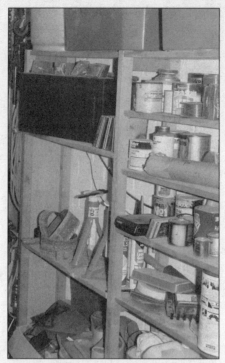

4.27 This wooden storage system was salvaged from the town library

27 An alternative is to use wooden racking and shelving built to suit the workshop **(see illustration)**. Remember that wooden shelving needs to be much bulkier than metal systems of equivalent strength. Discarded domestic bookshelves, cupboards and other furniture is a cheap source of workshop storage. Note however, that re-cycled furniture may not be able to cope with very heavy objects as well as purpose-made storage systems, and may not actually make the best use of workshop space.

28 Small parts are conveniently stored in moulded plastic bins mounted on metal racks screwed to the wall. These are available from most DIY outlets or from tool shops **(see illustration)**. The bins are available in various sizes and normally have slots for labels on the front lips. Larger free-standing bins and crates are also available and are ideal for larger parts and assemblies. These are also available in a

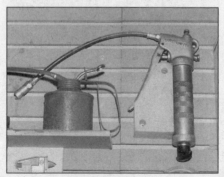

4.30a Mountings can be easily fabricated . . .

4.28 Small box racking. Not cheap but very tidy

range of sizes, and will normally stack securely. Alternatively, the shelving can be arranged to take the various sizes of bin. There are numerous bin and racking systems available, and all do a similar job. Bear in mind that those produced by one manufacturer will not normally fit rival systems; choose one manufacturer and stick to his products.

29 If you are stripping down bikes on a regular basis, it is worth making special boxes or trays in which to store particular components. In this way they can be easily identified, and rebuilt into the same assembly from which they came. It is also immediately noticed if one part is missing from its place in the box or tray.

30 In addition to shadow boards or designer mountings for storing tools **(see illustrations)**, you can use the same idea for keeping bolts and screws. A silhouette of an engine cover painted on card or hardboard can be drilled to accept the cover bolts for example, thereby

4.30b . . . for frequently used tools

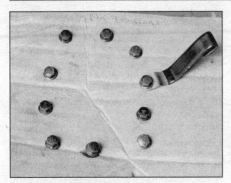

4.30c A cardboard template can be used to note bolt and wiring clamp positions . . .

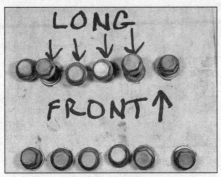

4.30d . . . and to note the position of different length bolts

keeping them together and in their correct positions **(see illustrations)**.

31 A range of plastic bags and tie- or stick-on labels will store items together and keep them clean.

32 Other containers can be used in the workshop to keep storage costs down, but try to avoid round tubs which waste a considerable amount of space. Glass jars are often advocated as cheap storage containers, but broken glass is a real safety hazard. Cardboard boxes are adequate for temporary use, but eventually the bottoms tend to drop out of them, especially if they get damp. Most plastic containers are useful, however, and large ice cream tubs, milk and oil containers are invaluable for keeping small parts together during a rebuild or major overhaul.

33 Fuel tanks often cause storage problems. A simple stand will prove useful, not only for keeping the tank undamaged, but also for holding the tank for repair work **(see illustration)**.

34 Where space is at a premium, look at the unused areas of the workshop as potential storage areas for larger or awkwardly-shaped items. Where there is sufficient ceiling height, part or all of this space can be made into a loft

4.33 A simple wooden tank stand provides a means of holding the tank for repair or paint jobs

area. Alternatively, fix hooks or racking to carry infrequently used parts or materials, removing them from the work area.

35 A mobile tool box can be used for the tools which you use most often and can be taken to wherever you are working. Tools can also be stored on purpose made boards mounted on the workshop walls. Paint a silhouette of the tool and label its position on the board.

36 Paints, solvent cleaners and other inflammables should be stored in a lockable steel container, preferably outside the workshop. An old metal office cupboard or filing cabinet, or a coal bunker, will do the job. There are rules and regulations governing the quantity and method of storing flammable and other dangerous substances. If in doubt check with your local fire service.

> **HAYNES HiNT**
>
> *Reducing the spare horizontal areas to a minimum will also restrict their use as 'temporary' storage. Unless your bike is permanently in pieces there will inevitably be spare storage space which will attract all sorts of odd items if you are not careful!*

5 The reference library

1 Keep a clean area on your bench, or preferably a separate small table or desk, on which you can leave the workshop manual, a note pad and pencils. It is also worth having a spirt-based felt tipped pen to hand for marking engine components – often it is necessary to mark Front, Back, In or Out on a component without scratching the surface.

2 A nearby shelf or fitted space is the place to keep other workshop tables, photographs etc.

3 Some mechanics like to keep a photographic record of their work for reference purposes. Information from other sources such as magazines, can be collected

in a reference file or folder. Whether this is kept in the house or in the workshop is up to you, however the use of plastic wallets in the folder will keep workshop paperwork clean.

6 Creature comforts

1 Whether you use a lift or work off the floor a useful addition to the workshop is a low stool. A purpose made one with a temporary storage tray for tools and small components under the seat is ideal.

2 A radio and tape/CD player can help on those winter nights when things aren't going as well as they might.

3 In addition to improving the safety in the workshop, a telephone extension, or mobile telephone is a useful workshop accessory.

7 Protective clothing and equipment

1 Use suitable footwear whenever you use the workshop. The best form of foot protection is provided by safety boots with steel toecaps. They can prevent serious injury if a heavy object should fall. The soles of the boots are also able to withstand oils and fuel. Ordinary shoes or trainers offer almost no protection at all.

2 Use a full overall or a boiler suit over your normal clothing. This has the obvious function of keeping you and your clothing relatively clean. Less obvious, but more important, the overall will offer less loose material which might otherwise become caught while working. Do not wear a tie while working (if you must do so, make sure that it cannot work free of your overall).

3 You should be constantly aware of the risk of catching clothing, rings, wrist watches or long hair on projections or moving machinery. Always remove all jewellery and watches before starting work. Any metal ring, bracelet or watch strap can also cause electrical short-circuits if it accidentally bridges the gap between a live terminal and earth (ground).

4 If you have long hair, tie it back or use some sort of hairnet to keep it well away from danger.

5 Eye protection is of vital importance during many workshop procedures. Filing, drilling, sawing or grinding metal all produce swarf or fine particles which can cause serious injury if they enter the eyes. It is a sound precaution to wear safety glasses during this type of operation, but when carrying out any form of grinding the risk of eye injury is much greater due to the small size of the particles and their high speed. For this type of work, use approved grinding goggles with full side protection. Welding work of any sort requires more specialised eye protection in the form of

7.5 A selection of eye protection. The spectacles have optical safety glass

masks or goggles designed to filter out the harmful ultra violet radiation **(see illustration)**.

6 Spectacle wearers can make use of face shields, although it is possible to get safety standard optical lenses.

7 Hand protection, in the form of barrier cream, should be used at all times. This will prevent dirt becoming ground into the skin, making it much easier to remove when the work is complete. More importantly, barrier creams are formulated to protect the skin from dermatitis, a condition often provoked by continuous contact with oils and similar products.

8 Physical hand protection is offered by gloves. Whilst it is almost impossible to manipulate hand tools with gloved hands, they are invaluable when lifting heavy, sharp-edged objects like engines, or when using wire brushes or similar tools. Industrial grade rubber gloves should be used during particularly dirty operations such as degreasing. If a high pressure air supply is used, keep the air jet well away from your face and never use it to dry your hands.

9 Precautions should be taken to avoid inhaling any volatile solvent product. Many solvents may simply make you feel sick if inhaled in any quantity, but some are more dangerous, especially over a long period. The best approach is to make sure that the workshop is well ventilated, and to minimise exposure to solvents and fuel vapour. If possible, work outside to allow solvent fumes to disperse quickly, and make sure that all solvent containers are kept closed when not in use.

10 Dust is another problem in the workshop, and whilst much of it is simply irritating, dust containing asbestos is definitely dangerous if inhaled. The fine fibres of asbestos can produce a serious illness, asbestosis, and extreme care must be taken to avoid inhalation of dust from products such as brake pads/shoes, clutch linings and gaskets. If in doubt, assume that such products do contain asbestos. The best course of action is to wear a particle mask whenever working on asbestos-based materials, to work outside if possible, and to avoid working methods likely to raise dust.

11 Ears should be protected from excessive noise, or the hearing may be permanently damaged. This is not likely to be a common problem in the home workshop, since although some power tools are quite noisy in operation, it is unlikely that they will be used for long periods. Even so, ear defenders are inexpensive, and worth having just to make life more comfortable. A lengthy session using an angle grinder may not cause permanent deafness, but it can certainly cause dull hearing and a headache for a while. Most motorcyclists have a set of ear plugs, and whilst they are unlikely to be as effective as industrial ear defenders, they will reduce the noise level.

8 Safety

Good practice

1 Remember that the workshop is a potentially dangerous place.

2 There is no way to make the workshop itself safe, and the topic of safety really relates to minimising the risk of accidents occurring by employing safe working practices, and to using the correct clothing and equipment to minimise injury if an accident should happen.

3 Try to get into the habit of thinking about what you are intending to do, and what might go wrong. A little common sense and foresight can prevent the majority of workshop accidents.

4 Asbestos is used in friction materials such as brake linings and shoes, and also in clutch friction linings. Of these, the braking system is the most risky area to deal with, since there will be asbestos dust on all brake parts as a matter of course. The golden rule is **never** to use compressed air to clean brake parts. Use instead a rag soaked in a cleaning solvent, or brake cleaner, to wipe away the dust, and then dispose of the rag immediately and safely.

5 Never allow a jet of compressed/high pressure air to contact your skin.

6 Take a regular look around your workshop, actively checking for potential dangers. The working area should always be kept tidy, and all debris should be swept up and disposed of after each working session.

7 Oil and other liquid spills should be cleaned up immediately. Sand, sawdust, cement powder, or even cat litter is handy for soaking up oil spills.

8 Check all fixtures and fittings for security, and make any necessary repairs or alterations as soon as a fault is noticed – don't wait for a shelving unit to collapse on top of you before you take action.

9 Exhaust gases produced by motorcycle engines contain carbon monoxide, and this should be avoided by running the engine outside only, or by using an approved exhaust gas extraction system. It is quite easy to position the machine so that the exhausts face an open doorway before the engine is started, if it must be run inside the workshop.

10 We are legally responsible for the safety of ourselves and others who may visit the workshop and have to show that we have been taking a responsible attitude. By keeping the workshop and equipment clean and in a good state of repair, and by working safely and with common sense, we can reduce the risk of accident and legal action.

Fire!

11 Fire is a potential hazard which may have serious consequences and a suitable extinguisher is strongly advised.

12 Use a reputable supplier and explain your requirements in detail. Make sure that you get an extinguisher suitable for use on fuel and electrical fires **(see illustration)**. A water filled extinguisher is not adequate.

13 Read the instructions on the extinguisher and check that you know how to use it. Hang it by the hanger provided near a door to the outside.

14 Use an approved container marked as suitable for the storage of petrol (gasoline), if

8.12 Check that your fire extinguisher is suitable for electrical and fuel fires

8.14 Only use approved fuel containers for storing petrol (gasoline)

you need to drain fuel from the bike's tank **(see illustration)**.

15 Do not smoke or allow anyone else to smoke in your workshop.

Wipes, rags and paper towels

16 Old rags have been used for many years for cleaning hands, components and bikes. These are a potential source of skin irritation and dirty rags present a storage and disposal problem, Rolls of paper towels provide a much better solution.

17 Ideally the workshop should have a wash basin supplied with hot and cold water. Hands can be cleaned and other emergencies treated on the spot without contaminating other facilities in the house or causing a delay.

Lifting

18 Motorcycles and their engine components are heavy items and not always balanced for easy lifting. Use a proper lifting technique which involves bending your knees and keeping your back straight. The effort is then provided by your legs and there is little danger of hurting your back **(see illustration)**.

19 Do not try and lift things which are too heavy to lift comfortably. Seek help from another person or use suitable lifting tackle.

20 Prop lifted items on stands and secure them against slipping or toppling before beginning work.

21 When lifting rough and sharp edged and/or slippery and greasy loads, wear gloves and foot protection.

Accidents and emergencies

22 These range from minor cuts and skinned knuckles to serious injuries requiring immediate specialist attention. You should give some thought to what you would do in the event of an accident.

23 Every workshop should have a first aid kit which is kept in an accessible and visible position. These can be bought complete in a plastic box to suit any level of risk and activity. If you collect your own kit, keep it in a closed box, which is painted green and has a white cross similar to the standard pattern **(see illustration)**.

24 Think about what you would do if you were badly hurt and incapacitated. Is there someone nearby who could be summoned quickly if the need arose? If possible, never work alone just in case something goes wrong. At the very least, ensure that someone else knows that you are in the workshop.

> **HAYNES HiNT** *If you had to cope with someone else's accident, would you know what to do? Dealing with accidents is a large and complex subject, and it is all too easy to make matters worse if you have no idea how to tackle the problem. First aid training is available in the UK through the St. John's Ambulance Service, or your local FE college.*

Waste disposal

25 Used oil, coolant and fuel should be taken to the nearest waste disposal site. This is

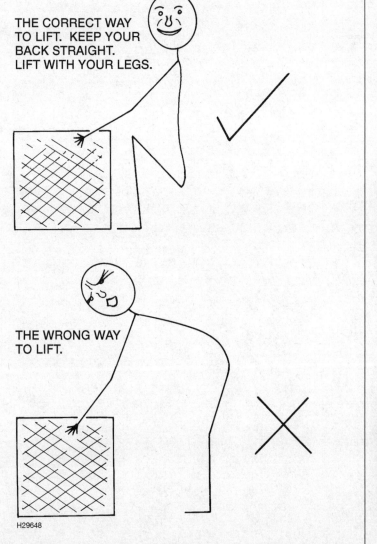

THE CORRECT WAY TO LIFT. KEEP YOUR BACK STRAIGHT. LIFT WITH YOUR LEGS.

THE WRONG WAY TO LIFT.

H29648

8.18 Lifting technique

FIRST AID

8.23 A workshop first aid kit, which should be refilled as items are used

OIL CARE

FOLLOW THE CODE

OIL BANK LINE

0800 66 33 66

Note: It is antisocial and illegal to dump oil down the drain. To find the location of your local oil recycling bank, call this number free (UK only).

usually at the local council refuse/ recycling tip. Your local garage may allow you to leave dirty oil. Note that in the US any oil supplier must accept used oil for recycling.

26 Metal swarf can also be taken to the tip, or to a scrap metal merchant. Small quantities are usually accepted by the normal refuse collection service.

27 Keep containers used for waste clearly marked 'WASTE', or 'DIRTY'. Dispose of any waste as soon as the job is finished, or at regular intervals, to prevent a collection of dangerous substances, which also takes up valuable space.

28 Dispose of batteries, antifreeze and other fluids, and tyres at approved facilities.

29 Contact your local authority for advice and information about disposal sites and recycling facilities.

Chapter 2
Tools and tool usage

Contents

1 Introduction

Which tools?

Most motorcycle owners will know only too well that the toolkit supplied by the motorcycle manufacturer is, at best, just about adequate for basic routine maintenance. Anything more demanding than this will require a more comprehensive selection of hand and power tools, together with measuring and test equipment. In this Chapter we will be looking at some of the more commonly needed tools and their uses.

Tools involved with particular tasks such as those carried out in the later Chapters will be described when the tasks are discussed.

Where possible purchase high quality tools, gradually expanding your toolkit as need and finances dictate. Economic decisions inevitably determine the extent and quality of the items in your tool kit. An aim of this Chapter is to give some idea of operations in which quality tools are essential, and also those where economies can safely be made. There is also some financial advantage, as well as pleasure, to be derived from making your own tools.

Modern materials, manufacturing processes and assembly techniques have affected the way in which we approach the business of home maintenance. The use of mass production and robot tools has meant that the assembly process, and therefore the disassembly process has been simplified. Improvements in quality control have reduced the amount of individual 'fitting' required. The unhelpful side of this is that improved reliability means that nuts and bolts remain in place for far longer than they used to do; so that when they need to be removed they are often corroded in place. As we said earlier, mass production has reduced the range of fastener sizes, however the number of special tools has increased.

British machines which were produced by batch methods and individual final assembly require a different approach. Special tools tended to be useful for a family of machines, and the bike's tool kit supplemented by a basic set of workshop tools was sufficient.

The problem of essential but infrequently-used tools is a difficult one, and affects just about every modern machine. The problem lies in the fact that motorcycles are no longer built with owner maintenance in mind. Some machines are worse than others in this respect, but with very few can you escape the need for special tools entirely.

Later in the book we will look at ways of improvising some of the more commonly-needed service tools. For the really specialised pieces it is best to refer to the Haynes Service and Repair Manual for the particular machine. Regular users of these manuals may have noticed that factory tools are only shown where their use cannot be avoided. When motorcycles are stripped and reassembled in the course of producing these manuals, a considerable amount of effort is directed to avoiding the need to buy special tools. Sets of factory tools are not kept in the Haynes workshop for the simple reason that it necessitates devising alternatives, just as the owner will have to do. Only occasionally is it necessary to advise purchasing the official tool, normally where damage or injury could result from improvised methods.

Tool manufacturer's and suppliers catalogues are a continual source of enlightenment and poverty.

Choosing tools of optimum quality

Optimum quality means getting value. You will not always need top quality tools where they are used only infrequently. Conversely, where a tool is used often, it pays to get the best you can afford.

Spanners (wrenches) tend to look rather similar, and it can be difficult to know just by looking at them how well they are made. As with most other purchases, there are bargains to be had, just as there are over-priced tools sold on a well-known brand name. On the other hand, you may well buy what looks like a reasonable value set of spanners only to find that they fit badly or are made from a poor quality material.

With a little experience, it is possible to judge the quality of a tool by looking at it. Often, you may have come across the name before and will have a good idea of the quality of tools sold under that brand name. Close examination of the tool can often reveal some hints as to its quality. Prestige tools are usually polished and chromium plated over their entire surface, with the working faces ground to size; a ground finish will have a matt, flat appearance. Ground jaws normally indicate that the tool will fit well on the fastener. The polished finish is largely cosmetic, but it does make them easy to keep clean.

A side-by-side comparison of a high quality spanner with a cheap equivalent will often prove illuminating. The better tool will be made from a good quality material, often a chrome-vanadium steel alloy. This, together with careful design allows the tool to be kept as small and compact as possible. If, by comparison, the cheap tool is thicker and heavier, especially around the working ends, it is usually because the extra material is needed to compensate for its indifferent quality. Given that the tool still fits properly, this is not necessarily a bad thing – it is after all cheaper – but on odd occasions where it is necessary to work in a confined area, the cheaper tool may be too bulky to fit.

A safe place to buy hand tools is from a specialist tool shop, although motorcycle mail order companies now stock good quality tools. You may not find cheap tools in the shop, but you should get a large range to choose from and also expert advice. Think carefully about your requirements before purchasing any item and explain what you want to the salesperson.

If you are unsure about how much use a tool will get, the following approach may help. If, for example, you need a set of combination spanners but are unsure of which sizes you will need, buy a cheap-to-medium priced set, making sure that the jaws at least fit the fastener sizes marked on them. After some use, examine each tool in the set to assess its condition. If all the tools fit well and are undamaged, you need not bother buying a better set. If one or two have become worn, replace them with individual high-quality items. In this way you will end up with top quality tools where they are most needed, the cheaper versions being sufficient for occasional use. On rare occasions it will become apparent that the whole set is of poor quality: in which case swallow your pride, buy a better set if necessary, and remember never to use that brand again.

Garage sales and auctions are a good source of second-hand tools. You may have little choice of sizes, but you can usually gauge from the condition of the tools if they are worth buying. You will end up with a number of unwanted or duplicated tools this way, but it is a cheap way of getting a basic toolkit together.

Fortunately wear and tear on second-hand tools is usually easy to spot. With new tools, which come pre-packed or mail order, it is not often possible to check the quality. Remember that you have rights as a purchaser, and can return any defective or substandard tools to the dealer as soon as a problem occurs.

⚠️ **Warning: To avoid the risk of a poor quality tool breaking in use, causing injury or damage to the component being worked on, always aim to purchase tools which meet the relevant national safety standards.**

2 Spanners and wrenches

A question of standards

1 Before tackling the matter of selecting spanners, however, it is best to dwell briefly on the systems used in spanner sizing. A quick check through the contents of the tool kit supplied by the manufacturer will give a good indication of the most commonly-needed sizes, though there may well be significant omissions.

2 Just about every machine produced in recent years will use metric fasteners, and in general the width in millimetres (mm) between the spanner jaws will be denoted by a number stamped near each end of the tool.

3 In the case of metric tools, the number corresponds to the size of the fastener hexagon, measured across the flats, not the diameter of the fastener thread. As an example, a 6 mm bolt commonly used on Japanese machines will almost invariably have a 10 mm hexagon, and this will be the size of spanner required to tighten or loosen it.

4 At the risk of confusing the issue, it should be mentioned that the relationship between thread diameter and hexagon size does not always hold true; in some applications, an unusually small hexagon may be used, either for reasons of limited space around the head, or to discourage over-tightening. Conversely, in specialised areas, fasteners with disproportionately large hexagons may sometimes be encountered.

5 On older British machines, a range of fastener types may be found. Early examples usually used Whitworth or BSF standards, though the actual thread form varied according to application. With these, the size marked on the tool refers to the thread diameter, not to the hexagon size, and thus a tool marked 1/2 in WHIT 9/16 BSF would be found to have a hexagon almost an inch across the flats. During the 1960s there was a gradual change to Unified fasteners. These used spanners marked with the across-the-flats measurements, in fractions of an inch, eg 1/2 in AF, 5/16 in AF.

6 Although some spanners will appear to fit both metric, unified and imperial standards, you should provide yourself with spanners specifically for each. The exception to this is the newer range of spanners especially designed to fit both metric and imperial standards.

Open-ended spanners (crescent wrenches)

7 The open-ended spanner, or crescent wrench, is the most commonly encountered type of spanner, chiefly due to its general versatility. It normally comprises two open jaws connected by a flat handle section. The jaw sizes normally differ by one size, with an overlap of sizes between consecutive spanners within a set. This allows one spanner to be used to hold a bolt head while a similarly-sized nut is released. A typical metric spanner set might thus run in the following jaw sizes: 8 – 9 mm, 9 –10 mm, 10 – 11 mm, 11 – 12 mm, 12 – 13 mm and so on.

8 Typically, the jaw end is set at an angle to the handle of the tool. This feature makes them particularly useful in a confined space; by turning the nut or bolt as far as the obstruction allows, then removing the spanner and turning it over so that the jaw faces in the other direction, it is possible to move the fastener by a fraction of a turn at a time **(see illustration)**.

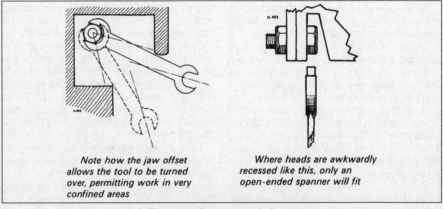

Note how the jaw offset allows the tool to be turned over, permitting work in very confined areas

Where heads are awkwardly recessed like this, only an open-ended spanner will fit

2.8 The versatile open-ended spanner

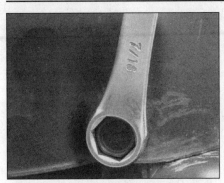

2.13a The six point ring spanner provides better grip . . .

2.13b . . . than the twelve point spanner

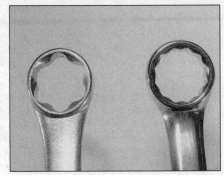

2.14 A comparison of surface drive ring spanner (left) with the 12 point type (right)

9 The common open-ended spanner of this type is usually sold in sets, and it is rarely worth buying these tools individually unless it is to replace a lost or broken tool from a previous set. Tools invariably cost more bought singly, so the best course of action is to check the hexagon sizes that you are most likely to need regularly, and to buy the best set of spanners that you can afford in that range of sizes.

Ring spanners

10 The ring spanner comprises a ring-shaped working end inside which is formed a bi-hexagon. This allows the tool to fit onto the fastener hexagon at 30° intervals, rather than at 60° intervals as would be the case were a simple hexagon end used. Normally, each tool has two ring ends of differing sizes, allowing an overlapping range of sizes in a set, as described for the open-ended spanners.

11 Although available as simple, flat pattern, tools, most ring spanner sets are of the offset pattern. With these tools, the handle is cranked downwards at each end to allow it to clear obstructions near the fastener. Normally, this is an advantage, though on occasions the flat pattern may be needed. In addition to normal length ring spanners, it is also possible to buy long pattern types. These have elongated handles to permit more leverage, and are very useful when trying to shift rusted or seized nuts. It is, however, easy to shear nuts if care is not taken with these tools, and sometimes the extra length impairs access.

12 Specialised ring spanners are also

available, and these can sometimes be invaluable when trying to reach awkwardly-positioned fasteners. Again, these tend to be available singly from specialist tool shops, and are quite expensive because they are made in limited quantities.

13 You will see that the internal shape of the ring spanner may have 6, 8 or 12 corners. The 6 point version gives better grip and is less likely to slip on a fastener with a damaged head **(see illustrations)**.

14 There is now a family of ring spanners which grip on the flats of the hexagon head and not on the corners **(see illustration)**. This type gives a more secure grip allowing more force to be used; the undoing of old nuts with damaged corners is therefore made easier.

15 Ring spanners are also available with their own ratchet device. They permit working on hexagons in confined spaces, however they are an expensive luxury.

16 As with open-ended spanners, ring spanners are available in varying quality, and again this is often indicated by finish and the amount of metal around the ring end.

Combination spanners

17 These tools combine a ring and open jaw of the same size in one tool, and offer many of the advantages of both **(see illustration)**. Like open-ended and cranked ring spanners, they are widely available in sets, and as such are probably a better choice than a set of flat ring spanners.

18 They are generally compact, short-handled tools, and are well suited for motorcycle work where space is often restricted. The compact shape also makes them ideal as a supplementary or replacement spanner set for the motorcycle's toolkit.

Box spanners

19 Box spanners are essentially lengths of tubing with a hexagon formed on one or both ends **(see illustration)**. The tubing is drilled at one or two points across its diameter to allow a round bar, generally called a tommy bar, to be inserted to turn the spanner. This type of spanner was once very popular, but has largely been replaced by the socket set. You are most likely to encounter a box spanner in a machine's toolkit supplied as a spark plug spanner.

20 The main advantage of a box spanner over all other types is its ability to fit closely around a hexagon where it is deeply recessed. It does, however, need plenty of clearance above the fastener, and sufficient room to turn the tommy bar. Another important asset of the box spanner is its cheapness.

21 Although no longer an essential purchase if you have a socket set, it is occasionally useful to have some in the workshop, and they can be an inexpensive alternative where a single, very large socket would otherwise have to be purchased for a one-off job.

Adjustable spanners

22 These tools come in innumerable shapes and sizes, and with various methods of

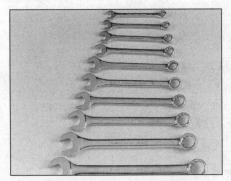

2.17 A typical combination spanner set

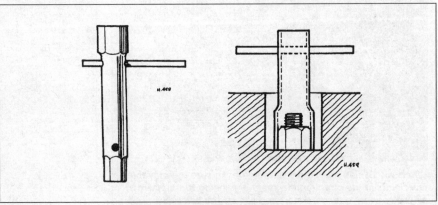

2.19 The simple box spanner

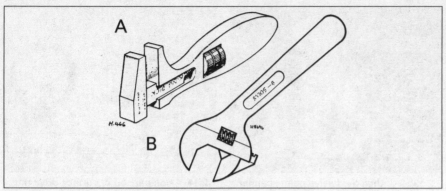

2.22 Two types of adjustable spanner. Type A is more robust, however type B is now more commonly found in tool shops

2.23 The versatile adjustable spanner is used here to hold an hydraulic hose union whilst the banjo bolt is tightened

operation **(see illustration)**. The principle is the same in each case; a single tool which can cope with fasteners of various sizes. It cannot be argued that any type of adjustable spanner is as good as a specially designed, single-size tool, and it is easy to wreak havoc on unsuspecting fasteners with them.

23 That said, they are an invaluable addition to any toolkit, provided that they are used with discretion. Adjustable spanners are in their true element in a heavier duty world than that provided by the motorcycle. The smaller the fastener and the more restricted its location, the less likely it is that the adjustable spanner will fit. On odd occasions, though, the adjustable spanner is worth its weight in gold **(see illustration)**.

24 The most commonly-known type of adjustable spanner is the open-ended type in one of its numerous guises. Common to each is a set of parallel or curved jaws which can be set to fit across the flats of a range of hexagons. Most are controlled by a threaded spindle, though there are various cam and spring-loaded versions available.

25 For motorcycle use, do not be tempted by large tools of this type; you will rarely be able to find enough clearance to use them.

Socket sets

26 The socket consists of a forged steel alloy tube section with a bi-hexagon or hexagon formed inside one end. The other end is formed into the square drive recess which engages over the corresponding square end of the various driving tools.

27 Sockets are available in 1/4 in, 3/8 in, 1/2 in and 3/4 in drive sizes, the 1/2 in type being the most common. The 1/2 in drive sockets and accessories will cope with most jobs, although a 1/4 in set is a good companion being useful where space is limited.

28 Work out what you need before you set out to buy a set. If you only ever work on metric fasteners, there is no point spending money on combined metric/AF sets. Decide what is the smallest hexagon fastener on your motorcycle (usually 6 mm or bigger) and also the largest (probably around 24 mm) and make sure that the set you buy covers this range comprehensively. Count anything bigger or smaller as a bonus, but don't let it sway your choice.

29 Frequently used sockets do wear out. Replacing them with high quality items is worth doing.

30 You will need a ratchet handle, at least one extension bar (one end of this bar fits into the socket and the other into the ratchet or T-handle) , and a T-handle or tommy bar. Other useful items are a speed brace, a flexible joint, extension bars of various lengths and adapters from one drive size to another. A typical set is shown in the illustration **(see illustration)**.

31 Some of the sets you may find combine drive sizes; these are well worth having if you find the right set at a good price, but avoid being dazzled by quantity of pieces.

32 Some combined-size sets may have a range of 1/4 in drive sockets and a screwdriver handle; very handy for running nuts onto their threads before tightening. It is also worth having an overlap in socket sizes. A 10 mm, 1/4 in drive socket is a good deal less bulky than a 10 mm, 1/2 in drive socket. Occasionally the extra clearance this gives you will be vital.

33 In line with developments to the ring spanner, socket sets are now produced with sockets which grip on the flats or wall of the hexagon and not on the corners. These are worth having.

34 Most socket sets include a special deep socket for 14 mm spark plugs. These have

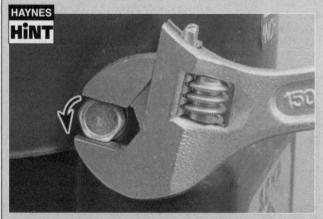

When you use an adjustable spanner, make sure the movable jaw points in the direction the spanner is being turned (arrow) so the spanner doesn't distort and slip off the bolt head

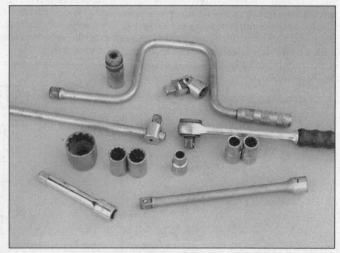

2.30 The usual socket set accessories

2.37 Socket set adapters are available to fit spin-on type oil filters

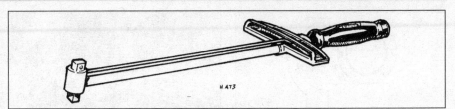

2.40a The basic beam torque wrench

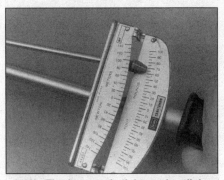

2.40b The fastener is tightened until the pointer aligns with the desired torque reading on the scale

2.41a The torque figure is set prior to tightening on the pre-set torque wrench

rubber inserts which protect the insulator, and which also hold the plug in the socket to avoid burnt fingers. Other spark plug hexagon sizes are available if needed.

Socket set accessories

35 One of the best things about a socket set is the facility for expansion. Once you have a basic set, you can purchase extra sockets where necessary, and you can also renew worn or damaged sockets.

36 There are specialised sockets having extra deep sections to reach recessed fasteners, or to allow the socket to fit over a projecting thread.

37 You can also buy screwdriver, hexagon (Allen), Torx and spline bits which will fit the various drive tools, and these can be handy for some applications. Adapters are available for unscrewing spin-on oil filters **(see illustration)**.

38 Odd pieces can often be picked up at little cost at autojumbles or garage sales, and these are worth considering if you remember to check that they are not worn out.

Torque wrenches

39 Torque wrenches can be considered as complimentary to the socket set, since they require the addition of a socket so that a fastener can be tightened accurately to a specified figure. To attempt an engine overhaul without a torque wrench is to invite disaster in the form of oil leaks, distortion, damaged or stripped threads, or worse.

40 The cheapest form of torque wrench is the beam type. This consists of a long handle which is designed to bend as pressure increases **(see illustration)**. At the drive end is fixed a long pointer, and this reads off against a scale near the handle **(see illustration)**. This type of torque wrench is simple and usually accurate enough for most jobs.

41 A far more satisfying version is the pre-set type, in which the torque figure required is set up on a scale before use **(see illustration)**. The tool gives a positive indication, usually a loud click. when the desired setting is reached. Needless to say, the pre-set type is far more expensive than the simple beam

type. Whichever type is chosen, think about your requirements before buying. Torque wrenches are available in a variety of ranges, to suit particular applications **(see illustration)**. For motorcycle use, the range of settings required is likely to be lower than those normally found on cars; on a typical machine these might run from around 7 Nm for small bolts and casing screws, up to about 100 N-m in the case of items like wheel axles.

42 Newton metres are the metric preferred units. See the Chapter 6 for conversion tables from the old imperial system.

43 Check the torque wrench settings applicable to your machine, and select a torque wrench which covers that range.

Impact drivers

44 The impact driver is mentioned here since it can also accept sockets **(see illustration)**.

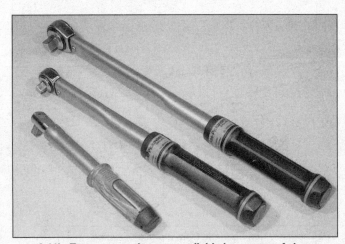

2.41b Torque wrenches are available in a range of sizes

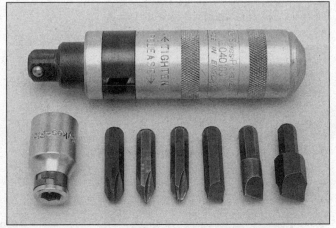

2.44 An impact driver set with screwdriver attachments

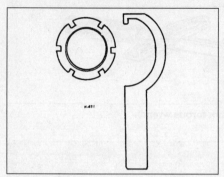

2.48a A sketch of a typical C-spanner

2.48b An adjustable C-spanner being used to set the rear suspension preload

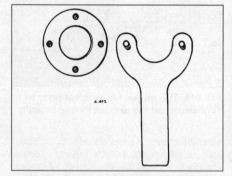

2.52a A sketch of a typical bearing retainer and a pin spanner which may be fabricated in the workshop

2.52b A fabricated pin spanner in action removing a thread retainer

The impact driver works by converting a hammer blow on the end of its handle into a sharp twisting movement. Whilst this is a great way to jar free a seized fastener, the loads imposed on the socket used are high.

45 An adapter is fitted to the square drive of the driver to accept screwdriver, Torx and hexagon tips.

46 Use this method only with discretion, and expect to have to replace the occasional split or rounded socket.

Special spanners and wrenches

47 In addition to the various types of standard spanners and wrenches described in the earlier part of this Section, there are also innumerable specialised tools designed to perform a particular job. Some of these are of limited general use, being useful on a range of different machines, whilst others are model-specific.

48 C-spanners, for example, will be needed on almost every machine. The C-spanner consists of a flat strip handle, the end of which is formed into a 'C' shape with a small hook at its end **(see illustration)**. The tool fits around a special slotted nut, the hooked end engaging in one of a number of slots machined around its edge. These nuts will normally be used to adjust and secure the steering head bearings, and a similar tool may be needed to adjust rear suspension spring preload on some models **(see illustration)**.

49 It is not an easy matter to do without a C-spanner for these jobs, the problem being that any given size of C-spanner will fit only a narrow range of nut diameters.

50 It is possible to obtain adjustable C-spanners which have a joint in the C section to accommodate a greater range of sizes, but several of these will be needed to cope with all the nut sizes likely to be encountered. Most manufacturers list a set of service tools applicable to a particular model, and the local dealer for that make will be able to order the appropriate tool for you, if required. Alternatively, measure the diameter of the nut, and purchase that size of C-spanner from a tool shop.

51 It is possible to make your own spanner using the measuring, cutting and filing skills described in later Chapters.

52 Rather more specialised is the pin spanner, another flat-handled tool with pins at each end of crescent-shaped jaws **(see illustrations)**. These tools are needed on a few machines where threaded retainers are used to secure wheel bearings.

53 A variation of this design requires a special peg socket to deal with recessed slotted nuts **(see illustration)**. These are typically found on clutch centres and engine mountings on Honda engines. Although they are not used every day, it is almost impossible to do without them. A friendly dealer may be prepared to let you borrow the tool. Alternatively you can make up the tool in your own workshop **(see illustration)**, although note that the manufacturer's service tool may still be necessary to tighten

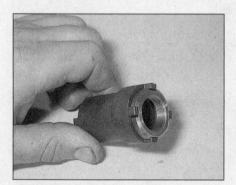

2.53a Peg spanner is required to engage slots of nut

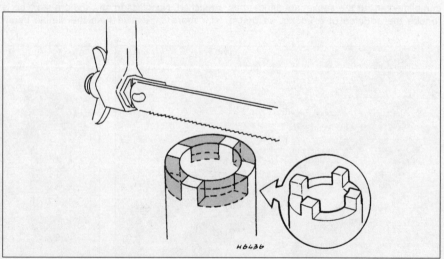

2.53b A peg spanner can be made from a piece of tubing

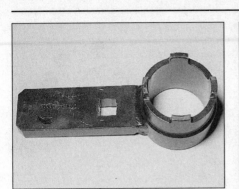

2.53c This type of peg spanner . . .

2.53d . . . allows the slotted locknut to be tightened whilst the central bolt position is held

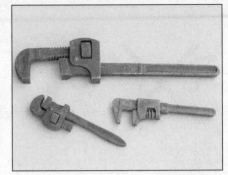

2.54 Examples of large and small Stillson wrenches and a heavy duty square jaw adjustable

the nut to the specified torque **(see illustrations)**.

Adjustable wrenches

54 The Stillson type wrench is mainly used for gripping round bar or tube **(see illustration)**. As more force is applied to the handle the tighter the jaws grip. It is again useful for dealing with damaged nuts and bolts, however it should be used as a last resort as the hardened jaws will destroy the surface of whatever they are holding. The smaller sizes may be more suited to motorcycle work.

55 Pipe grips are used for general holding jobs. The linked pivot holes in the handle allowing a wide range of jaw openings **(see illustration)**.

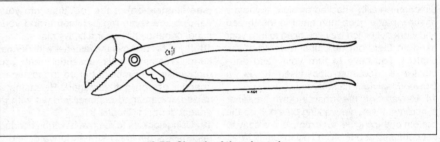

2.55 Sketch of the pipe grip

3 Using spanners and wrenches

1 In the last Section we looked at some of the vast range of spanners and wrenches available, with a few suggestions about building up a tool collection at reasonable cost. Here we are more concerned about using the tools in practice. Although you may feel that this is self-explanatory, it is worth giving the whole matter a little thought; after all, when did you last see instructions for use supplied with a set of spanners?

Which spanner?

2 It is instructive to sit down with a few nuts and bolts and your tools, and to look at how the various tools fit the heads.

3 A golden rule is to choose the tool which contacts the maximum amount of the hexagon. This distributes the load as evenly as possible, and lessens the risk of damage. The shape most closely resembling that of the bolt head or nut is another hexagon. It follows that a well-fitting hexagonal socket (or box spanner) is the best choice of all.

4 Generally though, sockets, like ring spanners, have bi-hexagonal working surfaces. If you fit a ring spanner over a nut,

look at how and where the two are in contact. The corners of the nut engage in alternate corners of spanner head. When the spanner is turned, pressure is applied evenly on each of the six corners. The newer shapes put pressure on the faces of the hexagon which allows you to apply more torque.

5 If you fit an open-ended spanner over a hexagonal head you will see that the tool is in contact on two faces only. This is acceptable provided that the tool and the head are in good condition. If either the spanner jaws, the bolt head or both are damaged, the spanner will probably slip, rounding and distorting the head.

6 In some applications, the open-ended spanner is the only choice due to limited access, but always be careful to check the fit of the spanner on the head before attempting to shift it; if it is hard to get at with a spanner, think how hard it will be to remove it after the head is damaged.

7 The last resort of all is the adjustable spanner or self-locking wrench. Use these tools only where all else has failed. In some cases, a self-locking wrench may be able to grip a damaged head that no spanner could deal with, but be careful not to make matters worse by damaging it further.

Using spanners, wrenches and sockets

8 Bearing in mind the remarks above about the correct choice of tool in the first place, there are several points worth noting about the actual use of the tool.

9 First, check that the hexagon head is clean

and undamaged. If the fastener has rusted or is coated in paint, the spanner will not fit correctly. Clean off the head, and clean it up with a file if possible. In extreme cases it may be necessary to file two good flats to fit a slightly smaller size spanner.

10 If the threads are rusted, apply some penetrating oil or a proprietary releasing fluid, Leaving it to soak in for a while before attempting removal.

11 It may seem an obvious thing to say, but have a close look at the fastener to be removed before wielding a spanner. On most mass-produced machines, one end of the fastening is fixed or captive. This speeds up initial assembly, and *usually* makes subsequent removal simpler. Where a nut is fitted to a stud, or a bolt screws into a captive nut or tapped hole, you have only one moving component to contend with.

12 If, on the other hand, you have a separate nut and bolt, you must make provision to hold the bolt head whilst the nut is released. In some areas this can be quite difficult, particularly where engine mountings and the like are involved. In this sort of situation you will need an assistant to hold the bolt head with, say, a ring spanner, while you remove the nut from the other side. If this is not possible you will have to try to fit a ring spanner so that it lodges against the frame or engine to prevent it from turning.

13 Be on the lookout for left-hand threads. These are not common, but are sometimes used on the ends of rotating shafts to make sure that the nut cannot come loose in use. If you can see the shaft end, the thread

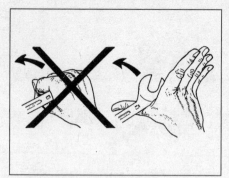

3.17 If you can't pull on the spanner to loosen a fastener, push with your hand open (right)

4.3 The hexagonal portion on the shank allows the screwdriver to be turned with a spanner

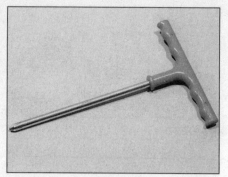

4.8 T-handled screwdrivers allow pressure to be applied whilst the fastener is turned

direction is easily checked by sight. If you are unsure, place your thumbnail in the thread and work out which way you need to turn your hand so that your nail 'unscrews' from the shaft. If you have to turn your hand anti-clockwise (counter-clockwise) it is a conventional right-hand thread.

14 Beware of the upside-down fastener syndrome. If you are working on a bolt on the bottom of the engine, for example, it is easy to get confused about which way to turn it. What seems like anti-clockwise to you can easily be clockwise, from the bolt's point of view. However long you work with nuts and bolts, this can still catch you out once in a while.

15 Watch out for semi-captive nuts or nut plates. These are sometimes used on engine mounting points, and you should start to suspect them when a half-removed bolt can be pushed in and out. Check what it is screwed into, and take care to catch it if it drops free. Take even greater care if it happens to be inside the spine frame of a step-thru moped or similar machine, or it may drop down into a dark and inaccessible corner when it comes free.

16 In the majority of cases, the fastener can be removed simply by placing the spanner on the head and turning it. Occasionally, though, the condition or location of the fastener may make things more difficult. Check that the spanner is fitted squarely over the head. You may need to reposition the tool or try another type to achieve a good fit. Make sure that the assembly you are working on is secure and unlikely to move when you turn the spanner. If necessary, get someone to help steady the workpiece for you. Position yourself so that you can get maximum leverage on the spanner, wherever possible.

17 If you can, arrange the spanner so that you pull the end towards you. If the situation makes this impossible and you have to push the spanner end towards the item being worked on, remember that it may slip, or the fastener may move suddenly. For this reason do not curl the fingers around the spanner handle or you may crush them when the fastener moves; keep the hand flat, pushing on the spanner with the heel of the thumb

(see illustration). If the tool digs into your hand, place some rag between it and your hand, or better still, wear a heavy glove.

18 If you fail to move the fastener with normal hand pressure, it is essential that you reappraise the problem before the fastener, spanner or you get damaged. Releasing a seized or damaged fastener is dealt with in greater depth in Chapter 6.

19 Using sockets to remove hexagon headed fasteners is generally straightforward, and if used correctly, is less likely to result in damage than is the case with spanners. Check that the socket fits snugly over the fastener head, then fit an extension bar if needed, and the lever bar (tommy bar).

20 A ratchet handle should not be used for freeing a fastener or for final tightening because the ratchet mechanism may be overloaded and could slip. In some instances, the location of the fastener may mean that you have no choice but to resort to the ratchet handle, in which case take care to avoid injury in the event of the ratchet failing.

21 Never use extension bars where they are not needed, and whether or not an extension is used, always support the driving end of the lever bar, **not** the socket, with one hand whilst turning it with the other. Once the fastener is loosened, the ratchet handle, or the speed brace, can be fitted to speed up removal.

4 Screwdrivers

1 A survey of any tool catalogue will show that screwdrivers come in a large range of lengths, blade sizes and shapes. A suitable screwdriver for the workshop will have a good quality steel blade, of chrome vanadium steel which extends through the handle.

2 With such a screwdriver, applying a little pressure to the handle, twisting it, and simultaneously striking the end with a hammer, a screw can usually be shocked loose without damage to the head. This

approach should only be used with screwdrivers designed for this type of use – if you strike the handle of an ordinary screwdriver, in which the shank extends only partly through the handle, you will shatter it.

3 It is useful on the larger sizes to have a square or hexagonal portion on which a spanner can be used to help rotation **(see illustration).**

4 The traditional slotted head screw has now largely been superseded by the simple cross-headed screw. A development of the cross-head which is more generally known as a posidrive' or 'super' drive screw will be found mainly in wood working applications.

5 The posidrive has a different internal shape to the screwdriver cross and demands a different type of blade to the simple cross-head. The posidrive type of screw is identified by two lines scribed on the screw head at 45° to the screwdriver slots. Refer to the information below.

6 Having stated the need for both slotted- and cross-headed screwdrivers the choice of length depends on the job in hand. Any tool box needs a selection from short, 'dumpy' drivers to drivers with long blades. There are also different styles of handle, so chose one which is comfortable for you and which you can grip easily.

7 For awkward or confined spaces there are cranked screwdrivers and ranges of hexagon bodied driver tips which can be used with a socket set, in an electric powered driver, or in your electric hand held drill.

8 It is possible to obtain T-handled screwdrivers, and these are very helpful in this respect **(see illustration).** Using the T-handle, pressure can be applied to the screw head to discourage it from throwing the blade out of the head recess.

9 You will also find a range of ratchet driven screwdrivers which allow screws to be tightened and removed from various angles. This equipment is a trifle bulky for some motorcycle applications.

10 Screwdrivers do get abused and, although flat-bladed items can be reclaimed, using a damaged screwdriver will result in damaged screws and components and

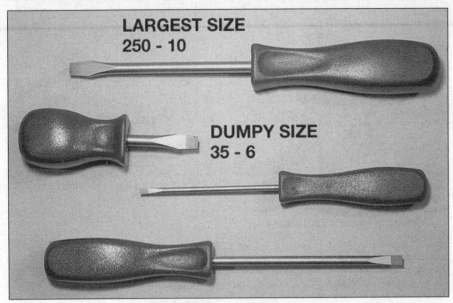

4.11 A set of flat blade screwdrivers

LARGEST SIZE
250 - 10

DUMPY SIZE
35 - 6

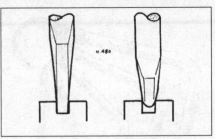

4.13 The tip of the shank should be ground to a parallel, flat profile (left) and not to a taper or wedge shape (right)

possibly hurt the operator's hands. Recycle old drivers as levers, scrapers and hole aligning tools.

Flat-blade screwdrivers

11 These are used to remove and fit conventional slotted screws, and are available in a wide range of sizes. The size is given as the length of the blade by the width of the blade tip. A typical set is shown in the illustration **(see illustration)**.

12 It is important to have a selection of screwdrivers so that screws of various sizes can be dealt with without damage. The blade end must be of the same width and thickness as the slot to work properly. Too wide a blade will damage the work piece, too narrow a blade will damage the screw, and too thick a blade will slip out of, or burr the slotted head.

13 The tip of the shank should be ground to a parallel, flat profile (hollow ground) and not to

a taper or wedge shape which will twist out of the slot when pressure is applied **(see illustration)**.

14 All screwdrivers wear in use, but the flat blade type has the advantage that it can be re-ground to shape a number of times. When doing so, start by grinding the end of the tip dead flat, at right angles to the shank. Make sure that the reprofiled tip fits snugly in the slot of a screw of the appropriate size, and take care to keep the sides of the tip parallel. Remove only a small amount of metal at a time to avoid heating the tip and destroying the temper of the steel.

15 A set of precision screwdrivers is a useful addition; they have blades ranging from 1 to 5 mm wide and incorporate a swivel handle **(see illustration)**. They are generally used for electrical work or clockmaking, but have their uses in repairing switch gear and instrumentation.

Cross-head screwdrivers

16 The idea of all cross-head screw designs is to make the screw and screwdriver blade self-aligning; provided that you aim the blade at the centre of the screw head it will engage correctly, unlike conventional slotted screws which need careful alignment. This makes the screws suitable for assembly with air tools on automatic machinery.

17 Do not use plain cross-head drivers with posidrive screws and vice versa. The tip will either slip out of the screw or damage the slot, making loosening difficult.

Plain cross-head or Phillips screws

18 It is essential that only plain cross or Phillips type screwdrivers are used on these screws; other cross-head patterns being of a different design will succeed only in damaging the head and the screwdriver tip. The tip is shaped into a cross which comes to a point.

19 The screwdriver is identified by its length and a number from 0 to 6. The number corresponds to the size of screw, '0' representing the smallest.

20 Choose the largest diameter which will fit snugly into the cross slot, and keep the driver in line with the screw whilst applying the turning force.

21 The set illustrated will satisfy most jobs **(see illustration)**.

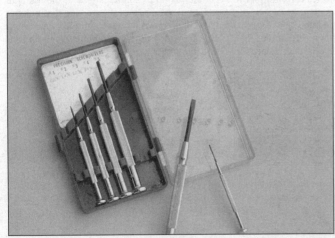

4.15 A set of precision screwdrivers for use on switches and other electrical components

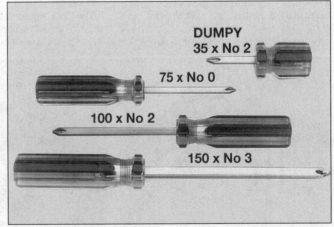

DUMPY
35 x No 2

75 x No 0

100 x No 2

150 x No 3

4.21 A typical set of plain cross-head screwdrivers

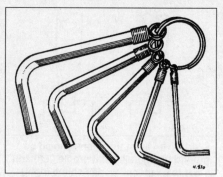

5.1a Sketch of an hexagon key set suitable for inclusion in the bike toolkit

5.1b Hexagon keys can be bought singly to build up your workshop collection. Hexagon keys with socket drive are worth having in frequently used sizes

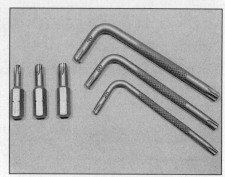

5.6 A set of Torx keys and bits for socket screws

Posidrive cross-head screws

22 Screwdrivers for these screws are identified the same as the Phillips screw by blade length and screw number, however if you examine the tip you will see that in between the main arms of the cross there is another smaller raised section dividing each main groove.

23 These smaller sections are at 45° to the main cross and correspond with the scribed lines on posidrive screws.

Nut runners

24 Although not strictly screwdrivers, these tools have a screwdriver handle and a socket at the tip of the blade in place of the cross or flat. Runners for the smaller common sizes are useful additions for quickly hand tightening covers and the like.

5 Socket screws and keys

Hexagon types

1 Hexagonal socket/Allen screws are normally turned using one of a set of hexagonal steel keys **(see illustrations)**.

2 Each key is made in a size which suits a particular diameter of screw, and this combined with the length of the key effectively limits the amount of torque which can be applied by hand. Even so, socket screws are easily tightened to greater torque settings than is possible using a screwdriver, so some care must be taken to avoid stripping the threads in soft alloy components. Allen keys are sized in millimetres, as measured across their flats.

3 In addition to the normal set, ball ended keys are available allowing the fasteners to be turned from a slight angle, which can be useful in awkward spaces.

4 Hexagon-ended sockets, used as an add-on to the normal socket set, and screwdriver handled keys can provide easier options. These allow recessed screws to be reached easily, and will also allow a torque wrench to be used on the screws if necessary. For occasional use, perhaps to reach a recessed screw head, you might consider cutting off a straight length from a normal key, using this held in a normal socket to allow access.

5 Should the end of the hexagon become rounded, it can be sawn or ground off until the full hexagon profile is recovered.

Torx types

6 A range of keys are available similar to those used for the hexagon sockets **(see illustration)**. They are not interchangeable with the hexagon key.

7 The 'Torx' shape can be internal or external and size therefore requires a socket and key. The keys are given a code reference related to their size and type, eg T25 (internal) and E6 (external).

8 For a further explanation of the Torx standard refer to the Chapter on fasteners.

Spline keys

9 Although not in common use on motorcycles, this standard requires its own set of keys. Spline keys can be purchased in sets and are sized in millimetres **(see illustration)**.

10 A comparison of the three types of head both external and internal form is shown in the illustrations **(see illustrations)**.

6 Hacksaws

1 A hacksaw comprises a handle to which is attached a frame supporting the flexible steel blade under tension. Blades are available in various lengths, and most hacksaws can be adjusted to accommodate the different sizes.

2 Blades can be bought with different numbers of teeth; usually quoted as the number of teeth per inch. The choice of blade is determined by the thickness of the material to be cut. As a rule of thumb, see that at least three teeth are in contact with the metal being cut at any one time. In practice this dictates a fine blade for cutting thin sheet materials,

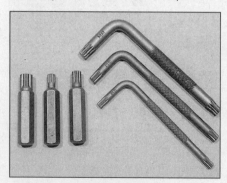

5.9 A set of splined bits and keys for socket screws

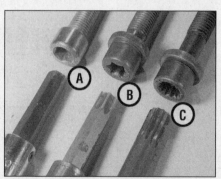

5.10a The three socket forms: hexagon (A), Torx (B) and splined (C)

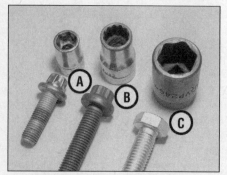

5.10b Showing the external forms: Torx (A), splined (B) and hexagon (C)

whilst a coarser blade can be used for faster cutting through thicker items such as bolts or bar materials.

3 The blade is fitted to the saw frame with the teeth pointing forwards, it will only cut when moving forward with the operator pushing, and the adjusting nut must be tightened to put the blade under tension **(see illustration)**.

4 When cutting thin materials it is useful to angle the saw so that the blade cuts at a shallow angle. In this way more teeth are in contact and there is less chance of the blade snagging and breaking or teeth being broken off the blade. This approach can also be used when a sufficiently fine blade is not available; the shallower the angle, the more teeth are presented to the work piece **(see illustrations)**.

5 When buying, chose blades made from high speed steel, or 'unbreakable' blades in which only the teeth are hardened, leaving the rest of the blade flexible.

6 The basic stance for right-handed people when sawing at the vice is to balance with your left foot a short pace in front of the right. The right hand can then hold the saw handle to push the saw, with the left acting as a guide holding the blade tightening nut end. Reverse the stance for left-handed people.

7 Listen to the sound generated by the saw. The change in note will tell you when the work piece is about to part so you can reduce the force and avoid damage to the work piece and yourself.

8 In some applications a full-sized hacksaw will be too big to allow access. Sometimes this can be overcome by turning the blade at 90° to the work piece, and most saws allow this to be done **(see illustration)**. Occasionally you may have to position the saw around an obstacle and then fit the blade on the other side of it.

9 For cutting screwdriver slots it is possible to fit two similar blades side by side.

10 Where space is really restricted, you may have to use a junior hacksaw, which as its name suggests is a scaled-down version of the normal hacksaw which uses miniature blades **(see illustration)**.

11 Another useful tool is a pad handle which allows a hacksaw blade to be clamped into it

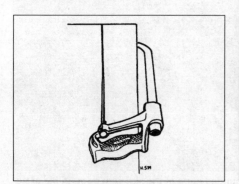

6.8 Sketch showing the saw blade fitted at 90° to allow long cuts to be made

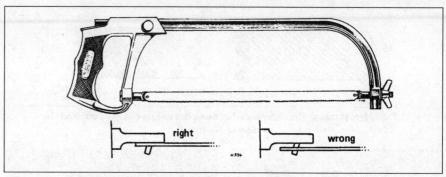

6.3 Sketch showing the hacksaw and the correct way to fit the blade

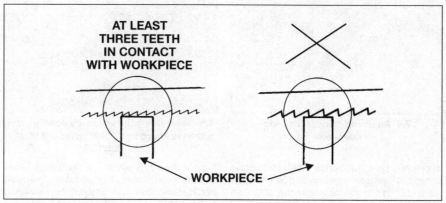

6.4a Sketch showing the recommended three teeth in contact with the workpiece

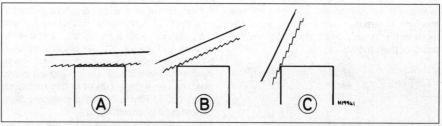

6.4b The correct cutting angle is important. If it is too shallow (A) the blade will wander. In (C) the angle is too steep and the blade will be inclined to jump out of the cut. The angle at (B) is correct when starting the cut, and may be reduced slightly once underway

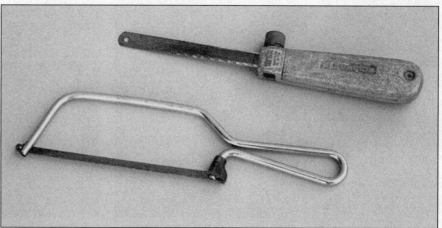

6.10 A padsaw, which uses the normal hacksaw blade, and a junior hacksaw

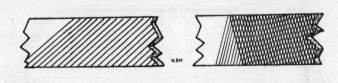

7.2 Sketch showing the difference between the single cut file (left) and the cross-cut file (right)

7.4 An assortment of files and swiss files

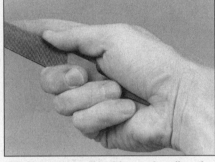

7.5 Never use a file without a handle – the tang is sharp and could puncture your hand

at one end **(see illustration 6.10)**. This allows access to awkward corners, and has another advantage in that you can make use of broken off hacksaw blades instead of throwing them away. Note that because only one end of the blade is supported, and therefore under tension, it is difficult to control and less efficient at cutting than a proper saw. The teeth in this case point backwards and the operator pulls the saw to cut.

7 Files

1 Files are available in a wide variety of sizes and types to suit specific jobs, but are all used for the basic function of removing small amounts of metal. For most motorcycle applications this will amount to removing rough edges where a piece of metal has been cut or drilled (deburring) or final finishing of a made-up part to size.
2 Files come in a wide range of sections, including flat, half-round, round, square and triangular. Each of these is available in a range of sizes and grades. The file blade is covered by rows of diagonally-cut edges which form the cutting teeth. These can be aligned in one direction only (single cut) or in two directions (cross-cut) to form a diamond shaped cutting pattern **(see illustration)**.
3 The depth and spacing of the teeth control the grade of the file, ranging from coarse to smooth in four basic grades; rough, bastard, second and smooth. Often one side of the flat will be rough and the other fine.
4 You will need to build up a range of files, and this can best be done by purchasing tools of the required shape and grade as they are needed **(see illustration)**. A good starting point would be one each of flat, half-round, round and triangular, in bastard or second cut grades.
5 Although many suppliers offer files already fitted with plastic handles, you will need one or more file handles. A file tang is fairly sharp, and you will almost certainly end up stabbing it into the palm of your hand if you use a bare file **(see illustration)**.
6 Exceptions to the rule on handles are the fine swiss files, which have a rounded handle section in place of the normal tang. These small files are usually sold in sets of a number of different sections and shapes. Originally intended for clockmaking and similar fine work, they can be very useful for detail finishing or use in inaccessible corners. Swiss files are normally the best choice where piston ring ends require filing to obtain the correct end gap in a bore.
7 The procedure for using files is fairly straightforward. As with saws, the work should be clamped securely in a vice wherever possible to prevent it from moving around while being worked on. Take the same balanced stance as for sawing, hold the file by the handle with the right hand, using the left at the far end of the blade to guide it (reverse this for left-handed people). Keep it flat in relation to the surface to be filed. Use smooth cutting strokes, taking care not to rock the file in an arc as it passes across the surface. This operation is helped if your vice is at the right height.
8 Typical filing jobs are shown in the illustrations **(see illustrations)**.
9 A very smooth finish to the work can be made by draw filing. To do this, hold the file by the ends in both hands and pull the file

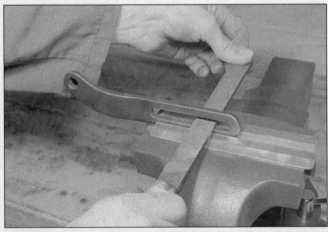

7.8a This flat file is being used to finish a slot drilled and sawn into a bracket. Note how the file is being controlled by both hands to ensure a 90° edge

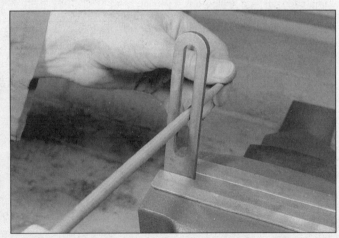

7.8b Finishing the rounded ends of the slot with a round file of the correct diameter for the end radius

7.8c The round file can be used for enlarging a round hole or making good a hole which has worn oval

7.8d Half round files are used for curves and irregular shapes. Here a curved recess is being finished after the shape has been roughly sawn

7.9 Draw filing gives an improved finish to the work

7.12a Rubbing a stick of chalk over the file teeth . . .

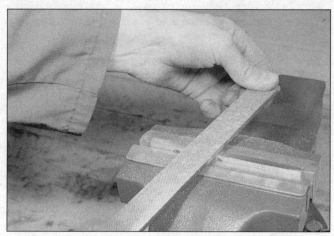

7.12b . . . prevents them clogging when filing aluminium

over the work in a direction of 90° to the file **(see illustration)**.

10 Most files have one edge which is smooth without teeth, and the other with a coarse set of teeth. When cutting into a corner for example, use the file so that the smooth edge rubs against the corner and this will avoid cutting into the adjacent side.

11 Files should be kept clean and free of swarf and filings. General cleaning is carried out using a file card, or failing that, a fine wire brush.

12 Softer metals like aluminium tend to clog the file teeth very quickly **(see illustrations)**. This can be avoided by rubbing the file surface with a stick of ordinary blackboard chalk before commencing work.

13 Kept clean, files will last a good while, but when they do eventually become blunt they must be renewed; there is no satisfactory way of sharpening a worn file.

8 Hammers and mallets

1 Basically there are two types of hammer suitable for the workshop: a heavy hammer with drop forged steel head, and the mallet or soft-faced hammer.

2 The steel-faced hammer known as the ballpein is the general purpose tool in any workshop. This type of hammer has a head with a conventional flat cylindrical face at one end and a rounded ball end at the other.

3 Mallets come with a variety of head materials. A black rubber-headed item is suitable for most work where damage to the struck part must be avoided. A white rubber-headed mallet is useful for beating metal panels as it does not mark the material. Nylon-faced mallets are also available.

4 A compromise between the weight of the steel hammer and the softness of the mallet is made by having a hammer head made from copper. Often the hammer has one side of the head in copper and the other made from compressed raw hide.

5 All the hammers come in a range of sizes, traditionally still classed in imperial pounds weight. Choose a hammer which is the maximum weight which you can control. Generally this means a hammer weighing one, or one and a half pounds (450 or 680 g). You should be able to strike an effective blow, on a specific spot, at a controlled angle.

6 Hold the hammer handle near the end, not near the head, and grip firmly but not too tightly. Allow the weight of the hammer to make the blow, there is often no need to exert a lot of effort with your arm.

7 Use the minimum of force required. With practice, a hammer can be used with great finesse. Within the bounds of your control strength it is easier to use a heavy hammer gently, than a light hammer wildly.

8 Your basic kit should include a ballpein hammer, one soft-faced, and one plastic-faced mallet **(see illustration)**.

8.8 The basic hammer and mallet kit; on the left the ballpein, a plastic-faced mallet in the centre, and a hard rubber mallet on the right

9.2 Length of round bar being used as a drift to remove a bearing

9.6 Sockets make good drifts and are always at hand in a large range of diameters

9 Although the carpenter's claw hammer is limited in the motorcyclist's workshop, the smaller version with one flat, and one narrow face can be useful in seat and sidecar body restoration.

10 Care should be taken to check the condition of hammers on a regular basis. The danger of a loose head coming off is self-explanatory, but check the head for signs of chipping or cracking too. Don't allow the flat face of the hammer to become rounded or greasy.

11 Wear eye protection when hammering.

9 Drifts, punches and chisels

1 These tools are used along with a hammer for various purposes in the workshop. In operations like these, especially where there is a risk of flying metal splinters of metal, use eye protection.

Drifts

2 Drifts are often simply a length of bar, purpose made or improvised, used to drive a component out of its location (see illustration).

3 Many manufacturers offer specialised drifts for the various bearings on a particular model, and these can be ordered through dealers.

4 For the majority of uses steel bar is suitable, however to avoid damage to the component drifts can be made from softer materials such as copper, or brass. For example when drifting a stubborn bolt out of a frame, a soft drift will not cause any damage to the threaded portion.

5 Another common operation using a drift is removing or fitting a bearing. A drift of the same diameter as the bearing outer race is placed against the bearing, and is then tapped with the hammer to knock it in or out of its bore.

6 For bearing removal and fitting a socket of the appropriate size may be used to tap the bearing in or out; an unorthodox use for a

socket, but one which will save time and expense (see illustration).

7 The hammered end of the drift should be kept free of burrs and splits.

Punches

8 Punches are available in various shapes and sizes, and it is useful to obtain a set of assorted types as and when the need arises (see illustration).

9 The most common of these is the centre punch, a small cylindrical punch with the end ground to a point. This will be needed whenever a hole is to be drilled. The centre punch is then used to place a small indentation at the intended hole centre. This acts as a guide for the drill bit, ensuring that the hole ends up in the right place. Without a punch mark the drill bit will wander, and you will find it impossible to drill with any real accuracy. The centre punch can also be used to stake components together to prevent loosening (see illustration).

10 You can also buy automatic centre punches. These are spring-loaded and need

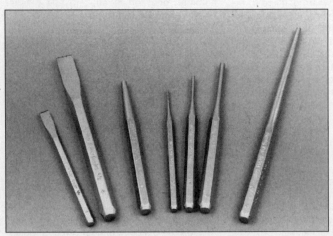

9.8 A set of cold chisels and punches

9.9 Using a centre punch to stake a bearing plate screw to prevent loosening

9.12a A parallel pin punch being used to stake a section of the clutch nut . . .

9.12b . . . into the input shaft groove

only be pressed against the surface to be marked. An internal spring mechanism fires the point at the surface, marking it without the need to use a hammer.

11 To position the tip of the centre punch accurately lean the punch away from you so that you can see the point. Then place the point exactly over the marked hole centre, tip the punch to the upright position without moving the tip and give it a gentle tap to indent the centre point. Check the position. Small errors can be corrected by using the punch at an angle toward the correct centre and tapping the hole towards it. When the small indentation is positioned correctly a larger mark can be made. Only make as large a mark as will locate the point of your pilot drill.

12 Parallel pin punches are intended as tools for removing devices like roll pins from their holes **(see illustrations)**. Roll pins (semi-hard hollow pins formed from steel sheet, and a fairly tight fit in their holes) are relatively uncommon on motorcycles, though you may encounter them on fuel filler cap and seat hinges and on the gear selector drum. Parallel pin punches have other uses, however. You may on occasion have to remove rivets or

bolts by cutting off the heads and driving out the remains, in which case a close-fitting punch is necessary.

13 When using a pin punch, hold it firmly against the work piece and strike the head with the hammer so that all three are in line at the point of impact.

14 Pin punches are also very handy for aligning holes in components while retaining bolts or screws are inserted.

15 Pin punches can be made to order on the workshop lathe.

Cold chisels

16 The simple cold chisel was once considered essential in the motorcyclist's workshop, however the increasing use of hand held powered tools has reduced its uses. The typical chisel is normally about six inches long, with a blade about 1/2 in wide. The blade end is ground to a rather blunt cutting edge (usually around 80°), the rest of the tip being ground to a shallower angle **(see illustration)**.

17 The primary use of the cold chisel is rough metal cutting, and this can be anything from sheet metal work to cutting off the heads of seized or rusted bolts.

18 Smaller chisels have their use in awkward or confined spaces.

19 The heads and the working ends of these tools will inevitably become worn or damaged in time, so it is a good idea to have a maintenance session on all such tools from time to time **(see illustration)**. Using a file or a

bench grinder, remove all burring, or mushrooming, from around the head area. This is an important task because the build-up of material around the head can fly off in the form of splinters, and is potentially dangerous.

20 At the working end, make sure that the tool retains its original profile, again filing or grinding away any burrs. In the case of cold chisels, the cutting edge will have to be re-ground quite often because the material in the tool is of necessity not much harder than the material being cut. Check that the edge is reasonably sharp, but do not make the tip more acutely angled than it was originally; it will just wear down faster.

21 In use, place the chisel firmly against the work piece. This will prevent the chisel edge from slipping and reduce the amount of 'bounce' felt through the hammer.

22 Use another piece of metal underneath the work piece to act as an anvil, otherwise the chisel will just distort the work piece.

10 Clamps and locking pliers

1 The traditional G or C clamp is of limited use as its swivel foot tends to slip off any rounded surface. A great deal of pressure can be put on the screw, so it is important to provided some sort of packing between the jaws to avoid damage.

2 The tool maker's clamp is more suitable to engineering operations **(see illustration)**. Like the G clamp there is a range of sizes available. The advantage of this type of clamp is that the jaws remain parallel. The jaws are closed on the work piece using the screw nearest the jaws, and then the other screw is tightened to effect the clamping action. The screws are tightened so that the jaws remain parallel.

3 This type of clamp is ideal for holding components which are to be drilled, filed, or welded. Making your own clamp is a good exercise in basic engineering skills.

4 Commonly known by its most popular brand names; *Mole Wrench* in the UK and *Vise-Grip* in the US, the locking pliers fall somewhere between being an adjustable

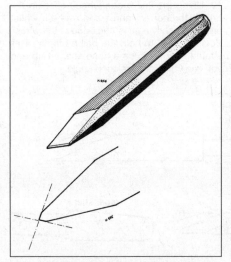

9.16 A sketch of a cold chisel showing the correct angle at the cutting edge

9.19 The chisel at the bottom should not be used until the damage to the blunt end has been removed as on the top example

10.2 A toolmaker's clamp

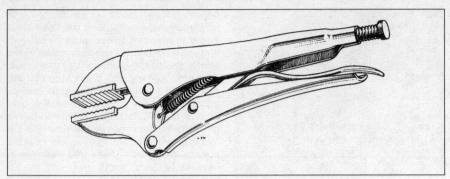

10.4a A sketch of the locking pliers or Mole grips

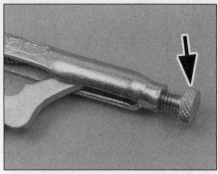

10.4b Place the jaws of the locking pliers over the part you want to hold, then tighten the knurled screw until the jaws are in firm contact with the part. Snap the handles together to grip the part.

spanner, a pair of pliers and a portable vice **(see illustration)**. It is a third hand. The jaw opening is set by turning a knurled knob at the end of one handle **(see illustration)**. Placed over the head of the fastener, the handles are squeezed together until the lower jaw linkage goes over centre, locking the tool onto the fastener.

5 The design of the tool allows considerable pressure to be applied at the jaws. This makes it very useful for holding nuts and bolt heads which have been damaged so that a conventional spanner will not grip.

6 Variations in the basic design allow it to cope with a variety of specialist holding and clamping jobs.

11 Drills

1 Drilling operations in the workshop are carried out using twist drills, either in a hand brace or in an electric drilling machine. The pillar drill is discussed in Chapter 15.

2 Twist drills (or drill bits, as they are often known) consist of a cylindrical shank, along about two-thirds of which is formed spiral flutes which clear the swarf produced while drilling, keep the drill true in the hole and finish the sides of the hole. At the working end of the drill, two cutting faces are ground, forming a roughly conical point. These are generally angled at about 60° from the drill axis **(see illustration)**.

3 The point can be re-ground to other angles for specific applications as described below. For general use, though, the standard angle is correct, and this is how the drills are supplied.

4 The remaining length of the drill is left plain and it is this which is used to hold the drill in the chuck. Large diameter drills may have reduced shanks in order to fit a smaller chuck. Twist drills for larger pillar drills usually have a tapered shank which is a more accurate fixing **(see illustration)**.

5 Make sure that the drills are marked 'High Speed Steel' or 'HSS'.

Twist drill sizes

6 Twist drills can be obtained in a vast range of sizes, most of which you will never need. There are three basic systems of drill sizing.

7 The metric sizes which you are likely to need range from 2 to 12 mm diameter. In addition to the whole number increments you will see a number of seemingly odd fractional sizes. Some of these you will need as tapping size drills when you need to make threaded holes.

8 Imperial drill sizes start at 1/64 in diameter and progress in 1/64 in steps. There is also a range of drill sizes which are identified in the smaller sizes by a number, 80 (0.35 mm) to 1 (5.80 mm), which changes at this point to a letter sequence beginning with A (5.85 mm) to Z (10.50 mm).

Sharpening twist drills

9 Like any tool with a cutting edge, twist drills will eventually become blunt. A good indication of the condition of the cutting edges is to watch the swarf emerging from the hole. If the tip is in good condition, two even spirals of swarf will be produced; if this fails to happen or the tip becomes hot, it is safe to assume that sharpening is required.

10 The drill bit makes the hole by a cutting action. In order to cut cleanly the edge must come into contact with the metal so that as it is advanced and rotated, metal which has been cut is pushed away from the line of cutting and allowed to escape. The internal shape of the flutes makes this possible. There must also be some clearance so that the cutting edge can bite into the metal without rubbing, but there must be sufficient material behind the cutting edge to give it strength. Hold a new 10 mm drill at right-angles against a flat surface and slowly twist it to give you an idea of how it works.

11 A bench grinding machine is the best piece of equipment for re-sharpening drill bits.

12 Using the fine grade wheel, offer up the drill at the correct angle and rotate it whilst pressing gently against the edge of the wheel. You will need to hold the drill bit firmly. This should now produce a cone shaped tip and you can check the included angle.

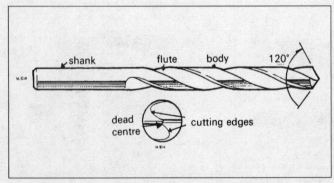

11.2 The names of the main parts of a twist drill. Note the chisel like tip between the cutting edges

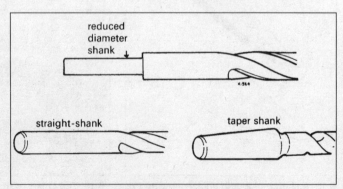

11.4 Sketches showing different shank types

13 To provide the required clearance a little material is removed from behind the cutting edge, so present the drill bit to the wheel starting at the heel of the drill and roll it round in your fingers almost up to the cutting edge. The movement is easier if you start with the drill pointing slightly upwards and to your right. Right-handers will have the drill held in the left hand controlled by the right hand fingers. As you roll the drill bit, bring the drill bit down until it lays horizontally on the tool rest. While this is happening you must retain the basic cone shape.

14 You will notice that the drill bit gets hot. Keep a small container of water close by into which you can dip the bit to cool it off. Don't allow the bit to get hot enough so that you can see a colour change at the tip. With the smaller sizes, it is important not to overheat them whilst drilling or re-sharpening, and not to weaken them with too much clearance.

15 You are aiming to maintain the correct angle with straight cutting edges of the same length and a small chisel edge between them. Try out the freshly sharpened drill on a bit of wood. The wood should come out as flakes and the force needed to advance the drill bit should be easy and constant.

16 It is possible to buy special kit which allows you automatically to produce the correct angles and clearance. These are mounted onto the grinder or onto the chuck of an electric drill. They can be a bit fiddly to set up and it is inconvenient if you need the drill immediately after sharpening to drill the hole.

Reclaiming damaged twist drills

17 Roll the drill bit on a flat surface. This will quickly show if the drill is bent. If it isn't straight, replace it.

18 Before you start to re-sharpen, examine the drill bit for damage such as chips in the cutting edges, a rounded tip or signs of over heating. These defects must be ground away before putting on a new point.

19 Re-claim the bit using the coarse wheel to grind away the damaged portions and produce the basic shape before moving onto the fine wheel for finishing.

Grinding the point

20 The approved point angle is 118° for steel, and there is also a recommended clearance. For practical purposes, the angle is almost 120°. This is an angle which we can picture, and is within our tolerance limits as we learn to grind accurately **(see illustration)**.

21 You could make a template with the angle accurately measured out of a piece of tin plate, or scribe on the grinder tool rest a line 60°, more correctly 59°, to the edge of the grinding wheel as a guide.

22 For drilling thin material it is recommended that the point angle is greater, ie the tip is flatter. This prevents the outer edges of the cutting edge catching on the sides of the hole. As we use a lot of thin material, it would be worth grinding a few drill bits in the most used sizes to this larger angle and keeping them for thin material only.

23 It is easy to make mistakes when grinding the angles, especially on the smaller sizes. It is a good idea to save up worn drill bits and sharpen them all at one session when you have a longer period to practice. Like wise, keep an extra drill in the sizes you use most.

Hand drills

24 The most common and useful powered hand tool is the electric drill. Not only is it used for drilling, but also driving screws and bolts, polishing, grinding, and wire brushing **(see illustration)**.

25 A good general purposes drill will have a power rating of 500 watts and a no-load speed of 1500 rpm. The maximum diameter which can be drilled reasonably by hand is 13 mm (1/2 in) and the chuck should accommodate this size.

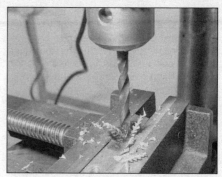

11.20 A correctly sharpened point will produce twin spirals of swarf from the cutting edges

26 Variable speed control is very useful for drilling the larger sizes and for screwing operations. You have the option of setting the maximum speed when the trigger is fully squeezed and a variable controlling in which the speed increases from zero to the maximum in proportion to the amount of squeeze. This feature is useful for starting drilling.

27 Cordless or battery operated drills are a complement to the mains operated drill **(see illustration)**. They are often more convenient to use, although they are limited in speed.

28 The hammer drilling facility only comes into its own when hanging shelves etc. in the workshop and for all those other household jobs.

29 A drill in which you can reverse the chuck direction comes into its own when screwdriving.

30 If you have compressed air in the workshop, an air drill is an alternative which is lighter and faster, however it has a smaller capacity for the equivalent price.

31 The drill is obviously best designed to handle the forces associated with drilling. When using the other types of attachments

11.24 An electric drill capable of drilling 10 mm holes with a range of useful accessories

11.27 A cordless or battery operated drill

and accessories take care not to impose heavy side ways forces on the drill which will cause early failure of bearings and motor.

32 We must not forget the humble hand powered drill, which has its place drilling thin sheet, making countersinks and de-burring, and as a general back up.

Drilling

Straightforward holes

33 Make sure the work piece is securely held either in the bench vice, clamped to the work table of the pillar drill in a machine vice or directly to the table. If the part to be drilled is still on the machine, make sure that the part and the bike are stable, and that nothing will be damaged should the drill break through the component.

34 Wearing eye protection, take a balanced stance so that you are able to control the pressure on the drill accurately. Hold the drill tip in contact with the punch mark, and make sure that if you are drilling by hand, that the drill is perpendicular to the surface of the workpiece. This is important if you are not drilling on the bench or pillar drill.

35 Start drilling without applying significant pressure, until you are sure that the drill is positioned accurately. If the hole starts off centre, it can be very difficult to correct this. You can try angling the drill slightly so that the hole centre moves in the opposite direction, but this must be done before the flutes of the twist drill have entered the hole.

36 It is at the starting stage that a variable-speed machine is invaluable; the low speed allows fine adjustments to be made before it is too late. Continue drilling until the desired hole depth is reached or until the drill tip emerges at the other side of the work piece.

37 Cutting speed and pressure are important during drilling operations. As a general rule, the larger the diameter of the twist drill, the slower the drilling speed should be. With a single-speed machine there is little that can be done to control this, but two-speed or variable speed machines can be controlled with this in mind. If the drilling speed is too

high, the cutting edge of the drill will tend to overheat and be damaged.

38 Pressure should be varied during drilling. Start with light pressure until the drill tip has located properly in the work. Gradually increase pressure so that the drill cuts evenly. If the tip is sharp and the pressure correct, two distinct spirals of swarf will emerge from the flutes **(see illustration 11.20)**. If pressure is too light, the drill will not cut properly, whilst excessive pressure will overheat the drill tip.

39 Care should be taken to decrease pressure as the drill tip breaks through on the far side of the hole. If this is not done the drill may jam in the hole, and if you are working with a portable machine of any size there will be a tendency for the machine to twist out of your hands, especially when using larger sizes of drills.

40 It is good practice to drill a small diameter pilot hole first and follow up with the correct size. It makes for a truer finished hole if you also drill a fraction under the required size and then finish with the correct drill.

41 When drilling steel, especially with smaller sizes of twist drill, no lubrication is needed. If using larger drills, it can be advantageous to use a little cutting lubricant to ensure a clean cut and to limit heating of the drill tip. With aluminium, which tends to smear around the cutting edges and clog the flutes, use paraffin (kerosene) as a lubricant.

42 After the hole has been drilled to the correct size, remove the burring which will be left around the edges of the hole. This can be done using a small round file, or by putting a small chamfer on the edges of the hole, using a countersink bit, or a larger twist drill. Choose a twist drill that is much larger than that used for the hole, and simply twist it around each side of the hole by hand until any rough edges are removed.

Angled holes

43 Drilling at an angle to a surface can be tricky as the drill bit will try to slide away. Begin by making a centre pop and drill through at 90° or deep enough so that the

angled twist drill will locate, with a small diameter drill. Adjust the workpiece so that it is at the right angle, or position yourself so that you can operate a hand held drill at the required angle. Using a drill bit larger than the pilot hole drill through at a slow speed until the drill bit is cutting on both flutes. Then finish drill.

44 If the shape allows, it is convenient to file a small flat at the required angle before making the centre pop. This will stop the drill skidding away from the correct place.

45 The pillar drill, which has a rotating and tipping work table is best for angled drilling.

12 Reamers

1 The hole size produced by drilling will be close enough for most applications, you cannot guarantee a precision hole size by drilling alone. It is good practice again to finish your holes with a reamer.

2 This is a tool which looks a bit like a cross between a drill and a tap **(see illustration)**. As you will see from the illustration, it has straight sides which are fluted with a cutting edge. It produces a truly round clean hole. For holes up to 10 mm (3/8 in) diameter, the finish drilling is done with a drill which is 0.30 mm (0.010 in) smaller than the finished size, holes larger than this usually are drilled 0.40 mm (1/64 ins) smaller. You will need to check your imperial/ metric, and drill charts to choose a suitable drill.

3 Reaming is done by hand with the reamer in a tap wrench. Feed the reamer into the drilled hole and rotate clockwise to take the finish cut. Removing the reamer with a clockwise action prevents the cutting edges from rubbing and becoming dull.

4 You can hold the reamer in the lathe tail stock chuck or in the chuck of the pillar drill. The reamer can be then be fed in by running the machine at a very slow speed.

5 The detachable side handle from a hand held pistol drill clamped around the drill chuck as a convenient means of rotating the chuck by hand for operations like these.

6 Solid reamers come in the usual hole size diameters, however you can buy adjustable reamers **(see illustration)**. The adjustment will cover two or three of the usual sizes, and will allow you to cover for both metric and imperial size holes. You can also adjust the size as you wish to give you as closer fit to the mating part.

7 The core hole still needs to be drilled accurately with a good and sharp drill. Reaming is not a corrective measure; it is a finishing operation.

8 An accurate reamed hole, which is a good sliding fit with the bolt, will reduce the risk of fretting and wear on the hole.

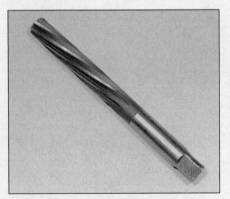

12.2 The standard reamer for hand or machine use

12.6 An adjustable reamer. The cutting edges are expanded or closed in by screwing the sleeve along the threaded shank

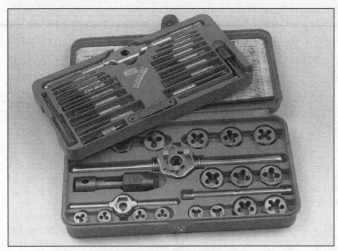

13.1a A typical tap and die set

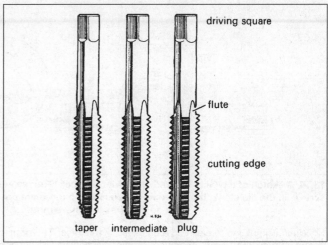

13.1b A sketch showing the three forms of tap

13 Taps and dies

Taps

1 Taps provide a method of forming internal threads, and are also very useful for cleaning up damaged threads **(see illustration)**. Each tap consists of a fluted shank with a driving square at one end. It is threaded along part of its length, a cutting face being formed where the flutes intersect the threads **(see illustration)**.

2 The tap is made from hardened steel, and is thus able to cut a thread in most materials softer than itself.

3 The profile of the threaded portion of the tap varies, giving three profiles described as Taper, Intermediate and Plug. Taper taps, as the name suggests, have a heavily tapered profile in which the thread is almost missing at the tip. This allows the tool to be started in a plain hole where the first few threads serve to locate it and to cut shallow grooves in the hole walls. As the tap is screwed in further, the thread form becomes progressively more developed, and so the final thread form is cut gradually. Only the last few threads are fully formed, and so the tap must pass completely through the workpiece before the finished thread is cut properly along its length.

4 Whilst the Taper tap is suitable for threading through holes, a problem arises where the hole is blind; the fully threaded section of the tap never reaches the bottom of the hole. To cope with this, Intermediate and finally Plug taps are used, after an initial thread has been formed with the Taper tap. The intermediate tap has a steeper taper near the tip, and thus can reach deeper into a blind hole. The Plug tap has only a slight taper over one or two threads and can effectively thread the hole to the bottom.

5 Taps are normally used by hand. The square driving end of the tap is held in a stock; an adjustable T-handle **(see illustration)**. For smaller sizes a T-handled chuck is also used.

6 The tapping process starts by drilling a plain hole of the correct core diameter. For each tap size there is a corresponding twist drill which will produce a hole of the correct size. This sizing is important, given that too large a hole will leave the finished thread with the tops of each thread missing, producing a weak and unreliable fastening. Conversely, too small a hole will place excessive loads on the hard and brittle shank of the tap, and this can result in it breaking off in the hole. Tapping drill sizes are also in thread tables and sometimes marked on the shank of the tap.

7 Once the initial hole has been drilled, the tap can be fitted into the stock and threading can commence. It is preferable to use a cutting lubricant on the tap; this will minimise the risk of breakage and will produce a cleanly cut thread. When starting the thread, using a taper tap, make sure that the tool enters the hole squarely. Once three or four threads are into the material the tap will guide itself, but

careful alignment when starting the cut is essential.

8 Check squareness if possible with a small engineers square, or small plastic set square, by testing at two positions at right angles. A practised eye will also be able to give a god indication, but again check from two positions.

9 Once the tap has started cutting the thread, the tap must be unscrewed by half a turn for each revolution in order to break the metal swarf away from the hole. Taps with four flutes may need reversing after half a revolution. If this is not done, the swarf can jam the tap into the hole which could cause the tap to break **(see illustration)**.

10 Occasionally, on large diameter or particularly deep threads, it is wise to remove the tap for thorough cleaning. The hole should be cleaned out too, and fresh cutting lubricant applied before re-starting the threading work.

11 When working on a blind hole, take care not to force the tap when its tip reaches the bottom of the hole. The tap should be unscrewed and it and the hole cleaned out before repeating the operation using the intermediate and finally the plug tap to take the thread to the bottom of the hole.

13.5 A tap wrench or stock with the tap held firmly by the squared shank end

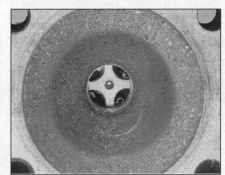

13.9 The tapping operation in progress, showing the curls of swarf ahead of the cutting edges

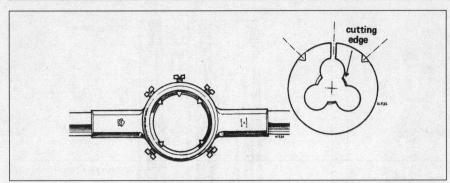

13.14 A sketch of a typical die, and die holder or stock. The arrows line up with the three screws in the die stock, the two screws opposite the three are not required for every day work on the sizes which we meet

12 When using a tap to clean up a damaged thread, check the exact condition of the thread before starting. If the first few threads are damaged it must be remembered that it is essential that the tap engages with the good threads past this point. If you simply screw the tap through the damaged area this is unlikely to happen, and you may well end up destroying the sound threads as a result. You may need to use a drill bit to remove the damaged area so that the tap can locate in the surviving threads accurately. Minor damage and burring can then be cleaned up.

Insert taps

13 These are special taps used with thread inserts for reclaiming damaged threads. They are used in the same way as the conventional tap. See Chapter 6 for details.

Dies

14 Dies are used in a similar fashion to taps, but for cutting external threads. Most dies take the form of a cylindrical block of hardened steel, the central thread being interrupted by several circular cutouts. These equate to the flutes on taps and allow swarf to escape during the threading process **(see illustration)**.

15 The die is located in a T-handle holder, or stock, in which it is clamped by screws. One side of the die will have a lead in to the main thread which is comparable to the taper on a tap. For a new thread this should face out of the stock. Usually the inscription is written on

this face. The other side can be used when engaging with undamaged threads.

16 The die is normally split at one point, and this allows it to be adjusted to some extent, giving fine control of thread clearances. The die is positioned so that the central of the three adjusting screws locates in the split. The other two screws push against the sides of the die and there are often dimples in the die to help locate them. Adjustment is made by slackening or tightening these screws in relation to each other.

17 The procedure for cutting threads with a die is broadly similar to that described above for taps. When using an adjustable die, the initial cut is made with the die fully opened, the adjustment screw being used to reduce the diameter of successive cuts until the finished size is reached.

18 As with taps, a cutting lubricant should be used, and the die must be reversed, as when using a tap, to clear swarf from the cutouts. The use of dies is less common than taps; it may be cheaper and easier to buy and fit a new bolt than to attempt to make one. Nevertheless, it can be useful to be able to extend, or clean up, the threaded area of a standard bolt or stud **(see illustration)**.

19 This restoring function can be carried out using die-nuts, a simplified type of die having an external hexagon which allows it to be used with a spanner rather than a die stock **(see illustration)**. Die-nuts are non-adjustable, and thus less suitable for cutting new threads.

1 During almost every engine overhaul there will be a need for some sort of extractor or puller, either to remove a gear from a tapered shaft or to extract bushes or bearings from their housings.

2 Common to all of these jobs is the need to exert pressure on the part to be removed whilst placing minimal strain on the surrounding area, and the best way of achieving this is to use an extractor specifically designed for the purpose.

3 Although levering components apart is not generally good practice, in some cases the use of two screwdrivers or tyre levers is a simplest and most effective method **(see illustration)**.

Specialised extractors

4 A good example of the need for a specialised extractor is demonstrated by the method of removing the alternator rotor. On certain machines, the alternator rotor (or flywheel generator rotor) fits over the tapered crankshaft end, where it is secured by a retaining nut or bolt and located by a Woodruff key. Even after the nut/bolt has been removed, it will still be necessary to exert considerable pressure to draw the rotor boss off the shaft. This is because the securing nut will have drawn the tapered faces tightly together during assembly and there will be corrosion between the tapered faces.

5 The method normally used to remove the rotor is to fit a specially designed extractor which screws into a thread provided for this purpose in the rotor boss after the rotor retaining nut or bolt has been removed. Pressure from the extractor is applied where it is most needed; at the centre of the rotor boss, rather than at the edge where it would be more likely to distort the body of the rotor than to draw the boss off the shaft end. For this reason, a legged puller is not recommended.

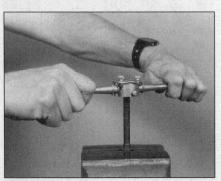

13.18 Using a die to clean up a bolt thread

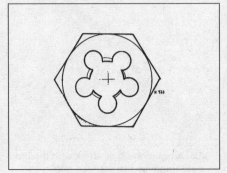

13.19 Sketch of a die-nut

14.3 A bearing being carefully levered off a gearshaft. The gear acts as a solid fulcrum, and there is space for two levers to work together

14.6a A centre bolt type extractor

14.6b The centre bolt extractor in use

6 If the centre bolt type extractor is needed **(see illustration)**, the extractor body is screwed into the rotor, then the centre bolt is tightened down onto the crankshaft end until the taper joint is broken and the rotor comes away **(see illustration)**.

7 The other type of extractor (common on most larger capacity engines) is screwed into the rotor threads until the taper joint is broken

and the rotor comes away **(see illustration)**. The rotor boss often has machined flats to enable it to be held as the rotor extractor is operated. Note that the type of extractor illustrated has four different size threads to enable it to be used on a range of engines.

8 The two types of extractor discussed in paragraphs 6 and 7 can be obtained from the motorcycle manufacturer, via the appropriate

dealer, or pattern versions can be purchased from dealer or mail-order specialists – of the two, the pattern version is likely to be cheaper. Note that if the thread size is known, a rotor removal tool can be made at home, and would be a good exercise in lathe work.

9 It is sometimes possible to draw the rotor off using an adaptation of the extractor described in paragraph 7. If the thread diameter and pitch of the rotor is known, a bolt of the exact same size can be used instead. In the example shown, a spacer is inserted through the rotor and the bolt tightened down on to the spacer to draw the rotor off **(see illustrations)**. Note that it is important that the spacer does not damage the end of the crankshaft if this method is used.

10 It is common practice to tap the head of the extractor bolt to 'shock' the joint apart, and this procedure must always be applied in preference to using excessive force with the extractor. Tighten the extractor bolt firmly then tap the bolt head smartly to jar the taper joint apart. Some discretion must be applied

14.7 This type of extractor offers four thread sizes

14.9a A spacer is inserted into the rotor . . .

14.9b . . . and the suitably sized bolt threaded into the rotor boss

14.9c The rotor boss is held whilst the bolt is tightened

14.11a Adapter is screwed into the rotor boss . . .

14.11b . . . and the slide-hammer is operated to jar the rotor off its taper

when doing this, though; it is possible on some machines with pressed-up crankshafts to drive the mainshaft out of line if it is struck too hard.

Caution: Although heat is often used in conjunction with a puller to aid separation of a taper, note that heat will destroy the rotor's magnetism and should not be used.
11 There are sometimes exceptions to the two common types of extractor, such as an adapter which threads into the rotor to which is attached a slide-hammer **(see illustration)**. The slide-hammer is operated to pull the rotor off the crankshaft **(see illustration)**.

General-purpose extractors and pullers

12 You are likely to need some sort of general-purpose extractor at some stage in most overhauls, often where parts are seized or corroded, or where bushes or bearings need to be renewed. Universal two- and three-legged pullers (sometimes described as sprocket pullers) are widely available in numerous designs and sizes.

13 Whilst these can be invaluable, it should be noted that they are of less use on current motorcycles than was once the case, mostly due to the different design and manufacturing techniques employed. The usual problem is that there is just not enough clearance around the part to be removed to allow this type of tool to be used. Nevertheless, the universal puller makes a good basis for an improvised tool.
14 The general design of these tools is based upon a central boss, to which is attached two or more arms **(see illustrations)**. The ends of the arms terminate in hooked jaws which locate on the part to be drawn off. Normally, the arms can be reversed to allow the tool to fit internal openings if needed.
15 As with specialised extractors, the boss is threaded to accept a central extractor bolt, and it is this which does the removal work.
16 Remember that the extraction force should be concentrated as near to the centre of the component as possible to avoid placing undue strain on it. In use, the tool should be assembled and a careful check made to ensure that it does not foul the adjacent

casing, and that the loadings on the part to be removed are even.
17 Where you are dealing with a part retained on a shaft by a nut, slacken the nut, but do not remove it entirely. This will support the shaft end and reduce the risk of it bellying out under pressure, and will also stop the assembly from flying off the shaft when it does come free.
18 All extractors of this type should be tightened down gradually until the assembly is under moderate pressure. **On no account** should the extractor bolt be screwed down excessively hard or damage will be done. Once under pressure, try to jar the component free by striking the extractor bolt head a few times. If this does not work, tighten the bolt a little further and repeat the process.
19 If the parts refuse to separate stop and reconsider the problem. It is vitally important to be a little discriminating at this stage; at some point a decision must be made as to whether it is safe to continue applying pressure in this way. If the component is abnormally tight, something is likely to break before it comes off.
20 If you find yourself in this situation, you

14.14a A two-legged puller in use. Care must be taken to prevent damage by the hooks and the bolt slipping off the end of the shaft

14.14b A three-legged puller is less likely to slip than the two-legged variety. The nut is left on the thread to prevent possible damage to the shaft

14.24 This specialised set up is for separating crankcase halves. Kit like this can be made in the home workshop

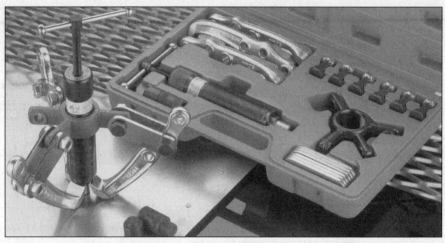

14.26 An hydraulic puller kit available from tool suppliers

could try applying a releasing fluid around the taper and leaving it overnight, with the extractor in place and tightened firmly, to work into the joint. With luck, the taper will have separated and the problem will have resolved itself by the next morning.

21 If you have the necessary equipment. and are skilled in its use, you can try heating the component with a blowlamp or gas welding torch; this is often a good way of releasing stubborn tapers, but is not to be recommended unless you have some experience of these methods. In particular, this approach should never be tried on rotors because the heat can easily demagnetise it or cause damage to the coil windings. The heat should be applied to the boss area of the component to be removed, keeping the flame moving to avoid uneven heating and the risk of distortion. Keep pressure from the extractor applied, and make sure that you are able to deal with the resulting hot sprocket or gear, and the puller legs if it does come free.

22 Be very careful to keep the flame well clear of any light alloy components, which are inclined to melt suddenly and unexpectedly in such situations.

23 It may be possible to leave the offending sprocket or gear in place, continue the dismantling process, and then to make another attempt at removal when access is improved.

24 The basic puller theme can be modified using spacer bars and link bolts to solve more complicated problems **(see illustration)**.

25 If all rational methods fail, never be afraid to give up the attempt; it is cheaper to do this than to repair a badly damaged engine. Either buy or borrow the correct tool, or take the engine to a dealer and ask him to remove the part for you.

26 An hydraulic version of the standard type puller is available **(see illustration)**. On this type tightening the screw increase the hydraulic pressure on a ram which is pressed against the end of the shaft. The advantage of this type of puller is that a greater pressure can be applied and the application is smoother and more controlled than that provided by turning a bolt with a big spanner. The disadvantage is the increased cost.

27 The hydraulic puller is available with attachments to suit various applications **(see illustration)**.

Drawbolt extractors

28 The simple drawbolt extractor is easy to make up and invaluable in every workshop. There is no standard extractor of this type;

you simply make up a tool to suit a particular application. You can use a drawbolt extractor to deal with stubborn piston pins (gudgeon pins), or to remove bearings or bushes.

29 To make up a drawbolt extractor you will need an assortment of threaded rod (studding) in various sizes, together with nuts to suit. These can be obtained from engineering suppliers, builders merchants and DIY stores. In addition you will need assorted washers, spacers and tubing. In the case of the tubing, fairly thick-walled material is best. Don't forget to improvise where you can. Your socket set offers a range of sizes for short parts like bushes, though for things like piston pins you will usually need a longer piece of tube. Note that you can purchase a drawbolt tool from mail-order suppliers for removing piston pins.

30 Some typical drawbolt arrangements are shown in the accompanying line drawings, and these also give some idea of the order of assembly of the various pieces **(see illustrations)**.

14.27 The hydraulic puller and attachments used to pull an unusually tight bearing from its shaft

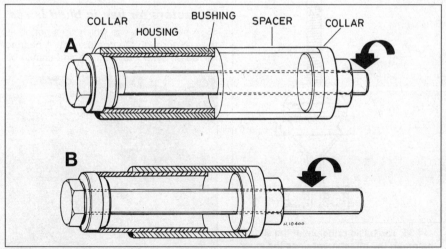

14.30a In A the nut is tightened to pull the smaller diameter collar and the bush into the spacer, whilst in B the spacer is omitted and the drawbolt rearranged to draw the new bush into place

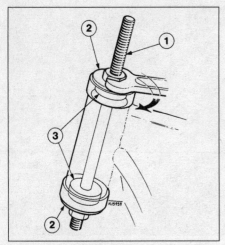

14.30b A length of studding (1) and two nuts are used instead of a bolt. The large washers (2) are used to pull the bearing races (3) into their bores in the steering head

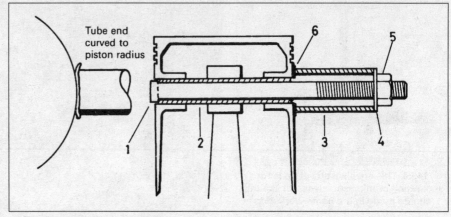

Tube end curved to piston radius

14.32 The use of a bolt with its head turned down to convert the drawbolt into a piston pin remover

1 Drawbolt   2 Piston pin   3 Tube   4 Washer   5 Nut
6 Nylon washer (to protect piston surface)

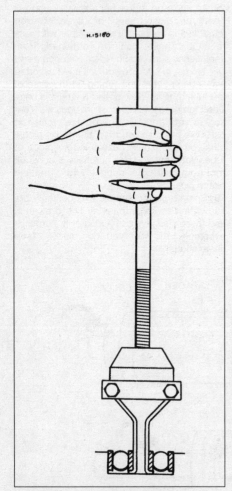

14.36 The basic principle of the slide-hammer; the attachment grips the inner race of the bearing and the weight slid forcefully by hand along the bar to jar the bearing out of its housing

31 The same arrangement, less the tubular spacer section, can normally be used to draw the bush or pin back into place. Using the tool is reasonably obvious, the main point to watch out for is to ensure that you get the bush or pin square to the bore when you attempt to fit it, and to lubricate the outside face to ease fitting, where appropriate.

32 If you make up a piston pin extractor using this method **(see illustration)**, it is worthwhile making it well, and also a little on the big side so that it can be kept as a permanent workshop tool and used on other machines. The end of the tubular spacer that contacts the piston must be smooth, and it is a good idea to file a radius to match that of the piston surface.

33 To prevent damage to the soft alloy of the piston, use some thin-walled plastic or neoprene rubber tubing slit lengthways and pushed over the edge of the tubing.

34 The Sections dealing with bearings and bushes show some more practical examples.

Extractors for use in blind bores

35 A blind hole is one which does not go all the way through the component. A bearing will be pressed into the hole and should be fitted so that there is a small gap between the bearing and the bottom of the hole.

36 If an extractor is needed, it will probably take the form of a slide-hammer with appropriate attachments for the working end. The slide-hammer consists of a steel shaft with a stop at its upper end. The shaft carries a sliding weight, and this is slid along the shaft until it strikes the stop. This hammer action pulls the bearing from the casing **(see illustration)**.

37 These range from universal legged puller arrangements, to specialised bearing extractors. The latter take the form of hardened steel tubes with a flange around the bottom edge. The tube is split at several places, and this allows a wedge arrangement to be used to expand the tool once fitted. The tool fits inside the bearing inner race, and is then tightened so that the flange or lip is locked under the edge of the race **(see illustrations)**.

38 A bearing extractor set is expensive and not frequently used. As such it is probably preferable to hire this type of equipment when it is needed.

39 A slide-hammer is well within the manufacturing capabilities of the home workshop.

14.37a A two-legged puller attachment in use

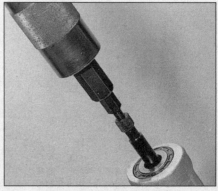

14.37b An internal wedge type attachment

15 Holding tools

1 During engine rebuilds, it is not uncommon to be faced with the problem of holding certain components stationary while a retaining nut or bolt is slackened. This applies to almost all clutches, where the clutch centre is free to rotate when the pressure plate has been removed to gain access to the retaining nut. It also applies to most alternator rotor nuts and the gearbox output shaft nut.

2 As you may have guessed, nearly every manufacturer supplies some sort of holding tool as part of the dealer workshop tool set for that model, and these tools can often be specific to one model or a small range of similar models. Whilst this is fine for the dealer, it is a less than satisfactory situation from our point of view. In this Section we will consider some of the possible alternatives to the official tool.

Ready-made tools

3 There are a few commercially-produced tools which can be useful when attempting to stop an engine component from turning, namely strap wrenches and chain wrenches. In the case of the strap wrench, an adjustable loop of tough nylon webbing is fastened to a handle. With the loop tightened around the part to be held, the loop grips onto the metal quite securely when the handle is pulled against pressure from the spanner.

4 The chain wrench works in exactly the same way, except that a loop of chain is used instead of the webbing. This tends to grip more positively, but the chain links tend to dig into the part being held, and can damage alloy parts quite badly.

5 Either of the above tools has its place in the

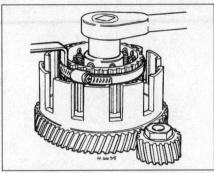

15.7 A sketch of the simple improvised clutch centre holding method

workshop, but be warned that the main drawback is finding some way of fitting the tool. As an example, it is almost impossible to use either tool on a clutch centre, because the outer drum masks it. The same problem applies to alternator rotors, though on small machines with flywheel generators, the large flywheel rotor is easily accessible, and thus ideal for holding by this method.

6 It must not be forgotten that any tool not specifically designed for a job may cause damage if not used with great care. It is possible to distort components like flywheel rotors, and where external ignition pickups are fitted, beware of causing damage.

An improvised clutch centre holding method

7 Use a strip of steel and a large worm drive hose clip, as a simple method of holding a clutch centre whilst the retaining nut is released (see illustration).

A fabricated clutch centre holding tool

8 Over the years countless one-off holding tools have been made up when dismantling

15.8 The home-made scissor tool in operation

various machines in the course of originating Haynes Service and Repair Manuals. These have ranged from pieces of scrap metal cut and filed to lock a component by wedging it, to more generally useful tools. Of these, the most successful and widely used tool has been a scissor-type clutch holding tool. No credit can be claimed for its design – many manufacturers produce a similar item as part of their service tool set for dealers. It is, however, easy to make and works on almost any clutch (see illustration).

9 The tool is constructed from mild steel strip (see illustration). The tool was made up into the scissor-shape shown with the jaws bent at 90° so that they lined up with the slotted clutch centre. The working edges of the jaws were filed to a shape which matched the profile of the clutch centre slots to reduce the risk of the tool slipping and subsequent damage.

10 There is no real need to harden the jaws – they will be gripping on aluminium alloy which is a good deal softer than mild steel.

11 The handles were made quite long so that the jaws would grip the centre firmly without having to apply undue pressure (see illustration).

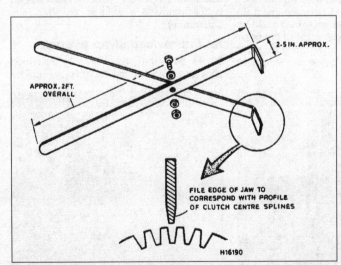

15.9 A sketch showing the scissor holding tool which can be adapted to hold almost any clutch centre. Note the profiled jaw ends

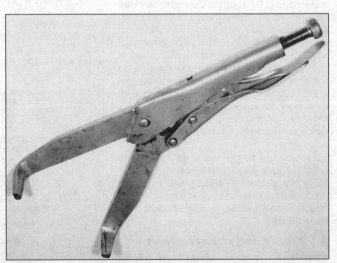

15.11 A development of the scissor type tool using self-locking grips

15.12 The rotor holding tool in use

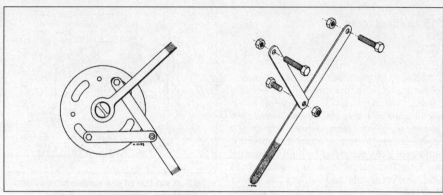

15.13 A sketch of the rotor tool showing its construction

15.14 Where circumstances permit, try bolting a steel strip to the gearbox sprocket as a holding method

15.15 Adjustable spanner clamped on rotor's machined flats whilst rotor bolt is slackened

15.16 The improvised chain wrench

A fabricated rotor holding tool

12 This is another useful tool which will work on the majority of machines. The tool requires that the rotor has slots or plain or tapped holes to accept a holding tool on the outer face (**see illustration**).

13 Once again, mild steel strip was used to make up a scissor-shaped device (**see illustration**). At each jaw end is a hole through which was fitted a high tensile bolt and a nut to secure it to the jaw. This arrangement will work on most rotors with either plain holes or slots in the outer face. Make sure the bolts do not extent too far into the rotor when the tool is fitted, otherwise the coils may be damaged. If the rotor has tapped holes, the normal bolts should be removed and replaced with a size which can be screwed directly into the holes in the rotor.

14 A variation on this design can be used to hold sprockets (**see illustration**).

15 Many alternator rotors have two flats machined on their boss to accept an open-ended spanner or adjustable spanner (**see illustration**).

An improvised chain wrench

16 If you find that you need a chain wrench when the tool shop is closed, it is relatively easy to make a quick improvised version using an old final drive chain and a length of steel tubing. Pass a loop of chain through the centre of the tube and fit this around the item to be held. Pull the handle as tight as possible, then pin it in this position by sliding a small high-tensile bolt or pin through the chain ends (**see illustration**).

17 The arrangement described is dependent on the strength of the bolt, which of necessity must be quite small to fit between the chain rollers. Despite this limitation (which could be overcome by a little modification of the basic design) the tool works adequately for most jobs, and is above all quick and simple to make up.

18 Often just the fact that the chain will grip if held tightly against a length of bar will be enough to turn a part without slipping.

19 Chain wrenches can be purchased from motor accessory shops. Note that whilst they have an application in the workshop, they can damage the surface of the component (**see illustration**). A typical use of the chain wrench is for removing a spin-on oil filter (**see illustration**).

An improvised strap wrench

20 As with the chain wrench described above, this is quick and easy to make up. The

15.19a A simple chain wrench used with packing to prevent damage to the fork leg

15.19b A typical use of a chain wrench is in removing a spin-on oil filter

simplest method is shown in the sketch **(see illustration)**.

21 Ideally, a length of nylon webbing should be used to form the strap, although in the absence of this a length of rope could be used. The handle could be made up as for the chain wrench described above, passing the loop of webbing through it, and then tightening it by passing a bar through the loop above the handle and twisting it until the webbing tightens around the object to be held **(see illustration)**.

22 You could also employ a pair of ring spanners as shown in the accompanying photograph. Used in this way the spanners act as a handle and also lock the webbing in position **(see illustration)**.

Ways of avoiding the need for holding tools

23 Before we leave the subject of holding tools, it is worth mentioning that as an alternative to the methods described above, it is often possible to avoid the use of holding tools if the matter is considered early enough in the dismantling operation.

24 If working on a motorcycle with a conventional transmission system, note that the entire gear train can be locked via the rear brake if the engine is still in the frame. If top gear is selected and the rear brake applied hard, the engine will be effectively locked in position through the gears and final drive. If the engine is out of the frame, the output shaft can be held as shown in illustration 15.14.

25 Once the cylinder head, block and piston(s) have been removed, crankshaft rotation is prevented by passing a smooth round bar through the connecting rod small-end eye and supporting the ends of the bar on wooden blocks placed across the crankcase mouth **(see illustration)**. If using this method, make sure that the bar is smooth, or damage may be done to the connecting rod. The wooden packing pieces are essential too, both to prevent the crankshaft from turning

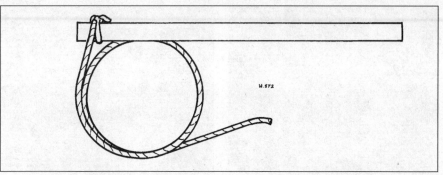

15.20 The simplest form of strap wrench; a cord and a length of wood

15.21 An improvised strap wrench being used to undo an oil filter

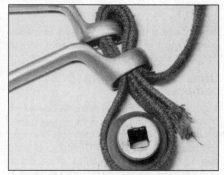

15.22 The two ring spanners and rope trick

past bottom dead centre (BDC), and to spread the load applied to the crankcase and thus avoid damage to its gasket face.

26 Two gears in mesh can be prevented from rotating by trapping a cloth rag between them.

16 Spring compressors

Valve spring compressors

1 A valve spring compressor is the only safe means of dismantling the valves on a conventional 4-stroke engine. When purchasing a valve spring compressor make sure that it is suitable for motorcycle use, many types sold in tool shops are made for car engines **(see illustration)**.

2 The valve spring compressor has a large C-shaped frame with one end ground to a blunt taper to locate on the valve head, and the other end formed into a fork or carrying a tubular foot which locates on the valve spring retainer. On certain types of compressor, the tubular foot can be detached to allow for the fitting of a different size foot.

3 When using the spring compressor, ensure that it locates centrally in the valve head **(see**

15.25 A long extension bar from a socket set used to prevent rotation of the crankshaft. The wooden blocks prevent damage to the gasket surface

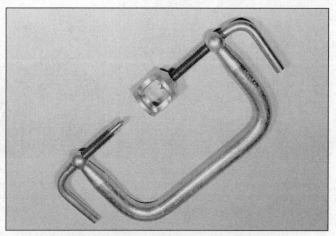

16.1 A typical motorcycle valve spring compressor

16.3a Valve spring compressor engaged with centre of valve head . . .

16.3b . . . and against the face of the valve spring retainer

16.5 An hydraulic spring compressor being used on this driveshaft shock absorber assembly to ensure that the spring is released safely

illustration) and that the tubular foot makes good contact with the spring retainer without danger of slipping (see illustration).

Other types of spring compressor

4 Occasionally, you will need to compress other springs during dismantling operations, suspension springs being the most common candidates. These are not easy to deal with, due to the high spring rates often used, especially on single-shock rear suspension units.

5 Whatever method you use, you should be sure that it is safe; if the arrangement used slips during use you could be badly injured as a result (see illustration).

6 You may be able to use a car-type

suspension spring compressor, though given that these are made for use on car suspension struts, they may prove too bulky for motorcycle use.

7 Before contemplating the removal of this type of spring, find out whether you will gain anything by doing so. All too often the manufacturer does not supply replacement parts, only complete units, and this makes the attempt futile. It is worth seeking advice from either a dealer or by consulting the appropriate Service and Repair Manual for the machine concerned for advice about removal and fitting procedures before attempting this job. If all else fails, take the unit to the dealer who will have the necessary equipment to do the work safely.

17 Soldering irons and blowlamps

1 Soldering irons are most often electrically operated, but you can get versions which will run off small gas cylinders, or gas lighter refills (see illustration). A fairly large electric soldering iron of about 100 watts will be suitable for soldering larger terminals and for

sweating soldered joints. For instructions on soldering refer to the Chapter 7.

2 The smaller soldering irons rated at approximately 25 watts and are intended for finer work on small terminals and electronic circuitry where excessive heat can damage the components.

3 A butane gas blowlamp of the type used by plumbers is useful for larger tinning and sweating jobs in addition to general heating duties.

18 Wood working tools

1 Wood working is only an occasional activity in the motorcycle workshop. However a basic set of wood working tools will also be useful for pattern making and special storage tray manufacture as well as repairs and improvements to the fabric of the workshop (see illustrations).

2 Take care not to mix posidrive and plain cross point screwdrivers.

3 A small block plane, pin hammer, and a range of chisels form 6 mm to 25 mm make useful additions.

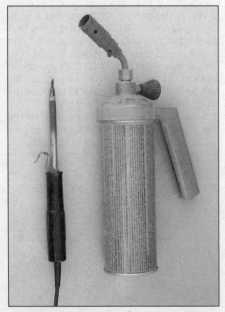

17.1 An electric iron complemented by a small gas blowlamp should be adequate for most jobs. Work on electronic components will need a smaller electric iron

18.1a A basic wood working kit comprising saw, plane, chisels, claw hammer . . .

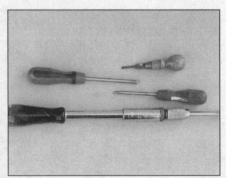

18.1b . . . with flat blade and posidrive screwdrivers in small and large sizes

Chapter 3
Materials

Contents

1 Introduction

This Chapter looks at the materials likely to be found in the workshop and on motorcycles.

The choice of raw materials is governed by a number of factors, the most important being to ensure that it is of adequate strength. On motorcycles there is a fairly high level of stress due to vibration, and the proposed fitting must be able to withstand this. There is also the effects of climate to be considered and consideration given to preventing corrosion. Add to that the need for a good finished appearance due to the exposed nature of most components on a motorcycle.

2 Ferrous metals

Cast iron

1 This is an alloy of iron (which gives us the general term ferrous metal) and carbon, where the carbon content is within the range 2 to 4%.
2 It is a brittle metal and has little strength except when it is compressed, but it casts well and, once the outer skin has been cut through, it also machines well. As it is fairly dense it absorbs vibration and sound, making for quieter engines.
3 The surface is hard wearing and has good bearing qualities.
4 The addition of small amounts of other metals such as nickel, molybdenum copper and chromium produces a cast iron which is tough and is used for casting crankshafts.
5 Cast iron is not used much in today's motorcycles, but was the material for cylinder barrels and piston rings in early engines, and more latterly brake discs.

Steel

6 Steel is the basic engineering material. It is again made up of two main ingredients: iron and carbon. Any ferrous metal containing less than 1.5% carbon is called a steel. By varying the amount of carbon in the mix, different properties can be obtained in the alloy. The higher the proportion of carbon, the harder and more brittle the material will be.
7 At the lower end of the scale of carbon content, we have what is often called dead mild steel. This has a carbon content of 0.1 to 0.15%. It is a dull grey in colour and is used in pressed car bodies for example.
8 Common mild steel has a carbon content of about 0.15 to 0.3%. It is silvery in colour, is easy to bend and cut and has reasonable strength. It is the most commonly used steel and can be used for frameworks, brackets and most general components. It can be drilled, tapped, cut and welded where necessary and it is cheap and easily obtained in numerous shapes and sizes. The main drawback is that it rusts easily, and thus must be painted properly before fitting.
9 A higher carbon content produces the type of steel used for cutting tools, chisels and hacksaw blades. It can be hardened to take a cutting edge, but is more brittle.

Alloy steels

10 In addition to carbon, other elements are added to steel to give special properties These are the alloy steels.
11 A most common addition is chromium, which when added to steel gives it anti-rust properties; stainless steel in fact. Stainless steel is a useful material for motorcycle use, having a natural bright finish and is capable of being polished to a mirror finish, if desired. In most respects it is similar to mild steel to work with, though slightly less easily worked.
12 Most commercially-used grades of stainless steel are alloys of steel and metals such as nickel and chromium, plus traces of other metals. The percentages of nickel and chromium denote the degree of corrosion resistance, the most common grade being 18/8 (18% chromium and 8% nickel). This grade has a high degree of corrosion resistance, and is non-magnetic.
13 Small additions of an element called vanadium to stainless produces a very strong steel which is commonly used in spanners

and springs. If nickel is added to carbon steel on its own it improves the strength and toughness of the material yet still allows the steel to be worked easily. In this form it can be used for axles suspension links and chassis members.

14 If we have a combination of steel, nickel and chromium it forms high tensile steel which is used for bolts, screws etc. Manganese is also added to steel to toughen it and make it withstand long use and wear. This alloy is used for springs and axle shafts.

15 Whilst some of the characteristics of a metal are decided at the time the original steel was manufactured, others are imparted at later stages of production. In its original state, the molten steel is poured into moulds to produce cast ingots, and these can be treated in various ways to impart certain properties. In its ingot form, the steel will have a hard, grainy and crystalline structure, similar to that of cast iron. If this material is then 'worked', by forcing it through rollers or by hammering or forging it in a hot state, the structure can be altered to produce a more resilient material with a directional structure to the grain, rather like wood.

16 Further treatments can impart hardening, either throughout the material, or more usefully, as a hard layer on the outside of a softer but tougher core. This allows items such as crankshafts and camshafts to be made, combining the tensile strength of a ductile steel with a hard working surface to resist wear.

17 Simple case hardening and heat treatment may be carried out in the workshop.

Stock supply

18 Steel bar is supplied in a variety of solid round, hexagon, square and flat cross section, in addition to round and square hollow section (tube) and angle.

19 The most useful grades are bright drawn mild steel which has accurate size and shape, and free cutting mild steel which is easier to machine.

20 Steel sheet is available in a range of thicknesses which are measured still in standard wire gauge (SWG); refer to the table for metric and imperial conversions **(see illustration)**.

21 Steel plate can also be coated with various materials to provide a corrosion resistant or decorative finish. Tin plate is steel with a layer of tin coating, however steel can be galvanised using a zinc coating or plastic material can be for a thin protective finish.

22 Hollow section is either cold drawn from a solid block, or formed from flat sheet and seam welded. The latter was thought to be inferior in quality, but modern production techniques make that questionable.

23 All or a selection of materials will be available form a local stock holder in larger quantities than you will need. Small quantities and off-cuts can be had from local engineering firms. The companies selling stainless fasteners and other items may also supply stainless steel stock in suitable sizes.

24 Local scrap yards and breakers are also sources of material. You will not be absolutely sure what grade of material it is, nor what treatment it has had, so exercise some care in your choice.

3 Non-ferrous metals

Aluminium

1 Aluminium has been used since the very early days of motorcycling as a casting material for the crankcase. Aluminium is a soft material and easily worked. Its use as a structural material require it to be alloyed with other metals.

2 The addition of copper and manganese forms an alloy called "Duralumin". This material has the curious property of "age hardening", so that it is easy to work and then hardens at room temperature over a few days. In this form it is suitable for brackets and engine plates.

3 Mixing copper and nickel with aluminium produces an alloy called Y-Alloy, which retains its strength at high temperatures making it suitable for pistons.

4 In sheet form it became popular for bodywork as it could easily be beaten or pressed to shape. Sheet aluminium comes in various grades of hardness: soft, half hard, and hard. Although still easy to indent, bending the harder grades is difficult in the home workshop. Half hard is the convenient compromise between workability and resistance to dents.

5 Aluminium can be cast by both the sand and die casting processes. Simple castings can be made in the home workshop.

6 The recent availability of MIG and TIG welding means that aluminium welding is now possible and there are some low temperature fusion processes which are within the scope of the home workshop.

Copper and copper alloys

7 Copper all by itself crops up in gaskets, wiring and electrical components. On older bikes it is used for fuel and oil pipes, however as we have seen with steel, it is more useful when alloyed with other metals.

8 The combination with zinc forms brass which is a very useful alloy. Depending on the relative proportion of the two materials, different grades of brass can be obtained from one that has high strength to one that is easily shaped and is corrosion resistant. In this latter form the most common use is for radiators.

9 Combining copper with tin produces bronze. This is a very good bearing metal with excellent low friction properties. It also has high resistance to corrosion combined with good strength. The addition of phosphorous to the bronze improves its qualities and in this form we find it in plain bearings, bushes and valve guides.

Other metals

10 Magnesium alloys, often called 'Elektron' are used where the need for lightness overcomes the disadvantage of cost on high performance vehicles.

11 Titanium is also used for its corrosion resistance and lightness. When alloyed with steel, the tensile strength of the material is increased.

12 Zinc has been used on simple castings which do not require stress resistance, eg carburettor bodies.

Stock supply

13 Aluminium and brass are available in solid bar, sheet and tube form in a variety of cross sections.

14 Aluminium sheet is also available with a raised pattern finish which may be used for foot boards for example. Thin sheet may also be salvaged from commercial vehicle breakers.

4 Plastics

1 It is very difficult to define a plastic. We have to go back to its molecular structure and make a definition which says that a plastic is made up of an extremely long chain of molecules, which have generally a carbon backbone and are made up of units which are repeated over and over again hundreds and sometimes millions of times.

2 There are two basic types of plastic: a

Standard Wire Gauge (SWG)	Metric thickness	Imperial thickness
10	3.30 mm	0.128 in
14	2.05 mm	0.080 in
16	1.60 mm	0.064 in
18	1.23 mm	0.048 in
20	0.92 mm	0.036 in
22	0.72 mm	0.028 in

2.20 Sheet steel sizes with metric and imperial conversions

thermoplastic and a thermosetting plastic. A thermoplastic is one that can be moulded and reshaped many times by heating. A thermosetting plastic can only be moulded once and then retains its shape.

3 Typical thermoplastics are polythene, polystyrene, polyvinyl chloride or PVC.

4 Formica and Bakelite, and epoxy resins are examples of thermosetting plastics.

5 The properties of each type of plastic can be modified by adding other materials to improve their impact resistance, strength and mouldability. As the basic plastic is virtually indestructible, additives are now added so as the make the plastic biodegradable.

6 The thermoplastic acrylonitrile/butadiene/styrene; more conveniently called ABS is probably the most common type of plastic used on motorcycles. ABS has a high impact resistance can be self coloured and is easily moulded. Self coloured means that the colour can be impregnated into the plastic on manufacture. The finished article does not therefore need painting, although it can be painted if required.

7 Some crash helmets are made from a material called polycarbonate. This plastic has a high impact resistance and is easily blown or sucked into shape. It is easy to clean and has a good finish. Unfortunately it is affected by the chemicals that occur in paints and glues; hence the warning never to stick transfers on to a polycarbonate helmet. I discovered that due to its strength and transparency it is used for the blue flashing lights on police cars!

8 Another thermosetting material, commonly known as Perspex, transmits light very well and is used in indicator lights and lamp lenses.

9 PVC is a good example of a plastic as it shows that a plastic can be manufactured in a variety of disguises. PVC can be soft and flexible or hard and rigid. In the motor industry it is used as a coating for fabrics and finds its way into seat covers and door trims in cars.

10 Nylon is a very useful thermoplastic which again illustrates the range of applications to which a plastic can be put. This was the first plastic to be discovered as a result of planned research. In engineering, nylon is useful as it has a high abrasion resistance, low coefficient of friction and is self lubricating. It can also be machined and so can be made into long lasting bushes and gear wheels.

11 Another plastic with engineering potential is polytetraflouroethylene; PTFE for short. It is one of the most slippery compounds known to man. Plumbers use it for taping the threads of pipe fittings to prevent leaks. We can use It on petrol fittings as it is oil and petrol resistant. Be wary though of fitting it where fragments could tear off, as it has little physical strength, and could clog up oil ways etc. It is used to coat metal and non-metal bearing surfaces to give an almost friction free surface, hence its use in modern forks.

Composite plastics

12 The term composite plastic refers to the group of materials which are made from fibres set in a resin matrix.

13 The most easily available is the glass fibre reinforced plastic or GRP. This has a variety of uses from patching a hole to building a complete fairing which can be carried out in the home workshop.

14 Fibres of a material called Kevlar have been used in such things as motorcycle helmets and other engineering applications.

15 Carbon fibres are now in common use in many engineering and motorcycle applications. It is possible to machine carbon fibre using conventional machine tools. This means that not only can its strength and fatigue resistance be put to use in structural and chassis work, but engine components can take advantage its lightness, and thermal properties.

16 Nylon is now being filled with fibre and the resulting compound can be used where impact and wear resistance need to be combined with fatigue resistance. The gears in your motorcycle engine could soon be made of this material.

Epoxy resins

17 Apart from acting as a cement to hold various fibrous materials as mentioned above, epoxy resins have a variety of uses on their own.

18 The two part mixture is used as an adhesive. In the car world in addition to riveting aluminium panels together they are also glued with epoxy. The cured resin has good electrical resistance and is fairly flexible which makes it excellent for encapsulating electrical components which might be subjected to bumps and vibration.

19 Epoxy resins can be filled with particles of metal, and form the basis of the repair pastes and putties which we use to mend castings etc.

Rubber

20 Rubber falls into our definition of plastics, however its properties depend on the type of materials with which it is combined and how it Is processed.

Stock

21 Motoring accessory shops stock smaller quantities of the most common epoxy resin compounds and glass fibre kits.

22 For larger quantities of GRP materials it pays to look for specialist supply, or user companies, as they are usually much cheaper than the shops.

23 Carbon fibre material can be bought through specialist suppliers.

5 Choosing a suitable material

Useful definitions

1 Tough - a tough material will withstand vibration and will not easily change its shape.

2 Brittle - a material which will snap or fall into fragments under shock load.

3 Soft - a soft material will scratch easily and may also bend easily.

4 Hard - a material which will resist scratching and has a high impact resistance.

5 Elastic - a material which when deformed will return to its original state.

6 Machineable - refers to a material which may have other properties, but which can be cut, turned and drilled easily.

In general

7 Repairs and modifications will probably be carried out using common mild steel, however you may want to improve the performance, durability or looks of your bike by replacing original parts with new.

8 When choosing a suitable material, use common sense and try and assess the forces and conditions with which your manufactured piece will have to cope.

9 Look at, and compare the design of similar components in successful applications.

10 Besides strength and wear resistance, there are other factors which might influence your choice of material. These may include the ease with which the metal can be cast or bent to shape, machined, or welded.

11 Materials have differing properties of heat and electrical conductivity which lend themselves specific jobs, but you may also be interested in increased corrosion resistance or ease of cosmetic finishing such as polishing or plating.

Notes

Chapter 4
Measuring and marking out

Contents

1 Introduction

1 During any overhaul or repair job, some measuring equipment is needed in order that wear can be assessed. In addition, some of the more basic devices, such as feeler gauges, are needed for routine servicing work.
2 For the manufacture of any replacement parts and tools, accurate measuring tools will be needed in order to prepare working drawings or sketches, and for marking out the stock materials.
3 In this Chapter we will look at the use of measuring and marking out tools and basic sketching in order to provide sufficient information for both the ordering of replacement items and the subcontracting of parts to local engineering firms.

2 Basic measuring equipment

Rulers

1 A basic steel ruler is an essential workshop item, which can be used both for measuring and marking out, and as a straight-edge for checking warpage of gasket faces **(see illustrations)**. Both 150 mm (6 ins) and a 300 mm (12 ins) rulers are worth having as is a 3 metre steel tape measure.

Feeler gauges

2 Feeler gauges are made from thin strips of steel, each identified by its thickness written on one side, and normally come as a set hinged together like a fan. These are an essential purchase for work on almost any machine.
3 The gauge is used by inserting the blade into the gap to be measured. The thickness of blade is progressively increased until the blade, or combination of blades just slides

2.1a Rulers can measure . . .

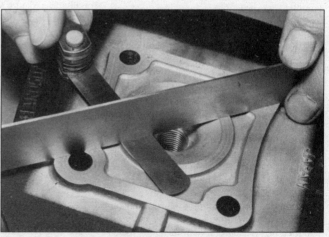

2.1b . . . and be straight-edges too

2.4 A comprehensive set of feeler gauges

2.5a Typical uses of feeler gauges are for valve clearance . . .

2.5b . . . crankshaft side play . . .

2.5c . . . and piston ring end gap measurement

into the gap. The size of the gap is read off the values of the blade, or is the addition of all the blades. In the smaller sets, different feeler gauges must be combined to make up thicknesses not covered directly.

4 Sets are available in either metric or imperial (inch) sizes. You should buy the range which suits your machine, although, as they are inexpensive, a set in both standards may prove convenient where older bikes or machine tools use imperial measurements **(see illustration)**.

5 You will need feeler gauges wherever it is necessary to make an accurate measurement of a small gap, typical applications being the checking of valve clearances on four-stroke engines **(see illustration)**, crankshaft side play **(see illustration)** and piston ring end gap measurement **(see illustration)**.

6 You can also use feeler gauges when assessing distortion (warpage) of gasket faces; the cover or casting is placed, gasket face down, on a surface plate, and any gap can then be measured directly using the feeler gauges **(see illustration)**. The feeler gauge

can also be used in conjunction with a straight-edge for measuring warpage **(see illustration 2.1b)**.

7 Feeler gauges should be treated with care and not bent or torn. Keep them clean and lightly oiled. Before sliding two or more blades together make sure that they are clean.

8 Twist drills can also be used as hole gauges

and feelers. A tip is to keep a set of old drills with the points ground off for this purpose.

Engineering square

9 This is a set square which will allow you to check right angles and the straightness of an edge and the flatness of a surface **(see illustration)**. Several sizes are available; one

2.6 Checking that a clutch plate is not warped

2.9 An engineer's square with a 150 mm blade will be adequate

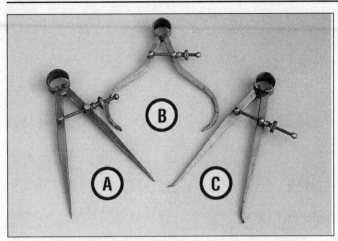

2.13 A pair of dividers (A) with external (B) and internal (C) calipers. The type with spring bows and screw adjustment is best

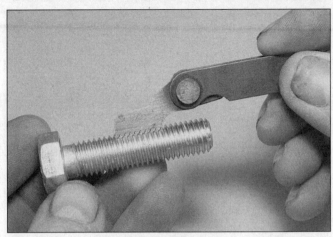

2.20 The thread gauge is very useful for identifying the threads on bolts, shafts etc.

with a blade 150 mm long will be suitable for most jobs.

Calipers and dividers

10 These are traditional engineering comparator tools. One set of calipers, which has the end of the legs bowed in, is used for measuring external dimensions, and the other, with the legs turned in, for internal dimensions. The best sort have the legs pivoted with a spring and the opening adjusted by a finely threaded knurled wheel.

11 The caliper is adjusted by feel until the legs just slide over, or between, the edges of the part being measured. For a reading of the size the caliper must be placed alongside a ruler, vernier gauge or micrometer.

12 Often it is only a comparison between say a shaft and a hole diameter that is required. It is possible to transfer the reading from the external caliper to the internal caliper.

13 Nowadays the use of calipers like these **(see illustration)** has been superseded by the vernier caliper from which a reading as well as a comparison can be made.

14 One version of the caliper which is still quite useful is the odd leg or Jenny caliper. This is used to mark a line at a given distance from an edge, and to find the approximate centre of a round bar.

15 Dividers have two points and are useful for scribing arcs and circles, and dividing lengths and arcs into equal divisions.

Surface plate

16 This is a flat surface used as a base when taking measurements or when marking out. Traditionally it is made of cast iron machined and scraped flat. A block of steel 25 mm (1 ins) thick with one face ground flat will do just as well, and an alternative substitute is a piece of thick glass plate. The useful minimum size is 200 mm (8 ins) square.

17 The surface plate acts as a reference point for taking measurements directly using a rule and a square.

18 As the surface is flat, any other surface

placed on it can also be checked for flatness. For example, the flatness of the mating face of a cylinder head can be checked by resting the head on the surface plate and then trying to insert a feeler gauge between the plate and the head. Should the feeler gauge slide between the two, then the head cannot be flat and if the distortion exceeds the service limit, remedial attention must be given.

19 Protect the surface by building a box cover, and only use it for measuring and marking out.

Thread gauge

20 This gauge is made from a thin strip of steel and along one edge is cut a profile of a thread form. The gauge should mate exactly with the thread on a standard bolt when the two are placed together **(see illustration)**.

21 The gauges usually come in sets determined by the thread form and include blades marked with increasing numbers of teeth per inch, or pitch sizes.

22 An unknown thread can be identified by trial of successive blades until the one that matches exactly is found. The identity of the thread is inscribed on the blade.

3 Vernier gauges

1 The vernier caliper may not provide the same degree of precision as measurement taken with a micrometer, but it is versatile in being able to measure internal and external diameters and usually incorporates a depth gauge.

2 The basic instrument has a friction controlled sliding jaw which is positioned by pressure from the thumb. More accurate and repeatable readings can be made on instruments which have a locking device which holds the sliding jaw at the approximate position and then fine adjustment is made by a knurled wheel operating on a fine thread **(see illustration)**.

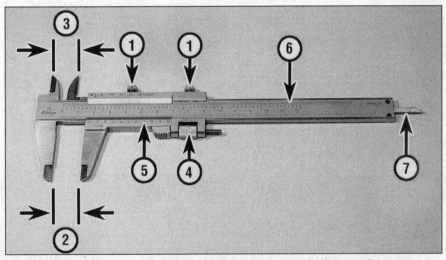

3.2 The component parts of the vernier gauge with linear scale

1 Clamp screws	3 Internal jaws	5 Sliding scale	7 Depth gauge
2 External jaws	4 Thumbwheel	6 Main scale	

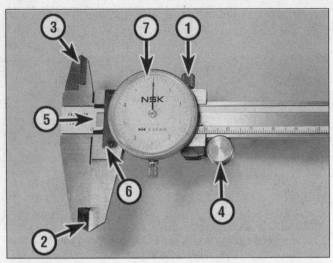

3.3a The component parts of a vernier with the scale on a dial

1   Clamp screw   4   Thumbwheel   6   Sliding scale
2   External jaws   5   Main scale   7   Dial gauge
3   Internal jaws

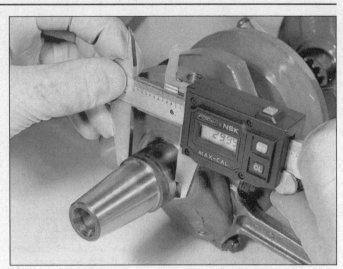

3.3b Digital readout verniers are much easier to read

The accuracy and repeatability of reading depends on the sensitivity of the user's fingers in finding the position where the jaws have just closed against the parts being measured.

3 Newer versions of the caliper are fitted with a direct reading dial for the fine measurement which makes reading measurement easier **(see illustration)**. More expensive models have a direct digital readout **(see illustration)**.

4 To use the conventional linear scale vernier, make sure the jaws are clean, slacken off the vernier clamp screws (1) and set its jaws over (2), or inside (3), the item to be measured **(see illustration 3.2)**. Slide the jaw into contact, using the thumbwheel (4) for fine movement of the sliding scale (5) then tighten the clamp screws (1). Read off the main scale (6) where the zero on the sliding scale (5) intersects it, taking the whole number to the left of the

zero; this provides the base measurement. View along the sliding scale and select the division which lines up exactly with any of the divisions on the main scale, noting that the divisions usually represents 0.02 of a millimetre. Add this fine measurement to the base measurement to obtain the total reading.

In the example shown the item measures 55.92 mm **(see illustration)**:

Base measurement	55.00 mm
Fine measurement	00.92 mm
Total figure	**55.92 mm**

5 On vernier calipers equipped with a dial gauge for fine measurement, set the gauge to zero before use by checking that the jaws are clean, then close them fully and check that the dial gauge reads zero. If necessary adjust the gauge ring accordingly. Slacken the

vernier clamp screw (1) and set its jaws over (2), or inside (3), the item to be measured **(see illustration 3.3)**. Slide the jaws into contact, using the thumbwheel (4) for fine movement. Read off the main scale (5) where the edge of the sliding scale (6) intersects it, taking the whole number to the left of the zero; this provides the base measurement. Read off the needle position on the dial gauge (7) scale to provide the fine measurement; each division represents 0.05 of a millimetre. Add this fine measurement to the base measurement to obtain the total reading.

In the example shown the item measures 55.95 mm **(see illustration)**

Base measurement	55.00 mm
Fine measurement	00.95 mm
Total figure	**55.95 mm**

6 The vernier is ideal for measuring clutch

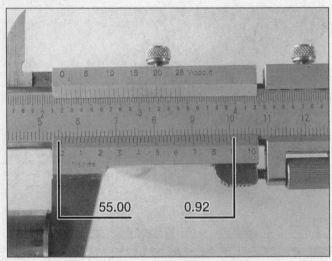

3.4 The vernier gauge reading is 55.92 mm

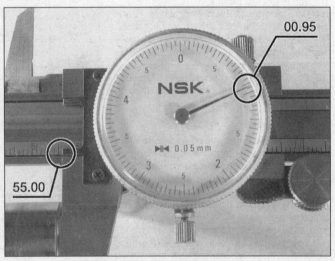

3.5 The reading on the dial is 55.95 mm

3.6a Example of external measurement . . .

3.6b . . . and internal measurement using a vernier

plate friction material and spring free lengths **(see illustrations)**.

7 Many auto jumble and second-hand sales fans carry a vernier as a convenient tool for inspecting and checking items before making a purchase.

4 External micrometers

1 External micrometers are used for measuring outside diameters of components, and are available in different size ranges, eg 0 to 25 mm (0 to 1 in), 25 to 50 mm (1 to 2 in), and upwards in 25 mm or one inch steps. Any one instrument can cover a limited range of sizes, and you would need a set of inside *and* outside micrometers to be fully prepared for any measuring job. However, considering the accuracy of the modern vernier, and as most components are less

than 25 mm (the largest precision measurement you are likely to take on a motorcycle is the piston diameter), larger micrometers than the small instrument might be a luxury.

2 The basic external micrometer comprises a U-shaped frame covering a limited size range **(see illustration)**. At one end is a ground stop, called the anvil, whilst at the other is an adjustable stop, called the spindle. This is moved in or out of the frame on a high-precision fine thread by means of a calibrated thimble, usually incorporating a ratchet to prevent damage to the mechanism and to help in maintaining the repeatability of readings.

3 The conventional analogue type metric instrument is described. The principles of measurement are exactly the same for the imperial instrument in which the sleeve scale is in steps of 0.025 in and the thimble in steps of 0.001 in.

4 It is possible to buy a micrometer set which use interchangeable anvils to allow a large range of measurements to be taken, however,

considering the points made in paragraph 1 above, it is not worth the expense.

5 Always check the calibration of the micrometer before use. With the anvils closed (0 to 25 mm type) or set over a test gauge (for the larger types) the scale should read zero **(see illustration)**; make sure that the anvils (and test piece) are clean first. Any discrepancy can be adjusted by referring to the instructions supplied with the tool. Remember that the micrometer is a precision measuring tool - don't force the anvils closed, use the ratchet (4) on the end of the micrometer to close it. In this way, a measured force is always applied.

6 To use, first make sure that the item being measured is clean. Place the anvil of the micrometer (1) against the item and use the thimble (2) to bring the spindle (3) lightly into contact with the other side of the item **(see illustration 4.2)**. Don't tighten the thimble down because this will damage the micrometer - instead use the ratchet (4) on the end of the micrometer. The ratchet mechanism applies a measured force preventing damage to the instrument.

7 The micrometer is read by referring to the linear scale on the sleeve and the annular scale on the thimble. Read off the sleeve first to obtain the base measurement, then add the fine measurement from the thimble to obtain the overall reading. The linear scale on the

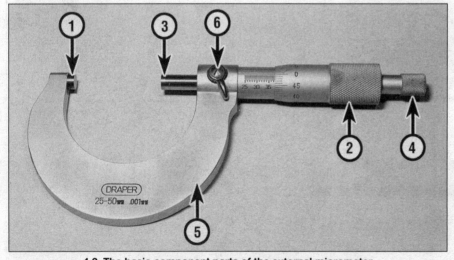

4.2 The basic component parts of the external micrometer

1	*Anvil*	3	*Spindle*	5	*Frame*
2	*Thimble*	4	*Ratchet*	6	*Locking lever*

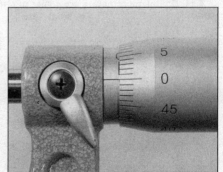

4.5 Check that the setting is zero when the anvils are closed before starting work

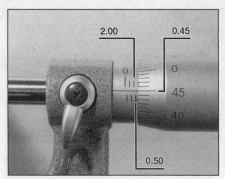

4.7 The micrometer reading is 2.95 mm

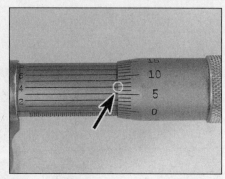

4.9a The micrometer is reading 46.99 on the linear and annular scales . . .

4.9b . . . and 0.004 mm on the vernier scale

sleeve will range from 0 to 25 or 25 to 50 mm depending on the measuring range of the micrometer. The annular scale on the thimble will be in graduations of 0.01 mm (or as marked on the frame) - one full revolution of the thimble will move 0.5 mm on the linear scale. Take the reading where the datum line on the sleeve intersects the thimble's scale. Always position the eye directly above the scale otherwise an inaccurate reading will result.

In the example shown the item measures 2.95 mm (see illustration):

Linear scale	2.00 mm
Linear scale	0.50 mm
Annular scale	0.45 mm
Total figure	**2.95 mm**

8 Most micrometers have a locking lever (6) on the frame to hold the setting in place, allowing the item to be removed from the micrometer.

9 Some micrometers have a vernier scale on their sleeve, providing an even finer measurement to be taken, in 0.001 increments of a millimetre. Take the sleeve and thimble measurement as described above, then check which graduation on the vernier scale aligns with that of the annular scale on the thimble. **Note:** *The eye must be perpendicular to the scale when taking the vernier reading - if necessary rotate the body of the micrometer to ensure this.* Multiply the vernier scale figure by 0.001 and add it to the base and fine measurement figures.

In the example shown the item measures 46.994 mm (see illustrations):

Linear scale (base)	46.000 mm
Linear scale (base)	00.500 mm
Annular scale (fine)	00.490 mm
Vernier scale	00.004 mm
Total figure	**46.994 mm**

10 All micrometers are precision instruments and are easily damaged if misused. They require regular checking and calibration if their accuracy is to be maintained.

11 Although more expensive than conventional types, digital micrometers are much easier to read (see illustration).

5 Internal telescoping gauges

1 Internal micrometers and dial type bore micrometers are available but are expensive and should only be considered for professional use (see illustrations).

2 A set of telescoping gauges (see illustration) and small hole gauges should be adequate for most bore measurements. Both of these need the use of an external micrometer for taking the actual measurement.

4.11 Digital micrometers are easier to read than conventional micrometers

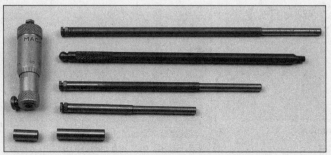

5.1a An internal micrometer with adapters

5.1b A bore micrometer with adapters

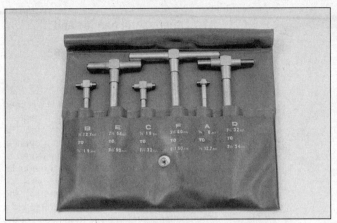

5.2 A set of telescoping gauges

5.4 The gauge is inserted into the bore, expanded to a sliding fit, and then the jaws are locked

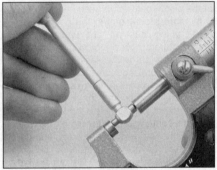

5.5 A micrometer is then used to take the actual measurement

5.6a A small hole gauge is used to measure the bore of the valve guide . . .

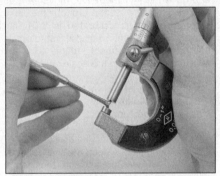

5.6b . . . and the measurement read off using a micrometer

3 For all but very small holes use a telescoping gauge. Select a gauge with a suitable size range, make sure that its ends are clean and insert it into the hole.
4 Expand the gauge, **(see illustration)** and lock it in position then withdraw it from the hole.
5 Measure across the gauge ends with the micrometer **(see illustration)**.
6 Very small holes, such as the bore in a valve guide, can be measured with a small hole gauge. Once adjusted to a sliding fit inside the bore, the ends are locked in position and measured with the micrometer after removal from the bore **(see illustrations)**.

6 Dial test indicator (DTI) or dial gauge

1 The dial gauge, or dial test indicator (DTI) as it is more correctly known, consists of a short probe attached to a clock-type gauge unit capable of measuring small amounts of movement accurately. Metric and imperial gauges are available A dial gauge set usually comes with a range of different probes and adapters and mounting equipment.
2 Typical uses are measuring shaft runout, end-float (sideplay), gear backlash, setting piston position for ignition timing on two-strokes, and setting work accurately in the lathe or milling machine **(see illustrations)**.
3 The gauge needle must point to zero when at rest. Rotate the ring around its periphery to zero the gauge.

6.2a The dial gauge will detect and measure any bend in the shaft as the latter is rotated on the vee-blocks

6.2b Dial gauge being used to measure shaft end-float, ie vertical movement of the shaft

6.2c A dial gauge being used to measure backlash between two gears

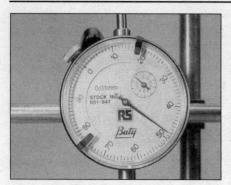

6.4 The dial reads 1.48 mm

4 Check that the gauge is capable of reading the extent of movement in the work. Most gauges have a small dial set in the face which records whole millimetres of movement as well as the fine scale around the face periphery which is calibrated in 0.01 mm divisions. Read off the small dial first to obtain the base measurement, then add the measurement from the fine scale to obtain the total reading.

In the example shown the gauge reads 1.48 mm **(see illustration)**:

Base measurement	1.00 mm
Fine measurement	0.48 mm
Total figure	**1.48 mm**

5 If measuring shaft runout, the shaft must be supported in vee-blocks and the gauge mounted on a stand perpendicular to the shaft. Rest the tip of the gauge against the centre of the shaft and rotate the shaft slowly whilst watching the gauge reading **(see illustration 6.2a)**. Take several measurements along the length of the shaft and record the maximum gauge reading as the amount of runout in the shaft. The reading obtained will be total runout at that point - some manufacturers specify that the runout figure is halved to compare with their specified runout limit. It is possible to carry out the same operation by using the lathe centres and mounting the DTI on the cross slide.

6 End-float (sideplay) measurement requires that the gauge is mounted securely to the

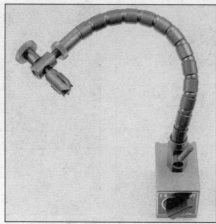

6.8 This flexible stand makes a useful mounting for a dial gauge

surrounding component with its probe touching the end of the shaft. Using hand pressure, push and pull on the shaft noting the maximum end-float recorded on the gauge **(see illustration 6.2b)**.

7 A dial gauge with suitable adapters can be used to determine piston position BTDC on two-stroke engines for the purposes of ignition timing. The gauge, adapter and suitable length probe are installed in the place of the spark plug and the gauge zeroed at TDC. If the piston position is specified as 1.14 mm BTDC, rotate the engine back to 2.00 mm BTDC, then slowly forwards to 1.14 mm BTDC.

8 It is obviously important that the gauge be mounted firmly. In the illustrations accompanying step 2 the gauge is mounted on a bar attached to a magnetic stand and there are also flexible arm mountings **(see illustration)**. This is fine for work on the surface plate or lathe. For other applications, a stand like those used in chemistry laboratories for holding burettes is very useful.

9 As you use the gauge more, you will find the need to make up brackets and clamps to suit each job. A typical example of this is mounting the gauge for wheel and disc runout checks.

7 Other useful gauges and equipment

Degree disc

1 In its simplest form it consisted of a printed card or thin metal disc calibrated in degrees around the edge similar to a protractor. The position for ignition timing, and cam opening and closing points can then be measured or checked as a figure representing the angular movement of the crankshaft.

2 The disc is fitted to the end of the crankshaft via a fixing hole at its centre, and a wire pointer arranged close to the edge of the disc, attached to a casing screw. The method can still be used if the required settings are expressed in degrees, rather than the position of the piston before top dead centre (BTDC).

3 In more recent times, the need to check cam timing has all but vanished; most manufacturers now prefer to express ignition timing settings on two-strokes in terms of piston position, and relevant timing figures are clearly marked on the flywheel or rotor. As a result the humble and inexpensive degree disc is all but forgotten. It is, however, useful if you are contemplating tuning modifications, especially where different cam timings are being tried, or when working on an old engine when engine specifications are not available.

4 Smaller diameter discs are also used to check fastener tightening where this is specified by degrees of rotation **(see illustration)**.

Angle protractor

5 This is a device which has a sliding ruler which can be set at an angle to the straight edge of a protractor. It is used for measuring and marking out angles **(see illustration)**. The sliding rule can also be used as a depth gauge.

Vee-block

6 This is a machined block with vee grooves on which you can rest round bar for measuring and marking out **(see illustration)**.

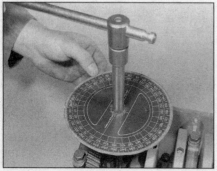

7.4 The degree disc used for setting the angular torque when tightening a bearing bolt

7.5 The angle protractor which can be used for approximate measuring of depths as well as angles

7.6 A tube clamped in the vee-block for marking out the slots during the fabrication of a peg spanner

7.8 A contour gauge in use

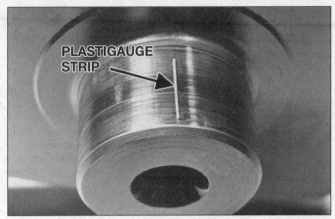

PLASTIGAUGE STRIP

7.12a A thin strip of Plastigauge is laid on the bearing

THE THIN STRIP HAS BEEN SQUASHED IN THE ASSEMBLY

7.12b After assembly using the correct torque settings, and stripping, the Plastigauge has been squashed

CIRCLE PLASTIGA

LE — HAGERSTOWN, INDIANA, U.S.A

7.14 The width of the strip is measured using the gauge supplied to check the bearing clearance

Usually a clamp is provided so that the position of the bar can be fixed. The vee block can also be used for machining operations such as the cross drilling of round components. Care must obviously be taken not to drill into the block itself.

7 Vee-blocks are also used for the measurement of shaft runout (**see illustration 6.2a**).

Contour gauge

8 This is a strip of plastic which holds a series of thin metal prongs. If the gauge is pushed up to a curved surface the prongs are pushed through the plastic until they take up the shape of the curve (**see illustration**). This is useful when you are repairing fairings or tanks for example, and can be especially useful as you get a profile of the external and internal shape.

9 Draughts persons also use a plastic strip which can be bent into a curved shape; this can also be used to follow the profile of a body panel etc.

Plastigauge

10 Plastigauge is a plastic material which can be compressed between two surfaces to measure the oil clearance between them. The width of the compressed Plastigauge is measured against a calibrated scale to determine the clearance.

11 Common uses of Plastigauge are for measuring the clearance between crankshaft journal and main bearing inserts, between crankshaft journal and big-end bearing inserts, and between camshaft and bearing surfaces. The following example describes big-end oil clearance measurement.

12 Handle the Plastigauge material carefully to prevent distortion. Using a sharp knife, cut a length which corresponds with the width of the bearing being measured and place it carefully across the journal so that it is parallel with the shaft (**see illustration**). Carefully install both bearing shells and the connecting rod. Without rotating the rod on the journal tighten its bolts or nuts (as applicable) to the specified torque. The connecting rod and bearings are then disassembled and the crushed Plastigauge examined (**see illustration**).

13 Arriving at the correct clearance demands that the assembly is torqued correctly, according to the settings and sequence (where applicable) provided by the motorcycle manufacturer.

14 Using the scale provided in the Plastigauge kit, measure the width of the material to determine the oil clearance (**see illustration**).

15 Always remove all traces of Plastigauge after use using your fingernails.

Measuring cylinder

16 Calibrated vessels are necessary for measuring specific quantities of oil or coolant. Depending on the quantity, either a jug, straight tube or syringe should be used (**see illustration**).

7.16 A measuring cylinder and a funnel are used for measuring and pouring oils etc.

8.3 An ideal cabinet for storing measuring equipment

Home-made equipment

17 You can make life easier by making up your own specialist equipment. This can take the form of a piece of bar turned to a set diameter or length which you need to check often, a clamping arrangement for mounting a dial gauge, or a specialist item such as a top dead centre (TDC) finder made from an old spark plug.

8 Care of measuring equipment

1 Treat all your pieces of measuring equipment as if they are precision instruments. Do not store them in the general toolbox.

2 Keep them clean and in their boxes or cases whenever they are not actually in your hands for measuring. Make up, or modify a wooden or plastic box if necessary.

3 A purpose tool/instrument chest with several drawers is a good addition to the workshop **(see illustration)**.

4 Various papers and sachets of rust preventative materials are available for storing with your instruments. They do not last forever and should be renewed at intervals.

5 Precision instruments need checking and re-calibration from time to time. The local technical college or a local engineering firm may be able to help in this respect as they will have the necessary equipment.

6 Always check second-hand equipment before you use it. Similarly if any instrument gets accidentally knocked or dropped it should be checked and re-calibrated if necessary.

7 Keep a section of the workshop or bench clean and use it only for measuring and marking out.

8 Don't try and measure dirty components.

9 Sketching and drawing

Sketching an existing part or assembly

1 Preliminary sketches can be done with an HB pencil or a ball-point pen, on any convenient piece of paper. Graph paper is very useful in this respect and can be chosen with a metric or imperial scale. A clip board made from a piece of hardboard and a bulldog clip makes life easier.

2 The first step then is to sketch the shape and take whatever measurements are necessary to be able to reproduce the component in its original shape **(see illustration)**. At this stage it doesn't matter

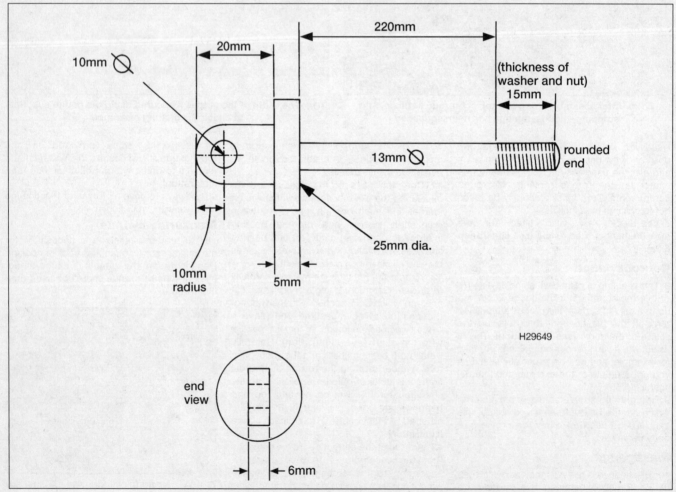

9.2 The first sketch of a component on which all the information is recorded

what units you use, provided that you clearly identify what standard you are using. It is important to take every measurement you will need to be able to reproduce the correct shape.

3 Having got what information you can from the old or original piece examine the mating or adjoining components. You may need to correct the dimensions to take wear into account for example.

4 Make a note of the materials from which the component is made.

5 At this stage you can also consider any modifications to the design or materials which you might want to introduce. For example, if a bolt hole has worn oval you may want to increase the diameter of the bolt.

6 Even if you are going to make the piece yourself, it is worth doing a reasonable drawing. If you have another original piece for direct comparison then perhaps it's not so important, but doing a proper drawing allows you to check that you have got all the necessary measurements and helps you plan how to make the piece; which operations should be done first for example. A classic case is the angle bracket with two holes in it. You drill the holes before bending the metal only to find that one of the holes is now in the wrong position.

7 If you are going to ask someone else to make the piece for you then it is essential to give them all the information they need, as they may not be able check with you if there is a problem without delaying the job.

The final drawing or sketch

8 Again graph paper is useful as you can make use of the grid lines to draw parallel lines and get a reasonable scale. Although engineering drawings are normally to scale, the component is made from the written dimensions not by taking measurements of the drawing. The picture or outline is to give the maker an idea of what the component looks like.

9 To get good clean lines on the paper you need to rest on something flat and hard. Use another piece of hard board or blockboard as a drawing board. If you make sure that two adjacent sides, say the left-hand side and the bottom are straight and smooth then you can use them as a guide for a rule or a plastic square.

10 It is possible to buy a small drawing board made of plastic with its own ruler which slides in a groove at the side. The ruler is held so that it is always at right-angles to the edge of the board and hence the paper's edge, and by butting a square up to it, lines can be drawn accurately at right angles to each other **(see illustration)**.

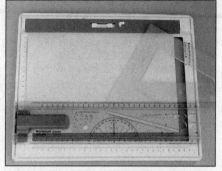

9.10 A small drawing board made of plastic can be worth purchasing

11 A4 size is probably big enough for all the things you are likely to draw and is also a convenient size for photocopying. The next preferred size up is A3 which can also be photocopied. Make your sketch the size of the paper. You can always do a freehand sketch to show the actual size.

12 Begin by drawing the basic shape of the component then add the dimensions (measurements).

13 Stick to some basic rules when creating the drawing. Don't write dimensions inside the lines of your drawing, use dimension lines as you can see on the finished drawing **(see illustration)**. Try and use three grades of line

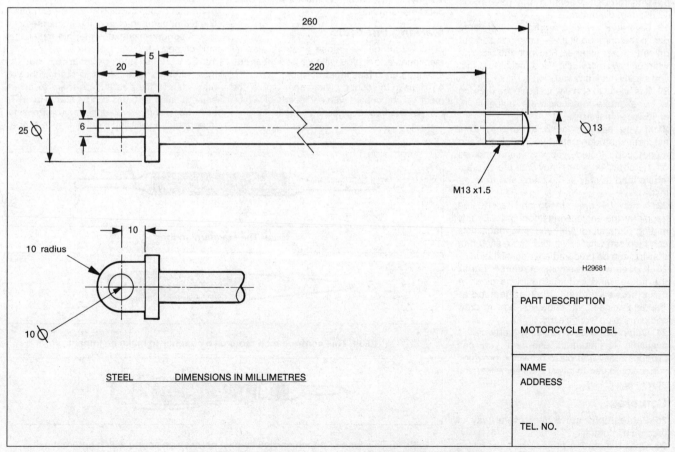

9.13 The final drawing of the bolt sketched in illustration 9.2

thickness: the boldest for the component outline itself, the thinnest for the projection lines which show where a dimension starts and ends, and an intermediate grade for the dimensions themselves.

14 Mark diameters as shown with a small circle crossed with an oblique line.

15 Many components involve a threaded section. There is no need to draw in the details of the thread. Use the method shown to indicate the threaded portion.

16 Again there are conventional ways in which all sides of the component should be shown. The draftsman draws another view of the component as if he or she were looking at the component from a point at right-angles to the first view. If there is any doubt draw a clear freehand sketch and add any dimensions to make all clear.

17 If the component was originally produced in inch units then dimension your drawing similarly, however as most machine shops work in metric it is useful to include the metric equivalent in a bracket after the imperial size. For example 1" (25 mm).

18 Using your vernier gauge or micrometer it is easy to get carried away and quote all sizes to the nearest thousandth of an inch. Don't be tempted. Think about the real need for accuracy. A bolt passing through a drilled hole need only be 13 mm diameter. A shaft passing through a bearing may have to be 12.995 mm diameter.

19 Give your drawing a title; use the same one in the parts book if you have one and put down the part number. Show on the drawing what units you are using and make sure that you clearly mark any variations.

20 It is useful to show what scale the drawing is. For example you could write "actual size", or "twice actual size".

21 If you have to send a drawing to a machine shop don't send your original. Send a photocopy. Include your name and address on the copy. Drawings stay with the job, but letters tend to stay in the office and may get lost.

22 It may be wiser to go and talk to the people at the engineering shop and take any mating parts along with you. The machinists can then see what is wanted and a sketch or drawing can be prepared after consultation.

23 It goes without saying of course that all the figures and writing should be clear. A quick browse through a magazine such as "Model Engineer" will show you how to draw and dimension work clearly.

24 Computer-based drawing software is available for amateur use and you can produce really first class drawings provided you are prepared to invest a little time learning how to use it.

Cameras

25 Photographs are a very useful way of recording information.

26 On a restoration project, besides giving you a record of how your bike was restored,

they can provide a library of information with photographs from similar models showing colour schemes, and the shape and relative position of components.

 Photographs taken of wiring and hose routing before engine removal, can save a lot of time working this out on the rebuild.

27 Photographic slides can also be projected to give an enlarged view from which general measurements can be taken.

28 Video tape, and even digital cameras working with computer software, will also provide help in storing information.

10 Marking out

1 Marking out is the process by which you draw on the base material the outline shape, and any holes or other features which have to be made.

2 For lathe work the dimensions are usually identified straight from a sketch or drawing so it is mainly fabrication operations which need detail marking out.

Marking out tools

3 In addition to those items already mentioned above, you will need a scriber and a centre punch **(see illustrations)**.

4 To make the scribed lines more visible, the metal can be coated with engineer's blue (you can get this from engineering suppliers or

good tool shops) and the lines scribed onto this. A small tin of this will last for years. A convenient alternative is to use a spirit-based felt tipped marker to darken the surface.

5 Work in an area where there is good lighting. A lamp on a flexible stand is ideal as it can be positioned to avoid shadows and glare hitting the work.

The method of marking out

6 Find a line or a point, which may be a hole position or a corner, which you can use as a reference. Ideally all independent dimensions should be made from this reference. Exceptions are where it is more important that two points be a certain distance from each other, mounting hole centres for example.

7 When marking out sheet or plate to fabricate a bracket or a similar item, you can work from a straight edge on the material, assuming it has been cut accurately. You will normally find that materials which have been cut to size on a guillotine will be quite good in this respect and it is easier to treat this straight edge as finished. To ensure accuracy it is better to allow about 1 mm or so and then file back to this after cutting the rough shape out of the metal.

8 Measure and mark out the shape of the work on the metal, using the scriber to trace the outline.

9 On thin material which is to be bent, use a fine felt tipped pen or pencil to mark the bend line. A scriber may cause the thin material to split on bending.

10 Corners should be marked out by intersecting scribed lines to start with; you may wish to file a radius on them to give a smooth finish, and this can be added later. To save work, and provided the radius size is not important, you will find it quite easy to scribe

10.3a The standard scriber

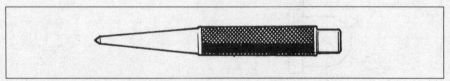

10.3b This centre punch requires a hammer to make an impact

10.3c This type of punch carries its own percussion spring which automatically makes a mark

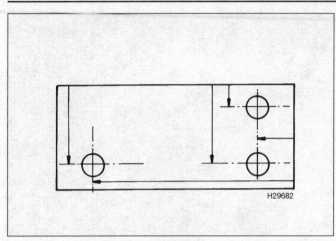

10.13a Marking out using the top and right-hand side for reference

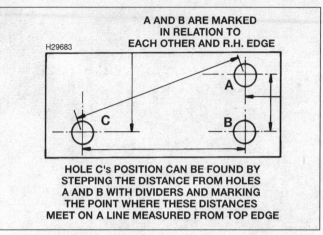

A AND B ARE MARKED
IN RELATION TO
EACH OTHER AND R.H. EDGE

H29683

A

C

B

HOLE C's POSITION CAN BE FOUND BY
STEPPING THE DISTANCE FROM HOLES
A AND B WITH DIVIDERS AND MARKING
THE POINT WHERE THESE DISTANCES
MEET ON A LINE MEASURED FROM TOP EDGE

10.13b Marking out where the hole positions relative to each other are important

around coins or washers to obtain a smooth, rounded corner.

11 Odd leg calipers, an angle/depth gauge with a scriber can be used to scribe a line at a given distance from a straight edge.

12 Dividers are used for scribing circles, radii at corners, and for stepping out distances to mark the pitch of a series of holes.

13 Holes are marked by finding the position of the hole centre; usually by making two lines at right-angles or by measuring from one edge to a point which intersects with an arc drawn from another point **(see illustrations)**.

14 A hole centre is marked with a centre punch using a light tap with a hammer. In fact any important reference point can be marked in the same way. This centre pop mark is not to locate the drill at this stage, therefore it does not need such a heavy mark.

15 If the component has to be bent, the position of any other features may not end up where they appeared when the material was flat. For accurate bending there are tables which state how much extra material to allow on the flat blank.

16 For practical purposes, especially where

bending is not done on a machine, use a reference point which does not have the bend between it and the feature, or finish marking out after the bending operation and with reference to the assembly of the part. This particularly applies to things like battery carriers and mounting brackets having bolt holes which need to line up with existing assemblies.

17 A right-angle bracket with a single bolt fixing for locating a component is marked out as an example **(see illustrations)**.

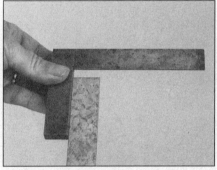

10.17a Checking that the end of the strip is cut square

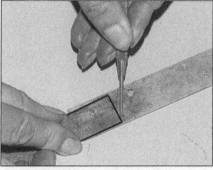

10.17b Marking the distance of the first hole from the end of the strip

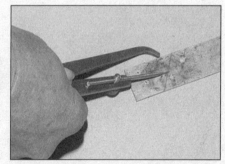

10.17c Using a pair of odd leg calipers to mark a line down the centre of the strip. Where the lines cross is the hole centre

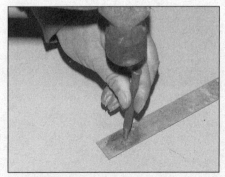

10.17d Using the centre punch to mark the centre of the hole

10.17e Marking the position of the bend with a fine marker

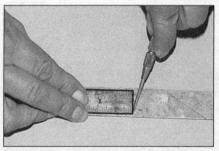

10.17f The line for the overall length of the bracket need not be exact at this stage. Allow a little extra which can be trimmed off after bending

10.17g After bending, the angle gauge is used to mark the position of the second hole from the outside of the bend

10.17h A scriber held in a block and set at the required height above the surface plate, is an alternative method of marking the position of the second hole. The odd leg calipers, at the same setting as above, identify the second hole centre

Chapter 5
General test equipment

Contents

1 Introduction

This Chapter includes some of the testing equipment in general use in the workshop. They are used as an important part of fault diagnosis, in addition to keeping your motorcycle running efficiently.

2 Compression tester

1 These devices are basically pressure gauges which connect to the engine via the spark plug hole and allow the pressure developed inside the cylinder to be measured. They consist of a clock, or stick type gauge connected by a short rigid or flexible tube which has either a male screw, or to a tapered rubber nozzle, for locating into the spark plug hole **(see illustrations)**. The screw-in variety is preferred.

2 In use, the gauge is connected to the engine, and the engine is then cranked for a few seconds. When the gauge needle reaches a stable reading it is removed and the reading noted, before the pressure is released to reset

2.1a The rubber push-in style of gauge is not really suitable for one person operation nor where access on multi-cylinder engines is restricted

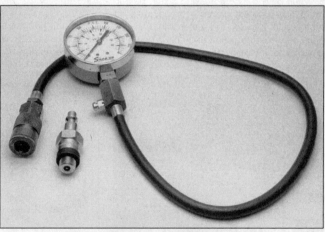

2.1b The screw-in type, with spark plug adapter is much more suited to motorcycle use

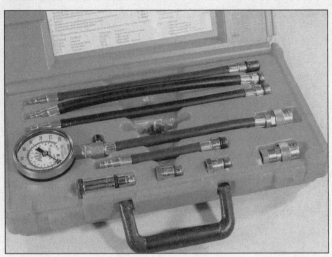

2.6 A compression tester with a set of adapters and flexible hoses

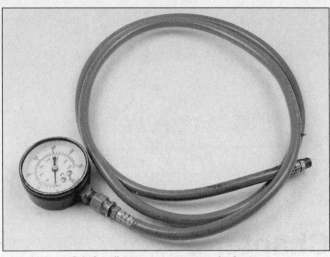

3.1 An oil pressure gauge and adapter

it. The exact pressure figure applicable varies widely according to the make and model of machine.

3 The purpose of the tool is to diagnose loss of pressure in a cylinder without having to dismantle the engine to check for physical wear. Used in the way described above, the gauge will show up bore or ring wear, and on 4-stroke engines additionally valve leakage. This can be extended on multi-cylinder engines to diagnosing compression differences between cylinders.

4 By introducing a little oil into a cylinder showing an abnormally low reading, a worn bore can be temporarily sealed; if the test is repeated, the pressure reading should have improved. Where the reading stays about the same, this points to the leakage being due to a worn or burnt-out valve, rather than in the bore. It follows that this last stage of testing is applicable only to 4-stroke engines.

5 It is useful to keep a record of compression checks over a period of time in your reference library.

6 When buying a compression tester, bear in mind the problem of restricted access on motorcycle engines. The tester with a flexible hose between the gauge and nozzle could be an advantage (see illustration).

3 Oil pressure gauge

1 An oil pressure gauge (see illustration) is used for measuring engine oil pressure when the engine is running at a speed specified in the relevant Service and Repair Manual.

2 Often the manufacturer will specify the pressure limits for a hot and cold engine; the pressure being different for each condition.

3 Most gauges come with a set of adapters to fit the thread of the take-off point, which is often at the oil pressure switch (see illustration). If the specified take-off point is an external oil pipe union make sure that the correct adapter is used to prevent oil starvation.

4 Vacuum gauge

1 Vacuum gauges are used to measure the vacuum effect developed in the inlet tract while the engine is running, and provide an

accurate method of setting up and synchronising two or more carburettors.

2 Two basic designs are available, having either clock-type gauge heads, or manometer types relying on mercury filled columns. Column type gauges are now available which do not contain mercury (see illustrations).

3 Both clock and column types will work satisfactorily, though with the clock-type instruments it is important that the gauge heads used are accurate.

4 Most vacuum gauge manufacturers will supply a set of gauges to suit four carburettor installations, with a range of adapters and hoses. Certain manufacturers will supply sets with two, three or six gauges to suit a different number of carburettors.

5 In use, the synthetic rubber hoses from the gauges are connected, via adapters (if necessary), to the inlet manifold for each cylinder. The manifold will either have tapped holes sealed with screws and sealing washers, or a brass stub sealed with a rubber

3.3 Measuring the oil pressure. The take-off point adapter is shown at the arrow

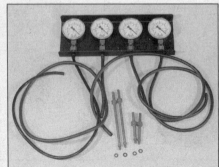

4.2a A set of clock-type vacuum gauges and adapters

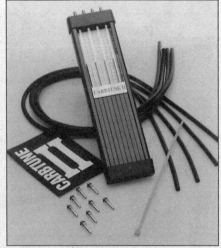

4.2b A mercury-free column type of carburettor gauge

4.5a Vacuum gauge hoses either fit over brass stubs (arrowed) on inlet manifolds . . .

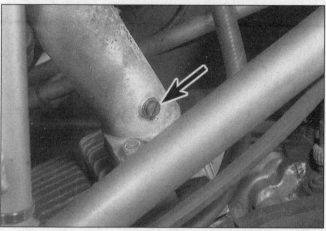

4.5b . . . or gauge adapters are screwed into threaded holes in manifolds (arrowed)

cap **(see illustrations)**. Before checking synchronisation, check whether the adjustment screws are accessible with the fuel tank in place – it is unlikely that they will. With the fuel tank removed, you can either run an extra long fuel pipe to the carburettors, or set up a temporary fuel supply **(see illustration)**.

6 With some gauge sets, you will have to attach each gauge to one cylinder in turn, so that the gauge damper valves can be set up so that each instrument gives the same reading. Other types use preset damping, and do not need setting up. Take care to position the gauges where they can be easily seen **(see illustration)**; some types come supplied with a clip for mounting to the handlebar.

7 Once connected, the vacuum reading for each cylinder will be shown with the engine idling and at normal operating temperature. Most manufacturers quote a reading for a particular model, though in practice it is more important to obtain an identical reading on each gauge than to get a specific figure (usually within 2 cm Hg of each other). Note that there are a few exceptions to this general

4.5c A temporary fuel supply set-up - ensure there are no fuel leaks and support the fuel container securely

4.6 Position the gauges where they can easily be seen

rule; some four cylinder models must be set up so that the inner pair of cylinders show a slightly different reading than the outer two.

8 If the readings differ widely, the synchronisation screws must be adjusted so that all readings are even **(see illustrations)**. The order in which the screws are adjusted depends on the number of cylinders and throttle operating arrangement – refer to your

workshop manual for details. Once the idle vacuum settings are correct, the engine should run noticeably smoother at tickover.

9 Blip the throttle open a couple of times to settle the linkage, and recheck the synchronisation. Once set up, re-set the idle speed, then stop the engine and disconnect the gauges. Install the inlet adapter plugs and roadtest the machine.

4.8a A long shafted screwdriver is usually necessary to access synchronisation screws

4.8b Typical synchronisation screw positions (arrowed) on a four cylinder engine

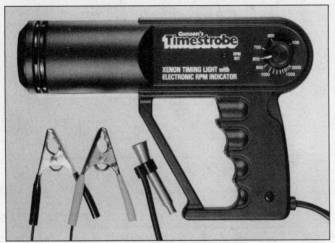

5.1 A xenon type stroboscope

5.4 The strobe beam is pointed at the timing marks on the exposed rotor

10 You should find that a few minutes work will be well rewarded, with the engine feeling smoother and more flexible. Keeping the carburettors in synchronisation will also tend to improve fuel economy and minimise mechanical wear due to backlash in the primary drive.

11 Setting up carburettors without vacuum gauges is possible, but far from easy. With twin-cylinder machines it is reasonably easy to do so by ear; a length of plastic tubing can be used as a stethoscope, and the sound of the intake hiss through each carburettor compared. If you can accrue enough experience in this method, you can get fairly good results, but for most people a set of gauges is a better bet. On engines with more than two cylinders, gauges can be considered essential.

5 Stroboscope

1 Stroboscopic test lamps, usually called strobes or timing lights, are used to check dynamically the ignition timing settings. There are two basic types, based on either neon or xenon tubes. The neon versions are cheap, but the weak reddish-coloured light produced is dim and poorly defined. Given that they are hard to see clearly unless it is dark, it is best to use the xenon tube types which give a much brighter white light and are far clearer in use (see illustration).

2 Xenon lamps normally require a power supply, usually from a 12 volt battery source, but occasionally mains voltage is used. If supplied from a battery it is preferable to use a separate battery; connecting it to the machine's battery can result in spurious signals triggering the lamp.

3 Two other leads are fitted, these connecting to the spark plug and plug cap of the cylinder under test, effectively connecting the lamp into that cylinder's high tension circuit. When the engine is running, the lamp is triggered each time the plug fires, producing a short pulse of light.

4 The light is aimed at the ignition timing marks (see illustration), which are usually found near the contact breaker assembly or pickup unit. The rapid pulses of light have the effect of 'freezing' the movement of the rotating pickup or cam unit, and the position of the marks in relation to a fixed index mark can be seen at the moment that the plug fires. If the two do not align, this indicates that the ignition timing setting is incorrect.

5 In the case of machines with contact breaker ignition systems (though mopeds and some small two-strokes are exceptions here) you can alter the ignition setting by turning the contact breaker baseplate once the retaining screws have been slackened. On most machines with electronic ignition, and in the case of the small two-strokes mentioned above, adjustment is not possible. If you are dealing with electronic ignition, incorrect timing usually means a fault in the ignition control unit, whilst on fixed contact breaker systems, worn or badly adjusted contact breakers are usually to blame.

6 On four-cylinder engines, and some twins, a spare-spark ignition system is used. With this arrangement, two plugs are run from a shared ignition coil. This means that both cylinders spark at the same time, even though only one is at compression.

7 In the case of most Japanese fours, the system is arranged so that the cylinders 1 and 4 fire together, as do cylinder 2 and 3, so two timing checks are made. The timing marks normally show which pair of cylinders they relate to, often being marked 1-4 F and 2-3 F.

8 You will note from the above that a strobe can be an invaluable piece of equipment when used on machines with adjustable ignition timing. On models where the ignition is fixed, they are of more limited use; the strobe can tell you if the ignition setting is incorrect, but it is not normally possible to do much about this, short of fitting new parts. With electronic systems it is debatable whether regular timing checks serve any useful purpose, though it is worthwhile being able to diagnose a suspected fault.

6 Multimeter

1 A multimeter is an invaluable piece of equipment if you are contemplating any work on the electrical system. Comprising a multi-purpose electrical test instrument (see illustration). Separate voltmeters, ammeters and ohmmeters are available although for motorcycle use the multimeter offers the best value. The multimeter is capable of measuring resistance (ohms or Ω) ac and dc volts, and in some cases current (amps). Most meters have several ranges in each of these categories.

6.1 A simple cheap multimeter which will be adequate for general electrical testing

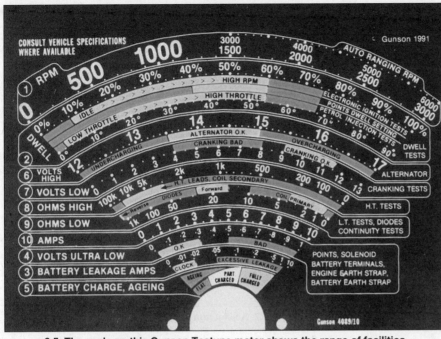

6.5 The scale on this Gunson Testune meter shows the range of facilities

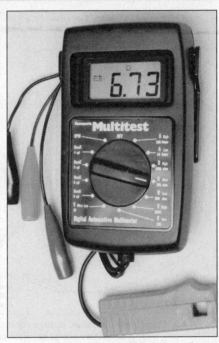

6.6 A multimeter with a digital reading

2 Multimeters are primarily intended for electronics work, and so the cheaper ones do not have current ranges capable of more than a few milliamps. You can either pay a little more to get this feature, or do without it (you can always buy a separate ammeter if you need it). Slightly more expensive versions have an internal resistance which allows current readings up to about 10A.

3 The single most useful function of the multimeter is its resistance ranges. In addition to its obvious application in checking the internal resistance's of electrical components, the resistance range allows the meter to function as a simple continuity tester; invaluable for checking for broken connections or short circuits. The meter may also feature a continuity buzzer, useful when you are not able to look at the meter during testing.

4 It should be noted that the polarity and internal workings of some meters means that the resistance readings you might get when testing a perfectly sound component could vary from those specified by the motorcycle manufacturer. This factor should be borne in mind when checking critical resistance values, and your findings confirmed by a motorcycle manufacturer before purchasing new components. In practice, any reasonable meter will give a good indication of a major fault, even if the values do not agree precisely.

5 Meters are available which have a comprehensive range of facilities which are useful to the motorcyclist **(see illustration)**. The model in the illustration measures a wide range of dc volts including an expanded scale of 12 - 17 volts for accurate measurement of

alternator and regulator performance. It also measures rpm, dwell, ohms and battery leakage which makes it a most useful piece of testing equipment.

6 Always disconnect the probes when changing ranges to avoid damage to the meter. Meters which give a digital reading are more accurate than the needle or analogue type **(see illustration)**. Although more expensive they also offer a range of useful facilities.

7 Familiarise yourself with the maker's instructions before using a new multimeter to avoid damage to the meter or bike electronics.

8 After using a meter, always switch it OFF to conserve its battery.

7 Continuity tester

1 A simple continuity test will tell you if there is a failure in the electrical supply to and from a component, ie a break in the wiring or poor connection. A continuity test can also be performed to check the operation of a diode.

2 A continuity tester is used to confirm that there is a unbroken electrical path between two points. It may have its own small dry cell battery or take power from the battery on the bike. Note that a multimeter (or ohmmeter) could also be used to check continuity (see Section 6).

3 Continuity testers either light a bulb or buzz when the circuit is complete **(see illustration)**. An audible reaction is preferable to a visual

one, especially when you are looking carefully at the position of the probes.

4 A workshop built model is a simple exercise using a door bell or buzzer with a dry cell battery; electronics DIY shops sell the parts. One lead should have a pointed probe, although a crocodile clip may be more useful on the other lead. Make the leads long enough to so that they can reach across the length of the bike without having to hang the buzzer unit in mid air or balance it on bits of the bike **(see illustration overleaf)**.

5 As the continuity tester is self-powered all checks are made with the ignition OFF. As a safety precaution, always disconnect the battery earth (ground) lead before making checks, particularly if working on the ignition switch.

6 Even though the self-powered tester may provide a small voltage, check that this will not damage any electronic units in the circuit you are testing.

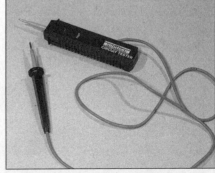

7.3 A self-powered continuity probe with light – similar types are available with a buzzer

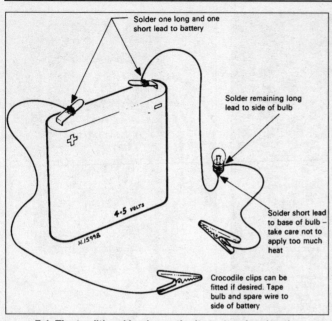

7.4 **The traditional basic continuity tester showing the arrangement of components**

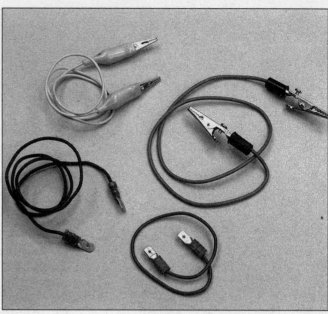

7.7 **A selection of insulated jumper wires**

7 A selection of wires with clips or connectors **(see illustration)** are useful items to keep with the test equipment.

8 Tyre pressure gauge

1 The most common type of pressure gauge is the pencil type. The calibrated scale is pushed out of the gauge body when the gauge is pressed onto the tyre valve **(see illustration)**. These are a convenient, pocket or toolkit accessory. Dial-type gauges are also available, which have a reset button **(see illustration)**.
2 A gauge capable of reading up to 50 psi (3.6 bars) will be suitable for motorcycle use. When purchasing a tyre pressure gauge, check that the gauge will fit between the valve head and brake disc – those with angled heads are best.
3 Electronic gauges which have audible 'bleep' measurement checks and digital read outs are available, but are more expensive.

4 It is difficult to check the accuracy of the stick gauge except by comparing the pressure reading with another gauge. Tyre pressure should be checked regularly and always when the tyre is cold – the pressure will increase when the tyre is hot (ie immediately after riding the motorcycle)

9 Tyre tread depth gauge

1 This is a device which measures the depth of tread remaining on a tyre **(see illustration)**.
2 In the workshop, you could also use the depth facility on a vernier gauge.

10 Wheel alignment gauge

Note: *Refer to Chapter 14 for more information on wheel alignment.*

Straight-edge gauge

1 This gauge can be constructed at home, and is simply two lengths of perfectly straight wood or metal which can be laid against the tyre sidewalls of both wheels on each side of the machine to check that the wheels are in line **(see illustration)**. The gauge is supported on a couple of blocks so that it contacts the tyres at a height roughly halfway between the axle and bottom of the wheel, although the disc/sprocket/final drive will have to be avoided. The rear tyre is usually much wider than the front, so measure the distance from the front tyre to the gauge and check that it is the same on each side of the wheel. Note that an uneven wheel offset is acceptable on some shaft drive machines – check with your workshop manual or a dealer for details.
2 The distance from the front tyre to the gauge can be calculated by subtracting the width of the front tyre from the rear tyre width and dividing the difference by two. Note that an uneven wheel offset is acceptable on some shaft drive machines – check

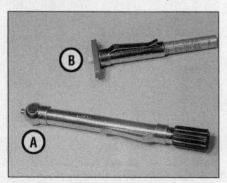

8.1a **The pencil type tyre pressure gauge (A), tread depth gauge (B)**

8.1b **The dial type tyre pressure gauge**

9.1 **Measuring the depth of tread at the centre of the tyre using the tread gauge**

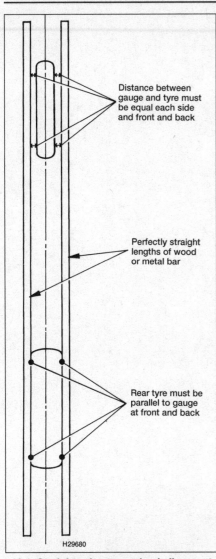

10.1 Straight-edge type wheel alignment gauge

Distance between gauge and tyre must be equal each side and front and back

Perfectly straight lengths of wood or metal bar

Rear tyre must be parallel to gauge at front and back

H29680

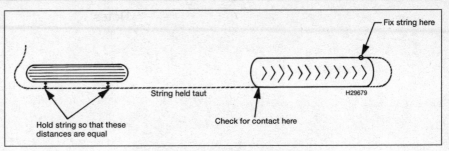

10.4 String type wheel alignment gauge

Fix string here

String held taut

Hold string so that these distances are equal

Check for contact here

H29679

with your workshop manual or a dealer for details.

3 Note that the machine must be off its stand, with the front wheel pointing straight ahead during the alignment check. It is preferable to have an assistant seated on the machine to hold it steady **(see illustration)**.

String gauge

4 The above straight-edge gauge can be substituted by a length of string. Have an assistant sit on the machine so that it is off its stand, with the front wheel pointing straight ahead. Fasten the string to one of the wheel spokes (at a height about halfway between the axle and the bottom of the wheel will do) so it comes round the rear tyre and pull it taut so that it is in contact with front and back edges of the rear tyre on the side being checked **(see illustration)**. Hold the string parallel with the front tyre and measure the distance from the string to the front tyre sidewall at the front and rear of the front tyre; unless the front and rear tyres are the same width, there will be a gap between the string and tyre – refer to Step 2 to calculate the gap.

5 Carry out the same test on the other side of the machine. The gap between string and front tyre sidewall should be equal on each side of the front tyre, and equal at front and rear points of the front tyre. Remember to keep the string in contact with the front and rear points of the rear tyre sidewall during the check.

Sprocket alignment gauge

6 It is possible to sight down the line of the final drive sprockets to check wheel alignment. To aid this, a gauge can be clamped to the rear wheel sprocket with its rod in line with the drive chain **(see illustration)**. Sight along the rod to check whether the sprockets, and thus rear wheel, are in line.

11 Exhaust noise and emissions

1 Although there are legal levels for exhaust noise, checking depends on the discretion of the tester and the expectations of a correctly fitted legally approved exhaust system in good repair.

2 It is possible to buy emission gas analysers, however if the engine is in a good condition and the carburettors and ignition timing correct, then the emission gases should be within acceptable limits.

3 A gas analyser may be needed where a catalytic converter is fitted into the exhaust system to check that it is functioning correctly.

10.3 Checking wheel alignment with the aid of an assistant to hold the motorcycle upright

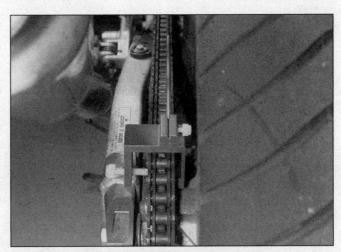

10.6 Sprocket alignment gauge in use

Notes

Chapter 6
Threads and fasteners

Contents

1 Introduction

This Chapter includes a brief discussion on the different types of thread found on a motorcycle and how to identify them.

As fasteners have often to be tightened to a specified 'torque', the meaning of this term is explained.

Advice is given on fitting fasteners and repairing damaged fasteners and threads.

This Chapter also contains a catalogue of the most common types of fasteners, washers, pins, rivets and retainers likely to be encountered on most recent models, together with an illustration to facilitate identification. Some additional types are listed where these are likely to be of interest in the home

workshop. The list is by no means exhaustive, but relates to the most common types.

Note that in the case of general-purpose fasteners used throughout the machine, ordinary mild steel or high tensile steel is normally used, with a bright zinc or cadmium coating to resist corrosion. If you purchase replacement fasteners of this type, it is more economical to buy them in quantity. Most motorcycle magazines will carry advertisements for suitable suppliers, many of whom will supply selections of popular sizes, together with suitable plain washers.

Assortments of fasteners will usually include a selection of bolts and setscrews in a variety of lengths and diameters. Bear in mind that these may have to be shortened to suit a particular application, and unless stainless steel is specified, cut ends of steel bolts will rust.

In some more specialised areas, such as stand pivot bolts, special materials or hardening processes may have been used to resist wear or breakage. These fasteners often have non-standard head sizes or shank diameters. Any replacement should be with an identical item.

If you need to renew any fastener in a highly-stressed application, be sure to replace it with a suitable equivalent to avoid subsequent failure, *not* with an ordinary mild steel item, or it may fail in use. The best way to avoid this risk is to purchase official replacement parts from a motorcycle dealer.

Fasteners are available in a range of materials to suit the application. For example, stainless steel nuts and bolts to replace existing mild steel items and aluminium fasteners in a range of anodised colours are available for fairing fittings.

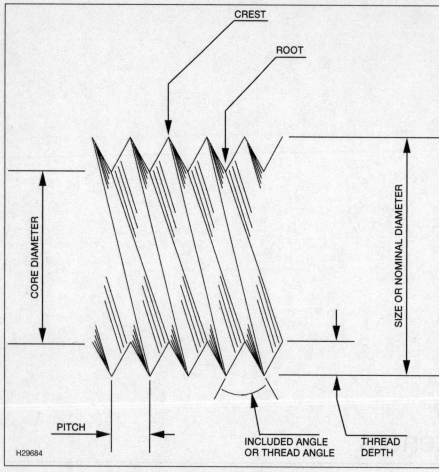

2.2 **The names given to parts of a screw thread**

2 Thread types

1 The ISO metric and the Unified series are the preferred standards in modern engineering practice, however anyone with an interest in restoring an older machine will have to familiarise themselves with the older thread forms and collect an appropriate range of taps and dies.

2 The thread shape or form and pitch is described in standard tables. This information is needed when cutting threads in lathe work and in identifying unknown threads on fasteners and components **(see illustration)**.

ISO Metric

3 This is the standard used on modern Japanese bikes and those produced in Europe **(see illustration)**. The thread is described by its diameter and the pitch of the thread. There may be a range of pitches given for any thread diameter so that the most suitable thread form can be chosen for a particular application. All ISO metric threads have a 60° angle.

4 Early machines made in Japan used a metric standard which is not in use today. Take care when working on these bikes to use the correct thread form.

AF size	Thread diameter and pitch
8 mm	M5 x 0.8
8 mm	M6 x 1.0
10 mm	M6 x 1.0
12 mm	M8 x 1.25
14 mm	M10 x 1.25
17 mm	M12 x 1.25

British Standard Whitworth, BSW

5 The earliest standard used in British engineering. The thread is described by its diameter and the number of threads per inch length of thread. The thread angle is 55° **(see illustration)**. Early bolts had a different width across the spanner flats to the later standard **(see illustration)**.

British Standard Fine, BSF

6 Used in general engineering applications alongside BSW and described by the thread diameter and the number of threads per inch. The angle is 55° **(see illustration 2.5a)**. The width across the spanner flats was at odds with early BSW but now they correspond. The Royal Enfields used BSF threads extensively.

British Standard Cycle, BSC

7 This was the most common thread form used in the British motorcycle industry. It has a 60° thread angle, and is described by the diameter of the thread and the number of threads per inch. The commonly used diameters between 1/4 and 1 in all have 26 threads per inch.

British Association, BA

8 This standard was devised for small threads such as those used in electrical fittings and components.

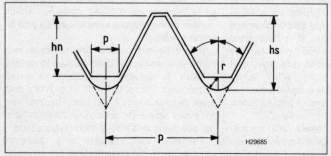

2.3 **The ISO Metric thread form information**

p Pitch   r Radius
hn Height of internal thread and depth of thread engagement
hs Height of external thread

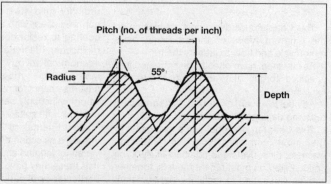

2.5a **Whitworth and BSF thread form showing the thread angle and relevant dimensional relationships**

BSW (Old standard)

Nominal size	Max across flats	Max across corners	Maximum thickness		
			Head	Nut	Locknut
1/4	0.525	0.606	0.22	0.25	0.166
5/16	0.600	0.694	0.27	0.313	0.208
3/8	0.710	0.821	0.33	0.375	0.250
7/16	0.820	0.948	0.38	0.438	0.291
1/2	0.920	1.062	0.44	0.500	0.333

BSW (New standard) and BSF

Nominal size	Max across flats	Max across corners	Maximum thickness		
			Head	Nut	Locknut
1/4	0.445	0.514	0.19	0.20	0.133
5/16	0.525	0.606	0.22	0.25	0.166
3/8	0.600	0.694	0.27	0.313	0.208
7/16	0.710	0.821	0.33	0.375	0.250
1/2	0.820	0.948	0.38	0.438	0.291

2.5b Hexagon AF sizes for Whitworth and BSF nuts and bolts

All dimensions are in inches

Unified

9 This standard was introduced following joint discussions between American, Canadian and British engineers, and is used on cars and motorcycles. The thread form is the same as the metric thread, and is described by its diameter and threads per inch and has a coarse and fine range of sizes, UNC and UNF.

3 Identification of thread types

1 It is important to know the names used to describe fasteners to avoid confusion when seeking replacements **(see illustration)**. As described above you can identify a thread by measuring its diameter and either counting the number of threads per inch length, or measuring the distance between each thread crest to find the pitch. This information can then be compared with the standard thread tables to find the correct thread description.
2 A useful addition to the measuring equipment is a screw thread gauge **(see illustration 2.20 in Chapter 4)**.
3 The width across the spanner flat can also give you a clue as to the type of thread form.
4 Strength marks indicating the material type can be seen on some types of bolt head. Generally these refer to bolts made of high tensile steel rather than common mild steel. Whereas the higher strength bolts can be

used to replace the common type, do not replace high strength items with ordinary mild steel bolts which may have a higher torque setting.
5 Do not mix nuts and bolts from different thread types. Although they may appear to fit, the strength of the thread will not be great and the fastener may prove difficult to loosen.
6 The standard thread can also be produced in 'left-hand' form. This modification means that to tighten the bolt or nut, you turn the head anti-clockwise, and clockwise to loosen it. Examination of the thread will soon show you if the thread is left-handed. However when in place, unless the head is marked, there may be no way of identifying it. The left-hand thread is often used to secure components which rotate and may loosen a conventional right-hand threaded fastener. If a bolt does not release on turning anti-clockwise, and is used to secure a rotating component, try turning it the opposite way, that is clockwise.

4 Repairing damaged threads

Internal threads

1 A tap or thread chaser can be used to clean up minor damage, or clean out old thread locking compounds **(see illustration)**.
2 Where there is sufficient material around the hole and a larger bolt or stud can be used, it is simple to drill out the old thread, and then drill with the tapping size drill for the next size up. The thread is tapped in the usual way.
3 Where a larger stud cannot be used because it would be of too large a diameter for the mating part, the diameter of the bolt hole in a mating cover for example, a special shouldered stud may be made on the

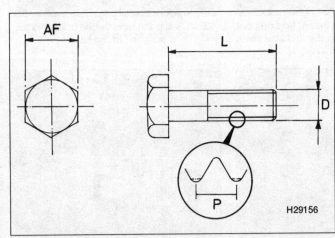

3.1 Thread diameter (D), pitch (P), fastener length (L) and across flats head size (AF)

4.1 A thread repair tool being used to correct an internal thread

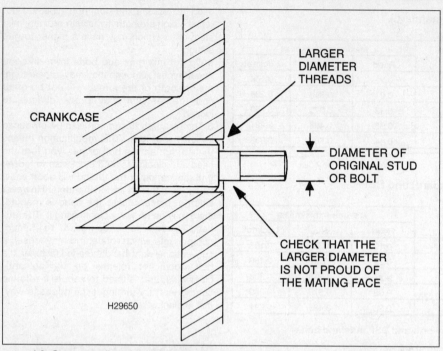

CRANKCASE

LARGER DIAMETER THREADS

DIAMETER OF ORIGINAL STUD OR BOLT

CHECK THAT THE LARGER DIAMETER IS NOT PROUD OF THE MATING FACE

H29650

4.3 Cross-section of a shouldered bolt used to repair a thread damaged hole

lathe to suit the larger threaded hole (see illustration).

4 A thread insert can be used if it is not possible to increase the size, for example on a spark plug hole, or drain plug where larger parts are not available or in the wall of a casing which may be too thin. The inserts can be bought in kits which included the correct size drill, tap and the insertion tool (see illustration).

5 The old damaged thread is drilled out to the correct size and the hole tapped with the special tap provided in the kit. The insert is then screwed in place using the tool supplied using a gentle downward pressure until the insert is between 1/4 and 1/2 a turn below the surface. The tang is then broken off to allow the normal bolt to be used (see illustrations).

6 There are now several epoxy type compounds which can be used to mould new threads. Although not quoted as being as strong as a metal thread, they can give a good service if the repair is done carefully.

7 The resin comes in two parts with a separate chemical which is applied to the male thread. Apply this release compound to a clean male thread first and then put it somewhere where it will not get dirty. Mix the epoxy resin and apply to the hole. Screw in the bolt and leave for the prescribed time before withdrawing it. After a further period of curing time the thread will be ready for use. Always use an undamaged, preferably new male thread. Don't use this method to repair vital components in brake and steering parts, or engine internals. It is a useful method of repair for other parts which would require dismantling to repair by any other method.

External threads

8 Special thread restorer files can be used to

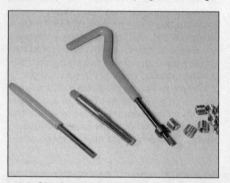

4.4 Obtain a thread insert kit to suit the thread diameter and pitch required

4.5a To install a thread insert, first drill out the original thread using the drill size given in the kit . . .

4.5b . . . tap the new thread using the tap supplied in the kit . . .

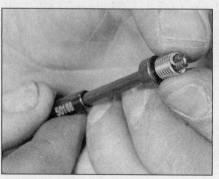

4.5c . . . fit the insert on the installing tool . . .

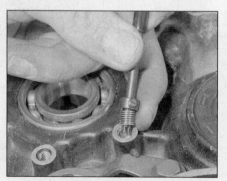

4.5d . . . and thread the insert into the component . . .

4.5e . . . then break off the tang

clean up a thread to remove burrs and old locking compound **(see illustration)**.

9 The thread can be cleaned up with using a conventional die, a thread chaser, or a die nut, which has a thread cutting internal form like the die, but with hexagonal spanner flats.

10 It is important that the die, or die nut **(see illustration)** is engaged correctly at the start of the thread so that it follows the original, and does not cut an additional thread. Where the end of the thread is damaged the use of the die may not be possible.

11 It is possible to use the screw cutting facility on the lathe to re cut the thread. As the lathe can be run in either direction, when the cutting tool is correctly positioned on a good part of the thread it can be moved over the damaged portion.

12 As with internal threads, if the damage has resulted in material being lost, then there will be gaps which will reduce the strength of the thread. If this is the case the bolt or threaded component must be scrapped.

13 Threads may be rebuilt using epoxy compounds as described above.

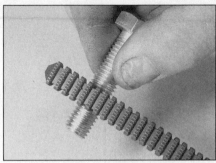

4.8 Using a thread restorer file

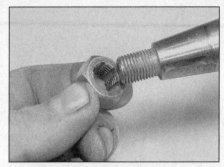

4.10 Take care that the die nut starts on the thread correctly

5 Dealing with damaged and broken fasteners

1 However careful you are, it is highly probable that at some stage you will be confronted by a damaged fastener. This can range from a casing screw with a chewed-out head to a broken off bolt or stud. All have something in common; they are difficult to deal with, and require a high degree of care and patience if the problem is not to be made worse. This Section describes some of the more common problems and suggests methods of dealing with them.

Damaged casing screw heads

2 This is probably the most common problem of all. The universal casing screw is invariably tight, and this combined with a soft cross-head means that damage is almost inevitable

unless great care is taken when removing them. If you are confronted with this problem it is essential that you take remedial action before the head gets too badly damaged, or you will be in real trouble.

3 The first thing to do is to examine the damaged screw head closely. If it has the remains of the driving tangs still evident, albeit distorted, you may not have too much trouble. Using a parallel punch, tap the centre of the screw so that the tangs are pushed down into the screw **(see illustration)**. With luck this will return them to a vaguely cross-head shape, even though a screwdriver will not fit them any more.

4 You will now need an impact driver and a range of cross-head bits. Using a similar screw head in good condition, find the bit which most closely fits the profile of the head. Hold the bit against the damaged head, and tap it into the head so that it fits snugly. Now fit the impact driver onto the bit, having checked that it is set to twist anti-clockwise. Push the tool hard against the screw head and tap the end sharply with a hammer **(see illustration)**. With luck, the screw will loosen and can then be unscrewed.

5 If the attempt fails, and access permits, you can try hacksawing a slot across the head. If you can cut a slot it should be possible to use a normal slotted bit in the impact driver to remove the screw.

6 Where the above methods fail to free the screw, you may have to resort to drilling out

the head of the screw. The remains of the head should suffice in locating the tip of the twist drill, though if necessary you can centre punch the head at the exact centre. Choose a twist drill slightly larger than the diameter of the screw shank, then drill into the head until it comes free of the shank. The cover can now be removed, leaving a short piece of the shank protruding from the case below. Apply a few drops of penetrating fluid and allow this to work for a few minutes. Grip the end of the shank between the jaws of self-locking grips and remove the remains of the screw.

7 In cases where the head has been damaged due to the screw being seized in the crankcase, or where the screw has broken off, refer to the text below for further information on dealing with this type of problem.

8 Whatever method has been used to remove a damaged screw, on no account re-use it or you will have similar or worse problems on the next occasion that removal is required.

> **HAYNES HINT** *It is well worth considering replacing cross-head screws with Allen or Torx screws, preferably in stainless steel. These can always be removed easily using the appropriate key, and the stainless versions will not suffer from corrosion problems.*

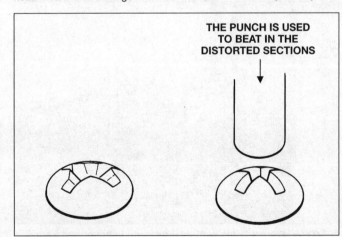

THE PUNCH IS USED TO BEAT IN THE DISTORTED SECTIONS

5.3 Reforming a damaged screw head using a parallel punch

5.4 Using an impact driver. Make sure that the assembly is solidly supported before striking with the hammer

5.17 Localised heat being applied with a hot air gun

9 If you choose to fit plated steel screws, it is worth guarding against problems in the future by applying a thin coat of a copper-based or graphite grease to the threads. This will help prevent corrosion of the threads by excluding moisture, and will also act as a lubricant to ease future removal.

Freeing seized fasteners

10 Casing screws, bolts and other types of fastener which have become seized in their threads will have to be tackled with care; it is all too easy to end up with part of the shank still seized in its thread after twisting off the head.

11 The usual cause of seized fasteners is corrosion of the threads, and if this gets bad enough it is possible for the threads to become firmly stuck together.

12 Another possible cause is that the screw has bottomed in the hole, causing the threads to distort and jam in position. This can be due to the wrong length of screw being fitted, or to accumulated debris at the bottom of the hole. In such cases, removal by normal methods may not be successful.

13 Start by applying penetrating fluid around the threads. This is likely to be more successful if the fastener can be persuaded to move, even slight movement indicates that

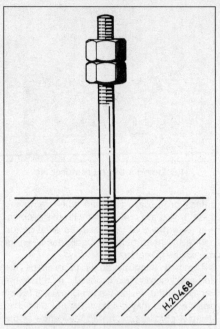

5.19a Sketch showing two nuts locked in position to loosen the stud

there is enough of a gap around the threads to allow the fluid to penetrate.

14 It is sometimes useful to try tightening the fastener very slightly and then backing it off again; this may work where attempts to unscrew it have failed. Using an impact driver may help by shocking the fastener enough to get slight movement.

15 Leave the penetrating fluid to work for as long as possible. If you can, let it stand overnight before further attempts at removal are made.

16 You may also care to try applying a little heat to the area; the differing rates of expansion between the steel and alloy may assist in breaking the bond between the threads. Be very careful how you do this; direct heat from a flame can cause the alloy to

melt very suddenly, and there is also a risk of distortion.

17 A hot air gun of the type used for stripping paint can be used to provide local heat **(see illustration)**, or the area treated with near boiling water (take care to avoid scalding yourself). A heavy-duty soldering iron applied to a screw head is also recommended.

18 Once you succeed in getting the fastener to move, start unscrewing it carefully. If it becomes tighter, this will be due to the corrosion locking the threads at one point. Do not continue forcing the fastener, but instead apply more penetrating fluid, screw it in by a turn or two to dislodge the corrosion, and then try again. Repeat this process until it can be removed completely.

19 If there is sufficient length of thread on a stud which is not too tight, the first means of loosening is to lock two nuts together on the stud, then unscrew the stud using a spanner on the first nut **(see illustrations)**.

20 Again if there is sufficient room and length of stud, a Stillson wrench or self locking grips may be used to good effect. The stem of the stud or bolt will invariably be damaged in this operation.

21 Another last resort method is to take a small cold chisel and hammer to work the fastener loose **(see illustration)**. This needs great care not to damage the surrounding metal and components.

Removing broken off fasteners

22 This can be a difficult undertaking, the chances of success being dependent on the original reason for the breakage. If it is a simple matter of an otherwise sound fastener being over-tightened and snapping off, the chances are that the remainder can be removed reasonably easily.

23 If on the other hand a fastener has snapped off because it was corroded in place or bottomed in its hole, you still have to deal with the seized threads, but without an easy method of turning it.

5.19b A couple of washers have been clamped between the nuts to make easier access for the spanners. The bottom, open ender will be used to unscrew the stud

5.21 A fastener being worked loose with hammer and a small cold chisel

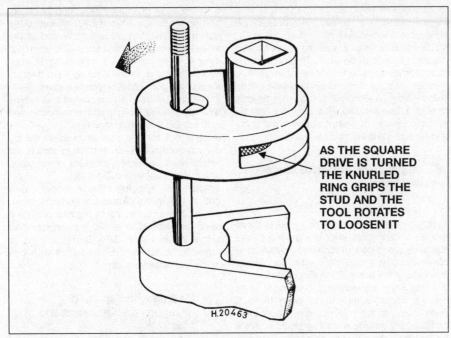

AS THE SQUARE DRIVE IS TURNED THE KNURLED RING GRIPS THE STUD AND THE TOOL ROTATES TO LOOSEN IT

H.20463

5.24a A sketch showing the method by which a stud extractor does the job

5.24b A stud extractor removing a broken crankcase stud

5.28 Drilling a hole for the screw extractor. Information on drill sizes is provided in the set

24 Where the fastener has a portion protruding above the hole, and space permits, a stud extractor tool can be used **(see illustrations)**. The extractor can of course be used on unbroken studs, where it will do less damage than a Stillson wrench or self locking grips.

Using a screw thread extractor
25 This is a tricky task especially as the host material is softer than that of the fastener as is the case with most motorcycle situations.
26 First mark the **exact** centre of the sheared fastener with a centre punch. This is easier to do if you first file the broken end flat, but in some situations this will be impossible.
27 It is vital that the punch mark is exactly at the centre of the fastener thread, so take time to ensure this. It is worth noting that the shock

from the centre punching may help matters; the impact itself might help loosen the fastener, and the compressive action can deform and thus loosen the threads a little.
28 You will now need to drill a small pilot hole through the fastener and finish with a drill size correct for the type and size of extractor needed. This is best done using a bench or pillar drilling machine **(see illustration)**. Where this is impractical, you will have to do the drilling work freehand, taking great care to ensure that the drill bit is kept perpendicular to the fastener.
29 You must also take extreme care that the twist drill does not snap off as it breaks through at the end of the fastener; you have enough of a problem already without having to extract a broken off drill bit! Try to gauge

the likely length of the fastener, comparing it to a neighbouring undamaged one, and ease off drilling pressure as the bit nears the end of the fastener.
30 The next step is to try to remove the screw with a screw extractor. These devices (also known as easy-outs or EZ-outs) are available in sets **(see illustration)**. There are two basic types, one of which employs a tapering left-hand thread. The tool is turned anti-clockwise, which screws it into the pilot hole and, hopefully, then unscrews the remains of the fastener **(see illustration)**.

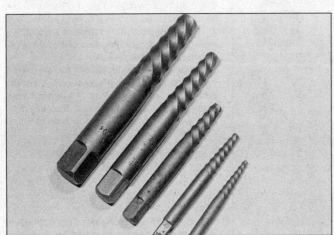

5.30a A typical set of screw thread extractors

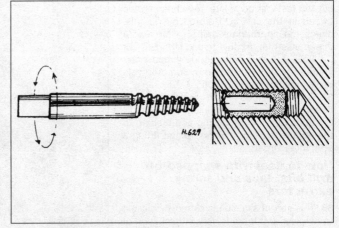

H.629

5.30b A sketch showing the screw thread principle

5.32 A broken fastener successfully removed with a screw extractor

31 The second type has a thin tapering square or cross-section shank which is tapped into the hole to locate it, and is then turned to remove the damaged fastener. Either type will work on most occasions, provided that the fastener was not originally sheared off **due to seizure**.

32 By holding the extractor in a tap wrench or turning with a small spanner you will be able to feel the screw start to turn **(see illustration)**. If all you feel is a slight spring in the extractor but no turning movement, then stop applying pressure immediately. The brittle extractors will easily snap leaving you with a bigger problem.

33 If the fastener is really stuck, the extractor may only succeed in spreading it outwards, making it even more securely stuck.

Drilling out a fastener

34 Where mechanical extraction methods fail, and assuming that you have not snapped off an extractor in the attempt, you will have to resort to drilling out the remainder of the fastener.

35 Use drill bits of progressively larger diameter, finishing with one at the core diameter of the damaged thread. If you are very lucky, this will leave just the thread remaining in the hole, and it is sometimes possible to peel this out of position to leave the tapped hole relatively unscathed.

36 As a last resort, it will be necessary to drill out the fastener complete, together with the thread in the casing. Before you do this, check the appropriate drill size for a wire thread insert tap for that thread size. Drill out the hole, and then either fit the thread insert yourself or have this done by a motorcycle dealer equipped for this work.

37 Other methods for reclaiming the threaded hole include aluminium welding to fill the hole, followed by drilling and tapping to the original size, or making up and fitting a solid thread insert.

How to deal with snapped-off drill bits, taps and screw extractors

38 This sort of situation is extremely difficult to resolve, and there is very little chance of coping with the problem at home. Even small engineering companies may be hard pressed to tackle the removal of hard steel tool fragments from a seized and broken off fastener in a soft alloy thread.

39 Specialist methods such as spark erosion machining, need to be used. Try and locate a local company who can offer this service through your local motorcycle dealer or the yellow pages. A technical college may be able to help. Once located, find out what will be required by way of preparation in order to try and reduce costs as much as you can.

6	Dealing with corroded studs and bolts

1 This problem is normally confined to those models where a fastener is exposed to the elements along part of its length, although in some circumstances corrosion can occur even where the fastener is fully covered.

2 Particularly vulnerable are cylinder head holding studs, where these pass through open finning at the front of the cylinder block, and similarly, engine mounting bolts, where a single long bolt or stud passes through two or more short lugs.

3 In countries where the roads are salted to prevent icing during winter, the deposited salt, water and repeated heating and cooling inevitably lead to corrosion of these fasteners.

4 Whilst this can be reduced or eliminated by coating the shank with copper-based grease during installation, this advice is of little comfort when you encounter a well-rusted example for the first time.

5 The best method of removal will have to be worked out to suit the particular situation, but in all cases start by using copious amounts of penetrating fluid, leaving this to work in for as long as possible. The location of the component, and that of surrounding parts will determine whether it is safe to apply heat; if it can be done without causing damage then it is worth trying.

7.8 A pair of nut splitting tools

6 In the case of engine mounting bolts, try drifting the bolt out. Start by unscrewing the nut, but leave it in place on the end of the thread to prevent the bolt spreading when it is struck. If you succeed in moving it even slightly, apply more penetrating fluid, then try turning the bolt until it begins to loosen.

7 Locking two nuts on the thread and turning will help release the grip of the corrosion and help spread the penetrating fluid.

8 Look out for this sort of problem during normal overhauls. Even if a bolt or stud is not seized in place, watch for signs of corrosion which might get worse if ignored.

9 Apart from applying a film of copper-based grease to minimise future corrosion, consider having the affected parts blasted and then cadmium plated to avoid the formation of corrosion at a later date. Better still, try to replace the affected bolt or stud with one made from stainless steel.

7	Dealing with damaged hexagons on bolt heads and nuts

1 Slight damage to the corners of the hexagon can be overcome by using ring spanners (preferably 6-point type) and sockets which grip on the flats rather than the corners.

2 An old trick is to jam a screwdriver blade between one flat of the hexagon and the spanner jaw.

3 It may be possible to hold the head using self locking pliers or a Stillson wrench. The latter may inflict more damage, and if this is the case the bolt should be scrapped.

4 Where space permits the fastener head may be filed to accept the next smallest spanner size. The bolt should be scrapped on removal.

5 Again where space permits the head can be sawn off and the bolt drifted out. Space must be available for both sawing and removal from the nut end.

6 It may be possible to weld a bar onto the head which then acts as a turning lever.

7 The methods outlined immediately above may be used in addition to a plentiful supply of penetrating fluid.

8 A device called a nut splitter can be used if space permits **(see illustration)**. This fits around the nut and the turn of a screw forces a chisel shaped bit into the nut. The nut is split and can be peeled off the bolt without damage to the thread.

8	Fitting bolts and screws

1 All threads must be clean before fitting. Any old grease or thread-locking compound must be removed. If dirt is present it can cause the thread to jam and give false torque readings.

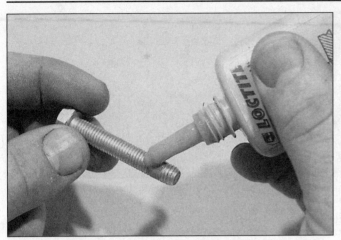

8.6 Only apply one or two drops of thread locking compound

8.8 A smear of copper-based grease will aid subsequent removal in critical locations

2 The threaded portion of a bolt should protrude through the nut so that the nut engages on the full thread. Check that on bolts where the nut has a locking insert that the threaded portion of the bolt does go through the inserted portion of the nut.

3 In locations where bolts are loaded at right-angles to the line of the bolt, engine mounting bolts for example, make sure that the components are located on the plain portion of the bolt and not on the threads, which will wear down and cause a sloppy fit.

4 If two components are to be held together, make sure that the mating faces meet before tightening the bolts.

5 Use thread-locking compounds as specified by the bike manufacturer. In other applications follow the instructions on the data sheet supplied with the product. Select a compound to suit the component being secured - a non-permanent general locking and sealing type is suitable for most applications, but a high strength type is needed for permanent fixing of studs in castings.

6 Apply a drop or two of the compound to the first few threads of the fastener, then thread it into place and tighten to the specified torque **(see illustration)**. Do not apply excessive

thread-locking compound otherwise the thread may be damaged on subsequent removal. Always install the fastener immediately after applying the locking compound.

7 Certain fasteners are impregnated with a dry film type coating of locking compound on their threads. Always renew this type of fastener if disturbed.

8 Anti-seize compounds, such as copper-based greases, can be applied to protect threads from seizure due to extreme heat and corrosion **(see illustration)**. A common instance is spark plug threads and exhaust system fasteners.

9 Check that set screws and studs do not bottom in blind holes. Do not overtighten as there is a danger of stripping the threads, particularly in aluminium.

10 On castellated nuts through which you are going to fit a split pin, tighten the nut to the specified torque and then align the nut with the next possible pin hole – never slacken the nut to align the hole. Fit the split pin on suspension and wheel components with the head (closed end) facing forward to avoid it being damaged or pushed out and bend the pin as shown **(see illustrations)**.

11 Generally threads should be assembled in

dry condition, and torque figures are normally given for fasteners in this condition. Where threads are to be oiled on assembly instructions will be given in the workshop manual.

12 After a period of running in, check the tightness of the nuts, screws etc. again.

9 Torque and angle settings

What is torque?

1 Torque describes the twisting force about a shaft. The amount of torque applied is determined by the distance from the centre of the shaft to the end of the lever and the amount of force being applied to the end of the lever; distance multiplied by force equals torque.

2 The manufacturer applies a measured torque to a bolt or nut to ensure that it will not slacken in use and will hold two components securely together without movement in the joint. The actual torque setting depends on the thread size, the bolt or nut material, the composition of the components being held,

8.10a Always ensure that exposed R-pins or split-pins are installed with their closed ends facing forward

8.10b Correct bending of split-pin arms on a castellated nut . . .

8.10c . . . and on a plain nut

and the required working condition of any gasket between the two components.

3 Always stick to the specified torque setting. This is given for specific fasteners in the workshop manual, but standard torque figures are given for fasteners in general situations (see paragraph 6 below).

Units of torque

4 Torque wrenches are available in Nm (Newton-metres), kgf m (kilograms-force metre), lbf ft (pounds-feet), lbf in (inch-pounds). Do not confuse lbf ft with lbf in. The preferred unit is the Newton-metre.

5 To convert kgf-m to N-m multiply by 9.804
To convert lbf-ft to N-m multiply by 1.356
To convert lbf-in to N-m multiply by 0.113
To convert lbf-in to lbf-ft multiply by 0.083

6 Where no torque setting is given fasteners can be secured according to the table below.

Fastener type (thread diameter)	N-m	lbf ft
5 mm bolt or nut	4.41 – 5.89	3.5 – 4.5
6 mm bolt or nut	7.84 – 11.79	6 – 9
8 mm bolt or nut	17.66 – 24.52	13 – 18
10 mm bolt or nut	29.43 – 39.24	22 – 29
12 mm bolt or nut	49.05 – 58.86	36 – 43
5 mm screw	3.43 – 4.91	2.5 – 3.6
6 mm screw	6.87 – 10.79	5 – 8
6 mm flange bolt	9.81 – 13.73	7 – 10
8 mm flange bolt	23.54 – 29.43	17 – 22
10 mm flange bolt	29.43 – 39.24	22 – 29

7 For practical purposes, and bearing in mind the scale of the torque wrench, use the nearest whole number.

8 A manufacturer sometimes gives a torque setting as a range (8 to 10 Nm) rather than a single figure - in this case set the tool midway between the two settings. Equally, the same torque may be expressed as 9 Nm ± 1 Nm.

Using a torque wrench

9 Check the calibration of the torque wrench and make sure it has a suitable range for the job.

10 On preset wrenches, adjust the tool to the desired torque on the scale **(see illustration)**. If your torque wrench is not calibrated in the units specified, carefully convert the figure using the information above in paragraph 5.

9.10 Setting the torque on a preset type wrench

11 Some torque wrenches have a method of locking the setting so that it isn't inadvertently altered during use.

12 Install the all the bolts/nuts in their correct location and secure them lightly.

13 Tighten the fasteners in the specified sequence until the torque wrench clicks, indicating that the torque setting has been reached **(see illustration)**. Apply the torque again to double-check the setting.

14 On the simple beam type torque wrench, pull the handle until the pointer lines up with the desired setting on the scale.

15 Where different thread diameter fasteners secure the component, as a rule tighten the larger diameter ones first.

16 It is good practice to tighten all the bolts on an assembly in stages rather than tighten one bolt fully leaving the others loose.

17 When a preset type torque wrench has been finished with, release the lock (where applicable) and fully back off its setting to zero - do not leave the torque wrench tensioned.

18 Do not use a torque wrench for slackening a fastener.

Angle-tightening

19 Manufacturers often specify a figure in degrees for final tightening of a fastener. This usually follows tightening to a specific torque setting.

20 A degree disc can be set and attached to the socket or a protractor can be used to mark the angle of movement on the bolt/nut head and the surrounding casting **(see illustrations)**.

9.13 Tightening the cylinder head nuts on a Suzuki engine

10 Loosening and tightening sequences

Loosening

1 Where more than one bolt/nut secures a component, loosen each fastener evenly a little at a time. In this way, not all the stress of the joint is held by one fastener and the components are not likely to distort.

2 If a tightening sequence is provided, work in the REVERSE of this, but if not, work from the outside in, in a criss-cross sequence **(see illustration)**.

Tightening

3 If a component is held by more than one fastener it is important that the retaining bolts/nuts are tightened evenly to prevent uneven stress build-up and distortion of sealing faces.

4 This is especially important on high-compression joints such as the cylinder head.

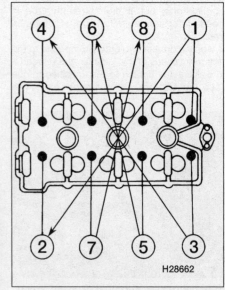

10.2 When slackening work from the outside inwards

9.20a Angle-tightening can be done with a torque-angle gauge . . .

9.20b . . . or by marking the angle on the surrounding component

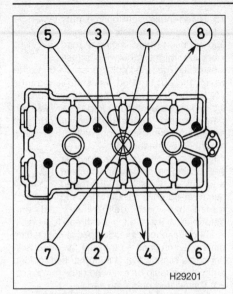

10.6 When tightening, work from the inside outwards tightening each bolt in stages until the final torque setting is reached

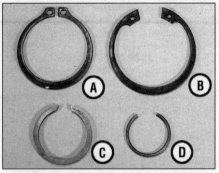

11.2 Showing an external stamped circlip (A), an internal stamped circlip (B), a machined circlip (C), and a wire circlip (D)

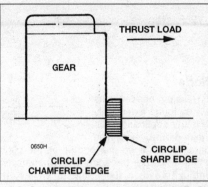

11.6 Correct fitting of a stamped circlip in relation to thrust load

5 A sequence is usually provided by the manufacturer, either in a diagram or actually marked in the casting.

6 If not, always start in the centre and work outwards in a criss-cross pattern **(see illustration)**. Start off by securing all bolts/nuts finger-tight, then set the torque wrench and tighten each fastener by a small amount in sequence until the final torque is reached.

7 By following this practice, the joint will be held evenly and will not be distorted. Important joints, such as the cylinder head and big-end fasteners often have two- or three-stage torque settings.

8 After a short running period it may be necessary to check and retighten bolts to the correct torque.

11 Circlips

1 Circlips of different types are found in various assemblies on the motorcycle, and are used to retain components on as shaft, or in a housing.

2 There are two basic types, flat-section stamped circlips (Seeger), and plain wire circlips **(see illustration)**.

3 Note that the two must never be interchanged – the retaining groove for the Seeger type must be parallel sided, and if this type of clip is fitted to a rounded groove it may work out in service. Circlips are available in a wide range of sizes, and as internal or external types.

4 Removal is generally by means of external or internal ears. The ears have holes which are used to locate the points of the circlip pliers.

5 Parallel sided (machined) circlips can be installed either way round in their retaining groove.

6 Stamped circlips have a chamfered edge

on one face, and must be fitted with the chamfer facing away from the direction of the thrust load **(see illustration)**.

7 Always use circlip pliers **(see illustration)** to remove and install circlips; expand or close them just enough for removal or fitting.

8 After installation check that the circlip is securely in its groove by rotating it.

9 A circlip used on a splined shaft should be installed with its opening aligned with a spline channel to ensure that the circlip ends are well supported, and unlikely to catch **(see illustration)**.

10 Circlips do wear and become loose in their grooves. For this reason, replacement is advised every time a circlip is disturbed.

11 Wire circlips are commonly used as piston pin retaining clips.

12 If the wire circlip has a removal tang, a long nose pair of pliers can be used to remove and refit it.

13 Plain wire clips need a small flat-bladed screwdriver to ease them out of the groove in the piston.

14 Wire circlips should be renewed every time they are disturbed.

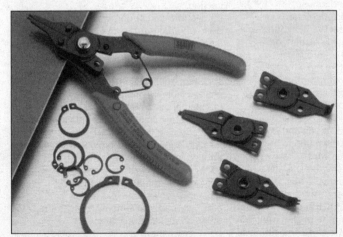

11.7 Circlip pliers with optional points for a range of sizes. The pivot can be arranged to suit internal and external circlips

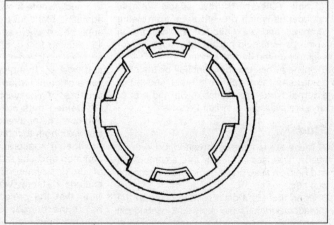

11.9 Correct position of the circlip ends on a splined shaft; the opening lines up with a channel in the shaft splines

12 Fasteners – common types

Bolts

1 Hexagon-headed bolts will be found extensively in many applications on most motorcycles. The parts to be joined are located on the plain shank area, the threaded section screwing into a thread in the frame or engine, or secured by a nut.

2 Hexagon-headed setscrews are similar in appearance to bolts, but note that the threaded area extends up to the underside of the head. Setscrews may be used where a thin fitting or bracket is attached to a frame lug or similar.

3 Flanged bolts or setscrews are often used in place of Phillips-headed casing screws, and in this application are less vulnerable to damage during removal and installation. Larger sizes are often used in place of conventional bolts or setscrews, where the need for a separate washer is avoided.

4 Socket bolts, also called Allen bolts, are driven by hexagon keys of appropriate size. In addition to the normal cheese head type shown, socket screws are also available in countersunk and button head forms, as well as grub screws.

5 Torx bolts have a hex-globe shape instead of the normal hexagon. The internal TORX is classified as the 'T' type and replaces the Allen bolt. The external is classified as the 'E' type and replaces the common hexagon. Special keys are required to tighten or loosen this type of bolt. The keys are given a code reference related to their size and type. Some 'T' type TORX bolts have special internal projections which prevent them from being removed and are used for applications in which parts should not be disassembled, for example on the throttle sensor.

6 Splined bolts can be identified by their 12-point head forms; either internal (socket) or external types are available. Splined bits or keys are available in millimetre sizes.

Studs

7 These are lengths of threaded rod with no heads. They screw directly into a component and hold an assembled component by means of a nut.

8 Often there is a plain section between the threaded portions which acts as a locating pin when other components are assembled to it. This type of stud should not be replaced with one without the plain section.

9 Where studs are screwed into aluminium or cast iron, the thread form is often different to that for the nut; a coarser thread being used in the softer material.

10 Studding, lengths of threaded rod, are a useful standby for the temporary replacement of studs and bolts. They are also useful in short lengths for holding work on the drilling table and in the lathe.

Screws

11 The casing screws used on many models are of the pan-head Phillips pattern shown. This type of screw head is very easy to damage during removal, and it is vital that the correct shape and size of screwdriver is used. It is preferable to slacken and tighten these screws using an impact driver, or to replace them with socket screws.

12 Self-tapping screws come in a wide variety of designs and sizes, and are used to retain some brackets and covers, particularly on thin steel panels. These screws have hardened threads which are capable of cutting their own corresponding thread in most thin materials, once a pilot hole has been punched or drilled to provide a starting point.

13 Wood screws may be used for repair of sidecar bodies. The modern favourite is the plated steel posidrive screw, although the conventional slotted brass screw may be preferred.

Nuts

14 Plain nuts will be found in many areas of all machines, and are used to secure the ends of bolts, 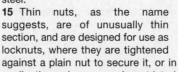 setscrews and studs. Like the bolts and setscrews, these should be bright plated to avoid corrosion, or better still, stainless steel.

15 Thin nuts, as the name suggests, are of unusually thin section, and are designed for use as locknuts, where they are tightened against a plain nut to secure it, or in special applications where space is restricted.

16 Washer faced, or flanged nuts are used in preference to a plain nut and washer. This type of nut often has a different torque setting to that expected of a conventional nut.

17 Domed nuts are used on the end of shafts or threaded studs and fasteners both to retain them and to provide a decorative finish, a common application being on the underside of the instrument cluster. They will also exclude dirt and water from the threads. Note that the projecting thread end must be of the correct length, or the nut will become bottomed out before the fitting is secure. Pack with plain washers where necessary.

18 Nylon-insert self-locking nuts are available in a variety of designs, and are used where engine or road vibration might otherwise cause loosening. The nylon collar grips the thread to which the nut is fitted, resisting accidental slackening in use. Note that nylon-insert self-locking nuts are intended to be renewed each time they are removed; they will not grip securely once the nylon collar has been deformed by the thread.

19 Stiff nuts are also used for their self-locking properties, and come in a variety of types. That illustrated has a raised collar inside which the thread has been deliberately split and deformed so that it grips the thread to which it is fitted. Variations include special nuts which have been crushed so that the threaded hole becomes slightly oval. Like other self-locking nuts, they should be renewed once removed.

20 Castellated nuts are used in conjunction with a split pin or R-pin to secure items like wheel axles. The nut is torque-tightened, and the R-pin or a new split pin fitted through the axle end, which is drilled for this purpose. The nut itself can be re-used indefinitely, but the split pin must be renewed each time the nut is refitted. Where an R-pin is used in place of a split pin, this too can be re-used.

Washers

21 Plain washers spread the load applied to items to be secured and allow the fastener to turn without damage to the fitting. Extra large diameter plain washers, called 'Penny washers' are used for even better load-spreading capabilities on soft or fragile materials.

22 Spring washers are designed to prevent a plain nut from working loose once tightened, and are available in square or rectangular section.

23 Double-coil spring washers are a variation on the plain single-coil spring washer shown above.

24 Toothed, or serrated, lockwashers are available in internal or external patterns and are used to lock plain nuts in place. Note that they can also be useful where the teeth cut through a paint film to provide a sound earth (ground) connection.

25 Wave washers in varying designs are sometimes used to take up freeplay, to avoid rattles or unwanted movement. These are often found on rocker arm shafts.

26 Tab washers are used to lock a nut in place by bending up part of the edge of the washer against the side face of the nut.

27 A tongued lock plate is similar to two tab washers made from one piece and used on adjacent nuts. With this sort of application the tabbed portion to be bent up must be positioned so that when the nut is set to the correct torque, the tab is next to one of the sides of the nut.

Pins

28 Split pins are used in conjunction with a washer or a castellated nut as a method of retention. Available in a wide range of sizes, the pin can be cut to the required length after fitting. Split pins should not be re-used.

29 R-pins are more durable replacements for the humble split pin 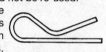 in some applications. They are especially useful in places where repeated removal is required, as in the case of the wheel axle nuts.

30 Roll pins (also called spring tension pins) are thin tubular steel pins with a longitudinal split. They are used in place of hollow dowel pins in some applications, and can also be used to retain a component on a shaft. They should be fitted and removed using a stepped parallel punch of the correct diameter, to prevent distortion.

31 Taper pins were traditionally used to secure items like pulleys to machinery shafts. In the workshop, small taper pins can be useful when pinning together a kickstart and its shaft to overcome stripped splines.

32 Cotter pins are a variation of the taper pin, having a 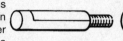 thread and a nut at one end to allow the pin to be drawn into position. They are used to secure components to shaft ends, a common application being the retention of pedal cranks to mopeds and bicycles.

Rivets

33 Plain rivets are the traditional method of riveting together two parts, provided that access to both sides of the workpiece is available. Materials include steel, brass and aluminium alloys, and head forms include domed and countersunk. Rivets are normally solid, though hollow copper rivets are used in some applications such as securing brake linings to shoes, on older machines.

34 Pop rivets, or blind rivets, allow pieces to be fastened from one side only. These rivets are available in a range of diameters and lengths, and head materials vary from steel to aluminium and Monel. Head designs include specialist shapes used to secure trim or upholstery. The rivets are set (fitted) using a special tool.

Circlips

35 Circlips are a simple method of retaining a component to a shaft end, or to secure a shaft or pin in a bore. Typical applications are the securing of piston pins, and holding gears on shafts. See Section 11.

Notes

Chapter 7
Workshop techniques with metals

Contents

1 Introduction

In this Chapter we will look at some of the general workshop techniques and procedures related to metal working which are commonly needed when working on motorcycles.

Becoming proficient in the handwork skills required when working with various metals and other materials will take time and practice. This is true also of other processes such as welding, riveting, lathe work and painting.

Safety

The use of welding equipment brings a greater safety risk. In industry, certain equipment may only be used by people who have been on an approved training course, and have been awarded a certificate to show that they have completed the course successfully.

It may be necessary for you as an individual to go on training courses run by industry, the local further education centres, or by equipment suppliers. This will help improve your skill as well as show you the safe way to work.

In addition to the basic safety rules outlined in Chapter 1 the following points are particularly relevant. For example, make sure that other members of your family and visitors to the workshop know when you are welding to avoid them suffering from arc eye. Do not allow your pets into the workshop for the same reason.

Being unexpectedly distracted does not help your concentration when you are measuring or at a crucial point when setting up your carburettors. An unexpected distraction when using a brazing torch for example, can be very dangerous – you must encourage safe working practice to all visitors to the workshop.

Compressed gas safety

Follow the makers/suppliers instructions when fitting or changing butane gas cylinders and the small disposable cylinders which are used with MIG welding equipment.

Oxygen and acetylene cylinder users should open an account with a local, bona fide supplier, which will mean that you become a registered user. The cylinders, which you exchange, are then part of a system in which proper safety checks are made. The supplier will also be willing to provide safety advice and up-to-date information. Note that this advice applies to readers in the UK, or other countries consult with your local suppliers and authorities.

Gas cylinders are heavy and should be stored vertically in such a way that they are prevented from toppling. Many welders use a properly constructed two-wheel trolley which also avoids long trailing hoses.

Compressed air equipment should also be regularly checked to ensure that it is safe at the working pressures you are using.

2 Simple bending and forming

1 Aluminium and thin mild steel sheet can be bent fairly easily by hand pressure across a suitable edge, though the thicker the material the harder this becomes.
2 Small lengths can be clamped in the vice and bent over the jaws, or a piece of wood clamped alongside the metal.
3 For longer work pieces, one method is to use lengths of hardwood clamped along the intended line of the bend. The projecting metal can then be folded along the edge of the hardwood, working up and down the line with a mallet or hammer. If necessary, you can shape the wood first as a former for the radius.
4 Take care when beating thin metal that you do not concentrate on one area. This will stretch out the material resulting in an irregular bend and also cause work hardening and weakening of the flattened section.
5 In an engineering press shop the metal is over bent slightly to allow for it to spring back to the correct angle. After bending check the angle with a square or angle gauge and make any corrections using a mallet or by squeezing in the vice.
6 In theory, the bend radius is calculated from the thickness of the material being used, and is listed in engineering tables for each type of material. In practice the material will tend to control the bend radius naturally, using normal workshop hand tools.
7 Angle iron, with the sharp external corner filed off to a radius can also be used as a former, although if you are intending to do a lot of bending work, the purchase of a simple folding machine is a worthwhile investment.
8 When two bends have to be made, check that the first bend will not prevent the material from being held in the vice or bender when forming the second bend. You may have to improvise some spacers from steel or hard wood blocks.

> **HAYNES HiNT**
> *Raised scars or nicks in the face of the hammer will damage softer sheet materials so keep a sheet metal hammer away from all those other hammering jobs such as nailing. Similarly your anvil or the bit of metal or hard wood on which you rest the work piece needs to be kept clean and unblemished.*

9 It is important that the material chosen is fairly malleable, and that you do not attempt to form too acute a bend. If this is not the case, the metal will be stressed across the bend and may fracture.

Forming with heat

10 When using heavier materials such as steel bar or thick strip, you will have to resort to the use of heat and a small anvil to form the bend successfully. The heat will soften the material, allowing it to be bent more easily and with less risk of cracking.
11 Wear stout industrial gloves and eye protection when using this method, and hold the work at one end, clamped securely in the jaws of self-locking pliers.

12 The heat source required will be dependent on the size of the workpiece, and thus the rate at which it can absorb heat. For small pieces, an ordinary blowlamp will probably prove adequate, whilst larger items will need much more heat. Any solid-fuel fire or stove will prove adequate for most applications.

13 Heat the metal until it turns bright red, then remove it and start forming the bend quickly, before it loses too much heat.

14 Lay the metal across the anvil, and start hammering along the intended bend, moving the hammer blows up and down the line, and keeping close to the intersection with the anvil.

15 Avoid moving the hammer too far from the anvil, or an irregular bend will be formed, and in the wrong place. As the metal cools and ceases to be luminous, apply more heat and continue the forming operation once red heat has been restored. When the bend has been formed, allow the workpiece to cool down in air to avoid embrittling it.

16 Remember that it will be hot enough to cause serious burns for some time after it has ceased to glow red hot.

17 The above technique will work well with all mild steel materials, including the softer stainless steels. Note that the latter will discolour due to the heat, though this can be filed and polished out if required.

18 You can apply the same principle to the straightening of items like footrests (if they are solid) and stands. Do make sure that the repair is safe; if badly bent, straightening will leave serious stresses in the component, which might lead to sudden failure at a later date. If you are unsure, play safe and renew the part rather than risk this.

Forming aluminium

19 With aluminium materials, choose a half hard grade when any bending has to be done.

20 Soft grade aluminium and soft alloys will bend reasonably easily, but are easily fatigued. If you have to use them, bend them only as much as you have to, and with the minimum of working. This will keep to a minimum the risk of work-hardening and fracture.

21 Where hard aluminium is required it is better to sketch what you want and seek professional help.

Bending angle and hollow section

22 Materials with these cross sections are very difficult to bend using normal hand tools.

23 For a bend with a single angle at the bend it is necessary to cut out a vee section from the side which will be on the inside of the bend. The size of this section can be calculated. The tube is then bent to the correct angle when the edges of the vee slot should come together.

24 If you are dealing with round or square section tubing, a bending machine and formers are needed to stop the tube walls from distorting and collapsing, though small

diameter thin-walled tube up to 15 mm diameter can be bent using a bending spring.

25 Depending on the application, the tube is then soldered, silver soldered, brazed or welded to form a solid join. Frame construction is a typical job requiring this type of work.

26 Curved bends require a series of slots cut almost through the material. The work piece is then bent into the curve and the slots welded or brazed to complete the join. Home made exhaust systems are usually made in this 'cut and shut' fashion.

3 Forming more complicated shapes

1 The first job is to cut out the shape that the metal must have if it is to be correct when it is formed up.

2 The basic shape, of the flat material is called the "blank" or "developed shaped".

3 This developed shape can be drawn from a sketch of the finished formed item. For most practical purposes it is easier to cut the blank from a template made from thick card.

4 The card can be bent up to shape and then be checked in position and any alterations made before starting work on the metal version.

5 Try to use card of a similar thickness to the metal being used; in this way the radius of the bend and the position of the fixing holes will be closer to the finished item.

A battery carrier

6 An example of this process is shown in the fabrication of a simple battery holder, mounted by two fixing holes and a small right-angle bracket **(see illustrations)**.

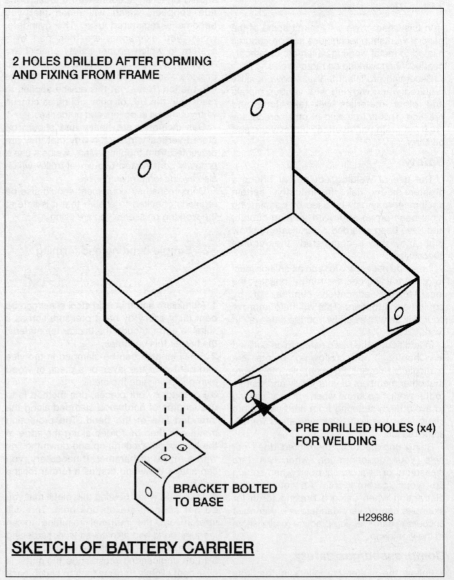

2 HOLES DRILLED AFTER FORMING AND FIXING FROM FRAME

PRE DRILLED HOLES (x4) FOR WELDING

BRACKET BOLTED TO BASE

H29686

SKETCH OF BATTERY CARRIER

3.6a Hand drawn sketch of the battery carrier

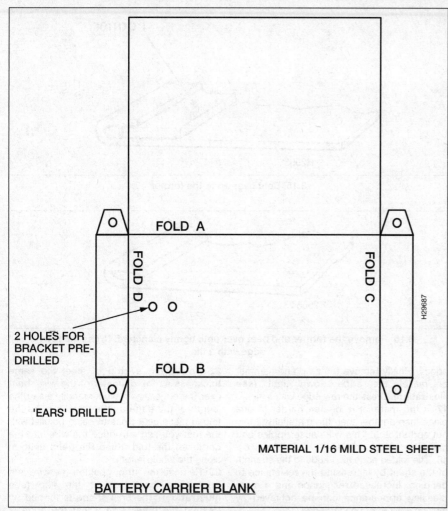

FOLD A

FOLD D

FOLD C

FOLD B

2 HOLES FOR BRACKET PRE-DRILLED

'EARS' DRILLED

MATERIAL 1/16 MILD STEEL SHEET

BATTERY CARRIER BLANK

H29687

3.6b Sketch of the blank to form the carrier

7 The carrier can be bent up in the vice using hardwood former blocks to allow for clearance to form bends C and D after bends A and B have been formed.

8 The ears were formed by clamping a metal former in the corner and tapping the ears round to 90°. The pre-drilled holes were then filled with weld.

A chain guard

9 The strip of steel was cut to length. To form the curve at the rear end, the blank must look like the sketch. The top side must be long enough to fold round the curve. If you wish the curve to be a certain radius to suit the radius of the rear sprocket, then you will have to calculate the length of the curve, or measure from an accurate drawing, to make sure the overall length of the blank is sufficient and the blank for the curved end marked out using a radius taken from the rear wheel sprocket as a guide.

10 The blank was then cut to shape **(see illustration)**. Note that the blank has to be long enough so that the straight tail is long enough to bend around the radius. A thin strip of steel is clamped in the vice between two pieces of angle. You could bend long pieces like this over the edge of your bench. Make sure that you can hold the fixed side of the workpiece flat and accurately. After bending along the length, the side of the chain guard is then clamped in the vice and using a small piece of angle iron and two tool makers clamps the curved portion is gradually pulled round the curve and welded in short stages. The finished join is then filed smooth. A curved former can be clamped in place to help position the top of the guard as it is pulled round.

11 After forming a right-angle bend using an angle iron former held in the vice, the tail was bent around a wooden former clamped to the curved side and welded in place.

12 The welded edge was then filed to give a smooth curved join.

Folded and beaded edges

13 Even when filed smooth, the edge of a thin steel sheet is dangerous. To avoid this the edges of mudguards and panels were traditionally given a folded or beaded edge.

Flat folded edge

14 To make a flat turned edge first scribe a line parallel with the edge and about 6 mm

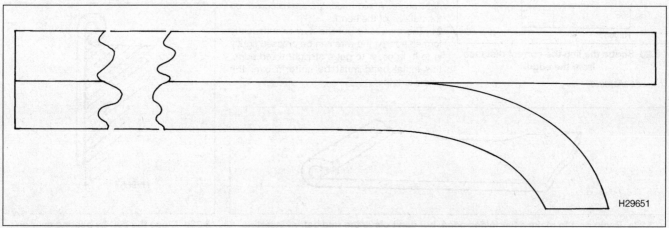

H29651

3.10 Sketch of the blank for the chain guard

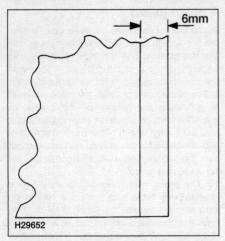

3.14 Scribe a line 6 mm from the edge and fold to 90°

(1/4 in) in from the edge (see illustration). Then using a vice with some of your angle iron if required, fold over the edge. You will only be able to get to 90° on the first folding.

15 Rest the metal on something solid and with your hammer or mallet beat over the folded edge flat. Hold a thin strip of metal of about the same thickness as that of the material you are using against the internal corner (see illustration). Take your time and move along the fold making the bend tighter as you go.

16 Avoid hitting the folded edge too hard. Hammering the steel on the folded edge will tend to split the material into two sharp

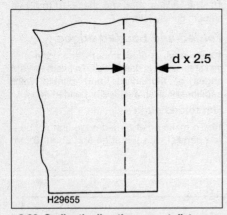

d = wire diameter

3.20 Scribe the line the correct distance from the edge

edges. Finally remove the strip and hammer or mallet the edge down tight (see illustration). Dress the raw edge with a file.

17 If the material is beaten harder in one place than another then the material will thin out and stretch. This will cause ripples and make the surface uneven.

18 The folded edge also adds to the strength of the sheet by increasing the resistance to bending. Increased resistance and a more pleasing appearance can be achieved by making a wired or beaded edge.

Beaded edge

19 A wire in this case is a single small piece of round small diameter metal rod, not the multi strand electrical type of wire. Usually the wire is approximately 3 mm (1/8 in) diameter.

20 First scribe a line 2.5 times the thickness of the wire in from the edge of the sheet (see illustration) and fold this over to about a right-angle. Avoid making a sharp corner on the outside of the bend.

21 The trick is to get the corner sufficiently formed so that the wire can be pressed tightly in to it. In order to get a straight wired edge, this initial bend must be uniform over the whole length.

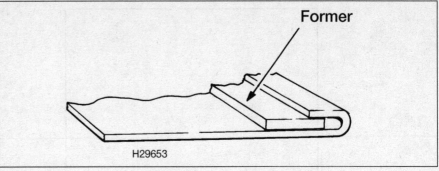

3.15 Beat over on to the former

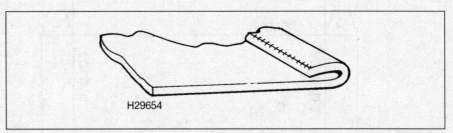

3.16 Remove the former and beat over until tightly clenched. Dress the raw edge with a file

22 Now using a strip of steel the same thickness as the diameter of the wire, beat over the edge. Again work steadily along the length of the edge a little at a time. As the folded piece gets close to being parallel with the rest you can introduce the wire into the corner of the fold. Keep the bend uniform along the whole length.

23 Remove the strip, position the wire and trap it by beating over the flap (see illustration). The final shape is formed by beating the outer side whilst the edge is rested on a flat support (see illustration).

24 For a curved edge such as a mudguard you will need to make a curved anvil. A hardwood former with a radius the same as that of the inner radius of the curved edge, having a steel strip screwed to it in a similar fashion to an old cart wheel will do the trick.

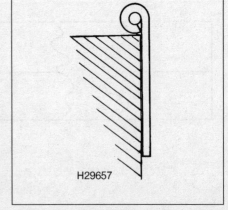

3.23b Close the curl by beating over on a solid edge

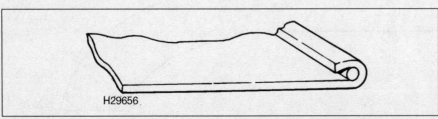

3.23a Begin as if to make a flat folded edge, but don't close the fold before inserting the wire

Chain case

25 This is usually too wide to be clamped in the vice or in a bender and so the right angle must be beaten to shape around a former. The former is made from hard wood in the shape required.

26 The former is clamped to the sheet material which is then beaten over the edge of the former. It is important that the material is not allowed to bow out from the former, so it is best to clamp the material between two pieces of hardwood; one being the shaped former and the other being say 10 mm less in overall size than the first.

27 The edge of the material is longer than the length of the curved portion. Therefore when it is bent over, small vee sections of the sheet must be cut away to allow the sheet to bend to the right angle. After forming the cut sections are welded or brazed together and filed or ground to a smooth finish.

4 Riveting

1 Amongst the methods of permanently joining materials, riveting is one of the easiest to carry out at home, though practice will be needed to form a good joint.

2 This technique is especially suitable where dissimilar metals have to be joined, though this does not remove the risk of electrolytic corrosion taking place between the two.

3 Rivets form a relatively strong and semi-permanent joint, and will have to be drilled out or the head filed off to remove them. In some applications, it may prove easier to use nuts and bolts, though rivets often take up less room.

4 Rivets are rarely found on modern bikes, but the restorer of older machines may need to rivet mudguard stays, brake shoe linings, and seat bases for example.

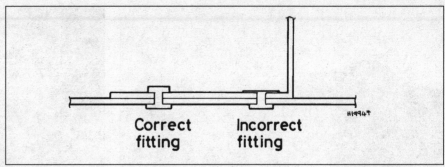

4.9 **The cold rivet must be set evenly on both sides of the join. The heads are often made dome shaped**

Cold riveting

5 In practice this means small rivets which can be 'set' without the need for heat to make them sufficiently workable. Rivets are available in innumerable shapes and sizes, and in various materials. The types normally used have round heads (snap-heads) and are made in steel and aluminium.

6 Other materials, such as brass or copper, are sometimes used for specialised applications, like riveting a soft material to a metal backing.

7 The basic principle requires a clearance hole to be drilled through the two parts to be joined. This is best done by aligning and clamping the two parts to ensure that the hole(s) align correctly. The rivet is passed through the hole and its head supported on an anvil or similar solid support and this is best done with the help of an assistant who can hold the assembly in place and make sure that the two parts are in close contact.

8 A hammer is then used to form the second head and to spread the rivet shank so that it is a tight fit in the holes.

9 The technique of riveting requires a certain knack; early attempts will almost invariably produce a rivet with a bent-over shank, instead of an evenly-formed head. The head should be formed gradually until it is about the same shape and thickness as the original head on the opposite side **(see illustration)**.

10 Aluminium rivets are much easier to set than steel ones. Despite this, do not be tempted to use aluminium rivets to join steel items. The close contact between the two metals will lead to rapid failure due to electrolytic corrosion. This condition occurs when two dissimilar metals react electrically, rather like a small battery.

11 Tubular rivets are easier to set in larger diameters than an equivalent solid rivet. It is best to start forming the head with a drift or a centre punch, and care must be taken to avoid shearing through the edge of the head.

Pop-riveting

12 This is a tubular rivet which is set from one side using a special tool. Each rivet has a shank which passes through from the far side of the rivet and emerges through the head. When the setting tool is operated, the shank is pulled into the tool, forming the head on the far side. At a predetermined tension, the shank snaps off, leaving the rivet in position **(see illustration)**.

13 These rivets are available in various lengths, diameters and materials, and can be bought as a kit together with the setting tool **(see illustration)**. The most common size for motorcycle work is 1/8 inch diameter.

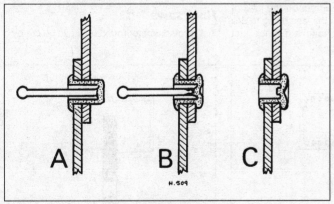

4.12 **Installing a pop rivet**

A   The pop rivet is inserted through the hole in both items to be joined
B   The head is being formed as the shank begins to pull
C   The shank has now broken off, leaving the two parts secure

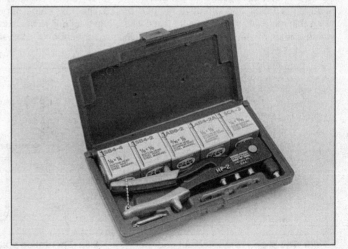

4.13 **A pop-rivetting kit**

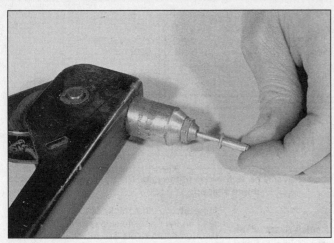

4.16a The rivet being inserted in the setting tool

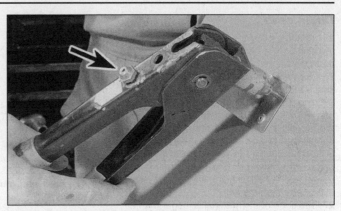

4.16b The tool handles are being squeezed to form the head on the other side of the material. This will form just before the shank snaps. This tool is suitable for setting rivets of more than one diameter; see the additional rivet holder (arrowed) which can be interchanged with the one in use

14 Line up the two pieces to be fixed together and clamp the two pieces which are to be fixed together using mole grips, a G clamp or a tool makers clamp. Drill through with a slightly smaller drill before using the recommended size for the rivet you are using. If you are using more than one rivet drill all the holes required before separating the pieces.

15 Next separate the pieces and deburr the holes. This will ensure that the top piece lies flat on the other, and that the rivet will have a solid base on which to squeeze.

16 Line up the holes and clamp the pieces together again. Insert the rivet and enter the shank into the nose of the setting tool (see illustration). Squeeze the handles until the shank snaps (see illustration).

17 Make sure the rivet is tight and that there is no movement between the two pieces. If they are not tight and are loose in the holes then they will start to fret and wear larger holes until they rattle and will eventually fall out.

18 The advantage of pop riveting is that it is a relatively a quick and effective method of fixing thin materials. Apart from the ease with which these rivets can be set, the main advantage is that you need access to one side of the workpiece only, and no form of anvil or support is required.

19 The disadvantages are that they are not removable except by drilling through, and they have an unsightly blob at the squeezed end which can also interfere with other components.

5 Cutting large and irregular holes

Chain drilling

1 The biggest practical size for twist drills used freehand is about 13 mm (1/2 in) due to the potential problem caused by the drill jamming and forcing the drill out of your hands. Large or irregular shaped holes can also be made by chain drilling.

2 The finished hole is carefully marked out onto the workpiece using a scriber.

3 The next stage depends upon the size of the twist drill to be used, the idea being to drill a sequence of almost touching holes just inside the finished outline of the hole. If you are using a 4 mm drill size, mark out a line about 2.5 mm inside the finished hole outline, then mark this line at 2.5 mm intervals. Centre punch each position (see illustration), then drill out the marked holes. It is important that these holes do not cross the perimeter of the required shape.

4 The size of the drilled holes is not crucial. Smaller holes mean that you get closer to the line and have less finishing to do. Bigger holes mean less drilling, but more finishing. One bigger hole will allow you to slide a junior hacksaw blade through, which can then saw its way from one small hole to the next.

5 The drilled holes are joined by filing, sawing or by chopping the bits in between with a small cold chisel (see illustration). A suitable file, flat for straight sided shapes or a half round for curves, is then used to finish the hole to the scribed line (see illustration).

6 This is a time consuming process, and success is dependent on your accuracy when marking out.

Hole saws

7 A large diameter round hole can be cut by a

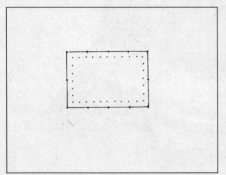

5.3 The shape is marked out and the position of the holes centre punched

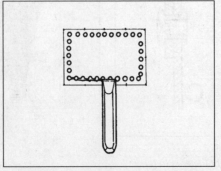

5.5a The drilled holes are joined in this case by chopping out the metal with a small cold chisel

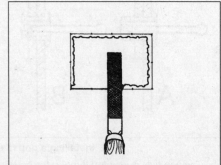

5.5b Finish off by filing back to the scribed line

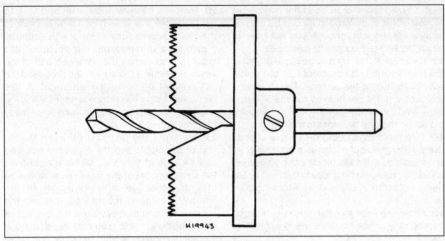

5.7 A hole saw set up for drilling

hole saw **(see illustration)**. You will need a high speed steel variety, not the type used for wood or plastic. Usually the saw comes as a kit with a pilot drill and a series of circular blades which fit into the holder to allow for a range of holes of different diameters.

8 As the hole saw has a normal drill bit at its centre, you only have to mark out the centre of the hole.

9 It is wise to drill a smaller pilot hole to ensure accurate positioning of the hole.

10 Use a very slow drilling speed.

6 Dealing with worn holes

1 If a hole needs to be enlarged slightly, a round, or half round, file is probably the best tool to use.

2 The repair of an hole worn oval is made difficult because re-creating the round hole depends on being able to determine the position of the original hole centre.

3 Even if an acceptable hole of larger diameter can be made by filing, the position of the hole centre needs to be identified in order to draw the new circumference.

4 The worn hole can be returned to its original size by filling with weld and redrilling, or by fitting a bush. For either of these methods the centre of the hole must be found.

Finding the centre of a hole worn out of shape

5 Inspect the hole. Often the wear has taken place in only one direction so by measuring using the internal jaws of your vernier caliper gauge you can identify one of the diameters of the hole. Mark the position of the jaws and then scribe a line across the hole and extended outwards by say twenty millimetres on each side.

6 Try and take two or three measurements at different points on the original, unworn hole diameter. This will give you a better chance to find the centre more accurately.

7 Another practical method of establishing the hole diameter is to use your drill set. Try various drills until you get one which just fits the shape of the unworn section of the hole. Fortunately designers tend to stick with a limited range of sizes. If the drills are well used, make sure that you don't just poke in the tip of the drill which may have been worn or improperly sharpened.

8 Once you have the hole size then you can measure from the drill to a fixed reference point such as an edge or another hole. To find the hole centre the distance from the reference point must have half the drill diameter added to it **(see illustration)**.

Making a new hole

9 A washer or short length of turned bar with a hole the desired size can be lined up with the scribe marks which show the position of the old hole. The new circumference scribed round and then the hole opened out to this new size with a file.

10 Alternately, clamp a flat piece of metal behind the hole and extend your scribed lines back into the hole to fix the centre. Centre punch this hole and scribe the new circumference with dividers.

11 Using the plate as above, clamp the workpiece to the table of the pillar drill, and drill a small pilot hole through at the centre punch. Turn the piece over and line up the pilot drill with its hole. Then drill through to the finished size. On larger holes you can use a round file to ease the hole back into a regular shape before drilling.

12 To return the hole to its original size you can use a bush or weld up the hole. Both the bush and the filled section can be redrilled by lining the workpiece up with its mating components and drilling through, or by marking the centre from the extended scribe lines as described in paragraph 8 above **(see illustration)**.

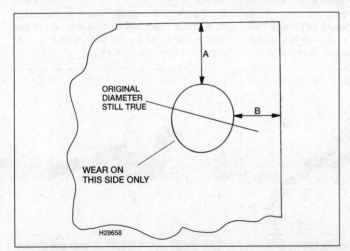

6.8 The hole centre can be found by taking measurements A and B from the unworn side and adding half the hole diameter to each

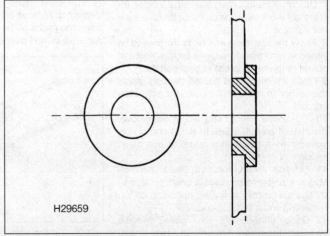

6.12 The locating hole for the bush need not be on the original hole centre. However, the centre hole must be drilled with the bush in place using the original centre

7 Soldering

1 Soldering is a technique for joining two metals using a third, usually an alloy of lead and tin. It is most often used for joining copper and brass, though there are other more specialised soldering processes. Strength is instead achieved by using the solder as a sort of combined glue and filler, allowing a mechanically strong joint to be made stable and secure.

2 Soldered joints are used extensively for making electrical connections, where the solder is useful as a good conductor between a wire and its terminal. The other common use is as a method of securing the nipples to control cable inner wires.

3 The process of soldering is entirely reliant upon cleanliness. This does not just mean that the worst of the dirt and grease has to be removed; the metal surfaces to be joined must be chemically clean with any oxide deposits removed with a file or abrasive paper. If this is not done, the solder will not take to the metal.

4 Once the parts have been prepared, the surfaces to be joined have to be 'tinned'. Tinning means coating the metal in the area of the joint with a thin film of solder.

5 'Sweating' is the term used when a joint is heated, so that when solder is put onto the surfaces it melts and flows into the joint. By moving the point at which the heat is applied, the solder can be drawn into and around a joint.

6 To assist in the soldering process a flux is used, and this cleans away surface oxides and helps the solder to flow. The most convenient form of flux is carried in solder wire in small cores, solder of this type being called 'multi-core'. Alternatively, plain solder can be used in conjunction with a paste flux which is applied to the metal before tinning.

7 Use only multi-cored electrical solder for electrical work as some of the paste fluxes are not suitable.

8 Apply the soldering iron bit to the area to be tinned. It may help to apply a small amount of solder to the bit to assist in heat transfer.

9 Once the metal has heated through, apply the solder to the metal (not to the soldering iron bit).

10 The solder should flow out smoothly over the heated area. If it fails to do so and simply collects in a bead, the metal is not clean enough.

11 Let the metal cool off, then use fine abrasive paper to produce a bright finish and try again. Repeat the tinning operation on the remaining piece to be joined.

12 Once tinned, the two parts can be sweated together. Arrange the two tinned surfaces so that they are in firm contact, then apply the soldering iron bit. The solder applied during the tinning operation will heat up and melt, flowing together to bond the two pieces of metal. This basic procedure can be applied to all soldering jobs, though you will have to adapt the technique in some instances.

13 If you are soldering a large piece of metal, the heat loss may be so great that the solder will not melt onto the surface. To get around this problem, try pre-heating the metal with a blowlamp, and supporting it on wooden blocks so that the heat loss is slowed.

14 To protect a part from the effects of heat, use a large piece of metal as a heat sink. As an example, a fragile electrical component could be protected by gripping the lead or tag being soldered in pliers or self-locking plier jaws.

15 Allow the joint to cool naturally. Forced cooling may create stresses which will reduce the strength of the joint.

16 Where a paste flux has been used it is important to wash the joint with water after it has cooled to remove any chemicals which may have been left on the surfaces which would then cause corrosion.

Soldering control cables

17 For most purposes, it is easier and quicker to buy ready-made control cables than to attempt to make them up at home, but on occasions it may be useful to be able to make up an emergency replacement cable, or to modify an existing one. In addition to solder and a soldering iron you will need a strong pair of side cutters capable of cutting cleanly through the inner and outer cable material. It is also preferable to have a selection of new cable nipples to hand. Whilst it is possible to re-use nipples on some occasions, many are now crimped onto the cable and thus not suitable for re-use.

18 If the purpose of the operation is to re-use a broken cable, this can be done provided that it has broken at or near one end. Check before starting that you can afford to lose a little of the overall length of the cable.

19 Clean the broken inner cable carefully. This is best done using aerosol contact cleaner to remove all traces of grease. Next, clean the metal of the inner with fine abrasive paper, and then degrease once more.

20 Heat the cable with the iron, and tin it to bind together the strands of the inner back to the point where they form a tight circular bunch **(see illustration)**; the object at this stage is to cut away the damaged end of the inner, and tinning the area of the proposed cut will prevent it unravelling when cut. A gas blowlamp with a fine nozzle is best for this job provided the plastic outer can be kept away from the flame.

21 Work out the distance between the far end of the nipple and the proposed cut, and make a note of this. You will have to remove the same amount of the outer cover to ensure that the effective working length of the complete cable is maintained. Cut off the inner cable, and then withdraw it a few inches down the outer cable. You may like to remove it completely so that both the inner and outer can be cleaned and lubricated prior to the new nipple being fitted.

22 With the inner removed, the outer cable can now be shortened to suit. Using the side cutters, remove the appropriate amount of the outer cable. The offcut piece will take with it the small metal ferrule which covers the cut end of the outer. You will need to fit a new one to the newly cut end, but with care it is often possible to work off the old one and re-use it.

23 Slide the inner cable back into position, and degrease and clean the tinned end ready for soldering.

Note: *Remember to refit in the correct sequence any adjusters or stops which are integral with the cable before the nipple is fitted! If you have no spare nipples of the appropriate size, you may be able to re-use the old one, provided that it was soldered on originally.*

24 Holding the nipple with pliers to avoid burns, heat it up until the solder melts, then shake out the old inner wire. You may need to use a piece of wire or a similar tool to dislodge the strands. While the solder is still molten, blow through the hole to remove excess solder.

25 If using a new nipple, heat it up and tin the hole at the centre. Fit the nipple over the end of the inner cable so that about 2 mm protrudes **(see illustration)**.

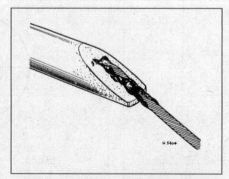

7.20 Tin the cable, using plenty of flux, until the solder runs freely through the cable strands. Do not allow the cable strands to fan out

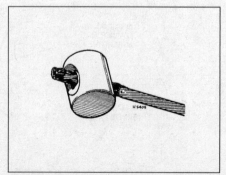

7.25 Position the nipple so that the solder holds it in place with about 2 mm of cable protruding. Allow to cool, without the position moving

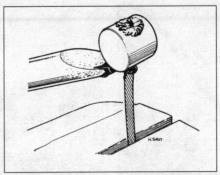

7.27a Peen over the cable strands, using a light, ball-ended hammer. The cable should be held in a vice fitted with soft jaws and the cable ends peened over sufficiently to stop the cable pulling through

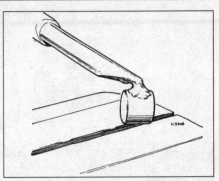

7.27b Heat the cable nipple until the solder melts and raise it upwards so that the cable end seats in the recess provided. Maintain the upward pull until the solder has cooled and set

7.27c Fill the recess with solder, holding the nipple in the vice clamps so that it cannot slide down the cable as the solder melts. Maintain a pull on the cable, if possible, throughout this operation

26 You will now have to flare out the individual strands into a fan shape. This is a vital stage in the operation, since it is this flared end consolidated with solder which gives the joint strength. If the cable end is left straight it will pull off the end of the inner cable. There are various ways of doing this, but I have found it easiest to clamp a self-locking wrench around the inner cable just below the nipple.

27 Alternatively, clamp the inner wire in a vice **(see illustration)**. If you are using new, untinned cable, it is quite easy to tease the ends apart, bending them into a fan shape. If the end has been tinned before cutting, heat the cable end first, keeping the solder molten while spreading the ends. The cable end and nipple can now be heated, and solder flowed into the end of the nipple to form a small domed end **(see illustrations)**.

28 Odd strands of inner wire should be smoothed off with a file to complete the job **(see illustration)**.

Soldering electrical connections

29 Soldering is without doubt the best way to make electrical connections, although crimped connections are commonly used these days.

30 Start by stripping back the insulation from the wire to be joined to the terminal. This is best done using a wire stripper tool, though if care is taken you can score through the plastic insulation with a sharp knife blade, taking care not to cut into the copper strands beneath. The insulation can then be slid off, and the strands twisted lightly together to stop them spreading.

31 Tin the bare end of the wire, keeping it on the bit just long enough for the solder to flow between each strand, but not long enough to melt the insulation. Remember to fit any insulating sleeves or other fittings over the end of the wire at this stage.

32 Tin the corresponding area of the terminal, then bring the two together and apply heat to flow the solder between the two.

Take care not to move the two parts as the solder cools.

33 A lack of cleanliness, forced cooling and pulling on the joint before the solder is solid will again result in a poor joint with little strength and poor electrical conductivity.

34 When it is cold, give the terminal a slight tug. It is better that it break now rather than in service.

Soldering banjo unions on pipes

35 Rigid oil pipes often have banjo union fittings at each end. In order to make a fuel tight seal between the banjo union and pipe, the banjo union is "sweated" onto the pipe.

36 First the pipe and the banjo union are cleaned using a fine wire brush or wire wool. Flux is then applied to both components where they are to be joined. Flux and wire wool can be had from the local builders merchants or DIY superstore.

37 Locate the pipe in the banjo union and grip the pipe gently in the vice using two pieces of wood or heat resisting material in the vice jaws. Arrange it so that the pipe is pointing downwards so that the molten solder will run down into the banjo union.

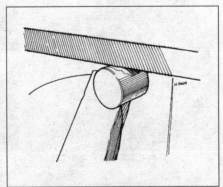

7.28 Smooth off the excess solder with a file, so that the original profile of the nipple is restored and it will move freely in the control lever

38 The solder, again from the builders or DIY store comes on a reel and is about 3 mm diameter. Stretch out a length of solder about 150 mm long. With the gas blowlamp lit and held in one hand, warm up the pipe and banjo union. Remember the hottest part of the flame is at the tip of the blue cone. The yellow part of the flame will take longer to heat up the job and as this part contains the carbon compounds there is a chance of sooting up the job and preventing good soldering.

39 With the end of the solder, just touch the pipe where it enters the banjo union. When the metal is warm enough, the solder will melt and flow into the joint.

40 By moving the flame you can encourage the solder to flow all round the pipe and into the joint. Remove the heat and let the job cool **(see illustration)**.

41 As the pipe becomes hot you will see the flux start to react and clean the pipe to a lovely salmon pink colour.

42 Many fluxes contain acids, so when the work is cold give it a good wash to remove any flux which may be left as this will corrode the pipe and prevent a paint or lacquer finish lasting.

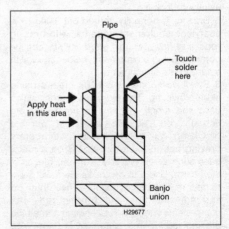

7.40 Soldering a banjo union fitting on an external oil pipe

8.3a Brazing is ideal for light fabrication jobs such as attaching brackets. Note that the bracket here has been positioned with a piece of brazing rod while it is tacked into place

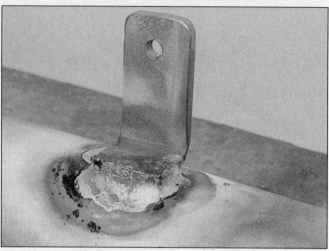

8.3b A brazed joint is reasonably strong and less prone than some welding to causing unwanted heat distortion. Note, however, that heat may cause discoloration or damage to plated parts

8 Brazing

1 Brazing is a process in which the pieces to be joined are heated to a temperature sufficient to melt a filler metal, which is allowed to flow into a joint in a similar way to soldering.

2 The filler is brass or bronze which is a mixture of 60% copper and 40% zinc and comes as a thin rod. The two pieces to be joined are held together and heated using a gas or oxy/acetylene torch until the filler melts and flows into the joint. The temperature of the metals at the point of the weld are about 750°C to 1000°C so there is less chance of distortion.

3 The joint may not be as strong as a welded joint, but it is tough and will allow some flexing **(see illustrations)**; it is currently used in chassis construction partly due to this reason.

4 A flux must be used which is then washed away after cooling.

5 Brazing is normally carried out using oxy-acetylene equipment, together with brazing rods and flux, though good results can be obtained using a simple arc welder fitted with a carbon-arc attachment.

6 Small components can be brazed using large blowlamp. The plumbers' burner which uses the small canister is not really big enough, but an old fashioned paraffin blowlamp will do. Make up a temporary brazing hearth using fire bricks on a metal base such as an old tray. Put your pieces in the hearth. Use a clamp or tie them with wire to hold mating pieces together, heat them up and add the flux and brazing rod. The components should be hot enough to melt the brazing rod when it is applied to them. You will not get a good joint if the flame melts the rod onto the join.

9 Welding

Warning: Refer to the Warning notice in Section 1 of this chapter concerning the dangers associated with welding and welding equipment.

1 Welding is the process of joining two similar metals (the term is also applied to plastics) using heat and a filler metal. The process is one of fusion in that the metals are joined together as one piece. This imparts great strength, and it allows a continuous joint to be made, unlike that made by bolts or rivets.

2 The heat is provided by burning gas or an electric spark. In some instances pressure is used as in spot welding.

Arc welding

3 The welding equipment comprises a metal cased transformer unit, normally with a dial control to regulate the welding current **(see illustration)**. To this are attached a mains lead and plug, and two heavy-duty output leads. One of these, the earth (ground) lead, terminates in a crocodile clip which is attached to the workpiece. The other is connected to an electrode holder.

4 The electrode is normally a steel rod, coated with a special flux which prevents oxidation of the weld during work.

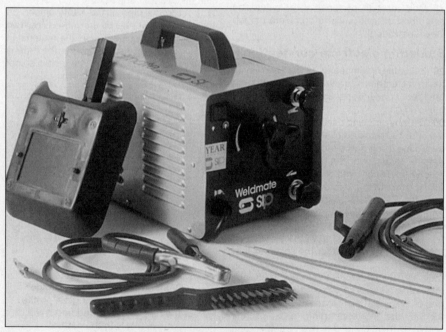

9.3 An arc welder kit with accessories

5 The key to the success of the process is to select a rod size and current setting appropriate to the thickness of metal being welded.

6 The machine is then switched on, and the electrode brought very close to the workpiece. As the tip of the electrode nears the workpiece, an arc is struck between them. This is almost exactly the same as a spark plug in operation, except that the spark is much hotter, and continuous.

7 The heat generated by the arc melts the rod, and also the pieces of metal in the area to be joined. The molten metal flows together to form the weld, while the flux melts and flows over the surface to exclude air from the weld. Once cooled, the slag formed by the flux is chipped away to reveal the welded joint.

8 The main advantage of arc welding is its low cost and general versatility. It is a good arrangement for home use, since there is no big outlay on equipment hire, as with gas welding. The range of thicknesses of metal covered by a particular welding set is invariably reflected in its price, but even the cheapest machines will suffice for tacking odd brackets into place or fabricating battery trays and similar items.

9 The main disadvantage with arc welding is that you will have to spend some time developing your technique before you can start serious work, and it is very easy to get things wrong during the first few attempts. As the arc burns the electrode rod, the position of the rod tip has to be constantly adjusted to keep the distance form the work constant in order to maintain the arc.

10 Also the arc is very fierce, and there is a danger of distorting thin materials out of shape and of burning holes in the work pieces.

Carbon-arc attachments

11 These devices replace the normal electrode holder with a pair of tapered carbon electrodes, one of which can be slid in relation to the other to regulate the gap between them.

12 In use, the arc forms between the two electrodes and produces a sort of flame, and this can be used to braze thin metal which would be burnt through when using welding rods. This extends the versatility of the arc welder considerably, and some manufacturers include a carbon-arc torch with their sets.

13 The only drawbacks are that it is a difficult process to master; all the problems of welding, plus an electrode gap to regulate. The carbon rods tend to be expensive if you use this method a lot, and the torch itself is bulky, and difficult to use in a confined space.

MIG welding

14 MIG (Metal, Inert Gas) welders avoid many of the problems of the arc welder, from which they were derived. A reel of wire, the charged electrode, is housed in the casing of the machine and fed by a motor and a capstan along a hose to the welding handset.

The speed at which the wire emerges from the welding tip can be varied, as can the welding current.

15 The flux is also eliminated, and instead an inert shielding gas is fed through the same hose to emerge around the welding wire. This prevents oxidation, and does away with the problem of slag formation.

16 The flow of gas also helps to keep the surrounding metal cooler, thus minimising distortion. The gas shield and lower current settings allow MIG welding to be done on much thinner metal sheet. A typical home workshop welder with a maximum current setting of 130 amp will weld steel up to 4 mm thick **(see illustration)**.

17 The wire and gas feed are normally controlled from a switch on the welding handset. This means that much closer control is possible than with arc welding, and that work in confined spaces is much easier. The electrode at the handset is only made live when the trigger is held. This means that the arc can be positioned at the start of a weld and the welding hand steadied before the view is hidden by the welding mask.

18 The only drawback with MIG welding is the higher initial cost of the machine, and also perhaps, the fact that brazing is not possible.

19 The relatively low-cost units designed for home or semi-professional use usually use miniature non-refillable gas bottles, and these can become expensive if much welding work is undertaken. It is possible to fit adapters to take industrial size gas bottles, however, and if necessary, larger wire reel sizes can be used.

20 By changing the wire and the gas you can also weld stainless steels and aluminium

which is an advantage in a motorcycle workshop.

21 It is possible to buy gasless MIG welding sets which have the flux inside the welding wire. This obviously means that repeated gas purchases are not required and that welding can be done in windy conditions which might blow the gas away from the joint.

22 The biggest advantage of MIG welding is that it is easy to learn how to use the kit and get a decent effective weld.

Oxy-acetylene welding

23 This is perhaps the most flexible welding method of all, allowing close control of the flame temperature. The possible range goes from low settings useful for heating metal and freeing seized fasteners, through brazing to welding and even metal cutting.

24 In essence, the system comprises two gas bottles, one containing oxygen and the other a fuel gas, normally acetylene. The gas is passed through regulators and anti-flashback valves to a handset, where the two gases can be mixed in differing proportions to permit various temperatures to be attained.

25 The main drawback for home use is the high initial cost of setting up a gas welding system **(see illustration)**. In the UK, the regulators, hoses, handset and nozzles must be bought, and then added to this is the cost of a rental agreement for the gas bottles, plus refilling charges.

Low temperature aluminium welding

26 This is a proprietary process for joining aluminium and various aluminium and zinc-

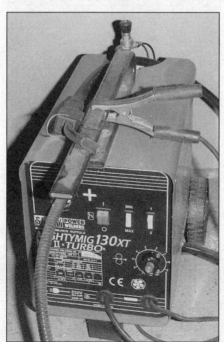

9.16 A MIG welder capable of most jobs in the motorcycle workshop

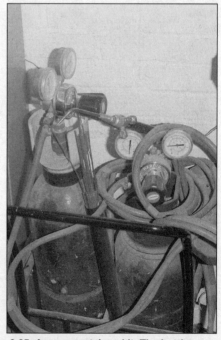

9.25 An oxy-acetylene kit. The bottles are strapped to the trolley and have gauges and regulators fitted

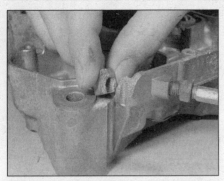

9.26a This broken crankcase lug is due for repair

9.26b The metal is cleaned using the stainless steel brush provided in the kit. The instructions also provide helpful information cleaning aluminium castings in preparation for welding

9.26c The metal is heated to the required temperature by burner flame. It can also be pre-heated in an oven

9.26d The surfaces are tinned with the filler rod and are agitated with a stainless steel rod to remove impurities from the surface

based alloys. As such it is of considerable potential use in the home workshop **(see illustrations)**. It is sold in kit form under the name Lumiweld.

27 As the name suggests, this process does not require the parts to be joined to be raised to melting point to allow a full fusion weld to take place. In this respect it is rather similar to soldering or brazing, though the manufacturer claims that a molecular bond is formed.

28 In use, the workpiece is raised to a temperature of about 390°C (730°F), at which point the filler rod will melt and flow between the parts to be joined. It should be noted that

this is far lower than the melting point of aluminium and related alloys (generally about 1100°F or 595°C) and so there is little risk of sudden melting of the parts being worked on. More significantly, it is normally possible to obtain these temperatures using no more than a butane torch.

29 Applications include casting repairs, building up stripped threads prior to re-tapping, repair of radiators and similar jobs which would otherwise demand professional attention or renewal of the damaged part **(see illustrations)**. It will also cope with zinc alloys, which are normally difficult or impossible to repair.

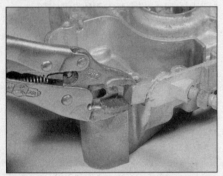

9.26e The broken part of the boss is held in close contact and 'sweated' in place

9.26f Once secure, the joint can be improved by filling in the cracks around the break

9.26g After cleaning and filing the lug is as good as new

9.29a Casing damage due to bearing failure . . .

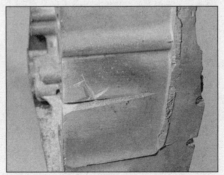

9.29b . . . is first filed into a V-shape to ensure a good bond

9.29c After the usual preparation, the notched areas were filled using the filler rod

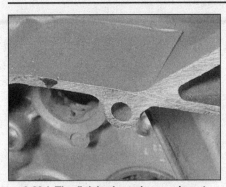

9.29d The finished repair was almost invisible, other than where the light caught the gasket face

30 Disadvantages are that the zinc content of the rods means that corrosion takes place where salt is present, and that anodising and heat treatment are not possible, though these are more than outweighed by its general usefulness.

31 Conventional alloy welding methods such as TIG (tungsten inert gas), and MIG welding are specialised skilled processes, effectively limited to professional engineering workshops equipped for this type of work.

Welding safely

32 Fire risks are a real problem when welding. Remember to remove all fuel sources, including the machine's fuel tank, before starting work.

33 Work in a well-ventilated area to avoid the risk of a build-up of fumes, and make sure the area is clear of paper or rags which might be ignited by the sparks.

34 Make sure that you have adequate fire-fighting equipment on hand in case of fire.

35 Always thoroughly clean any petrol from a petrol tank before attempting to apply heat to it. It is wise to flush the tank with water several times and leave in a warm well ventilated atmosphere for several hours before starting to weld.

36 Eye protection is especially vital when welding. Arc and MIG welders produce an extremely bright arc which can cause serious eye damage unless filtered through special dark glass. Use only an approved full welding mask, and make sure that the glass fitted is of the correct type for your welder.

37 The risk comes mainly from the high ultraviolet levels in the light emitted. You need only look at the arc with the naked eyes for moments to develop a condition called arc eye. This potentially serious condition is extremely painful, leaving your eyes feeling as

if they are full of sand or grit. In bad cases, permanent damage may be caused.

38 Do not forget that spectators and pets can suffer from this too, so keep them well away when welding. Oxy-acetylene welding requires a less dark glass, but gas welding goggles should be worn at all times.

39 Welding kits usually come with a small hand-held eye shield but many people prefer the head band type which has a flip up shield and keeps both hands free. This very useful when starting MIG welding as you can position the hand with the handgrip in the correct place supported by the other hand. Then a sharp nod, or with a gentle movement of the supporting hand, flip the eye shield down and then press the button to make the electrode live and start welding once your supporting hand is back in place.

40 Skin protection will be needed, both to fend off hot sparks, and to protect the skin from the intense ultraviolet light from the arc; you can easily get a nasty version of sunburn from arc and MIG welders.

41 You will need gloves to avoid burns to the hands, and a cotton boiler suit with no cuffs (these could trap sparks) which fastens to the neck. Wear work boots, preferably arranged so that sparks cannot get down inside them.

42 Machine protection is required whatever form of welding is employed, but especially so in the case of arc or MIG welding. If you are welding a bracket or lug to the frame, remember that the welding current will be passing through it, and this can easily damage sensitive electronic components.

43 Always disconnect (earth/ground lead first) and remove the battery, and also disconnect the alternator, regulator/rectifier and electronic ignition leads to prevent damage to these components.

44 A secondary risk is due to the passage of the welding current along the machine's frame. For example, if the earth (ground) clamp is attached to a fork leg while welding is carried out on the main frame, the current must pass through the steering head bearings to complete the circuit. Since this presents only a small contact point, the bearing balls or rollers may become welded to the races. Always attach the earth (ground) clamp close to the weld area to avoid this risk.

Welding practice

45 Whether welding or brazing there are common guidelines which must be followed in order to get a sound, strong joint. These guidelines relate to the cleanliness and

condition of the material to be welded, the amount of heat, the speed and angle of movement of the electrode, and the gap between electrode and joint.

46 The area where the weld is to be made must be clean and rust free to avoid any pollution entering the molten weld. Also the heat can cause unwanted fumes from painted and galvanised surfaces.

47 Butt joints need a chamfered edge to assist weld penetration. Chamfers can be filed, however It is easier to make these with an angle grinder.

48 The edges of the parts to be joined should be positioned close together and clamped if possible. Where tubes of different sizes are to be butted together, the small tube is inserted into the larger. Another tip to increase the amount of filler on a brazed joint is to pinch in the sides of the tube.

49 On thin material, it is usual to tack the pieces together and then fill in the gaps gradually working from different ends in order to avoid distortion.

50 Except where the joint is for cosmetic repair, it should not be ground flat to the parent material.

51 In the beginning you will need to take time to learn. There is a lot to learn: power settings, wire speed, gas flow, angle of electrode and speed and direction of movement. Keep trying and don't attempt anything too difficult until you have the basics **(see illustration)**. Follow the guidance on hand positions and direction of travel as given in the instructions with the equipment.

52 Set aside a day or two for learning. Collect bits of scrap metal so that you have plenty to practice on. Begin with pieces that are about 4 mm thick and compare your finished weld with the illustrations shown in the instructions. As you get more confident and competent use pieces of different thicknesses. Try butt welds, seam welds, welds on curves and where the pieces are at right-angles.

53 Keep a note of the settings when you do each piece including the type, shape and thickness of the work piece. This will help you learn from your mistakes and be a useful guide for future work. Test your work by trying to break the join and occasionally saw through the join and see how the weld has penetrated.

54 If possible enrol on a course at the local technical college or ask an experienced welder for advice.

10 Lathe work

1 A general description of the lathe and lathe tools is given in Chapter 15.

Lathe uses

2 With the basic turning skills it is possible to manufacture all manner of spacers, bolts, nipples, studs and nuts.

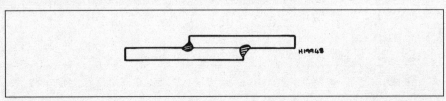

9.51 A welded lap joint. The fused section must penetrate right into the parent metal

10.3 A dial gauge is being run along a parallel bar held between centres. This operation will check the alignment of the centres prior to a turning job, or a runout investigation

10.4a Cleaning up the end of a bar by facing across with a left-hand knife tool

10.4b Centre drilling to provide a location for a lathe centre, or as the first step in drilling a hole down the centre of the bar

3 The lathe can also assist with maintenance jobs such as skimming brake drums and even discs if the swing is big enough. When fitted with centres, the lathe can also be used to make runout checks on a variety of components **(see illustration)**.

4 In this manual there are many references to tools and gauges which can be made on the lathe. Flywheel pullers, rotor extractors and bearing removers are all within the scope of the one machine **(see illustrations)**.

5 The lathe can also be used as a small milling machine, a drilling machine and as a grinding machine. The latter is not recommended as the normal lathe does not have the protection from the minute particles of grit which may damage slideways and threads.

6 Although primarily for metal work, a lathe will allow you to turn wood and a range of plastics and manufactured materials.

7 Begin with some of the simple projects suggested in this manual; the tubular peg spanner for example. There are many books about lathe work, but it is best to get some tuition from the start. There may be courses at local technical colleges on which you can enrol.

Lathe safety

8 Any machine tool demands a high level of safety awareness.

9 Make sure that the electrical supply is properly fitted and that the isolating switch is clearly marked and easily reached.

10 Always wear eye protection.

11 Do not carry out any inspection or touch any part of the work whilst the lathe is still rotating.

12 Never leave a chuck key in the chuck.

13 Make sure all tools and workpieces are tightened securely in place.

14 Don't allow any coolant on you, your clothes, or the floor.

15 Isolate the supply to the lathe when it is not being used.

10.4c Checking progress by measuring the diameter of the workpiece. Every millimetre advance of the tool removes 2 mm from the diameter

10.4d Cutting a thread using a die and die stock. The stock is supported by the tail stock. The chuck is turned by hand and the spindle of the tail stock advanced at the same time until the thread is properly started. The forward/reverse technique must be used

10.4e Setting up for screwcutting. The tool, which has been ground to the correct thread profile using the thread gauge as a guide, is being set at right-angles to the work. The thread gauge is held against the work, and the tool set so that it enters the profile cleanly

Chapter 8
Workshop techniques with plastics and composites

Contents

---

1 Introduction

Work with plastics will mainly be repair work as it is difficult to fabricate plastic items at home. It is possible to machine certain types of plastic using conventional tools and small fabricated items can be made using adhesives.

Glass fibre reinforced plastic or GRP can be fabricated at home and formed or moulded into a variety of shapes.

Note that most plastics have limited resistance to temperature. Therefore remove them if you are doing any repair work such as welding, or they may be damaged, melt, or catch fire.

2 Types of plastic

1 Before commencing any sort of repair work it is essential to know with which plastic you are dealing.
2 Each plastic has its own properties, which affect the way it is used and repaired **(see illustration overleaf)**.
3 Probably the most common plastic is Acrylonitrile Butadiene Styrene resin known as ABS which is used for fairings and body panels.
4 The plastic may carry an international identification symbol. However, this standard is not used universally.
5 Fortunately there are not a great many different types of plastic used in motorcycle manufacture and a clue as to the type of plastic can be taken from the part on which it is used **(see illustration overleaf)**.

Material name	ISO code	Resistance to petrol (gasoline) and solvents	Other cautions
Polyethylene	PE	Not affected by petrol and most solvents	It is flammable
Polyvinyl chloride	PVC	Not affected by petrol and most solvents if exposed for a very short time. Wipe off quickly	A poison gas is emitted when it burns
Polypropylene	PP	Not affected by petrol and most solvents	It is flammable
Acrylonitrile butadiene stryrene resin	ABS	Avoid contact with petrol and solvents	Avoid contact with brake fluid
Acrylonitrile ethylene styrene	AES	Avoid contact with petrol and solvents	
Polymethyl methacrylate	PMMA	Avoid contact with petrol and solvents	
Polycarbonate	PC	Avoid contact with petrol and solvents	
Polyamide (Nylon)	PA	Not affected by petrol and most solvents	Avoid immersing in water
Polyurethane	PUR	Avoid contact with petrol and solvents	Contact with alcohol may be used for very short periods when wiping clean or removing grease
Fibre reinforced plastics	FRP	Not affected by petrol and most solvents	

2.2 Precautions to be taken when handling the common plastics

Material name	ISO code	Thermosetting or thermoplastic	Design applications
Polyethylene	PE	Thermoplastic	Trim panels. Containers
Polyvinyl chloride	PVC	Thermoplastic	Seat covers and trim
Polypropylene	PP	Thermoplastic	Body mouldings
Acrylonitrile butadiene stryrene resin	ABS	Thermoplastic	Fairings, trim (may be reinforced with fibre glass mat, or polyethylene)
Polymethyl methacrylate	PMMA	Thermoplastic	Lenses, windshields
Polycarbonate	PC	Thermoplastic	Lenses, instrument panels
Polyamide (Nylon)	PA	Thermosetting	Body panels, trim, gears, bushes
Polyester	UP	Thermosetting	Resin for reinforced fibre composites
Polyurethane	PUR	Thermosetting	Body panels
Epoxy	EP	Thermosetting	Adhesives, resin for reinforced fibre composites, encapsulation of electrical components

2.5 Typical design applications of commonly used plastics

3 Repairing plastic parts

1 There are various repair systems available, but adhesives and plastic welding with hot air are the most common (see illustration).

Preparation

2 If the part has actually broken, collect as many pieces as you can: it may be possible to glue or weld them back into shape.
3 Remove any rough edges.
4 Where possible from the inside surface of the plastic, grind out along the damage to establish the true extent of the damage.
5 Cracks which are to be weld must be ground into a V to accept the weld material as you would do for normal metal welding.
6 The plastic must be clean and free of dust, and grease. On new plastic products there may be remains of the mould release agent which must also be removed.
7 Clean using detergent to remove the general muck, then use a high flash-point solvent. A special plastic cleaner is available from the suppliers of paint finishes and welding materials.

Adhesive repair

8 Adhesive repair does not require the use of heat and therefore does not carry the risk of distortion occurring to the plastic.
9 Apply an etching compound to prepare the surface for the adhesive.
10 One adhesive which may be suitable is the cyanoacrylate, or instant superglue type.
11 This glue does not work well on all plastics and a test is recommended before making the repair. There is also some doubt as to its ability to withstand exposure to weather.
12 Other adhesives are of the two-part type,

Material name	ISO code	Repair methods				
		Adhesive	GRP	Hot air weld	Anaerobic Superglue	Airless welding
Polyethylene	PE			Y		Y
Polyvinyl chloride	PVC	Y				Y
Polypropylene	PP			Y		Y
Acrylonitrile Butadiene Stryrene resin	ABS		Y	Y	Y	Y
Polyamide (Nylon)	PA			Y	Y	Y
Polyurethane	PUR	Y				Y
Polyester	UP		Y			

3.1 Repair methods for different plastics

an accelerator or catalyst and the adhesive itself.
13 Unlike other two-part resin adhesives the two are not mixed before application. The accelerator is sprayed onto the edges to be glued and then the adhesive is applied. The two edges are brought together and held for a short period of time until the adhesive is set.
14 The parent plastic product is flexible. It is important to choose an adhesive, and any repair material which you are gluing in, which has the same degree of flexibility. This information and a sample repair patch for comparison can be had from the repair product suppliers.
15 As products from different manufacturers may be slightly different, stick with one supplier or manufacturer for the whole of the repair.
16 Kits are now available from motorcycle

accessory shops which contain adhesives and GRP matting, and will work on most plastics.
17 The two-part epoxy or polyester resin may also be used for adhesive repair. These are mixed, and used as for normal applications. The problem with these compounds is that they may not have the flexibility of the parent material and will crack.

Repair by welding

18 Welding can be done on thermoplastic type materials (see illustrations).
19 Welding is done by blowing hot air under pressure onto the areas to be welded and applying a filler rod of the parent material.
20 Before beginning serious work, it is wise to carry out a trial weld on a hidden or damaged area to confirm that the material and filler can be welded successfully.

3.18a This mudguard can be hot air welded. Grinding the groove along the line of the split involves using a small grinding stone. This is more easily done using a hand-held electric grinder or a flexible drive from a motor

3.18b From the outside this looks like a simple adhesive repair, however . . .

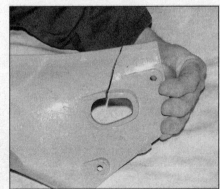

3.18c . . . inside the moulding is a shaped location for a mounting bolt, and there is the boss around the indicator mounting hole. Welding is the only method for permanent repair

21 Try several filler rods until one sticks. The rods are colour-coded so that when you have a rod that works you can identify the base material.

22 When welding, small beads of liquid should be seen where the rod meets the base material.

23 Keep a steady downward pressure on the rod. The rod should keep its round shape and neither rod nor base material should char or discolour.

24 Don't try and stretch the filler rod over the weld. The length of rod should match the length of weld.

25 Only use hot air, never oxygen or other inflammable gases.

26 Welding kits can be bought, but are quite expensive.

27 If the broken parts can be kept on their mountings or subframe, this will help keep them in shape whilst being welded and during cooling.

28 Avoid moving or flexing the welded parts until the are cool. A good weld will stick even when hot, but there is the risk if distortion.

29 When the weld is cool, smooth down the area ready for painting. A fine filler may be required to finish the external contours.

Home heat welding tool

30 Some owners have had some success using a modified low wattage soldering iron. The main requirement is to reduce the temperature at the bit, and the easiest way to do this is to attach an extended bit in the form of a length of thick wire.

31 This will act as a heat sink, and by progressively reducing the length of the wire tip it is possible to arrive at the desired temperature. This should be just enough to melt the plastic, but no hotter.

32 Using the improvised tool, melt across the split or join in several places to tack them together, ensuring that the parts are held level. Once you are sure that the parts are correctly positioned, work along the join with the bit, moving it from side to side slightly to help 'stitch' the parts together.

33 Be very careful not to allow the heat to penetrate too far; you need to fuse the plastic together as far as possible, but beware of burning through on the side that will show.

34 With luck, you should find it possible to repair light damage using this method. The join will not be as strong as the surrounding material, but this can be improved if you can find a piece of similar plastic to use as a filler.

35 This should be used in the same manner as welding rod, running the extra material into the weld to reinforce it.

36 The hot air gun used for paint removal might act as the hot air source provided it is fitted with a fine nozzle, which would need fabricating in the workshop.

Repair using GRP

37 An alternative approach is to attempt a repair using glass reinforced plastic (GRP)

methods. This is the basis of the repair kit mentioned above in paragraph 16.

38 The snag here is that resin may not adhere to some types of plastics, and not may be flexible enough.

39 Test the adhesion on a small area first, before carrying out a full repair.

A cautionary note

40 The main manufacturers are continually changing the specifications of the plastic used on their bikes. The addition of other chemicals, as fillers, colouring agents and strengtheners, change the properties and weldability of the plastic.

41 This makes home workshop repairs difficult and reduces the success rate of any repair.

42 Probably the best advice is to contact a repair specialist to carry out any work and ask how you can prepare the work so as to make the repairers' job easier and save costs.

---

4 Plastic windshields (screens)

Cleaning and renovation

1 The clear or tinted windshield fitted to fairings will eventually get scratched by the road dirt and is often vulnerable to knocks. Use a silicone-based spray polish which will help prevent road dirt sticking to the screen.

2 When cleaning **any** plastic surface, use copious amounts of water to soften the dirt first, then wash it off gently using a sponge or chamois leather.

3 If the screen is badly scratched it is worth trying to remove the scratches by polishing them out. This is a tedious process, and will work better on some materials than others.

4 Suitable polishes include specialised clear plastic scratch remover and polishes (try a boatyard or caravan accessory stockist) or most liquid metal polishes, like Brasso.

5 You can also try paint cutting compounds and haze removers, chrome or aluminium polish, or even toothpaste!

6 Experiment with various grades to see which seems best, working down to progressively finer grades to leave a clear finish.

7 Take care when polishing not to create too much heat which will soften the plastic surface and trap particles of polish and dirt.

8 Note that some light scratching will inevitably remain, and if you look through the screen rather than over it this will be dangerous; buy a new screen instead.

Fabricating a new windshield/screen

9 Most modern screens are moulded, rather than being produced from flat sheet materials. Any such screen will invariably have a double

curvature profile, which is difficult to reproduce successfully at home.

10 Older types used screens with a single curve profile and were usually moulded from *Perspex (Plexiglas)* acrylic sheet. These can be made up at home, provided that great care is taken; the material is brittle, especially when it is cold.

11 A good alternative material is one of the more modern flexible plastics like *Lexan*, though this is usually a lot thinner than the original and may flex too much in use. It does avoid the need to form a curve, however, and will withstand the odd knock and scrape without damage.

12 The new screen shape can be traced onto the sheet using the old one as a pattern, and is best cut out using a power jigsaw fitted with a fine blade. Support the sheet solidly when cutting.

13 Alternatively use a padsaw, and take great care not to let the blade snag in the cut or you may split the sheet.

14 Rough edges can be filed or sanded smooth. Straight lines can be planed.

15 It is reasonably easy to mould a single curve in flat acrylic sheet using boiling water. A handy method is to place the sheet in the bottom of the bathtub, and then to pour the boiling water over it until it softens and bends to the curvature of the tub.

16 Make any further adjustments to the curve by hand while it is still pliable, taking care to avoid scalding your hands.

17 Double curvature screens can be made by building a mould using GRP materials, or plaster on a wooden or wire mesh frame.

18 Cut a piece of plastic with a generous extra allowance and warm it with hot water or on a polished tray in the oven until it is just pliable. Then place the plastic over the mould and smooth it down. Use soft gloves to protect your hands from heat, and to protect the plastic from scratches.

19 A paper template, taken from the original can be laid over the completed shape in order to cut out the finished item.

20 Mark out the fixing holes carefully; they must be drilled accurately or great stresses will be placed on the screen. Using a sharp drill bit at low speed with water or soluble oil as a lubricant/coolant.

21 Drill through the sheet **from both sides** to prevent the material shattering when the bit emerges.

22 Check that the holes align correctly, and if necessary file them to make sure that there is no stress on the surrounding material.

23 Fix the screen using rubber washers or sealing strips so that the screen is allowed to flex slightly.

24 Even better would be to drill oversize holes and then to use rubber 'top-hat' bushes on one side and plain rubber washers on the other; that way the bolts can never twist directly against the screen.

5 Safety precautions when using resins and GRP

1 Avoid inhaling the resin fumes – always work in a well-ventilated area or outdoors.
2 Do not handle the matting without gloves on, or the tiny fibres will become embedded in your skin. Avoid skin contact with the resin, again using rubber or disposable plastic gloves during use.
3 If you need to sand down the hardened material, use goggles and a dust mask to avoid inhaling dust, which will contain fine glass particles and fibres.
4 Take note of the instructions supplied with the materials you buy. These normally explain safe working practices and any special precautions which must be taken. For example, where accelerator and hardener are supplied separately from the resin, you should keep neat accelerator well away from the hardener until the former has been mixed thoroughly with the resin. If the hardener and accelerator come into direct contact they can explode!

6 Using fillers

1 Cracks, stone chips or scratches in the surface of the fairing or body panels can usually be dealt with by filling. Given the amount of road and wind vibration experienced on fairings and luggage it is best to choose a type of filler designed to remain slightly flexible; if it gets too hard it may crack away after a while.
2 Before applying the filler, check that the gel coat in the vicinity of the damage is adhering to the underlying layers. If it is coming away, grind it back until it is sound.
3 Mix the filler and hardener in the proportions recommended by the manufacturer. Apply a thin film of filler using a spatula or plastic spreader, smoothing it to follow the original shape as closely as possible.
4 Once the filler is cured, sand the surface to blend it into the surrounding material. If you find odd low spots or holes these should be filled, and the sanding operation repeated, finishing with a fine abrasive to leave the surface ready for painting. Note that where the original item was colour impregnated during manufacture, it will be difficult to match this with paint. In such cases it is probably best to sand the entire surface to provide a key for the primer and then spray the whole item.
5 Fillers containing glass fibre strands are now available from accessory shops. They are used to bridge larger holes without needing to use separate GRP matting.

6 The filler is mixed and laid on a polythene bag which is the held over the hole until it is set. The bag is then peeled off.

7 Repairing glass reinforced plastic GRP

1 Before attempting to repair a split fairing or damaged luggage, have a look at how the original was made up. This tends to be the exact opposite of how you would expect it to be done, rather like starting with the paint and adding the underlying panel!
2 Normally, the part will have been made in one or more sections, each of which will have been laid up in a female mould.
3 The mould is coated with a release agent to allow the moulding to be removed easily, once finished.
4 The first coat applied to this forms the finished outer surface of the moulding and is called the gel coat. Sometimes this surface will have been painted, but more often the resin itself is coloured by adding a pigment to it.
5 Once the gel coat is completed and cured (the exposed surface never actually gets fully dry while it is in contact with the air, so that it adheres to the subsequent layers) the rest of the laminate is built up.
6 This consists of the glass fibres, in the form of chopped strand matting. Into this is worked the resin, then the air bubbles are stippled and rolled out, more glass mat is applied , and so on until the required thickness is built up. The inner surface is sometimes smoothed off a little by using a fine glass tissue as the final layer.
7 Once the resin has hardened fully, the moulding is freed from its mould and is ready for use once any attachments or fittings have been added.
8 For more complex shapes like full fairings, more than one original moulding is used and these are then bonded together with resin to form the final composite structure.

Repairing GRP

9 Minor damage to GRP mouldings is relatively easy to deal with at home, and you can buy all the materials you will need in the form of bodywork repair kits from car accessory shops.
10 If you find that you want to develop the technique for larger jobs, or to make up your own bodywork mouldings, then the materials can be bought in bulk quantities from specialist suppliers.
11 The materials needed are as follows:
a) Pre-accelerated lay-up resin (the correct grade of resin, with an accelerator added in the appropriate quantity).
b) Hardener to suit the quantity of resin.
c) Body filler, or inert filler powder to be

added to the resin to make up your own filler.
d) Chopped strand matting (some fine tissue is useful too).
12 You should also collect together some rubber gloves, a polythene container or a tin or similar for mixing the resin, a 1 inch paintbrush, and a mixing stick.
13 Some solvent, such as acetone or a proprietary equivalent, is useful for removing the resin from brushes, but for small jobs it is easier to buy a cheap brush and throw it away after use.
14 If you do use such solvents for cleaning, note that they can be flammable and dangerous if misused. Get advice on safety precautions from the supplier of the particular product.
15 Small holes and splits in the original moulding can be patched over from the back after bridging the front surface with masking tape to provide a temporary support for the matting. Fix the tape in position, then apply laying up resin with a brush to the back surface, overlapping the sound material to form a strong repair. Cut a piece of matting with scissors, then use the resin-soaked brush to stipple it into place. Make sure that the resin soaks well into the fibres.
16 Coat the first layer with resin and repeat the laying up process until a reasonable thickness has been achieved. On the final layer, fine mat or tissue can be used to give a smoother finish, though this is not necessary unless it is readily visible. Once the laminate has cured, strip off the masking tape and check the surface. If it stands up in relation to the surrounding moulding, file and sand it flush, then complete the repair using filler to give a smooth surface ready for painting.
17 Larger holes are repaired in a similar manner as described above, though you will need to contrive some sort of temporary mould to support the matting and resin until it cures. Care must be taken at this stage, since any large discrepancy in levels will be difficult to correct once it is dry. If you have the damaged section, this can be repositioned in the hole and held in place with tape or small metal strips pop-riveted to the surrounding moulding. Lay up fresh layers of matting and resin over the join, then remove the tape or strips from the front when dry. Fill and sand back the crack as described above.
18 Where a large section is missing, you will have to contrive a mould using hardboard or stiff card, riveting it in place until the repair has been made. This may not be appropriate where the hole covers an awkward double curve or complex shape. In such cases it may be necessary to form a support for the matting *inside* the hole, using this to hold the material in place and stippling the mat into the resin as best you can. Lay up just one or two layers and allow it to harden, then cut away and remove the support, and continue to lay up successive layers from the inside as normal.

8 Repairs using GRP

1 Assuming that they are non-structural items like mudguards, rusted or split pressings can be reinforced and repaired with fibreglass. The success of such repairs is entirely dependent on the standard of preparation. All dirt, paint and loose rust should be removed and the surface wire-brushed until it is bright.

2 A good way to make sure that all loose material has been removed is to prepare the metal as described, then lay up a single layer of matting. Allow the resin to harden until fairly stiff and rubbery, then tear it away from the surface. The resin should bring with it any residual dirt and rust, leaving the surface ready for repair.

3 Using the same technique as described above, and having taped over any small holes or splits, lay up several layers of matting, working them well into the resin to push out any air bubbles.

4 Once dry, trim off any stray fibres, then prepare and finish the outer surface of the part using filler to cover any small holes or splits.

9 Making parts using GRP

1 The method used depends on the number of items you want too make. If you want a mini production line the best method is to make a female mould, a three dimensional mirror image of what you want.

2 This mould can be made of metal wood or plastic. The surface of the required shape in this mould is finished to an extreme degree as the exterior of the finished product will be moulded by it.

3 This plastic mould is then coated with a chemical release agent and layers of the uncured plastic resin are pressed into the mould, beginning with the gelcoat, if this is required. Where necessary the glass fibre strands in the form of a matting are pressed into the plastic and the thickness is built up layer on layer, being careful to press out any bubbles of air. When the design thickness is achieved the material is left to set or cure and then removed from the mould.

4 For one-off parts, begin by building a skeleton framework of wood or metal strip and then using thin wire mesh, cardboard or even papier-mâché create your final shape. The finish needn't be absolutely smooth, but paint it with a gloss paint.

5 Coat the mould with release agent and lay on a first layer of fine mesh mat. Then continue layering on the resin and fibre matting until you have the required thickness, and finish with a smooth coat of the resin. On curing, you may have to sand the surface to get a smooth surface for painting, and to get the contours exactly right.

6 If you are making an item, like a cover, then you can form up your wire mesh and leave it in the plastic as it won't be seen. You can use this technique to build up new parts, or to modify the contours of an existing part which isn't quite the authentic shape you need.

7 With practice there is no reason why complicated shapes like seats and fairings could not be made in the workshop using one or multiple moulds.

8 Any bracket work can be made from steel and included in the moulding process. Heavy or load bearing components can be attached to a fibre-glass shell, but considerable thought has to go into the shape of the mounting bracket, the thickness of the plastic wall and the necessity of a strengthening plate on the opposite side.

10 Carbon fibre

1 This is an advanced composite from which items with high strength and low weight can be made.

2 The material can be constructed with the fibres aligned so that they provide maximum resistance to the forces applied to them. For motorcyclists carbon fibre offers good corrosion resistance and damage tolerance.

3 Carbon fibre components can be repaired using epoxy resin based adhesives.

11 Machining plastics and composites

1 For drilling, ideally a slow helix twist drill is used for thermosetting plastics and a quick helix for thermoplastics. Although a normal drill will be fine if you use a slow speed and advance the drill slowly.

2 Use water or soluble oil to prevent thermoplastic materials getting too hot and gripping the drill.

3 Thermosetting materials can be drilled dry.

4 Rigid plastics and composites can be machined on the lathe using a similar practice to that for light alloys. Remember to keep the material cool by using soluble oil rather than water.

5 Threads can be cut in rigid plastic materials, although the strength of these threads is not great. It would be better to use a threaded insert glued or moulded in place. Use a little water or soluble oil as a lubricant when cutting threads.

Chapter 9
Cleaning, finishing and protecting metals and plastics

Contents

1 Introduction

The problem of deteriorating paintwork and plating is one with which most owners will be familiar. Although regular cleaning and waxing will reduce the rate at which this deterioration occurs, each new stone chip or scratch provides a starting point for corrosion, and even sound paint will eventually fade and lose its shine.

In the case of bright decorative plating, usually chromium plate, this will last well if looked after, but once it does start to peel or rust little can be done at home to restore it.

In the Sections which follow, painting and plating techniques are discussed, together with ways of maintaining them and repairing minor damage.

2 Cleaning

The bike

1 Regular cleaning should be considered an essential part of routine maintenance for any machine. Apart from keeping the paintwork in good condition, cleaning will ensure that accumulations of road dirt are removed before they can encourage corrosion to start.
2 In the UK, as in many other countries, salt is spread on the roads during winter to prevent ice and snow building up on the surface. It is

inevitable that this will find its way onto the motorcycle in the form of spray from passing vehicles. If you combine salty water with a fresh chip in the paint film, rapid corrosion of the area will begin, so it makes sense to wash off the salt before this happens.
3 This is a necessary job before commencing any engine overhaul or major repair job; the work will be that much easier If the machine is cleaned thoroughly.
4 The process of cleaning a motorcycle should be fairly obvious, though it is worth mentioning one or two details worth bearing in mind.
5 The traditional methods involve a proprietary degreaser or detergent, brushes and a supply of water.
6 Wear overalls, industrial rubber gloves and some form of eye protection to guard against accidental splashes.
7 The degreaser should be applied according to the maker's directions, but as a general guide it is preferable to use a screwdriver or similar to dislodge any thick greasy deposits before work commences.
8 Most degreasers work better if they are left for a while to penetrate the grease film, and all are most effective if the degreaser is worked in with a stiff brush to make sure that it has penetrated fully. Once the grease film has been broken down, the machine can be washed off as normal, carrying the dirt and grease with it.
9 Degreasers are available in liquid or aerosol form, the latter covering the machine in a foam blanket which gradually subsides as the grease film breaks down. Whichever type you use, keep it away from the tyres and braking system components, and cover any

vulnerable electrical components or wiring connectors to prevent them being soaked when the machine is washed off.
10 If there are grease or oil deposits to be removed, apply a water-soluble degreaser before you start using water for general cleaning. Soak the dirt with water to which a little detergent has been added, and allow this time to soak in and soften the dirt film. You can use hot water to speed this process up.
11 A good method of applying the water, and for rinsing after washing, is to use a pump-type garden spray. These allow the water to be delivered as a jet or as a fine mist.
12 Once softened, use a soft brush or a cloth to dislodge the dirt, moving it gently over the surface to minimise scratching. Wash the cloth or brush regularly to prevent embedded dirt getting dragged over the surface.
13 Do not forget to clean the areas you can't see, like the underside of the machine.
14 Depending on the type and model of motorcycle, you may find it worth removing the seat, fuel tank and side panels to allow easier access. If you do this, do not omit to protect vulnerable electrical components and the air filter intake from water contamination.
15 When all the dirt has been loosened, wash it off using clean, cold water, preferably using a spray or a hose. To prevent water marks forming as the machine dries off, use a chamois leather to remove water droplets, rinsing and wringing it out frequently.
16 Washing will take off the film of road dirt, diesel fumes and other deposits which would otherwise attack the paint, but it also leaves the surface open to attack by the same deposits next time you use the machine.

High pressure washers

17 By far the easiest and least unpleasant method is to use a hot pressure washer. These machines deliver a high pressure stream of hot water, normally with a detergent mix, and this is played over the machine to blast away the mud and dirt. There are now a range of reasonably-priced home machines are now on the market, and whilst these are not normally capable of supplying hot water, they will shift most of the dirt using cold water with a detergent. In addition, coin-operated machines are available at many filling stations.

18 Before using a pressure washer, make sure that vulnerable areas, like the carburettors, air intakes and exposed electrical components are protected, or they will be swamped during the washing operation. It is a good idea to wear waterproofs while using the pressure washer, and an old riding suit is ideal for this purpose.

19 Take care not to direct the washer into areas where there are bearings such as wheel hubs and the steering head as the pressure of the jet will force water passed the seals and contaminate the bearings.

After engine removal

20 Once preliminary cleaning has been carried out, the engine unit can be removed, should this be required. The operations described above will have shifted the majority of the dirt and grime, though there will be more cleaning to be carried out on previously inaccessible corners and recesses.

 HAYNES HiNT *If the engine has been removed, take care to plug the exhaust ports, inlet manifold stubs and spark plug holes with rag, otherwise dirt will be washed into the engine.*

21 Place the engine on a suitably large collection tray to make disposal easy, or work in an area which can be washed clear.

22 Only after all external dirt has been removed should dismantling begin, or there is a risk of dirt entering the engine. If this happens it will be necessary to strip and clean the whole unit very carefully.

During engine overhaul

23 If the engine unit is to be stripped for inspection or overhaul, there will be further cleaning to be carried out. The inside of the cases, and the surfaces of the internal parts will be coated in a film of oil, and this usually carries a certain amount of dirt, fine metal particles and carbon.

24 All internal parts should be cleaned meticulously after dismantling has been completed. Clean one part or assembly at a time to minimise the risk of parts getting lost or interchanged.

25 Use a conventional degreaser, wash each part off in water and then dry it. Paper or rag

clothes can be used provided they do not leave bits of material on the surface which could clog oilways on reassembly. An air line can also be used, however ensure that no dirt can be blown into the oil ways.

26 Once clean, cover all parts with clean cloth or wrap them in rust inhibiting paper until they are required during reassembly. A thin film of clean engine oil or moisture repellent spray can be used to prevent corrosion on metal parts, however these do attract dust.

3	Maintaining and repairing paintwork on metal

Preventative maintenance

1 You can protect painted and plated surfaces to some degree by waxing them. Waxes and polishes are available in innumerable varieties and in liquid or paste form. The composition of these waxes varies considerably, some using mainly natural waxes, or mixtures of waxes and silicone, while others use polymer sealants to leave a tough detergent-resistant skin over the paint.

2 Some polishes include a fine abrasive designed to remove the outer layer of paint, and thus any oxidation of the surface. These are fine if the machine has been neglected for a while and the paint has gone dull, and in some cases can transform the appearance of a bike. Beware of using an abrasive polish on a regular basis, though, because each time you use it, your paint is getting a little bit thinner.

3 If the paint has got really dull, or is covered by fine scratches, it can be restored by using a haze remover or even a paint cutting compound. Again, this is an abrasive process which will wear the paint down, and must not be done too often. In particular, be wary of over-use on lacquered finishes, and be very careful near the edges of side panels and the fuel tank; it is quite easy to cut through to the primer in these areas.

Minor damage to steel frames and fittings

4 Minor damage, by which is meant stone chips and small scratches in the paint film, can be dealt with at home in most cases. In the case of the frame and its associated fittings, which are normally painted black on most machines, you can get by with touching in the scratches using a small brush.

5 You will need a small paintbrush (about 1/2 inch), some wet-and-dry paper in various grades, a good quality brushing enamel, thinners for cleaning the paintwork and brush, and some metal primer compatible with the enamel chosen.

6 The frame will probably be finished with a cellulose-based paint. In which case you can

use a spray or brushing cellulose. Most motor accessory shops will stock these, together with the appropriate thinners and primer.

7 You can also use an enamel brushing paint of the type used by modellers. This is a good paint as it is less likely to chip than a cellulose-based paint.

8 Another possibility worth considering is the oddly-named *Smooth Hammerite*, manufactured by Finnegans Speciality Paints, and again stocked by motor accessory shops and hardware stores. It can be applied to bare metal, and is touch dry within about twenty minutes, and is thus ideal for repairing stone chips.

9 Start preparing for painting by rubbing down the damaged area with medium wet-and-dry paper, used wet. Remove any corrosion and cut back to the sound paint, leaving a feathered edge. Apply a coat of primer, (unless you are using the *Smooth Hammerite* mentioned above) overlapping the feathered edge slightly, and allow it to dry, for the recommended length of time.

10 Once the primer is dry, use fine wet-and-dry paper to flat down the surface, removing any brush marks or runs and leaving the surface keyed ready for the top coat. Remove any residual surface dust using a clean rag moistened with thinners.

11 Using a clean, small brush, apply the top coat, carefully brushing out the brush marks and taking care not to apply too thick a film, which could cause sagging or runs on vertical surfaces.

12 Brushing is preferable to spraying as neighbouring components will not need masking from overspray.

13 If a second coat is needed, flat the first coat again using fine wet-and-dry, paper.

Damage to tanks, side panels and mudguards

14 On most machines, the main areas of decorative paintwork will be found on these areas, though it can be assumed to cover other items finished in the main colour.

15 The best way of dealing with scratches and chips will depend upon the type of finish used by the manufacturer. With a simple paint finish, you can adapt the procedure described above for the frame, but you will have to find a suitable colour matched paint. Motorcycle paint can be obtained in the form or touch-up sticks or aerosols from the relevant motorcycle dealer or from a mail-order motorcycle paint specialist. Alternatively you can ask a car paint specialist to match the colour of the existing paintwork.

16 If the damage is simply a scratch or small chip, the easiest method is to use a modelling paintbrush to touch in the damage. Spray a small amount of the paint into the can lid, and then carefully apply this along the scratch using the brush.

17 More extensive damage is rather more difficult to deal with, and the paint will have to be sprayed on.

18 Note that to achieve an exact colour match, you will have to use the correct shade of primer and undercoat.

19 If you intend to do any form of paint spraying, note that you should pick good conditions in which to do it. The air must be dry, and reasonably warm with no wind, or a poor finish will result.

20 Do not work in a dusty or badly ventilated area.

21 Do not use any type of open flame or electric heater, this would pose a serious fire risk, and will tend to stir up any dust.

22 You can try working outside if the weather is warm, dry and still. This does bring its own problems, in the form of flies which seem to find wet paint irresistible.

23 Wherever you decide to work, remember to take precautions to avoid spray drift landing anywhere it would not be welcome, wear a clean overall, and use a dust mask to keep the atomised paint out of your lungs.

24 Materials needed include various grades of wet-and-dry paper, aerosol spray cans of colour-matched top coat and primer, masking tape and newspaper.

25 Start your preparatory work by removing the part to be worked on, and remove all traces of wax or polish using a clean rag dipped in thinners. Using progressively finer grades of wet-and-dry, paper, again used wet, rub down the affected area until the damaged paint edge is blended into the metal below.

26 It should be noted at this stage that any decals in the vicinity may have to be renewed, see Section below, in which case order replacements well in advance. The old decal may peel off, but more likely you will have to sand it away.

27 Use masking tape and paper to protect the surrounding area from overspray, rubbing the edges of the tape down smooth with the thumbnail. Following the paint manufacturer's directions, mix the primer by shaking its can for the specified length of time (and don't cheat!) then spray on the primer coat. Start spraying on the masked area, positioning the spray head 150 – 200 mm from the surface, and moving the can smoothly and horizontally across the spray area and onto the masking paper before releasing the spray head.

28 Gradually move down, applying the paint in overlapping bands until the area is covered.

29 Do not be tempted to apply too much paint; several thin coats are preferable to one thick one, which will probably result in runs.

30 The primer coat(s) should now be flatted using fine wet-and-dry paper, having allowed sufficient time for drying. Wipe over the surface with a thinners-moistened rag to remove dust.

31 The top coats can now be applied. With these, the need for careful application is vital if runs are to be avoided. If a run does occur, let the paint dry fully, then remove the run with abrasive paper before continuing.

32 Once the final coat has been applied, let it dry, and then remove the masking tape and paper. There will almost certainly be an overspray line where the masking tape was, and this can be removed once the paint has hardened fully. Use a fine cutting compound to smooth away the excess paint, blending the new and old coats together.

33 Any decals can now be applied, and the paint surface waxed for protection.

34 Where the part was lacquered, it may me impossible to get a satisfactory small repair. the only alternative is to have the complete part repainted.

<table>
<tr><td>**4**</td><td>**Maintaining and repairing paintwork on plastic**</td></tr>
</table>

1 Plastic parts present a great many problems for the painter. For example, a paint has to be used which is compatible with the plastic, whose exact material type may not be known, and the paint must be as flexible as the plastic.

2 As the paint is only for cosmetic purposes, it is generally very thin, which causes problems when making small repairs.

3 Many of the paint schemes are pearlescent or metallic. To get a colour match you need to use the appropriate primers.

4 Matching a lacquered finish is difficult and may necessitate the repainting of the whole piece to achieve a good match.

5 For small repairs the methods above will be adequate, but bear in mind the notes below.

Glass fibre reinforced plastic

6 Any repairs must be done very thoroughly. Cracks must be ground out and filled using resin and tissue.

7 The surface must then be prepared using fine wet-dry paper to grade 320 or higher.

8 Take care using paint strippers on GRP. Use only water soluble strippers.

9 Also take care when using powered tools which can cut into, or through the soft GRP in a very short period of time.

10 Allow the paint and any thinners to stand for a while and stir to make sure that they are thoroughly mixed begin by using a synthetic primer surfacer, then you can use synthetic enamel or cellulose paint.

11 With cellulose paints, use the minimum of thinners to help prevent the thinners penetrating the GRP. If penetration occurs it tends to highlight any repairs and defects.

12 Leave a week between coats.

Plastics

13 Small chip damage can be repaired using the touch up sticks available.

14 Where the damage is greater and is not in the immediate eye line, it is possible to use a cellulose paint from an aerosol can. The range of colours available is enormous, and there are some vehicle paint suppliers who can match and mix paint for you.

15 Use a flexible filler on deeper scratches.

16 Take advice on types of paint, thinners, fillers and so on from a reputable paint supplier.

<table>
<tr><td>**5**</td><td>**Painting in the workshop**</td></tr>
</table>

1 If you should decide to undertake this sort of work yourself, be prepared for a considerable expenditure on equipment, and an investment of time in learning spraying skills. You may be able to find a training course for this purpose at a local college.

2 You will also need to establish the type of paint used originally so that a compatible product can be obtained. A local paint stockist will be able to advise if you take in a sample part and explain what you are attempting to do.

3 The basic procedure for dealing with larger areas is broadly similar to that described above, only bigger and thus more demanding if a good finish is to be achieved. A simple summary of the process would look something like this:

a) *Remove and clean the part to be sprayed.*

b) *Assess the type of paint originally used, and choose a colour-matched alternative. Seek advice from your paint supplier on this point. To ensure an accurate colour match, take a sample of the existing paint when ordering the new paint.*

c) *Use a spirit wipe to remove all traces of old polish (especially where silicones may have been used).*

d) *Wash down with warm water and detergent, then rinse with clean water.*

e) *Sand down and fill any damaged areas.*

f) *Fill any paint defects with a suitable stopper.*

g) *Flat the paintwork using medium (P240 to P400) grade wet-and-dry paper.*

h) *Check that all paint edges have been feathered.*

i) *Apply any necessary masking.*

j) *Apply the primer coat (a special type may be needed on some plastics and on aluminium parts).*

k) *Flat the primer when dry using fine (P400 to P1200) grade wet-and-dry paper.*

l) *Apply the top coat(s) noting that the masking pattern needs to be worked out beforehand if the part has more than one colour.*

4 Ideally painting should be done in a clean area of the workshop which can be left unused whilst painting and drying is in progress.

5 Be aware of the extra fire risk when using paints, and the hazards of breathing fumes, and skin contact with painting chemicals.

6 From the above you will probably appreciate that paint refinishing at this level becomes rather complex. Alternatives to attempting the work yourself or sending the whole job to a professional include doing your own rubbing down and flatting, thus saving a good deal of time and expense at the spray shop.

7 You could even apply the primer yourself, but agree this beforehand with whoever is going to do the final spraying work. In the case of side panels or other smaller parts, you could even consider buying a new (or even second-hand) replacement.

6 Steel frame refinishing

1 Sooner or later the frame on most machines will have got to the stage where touching up is insufficient to keep corrosion at bay. To avoid reaching the stage where the frame is in need of renewal, it will be necessary to refinish the frame and thus halt corrosion.

Preparation

2 The decision to have a frame refinished is not one which should be taken lightly. You will have to strip off **every** part from the frame. This means not just the engine and wheels, but the rear suspension, front forks and steering head, and the entire electrical system.

3 It goes without saying that you should only contemplate this sort of restoration work if the machine warrants it. If the machine is rare or valuable, or if you intend to keep it for some time, then fair enough, but it would not be worthwhile on an average machine nearing the end of its useful life.

4 Once all fittings have been removed, the frame should be examined closely for signs of damage, corrosion or similar problems. If any repair work is required, this should be carried out now, rather than after paint removal has been carried out.

5 The bare frame should next be cleaned with degreaser, and the remaining old paint removed. You can do this at home if you so wish, using a chemical paint remover or a blowlamp and scrapers. Both approaches require the use of suitable safety equipment, in the form of gloves and eye protection. The risk of burns from the blowlamp may seem obvious, but do not forget that chemical paint strippers are highly caustic, and can cause serious damage to skin and eyes.

6 Whichever method you choose it is a long tedious job, and best avoided unless you have nothing better to do for a few days. There may not appear to be much to a frame, but it is surprising just how long it takes to remove all traces of paint and corrosion by hand.

Blasting

7 A better solution by far is to have the frame stripped by blasting. In this process, compressed air is used to blast the frame with either abrasive grit or glass beads, removing all traces of the old paint and also any rust.

8 The frame, swingarm, stands and any other parts to be refinished should be completely free of grease and road dirt prior to blasting. You should also note that the blasting process will damage machined surfaces, so drive out any bearings or bushes which would otherwise be destroyed.

9 When you take the parts for blasting, specify either bead blasting, or **fine** abrasive grit blasting; coarse grit will leave the metal too rough for painting.

10 Make a list of all the parts you take so that you can check that they are all there when you collect them. The blasting process should result in a perfectly clean frame with a fine matt finish to the now-exposed metal.

11 Check that the blaster has got into all the corners and recesses – it is easy to miss a few.

12 It is important to apply the new paint finish on the blasted parts as soon as possible, preferably on the same day. If you leave them longer, surface rusting will occur, and even if this is not apparent the potential for further corrosion will be lurking under the new paint finish.

Frame finishes

13 In addition to the various conventional paint finishes available, you can also have the frame finished in several other coatings, many of which offer a number of advantages over normal air-drying paint. The most common choices are listed below.

14 It is worth enquiring about companies offering this type of finish when dealing with the blaster; many have reciprocal arrangements with a local powder coating specialist.

Stove enamels

15 These were once the traditional frame finish, and these gave a tough and reasonably hard gloss finish.

16 They are normally baked on at fairly high temperatures during manufacture. Traditional stove enamels have largely been superseded by modern synthetics, some of which require baking in much the same way during original manufacture.

Cellulose

17 Cellulose finishes are commonly used for car and commercial refinishing work, and are easy to use, relatively safe and air-drying. They are less than ideal on frames and stands of motorcycles, however, because they chip easily and are likely to lose their initial shine quite quickly.

Two-pack paints

18 These paint finishes work in much the same way as epoxy resins, that is they harden chemically rather than by air-drying. They give a good finish which is quite durable, but have the great disadvantage of being isocyanate-based products. This makes them toxic, and special breathing apparatus must be used when spraying them.

Epoxy powder

19 Powder coatings are used in general manufacturing, where an even and tough finish is required. Fortunately for us, epoxy powder is also an ideal finish for motorcycle frames.

20 The frame is hung up in a booth and an electrical charge passed through it. The spray gun applies a coating of powder which clings to the entire surface, attracted to the electrostatic charge in the frame. This tends to even out the coating as it goes on, and also helps to avoid any thin or missed areas.

21 Once coated, the frame is baked in a high temperature oven, where the powder melts, flowing out over the surface of the frame in a continuous smooth film. The resulting finish is quite acceptable cosmetically, and very tough.

22 The only disadvantage may be that a wide range of colours is not normally available, though this will depend on the range stocked by the local expert in this type of work. This will usually be dictated by the nature of the main part of his business.

Nylon coating

23 This is a similar process to epoxy powder coating, except that nylon is used as the coating medium. The resulting film is less smooth and inclined to be duller than with other finishes. The main advantage is that it is relatively resistant to stone chips in use. The drawback is that it is difficult to find a paint to touch in any damage that does occur, and like epoxy powder, is available in a limited colour range.

7 Finishing aluminium parts

1 Where alloy castings are easily visible, the traditional approach was to grind the rough cast surface smooth, and then to buff the metal to a smooth, bright finish. The resulting surface was attractive to look at, and had a secondary advantage, in that it was fairly easy to maintain in this condition, regular polishing restoring the shine if it became oxidised. An example of this can be seen on fork legs and engine covers.

2 An alternative way of finishing these areas involved the casting being sanded to remove the rougher parts of the surface, and then a coating of aluminium-coloured paint applied. This gives a bright and reasonably smooth finish and is often used on fork lower legs and cast alloy wheel rims.

3 A similar process is often used on the engine covers, where a lacquer coating is then applied. Alternatively, a heat-resistant satin black finish can be used, with detail areas like the edges of fins being polished up as highlights.

4 From our point of view, this treatment of castings can present problems once it becomes damaged and chipped. This sort of damage is inevitable during normal use, and spoils the appearance of the machine. Most owners will be familiar with the problem; the paint around the stone chips allows oxidation

of the metal underneath, and this then spreads, flaking off the surrounding paint or lacquer.

Removing the original or damaged finish

5 Once this occurs to any great extent, the only solution is to remove the old coating and start again, a process which will require the removal of the part(s) affected. Even where the original finish was not coated, general wear and tear or neglect will leave it looking discoloured and pitted, especially where road salt has been allowed to speed the corrosion.

6 The intricate surface shape of most castings will make the removal of the old coating difficult using normal chemical paint strippers, but it can be done this way. You will need to allow a good deal of time, and have available a selection of scrapers, wire brushes and steel wool to help dislodge the softened paint.

7 If you use this method, be sure to wear overalls, rubber gloves and goggles to avoid getting the corrosive stripper on the skin or in the eyes. Once removed, you will have to deal with the underlying corrosion, which will appear as unsightly pitting on the metal surface.

Bead blasting

8 The time needed for preparation and the corrosion problem can be reduced by having the part bead blasted. This process, unlike abrasive blasting, is safe for use on soft alloy and will dispose of both the paint and the corrosion, leaving the surface with a bright matt finish.

9 An additional advantage is that the blasting process works equally well on fairly rough cast surfaces, and thus can be applied to items like the crankcases on European models, maintaining the original finish.

10 If possible, choose aquabead blasting in preference to a dry bead blasting process; the resulting finish is finer and smoother.

11 The main point to remember is that any surface that you want to protect from the blasting process will have to be masked off thoroughly, and simply applying masking tape is often not enough.

12 The tops of fork legs can be plugged with rag or large corks, while in the case of engine castings, plug any small openings, and screw the cover down onto a wooden base using woodscrews through the normal fixing holes.

13 Once the corrosion and the old finish have been removed, you will have to decide on how to refinish the part. In some applications, it may be most effective to choose a simple polished surface. This will entail smoothing the surface with progressively finer grades of abrasive paper, and then using a buffing mop to polish it to a bright finish. The success of this process is somewhat dependent on the composition of the alloy, but with the exception of zinc alloys it will generally work quite well.

14 If you wish to duplicate the original finish, the choice of coatings is important. The matt black paints and clear lacquers available in aerosol cans, unless specifically designed for these applications, are unlikely to be tough enough, and may flake off in time. High temperature exhaust paints can work on the engine covers, but are not very resistant to wear and tear.

15 The best option is to consult a local metal coating specialist. You may find that the blasting company will be able to recommend a local company. Explain in detail what you want to do, and see if they can offer a suitable process. These companies specialise in applying various coatings to manufactured parts, and will probably have a coating which will suit your application.

16 Many of these may require high-temperature stoving, so check that this will not damage the component, and make sure you remove any fittings which might be affected.

Anodising aluminium parts

17 Anodising is a technique for stabilising and sealing aluminium surfaces, often with the addition of a dye in a range of basic colours, which is used to impart a translucent colour to the metal. It is frequently used on new parts such as aluminium wheel rims, handlebars and brake line fittings, and can be an effective cosmetic touch as well as good protection for the metal.

18 Most platers will carry out anodising work, though they may not be able to deal with items as bulky as a wheel rim. If you are carrying out a full rebuild, you might consider this technique for use on small parts and fittings.

8   Care of electro-plated parts

1 Many parts on motorcycles are finished by electro-plating, either as a decorative element, or simply to protect the metal from corrosion in use. The most common plated finish is chromium plating, and this will be found on almost all machines. Common applications include exhaust systems, headlamp rims, wire-spoked wheel rims, and some control levers and pedals.

2 Chrome plating is also found on items like the front fork stanchions, but in this type of application its main use is to provide a hard, smooth working surface. This type of chroming is normally described as 'hard chrome' or 'industrial chrome' to distinguish it from the decorative processes.

3 The plating process starts with the preparation of the bare metal, followed by a plating with nickel. After any necessary polishing of the nickel surface, the chromium layer is added. Hard though it is to believe, the chromium layer will be only 0.000005 inch

thick. Despite this, the chrome is what gives the part its blue-white sparkle, and prevents the normal dulling of the underlying nickel layer.

4 Less cosmetically-important items are often given a protective electro-plated finish. Fasteners, for example, are given a bright zinc or cadmium coating, and black chrome is often used for coating exhaust parts, an application in which it outlasts most paint-based finishes.

Cleaning and maintaining plated parts

5 From the above description of the plating process it will be appreciated that plated surfaces, though fairly tough, will not withstand too much wear before corrosion can occur.

6 The thin layer of chromium is hard and quite durable, but once worn through the underlying nickel layer is exposed, and it is the oxidation of this layer which produces the greenish-white deposits which form in corners of plated parts exposed to attack from road dirt and water.

7 Chrome plating which is in good condition can be cleaned and waxed in exactly the same way as painted parts, and if treated with care will last well.

8 Once surface rusting is seen it is fair to assume that the plating is well on the way to failure. The best that can be done at this stage is to remove surface corrosion using a fine metal polish. Application of a wax polish, or even a clear lacquer, will slow subsequent corrosion, but will not prevent it.

9 Owners of vintage machines will probably have only nickel finishes to clean. Care must be taken as the nickel is relatively soft.

Re-chroming

10 With plating work, preparation is the key to a good job, and you may not find out if this stage has been skimped on until your newly-plated parts start to peel some time later.

11 As a rule, you should contribute nothing to the preparation yourself, apart from carefully cleaning and degreasing the parts before taking them to the platers.

12 On no account should parts for plating be blasted; the resulting surface will need a great deal of polishing to get it smooth again, and on some parts the thickness of the metal may make this impossible.

13 It is feasible to plate many other items on the machine, though the cost of preparing items not originally plated will be high due to the large amount of polishing work needed.

14 Chromium plating does tend to weaken steel parts by making them brittle, however, and consideration should be given to the safety aspects before sending parts like wheel spindles to the platers.

15 It is also possible to chromium plate aluminium alloy, as you may have seen on custom bikes. Be warned that you cannot guarantee plating to stay on aluminium for

long – it will tend to flake off after a year or so. The plated layer will also tend to act as a heat barrier, and for this reason is best avoided where good heat radiation is desirable.

16 You should check around locally before sending parts for replating. Often there will be one local firm which has a good reputation for plating motorcycle parts.

17 When you deliver the parts for plating, take with you a list of the items taken, together with your name and address and daytime telephone number. Keep a duplicate of the list yourself so that you can check that everything is there when you collect them.

18 Often with small items it is quicker and easier just to fit a new one, or to visit a local breaker in the hope of obtaining a used part in better condition.

19 In the case of wire spoked wheels, the normal course of action is to have a new rim built onto the hub, usually with new spokes. Unless the machine is very old or has an unusual rim size, it is not normally worth having rusted rims polished and replated. Bear in mind that plated steel rims can often be replaced with aluminium alloy ones – check with your local wheel builder to establish the best choice for the replacement parts.

20 It is not generally worth having exhaust system parts replated, and many platers will not accept them anyway, due to the risk of their baths becoming contaminated. Remember that exhausts often rot through from the inside; if the plating has gone, it is safe to assume that the underlying metal is heading that way. The best cure for rusting exhausts is to purchase a replacement system made from stainless steel.

Cadmium plating

21 This is a good way of refinishing fasteners and odd brackets and fittings, being reasonably cheap to have large quantities plated.

22 The finish obtained will be a fairly bright satin silver colour with good resistance to rusting. If you decide to have the frame refinished, it is a good idea to send the various fittings away for cadmium plating at the same time.

23 Prepare the parts by carefully cleaning them and remove any surface rusting. Given that the finish will be matt anyway, you might consider having the parts bead blasted before plating.

24 Before you decide to have all the casing screws replated, consider replacing them with stainless steel Allen or Torx screws. These will never rust, and are far more practical than the standard cross-head types. If you intend to keep the machine for any length of time they are well worth spending money on.

Home plating kits

25 It is possible to carry out nickel plating at home using a kit of materials especially designed for this purpose.

26 This type of kit is best suited to those who restore older machines, where the original finish on plated parts may have been nickel originally, and you should bear in mind that, unlike chrome plating, nickel will require regular cleaning and re-polishing.

27 It is possible, however, to use nickel plating to build up worn parts for re-machining, and this may have uses in some applications. The kits contain the nickel anodes, chemicals and full details of how to set up your own plating bath. You will also need a power supply in the form of a battery charger or 12 volt battery, a suitable small tank, a bar from which to suspend the parts for plating, some bulb holders, bulbs and electrical cable. In addition, a small hydrometer and a thermometer are required.

28 Complete nickel plating kits and individual items can be obtained from companies who advertise in the motorcycle press.

29 The plating process is essentially a scaled-down commercial plating system and can give excellent results if the instructions are followed carefully. The bulbs and bulb holders are used as a method of regulating the plating current, and you must calculate this having worked out the surface area of the item to be plated.

30 Note that as supplied, the standard kits allow only small parts to be dealt with, but you may be able to expand your system to take larger parts if you find this necessary.

Caution: Take great care in the disposal of waste products from plating kits. Contact the local authority responsible for waste disposal for advice.

9 Stainless steel

1 The surface of stainless steel parts can be polished to a high shine and protected with a wax polish.

2 Minor scratches can be smoothed out using fine wet-dry paper.

10 Decals

Removing old decals

1 Old decals may be removed by first rubbing with solvent on a rag, or using a hot air gun.

2 Where the decal is under a lacquered finish, it must be scraped or sanded away.

3 If the decals are to be replaced, first sketch their position and take some measurements from a couple of reference points.

Putting on new decals

4 The main problems with mounting decals are to get them in exactly the right place so that they look right and lined up with the other decals, paintwork or body shape, and to apply them round curves without trapping air bubbles, making creases, or distorting the decal.

5 A decal kit for a particular model may have detailed instructions relating to the application.

6 You will need a flexible rule, a sharp knife of the sort modellers use, and some masking tape.

7 First, clean the surface on which the decal is to be mounted. Make sure every bit of dirt, wax, silicone, and release agent is removed.

8 On new paintwork, allow plenty of time for the paint to dry before sticking on the decals.

9 Some decals have a narrow strip on the top edge which can be used to temporarily fix the decal so that the position can be checked. However it is worth using masking tape to act as a guide. The tape can be stuck on to the surface and alignment checked on both sides of the machine.

10 Once the tape is removed, give the area a wipe with cleaner to remove traces of the tape adhesive if a decal is to be placed on that area.

11 It is a good idea to choose two or more reference points which can be duplicated on both sides of the bike. A reference point could be the corners of the fairing, a bolt centre, or even marks made on a strip of masking tape.

12 Although it may be easier for the actual application to remove the part from the bike, either do the alignment work on the bike, or refit the part before the final application. This will allow you to check the alignment with other decals and bodywork.

13 Remember that there are not many places where you can see both sides of the bike at the same time. Where decals can be seen on both sides their position should match side for side.

14 If the decal has a peel off adhesive back, peel a little of the backing strip away and position the exposed edge. Peel the backing away with one hand and smooth the decal down with the other. Be careful not to pull so hard that the decal is stretched or distorted. A second pair of hands is useful for larger decals. Note that some decals require immersing in cold water and are then floated into position and left to dry.

15 It is usually best to fix the narrow edge first and work from that, although this may not be possible due to the contours of the surface.

16 Some decals are marked for cutting where the surface curves would cause bubbles or creases. It is best to cut the decal before application. Work towards the cut from one side to fix its position, align the edges, and then work away.

17 The finished work can be protected by spraying with an acrylic lacquer. This will also hide the edges of the decal preventing the risk of peeling, and give a smooth finish to the surface.

Chapter 10
Assessing engine problems and repair

Contents

1 Introduction

This Chapter gives advice on when overhauls might be necessary and how to assess the nature of the repair.

Advice is also given on how to identify the various noises and symptoms related to engine problems.

The initial assessment before starting work is a useful exercise, and it is a good idea to make a written note of symptoms as well as any actual wear or damage found during this process.

Later, you can sit down and consider the best course of action, and decide which aspects you can deal with at home and which require specialist help.

2 Repair assessment

1 An important aspect of any overhaul is assessing the overall condition of the engine unit and then armed with this information, deciding on the best course of action.
2 If the machine is fairly new and just out of warranty, for example, the failure of a single component with no attendant damage to the rest of the engine is easily assessed; just purchase the new part and fit it.
3 In the case of older machines the situation is less straightforward. You must assess the nature of the immediate problem, just as you would with a newer machine, but in addition, you should also check the rest of the unit in detail to see whether it is worth carrying out the repair.
4 It is usual to find that when the engine is dismantled in response to an obvious problem, say worn valve guides, the rest of the engine is nearly worn out too. There would be little point in fitting new guides if the valves, bores, pistons and crankshaft bearings are worn out, and you will have to work out whether a full overhaul would be warranted if the machine in general has seen better days.
5 This might seem a rather pessimistic attitude to take, but it is a necessary one if you are to avoid wasting money. However fond you may be of that particular machine, if it is likely to cost more to repair than the bike is worth, it is time to consider cutting your losses and looking for a newer model.

6 Alternatively, if something disastrous has happened to the engine of an otherwise sound machine, think about obtaining a second-hand engine unit from a motorcycle breaker. Although you may be taking something of a chance regarding the condition of the new engine, this approach can be a great deal cheaper than attempting to repair the old one if wear or damage is extensive.

7 On restoration work you may not have the option of replacing a badly damaged engine. In this case a careful study of everything that needs attention is called for before you begin repair.

3 Sudden component failure

1 If something serious goes wrong with the engine or transmission while the machine is in use, the chances are that it will be readily apparent to the owner when this occurs. Any major component failing in use will invariably produce some sort of knocking, rattling or vibration, even if the engine continues to run **(see illustrations)**.

2 Should this happen, pull in the clutch immediately to prevent further damage. If the engine is still running, use the kill switch or ignition switch to stop it, and coast to the side of the road. Try to find a way of getting the machine out of the way of passing traffic in a gateway or lay-by if possible, then set about trying to diagnose the fault.

3 Where the engine stops abruptly with accompanying ominous rumblings or other noises, it is a fair assumption that something unpleasant has occurred. It is also probably safe to assume that little more can be done there and then; you will have to resign yourself to further investigation once the machine has been recovered.

4 There are, of course, exceptions, and you

should make a quick preliminary check on the roadside in case the fault can be dealt with easily there and then.

5 If the problem looks like being a serious failure, the first thing to do is to get the machine home so that you can check it in the relative comfort of the workshop.

6 The next thing to consider when trying to assess a sudden major failure is the most likely source of the trouble. Think about where you were at the time, how hard the engine was working, whether it was being revved hard, and whether there were other signs such as unusual noise or vibration just before the problem happened. If you have an oil pressure warning lamp (four-stroke models) was this lit when you first noticed the problem? If the engine stopped suddenly, did you notice any slowing down of the machine just before it did so? Try to get any such symptoms clear in your mind at the earliest possible opportunity.

7 Whether you intend to repair the machine yourself, or ask a dealer to do so, such information is invaluable, pointing to the general area of the failure before dismantling commences.

4 Overhaul assessment

1 Whilst the engine and transmission assemblies of modern motorcycles will run happily for many thousands of miles, given reasonable treatment and regular servicing, the time will come eventually when an overhaul will be necessary. It is impossible to define the point at which this will occur, and you will either have to assess this for yourself, or ask your local dealer for his opinion.

2 More often than not overhauls are prompted by a number of symptoms. You may, for example have noticed high oil consumption or leakage and have been

prepared to accept this condition for some time. If the engine then begins to get unusually noisy, however, you might feel that the time has come to check the whole unit over and put right these and any other problems.

3 It is difficult to establish the cause of a problem on a machine which is in need of general servicing; excessive play due to infrequent adjustment and failure to take up normal freeplay can cause a good deal of noise. It follows that regular services will make any fault diagnosis easier, and will also highlight developing faults at an earlier stage.

4 In the Sections which follow we will consider some of the problems that you are most likely to come across so that you are better able to make the decision to proceed with an overhaul. There are, inevitably, many other things which may go wrong with your machine, but the following should give you an indication of the checks you should make on faults in general when assessing their seriousness.

5 Excessive oil consumption in two-stroke engines

1 Two-stroke engines are lubricated by a total loss system in which oil is fed to the engine internals by a pump (oil injection), or as a mixture with the fuel in the fuel tank (pre-mix). In each case, the excess oil is burnt off after reaching the combustion chamber, and excessive oil consumption will produce dramatic smoking from the exhaust of the machine.

Oil injection system

2 If the level in the oil tank drops faster than normal, the probable cause is maladjustment of the oil pump cable or a damaged or worn pump. The first thing to check is that the pump control cable is in good condition and

3.1a Detonation damage can cause a hole in the piston crown

3.1b Here, where the piston crown has broken up, the worrying factor is how much damage has been done by the debris

correctly synchronised to the carburettor. The procedure for doing this varies widely, and you should consult your workshop manual for details.

3 Some pumps allow the volume of oil delivered on each stroke to be regulated, and whilst this setting should not normally require alteration, it should be checked in cases of high consumption. Once again, instructions for checking and setting the pump stroke will be found in the workshop manual. In other cases, the pump may not be adjustable and will have to be renewed.

4 If you find the typical symptoms of excessive oil consumption, such as heavily smoking exhausts and oil-fouled plugs, but the level in the tank drops at the usual rate, then the only other way the engine can burn oil is to draw it from the reservoir of lubricant held in the transmission area of the crankcase. It does this by drawing oil through worn crankshaft seals, and you should monitor the transmission oil level carefully to see whether it drops over a week or so. If this is the case, the crankshaft oil seals are leaking, and it is likely that the machine will be running poorly and is reluctant to start, due to the loss of crankcase compression through the seals. New seals will be required. You may well find that the main bearings will also need renewing, because play in the bearings is often the cause of damaged seals, though they may just be worn out through sheer age and the effects of heat on the sealing lips.

Pre-mix system

5 There is very little to go wrong with a pre-mix system, apart from getting the fuel/oil ratio wrong. Check that you are using the correct mixture ratio and measuring the oil out in the correct quantity.

6 If the mixture is correct, yet there is heavy smoke from the exhaust and the spark plug is fouled with oil, the crankshaft oil seals could be leaking as described in paragraph 4.

 HAYNES HiNT *Always use a two-stroke oil suitable for the type of lubrication system. Injector oils have different qualities than pre-mix system oils.*

6 Excessive oil consumption in four-stroke engines

1 Most current four-stroke designs are wet-sump, ie the reservoir of oil is held in a space at the bottom of the crankcases from where it is pumped under pressure around the engine and also to the transmission assembly which shares the same cases.

2 Older designs use a dry-sump system where the oil is held in an external tank. It is circulated by pump around the engine and then returned to the tank. In this system, the transmission is lubricated by a separate oil bath arrangement.

3 Since the oil is under pressure, the passages and joints through which it passes must be sealed to contain it. Oil can also be lost through being burnt in the engine, and in the case of four-strokes this points to wear in the cylinder bores, pistons and rings, or valve and valve guide wear.

4 To deal with leakage, you must first identify the source of the leak. Start by degreasing the engine thoroughly. Once cleaned, the exact point of any leakage can be established by running the engine. If the leak is serious, it will show up after a few minutes running on the stand. Note that care should be taken not to overheat the engine by allowing it to run with the machine stationary for too long a period.

5 With a less serious leakage you will have to ride the machine for a few miles to provoke the problem; some leaks may only occur when the engine is at full operating temperature. The leakage will show up quite readily in most cases, though bear in mind that oil will be swept back from the source of the leak by the airflow past the engine.

6 Check over the engine carefully and note where the oil is coming from, having removed any minor covers (eg sprocket covers) as necessary. Leakage around seals will be fairly obvious, as will most gasket leaks.

7 There are a few exceptions however. Most Japanese four-stroke engines pass oil through passages in the cylinder block and head to lubricate the cam and rocker gear. The joints at each gasket face are usually sealed by O-rings. Sometimes, oil can leak at the crankcase to barrel joint or around the base of a holding stud. From here it works up the stud to emerge at the head to barrel joint surface, giving a misleading impression of the location of the problem. Bear this in mind, and remember to check for such migrating leaks during the overhaul.

8 Finally, not all oil leaks are due to simple seal or gasket failure. Poor assembly of the engine or incorrect tightening of components or covers can be responsible.

9 You should also check all engine breather arrangements; these must allow air in the crankcase to be displaced as the engine runs. If the breather system gets blocked, pressure in the crankcase will cause oil to be forced out of otherwise sound joints and connections.

10 The same applies to the more sophisticated recirculating systems where oil vapour is redirected from the breather into the air filter chamber to be burnt before expulsion into the atmosphere.

11 If the loss of oil is not due to leakage, the engine must be burning it. This is almost always a good indication of general engine wear. Worn or damaged cylinder bores or piston rings will cause high oil consumption, the oil film on the cylinder wall being drawn up past the rings on the induction stroke and then burnt.

12 There are many causes of this type of problem, but all indicate the need for a top-end overhaul at the very least. Most problems of this type relate directly to worn or damaged pistons, piston rings or bores, and may be as simple as a stuck oil ring or as complicated as a cracked or deeply scored piston.

13 Less obvious areas include worn plain big-end or main bearing surfaces; these can allow excessive amounts of oil to be thrown onto the cylinder walls. The piston rings are unable to cope with the high volume of the oil, which finds its way past them and into the combustion chamber. Problems of this nature can go unnoticed for some time before exhaust smoke becomes significant.

14 Worn valve guides and valve guide seals allow oil to be drawn down from the cylinder head area into the combustion chamber, where it is burnt. One indication of this is a brief cloud of exhaust smoke at the moment the throttle is opened after the engine has been on overrun down a hill; the oil builds up in the combustion chamber and then burns off as the engine begins to pull once more. Get someone to follow you on a short ride and check whether this is happening rather than attempting to monitor the situation with the rear view mirrors.

15 There are several other causes of oil burning, though these are less common and less obvious than those mentioned above. If too much oil is added to the crankcase, burning of the excess may occur. This problem is easily resolved by draining off the excess oil to restore it to the correct level.

16 Very occasionally, an oil pressure relief valve may stick, causing the oil system pressure to become excessive. If noticed early enough, the valve can be cleaned to restore normal operation, but if left for any length of time, seals, O-rings or gaskets may be damaged by the abnormally high pressure.

17 Finally, the accumulated debris in the oil system of a neglected engine may block passages, causing either pressure leaks or oil starvation in localised areas. Even where oil starvation does not occur, the abrasive contaminants in the oil will cause rapid engine wear. This highlights the essential nature of regular oil and oil filter changes.

7 Identifying engine noise

1 Engine noise usually develops as a result of excessive clearance due either to wear, or the need for routine adjustment of certain wear-prone areas of the engine/transmission assembly. An example of the latter would be the valve clearances. These need to be checked and adjusted periodically to ensure that the small clearance required during normal running is maintained; if the gap is too small the valve will be unable to close fully

7.1 Inadequate valve clearances often result in burnt out valves

and will burn out **(see illustration)**. If the gap is too large, the extra clearance will result in the noisy operation that most owners will be familiar with.

2 All engines produce some mechanical noise during normal operation, this being an inevitable by-product of all mechanical devices. What we are concerned with are abnormal noises which indicate an internal problem. Becoming attuned to the various normal engine noises is an essential first step in being able to spot the abnormal ones, and this requires experience and a degree of familiarity with a particular engine.

3 If you ride one machine on a regular basis this will happen subconsciously; you will find that you can estimate your road speed quite accurately before you check the speedometer, for example, and this is largely due to an association of a particular engine note with that road speed. In the same way you will automatically notice a new noise quite readily. The skill comes in associating that noise with its probable cause, and this will require a certain amount of practice.

4 Describing even the most common engine noises is not easy; we simply do not have the vocabulary to do so concisely. If you ask several skilled mechanics to describe what a worn big-end sounds like, each will give a slightly different description.

5 This is simple due to the fact that any one person can only describe what they think the noise most resembles, and you may not agree with their subjective impression. However you care to describe a noise, if you hear a worn big-end on several occasions you will recognise it again in the future.

6 Bearing the above in mind, let us consider some of the more common engine noises and attempt to describe them.

Big-end bearing wear

7 This is caused by excessive clearance in the big-end bearing due to wear or bearing failure. It is normally described as a knocking or rattling sound, and increases with engine speed. It is likely to be loudest at low to medium engine loadings, especially during the transition from idle speed to acceleration.

8 If the cause is general wear, the noise is likely to be most evident when the engine is first started, diminishing somewhat as the oil pressure in the lubrication system increases.

Main bearing wear or damage

9 Wear or damage produces a similar noise to big-end wear, but is usually a duller rumbling sound. The noise will be less affected by engine speed or load than would a worn big-end bearing, but may be unnoticeable at idle speed.

10 The intensity of the noise will probably increase progressively as engine speed rises, and it is often possible to feel the resultant vibration through the footrests.

Piston and bore wear

11 This is characterised by piston slap, a light metallic rattle caused by the piston rocking in its bore at the top and bottom of each stroke. It is likely to be most noticeable when the engine is first started and will diminish as the piston warms up and expands.

12 If you suspect piston slap, try pouring a little engine oil into each cylinder through the spark plug hole. Refit the plugs and start the engine. The oil will tend to damp out the worst of the noise for a few moments, after which it will be scraped off the cylinder walls and the noise will return.

13 Another good indication can be gained by performing a compression test. Low compression is a good indicator of bore wear, and will often confirm your diagnosis of the noise. On four-strokes, add a little oil to each bore and repeat the compression check. If the reading improves, bore wear is confirmed, but if the same reading is found the compression loss may be due to leakage at the valves.

Piston pin and small-end bearing wear

14 Wear here normally results in a light rattling sound. Two-stroke engines are often susceptible to this type of wear or damage, particularly where the lubrication to the small-end has failed.

Valve train wear

15 Wear in the valve gear can be difficult to pinpoint due to the numerous possible areas in which wear can develop. You should check first of all that the valve clearances are set correctly to eliminate this as the cause of the noise.

16 If the noise is unchanged, check for wear between the rocker arms and their shafts, the camshaft bearings or bushes, cam lobes, cam followers or tappets and the camshaft drive.

17 In the camshaft drive area, check the cam chain, paying particular attention to the tensioner mechanism and guide blades. It is not unknown for these to fail or jam in use, and the problem can be recurrent and difficult to resolve with some models.

Pinking and pre-ignition

18 These conditions are due to incorrect combustion. They normally arise when the wrong fuel grade or fuel/air mixture is present, if the ignition timing is set incorrectly, or where the compression ratio of the engine becomes abnormally high due to carbonisation of the combustion chambers.

19 Other contributing factors are using the wrong grade of spark plug and general overheating of the engine. Although there is a subtle difference between the two faults, they are closely interrelated and give rise to similar symptoms; namely a light metallic-sounding rattle often referred to as pinking (or pinging in the US).

20 The problem is usually most evident when the engine is hot and being worked hard, and will often vanish when the machine is not accelerating. Without direct comparison it is not easy to distinguish between these conditions and mechanical faults such as wear in the small-end bearing which produces a similar sound.

21 Whatever the actual cause, this type of noise indicates the need for careful examination of the combustion chambers and pistons. If left unresolved, detonation can damage the pistons and overload the hard-pressed big-end and small-end bearings. In extreme cases the piston crown may become holed or collapse under the excessive pressure **(see illustrations 3.1a and b)**.

22 Pinking, or knocking, can occur as a result of over-advanced ignition timing, or an excessively high compression ratio. Part of the mixture charge in the combustion chamber burns normally, but the remainder is then provoked into exploding due to compression pressures. Many engines will suffer slight, barely audible, pinking, but if the problem becomes severe, damage can result.

23 Pre-ignition is caused by ignition of the fuel/air mixture at the wrong point in the engine cycle. This can be due to accumulated carbon deposits on the piston, combustion chamber and spark plug or by overheated components.

8 Identifying transmission noise

1 Transmission noises are due to wear or damage of the transmission components, which for the sake of convenience we will use to describe anything within the crankcases not covered above. There are innumerable possible causes, and the most likely ones will depend upon the machine in question. Some of the more common general problems are as follows:

Clutch and primary drive

2 Noise can result from general wear and tear, or from mechanical failure. Noises can

8.2 Damaged teeth on the clutch will cause a noise. The piece missing from the basket may have caused problems elsewhere

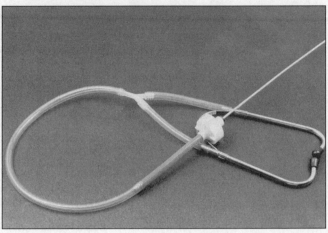

9.4 A stethoscope is an invaluable tool for diagnosing engine noises

range from whining primary gear teeth to rattles or knocking from a worn or damaged clutch **(see illustration)**.

3 On some four cylinder models, even carburettor imbalance can be enough to cause snatch and a resulting rattle from an otherwise sound clutch assembly!

Gearbox

4 Noise is generally confined to one ratio, though it can apply in all gears in cases where the input shaft or output shaft or bearings are involved. As a general guide, input shaft related problems will vary with engine speed, whilst those relating to the output shaft will be controlled by the road speed of the machine.

5 Do not forget that the whole of the final drive will be involved here, so check that the drive chain or shaft is not causing the problem.

6 Generalised rumblings or roaring noises are often attributable to worn bearings, whilst regular clicking or rattling noises are indicative of chipped or broken gear teeth.

7 Whining noises can often occur where general wear of the gear teeth has occurred and will build up slowly, rather than appearing suddenly.

9 Locating the source of noises

1 Mechanical noise can be produced from almost anywhere, and is largely dependent on the model producing them. For example, where balancer shafts are used on single-cylinder or twin-cylinder models, there are extra bearings to wear out. Similarly, ancillary items such as alternators, and minor gears driving oil pumps for example, can all contribute to a noisy engine.

2 Provided that you can provoke the noise while the machine is stationary, there are a number of ways of attempting to work out the general area of its source. This can be difficult

if you just listen unaided, because sound can be transmitted through the cases to emerge some way from the source.

3 The simplest method is to run the engine then place a large screwdriver against the engine at various points. If you place your ear against the handle, you will be able to hear the mechanical rumblings produced by the engine. By moving the tip around you should get a good idea of the location of the suspect sound.

4 To refine this process, use a length of fuel pipe as a makeshift stethoscope, or better still, buy a real stethoscope **(see illustration)**. These are often sold in engineering shops or tool shops for this very purpose.

10 Engine seizure

1 A seized engine is the usual result of lubrication failure or serious overheating. The overheating problem may have been caused by lubrication failure, though in other cases, a

condition such as an abnormally weak mixture may have caused it, and the subsequent failure of the lubrication film. In other words, overheating and loss of lubrication may either have been the cause or the symptom of the failure.

2 In most cases, it is the cylinder bore and piston areas which are most at risk; if the lubrication film breaks down for any length of time, the piston and cylinder wall come into direct contact, and the resulting friction generates a tremendous amount of localised heat.

3 The heat and friction will cause galling of the piston surface, and quite often significant amounts of the piston material will be smeared along the length of the piston thrust faces, trapping the rings in their grooves **(see illustration)**. Eventually the condition will become so severe that the piston may end up virtually welded into the bore. At this stage, if not before, the engine will stop abruptly.

4 Seizure can also occur as the result of component failure. In the case of the bore, ring breakage, the dislodging of one of the ring location pegs (two-strokes only) or a

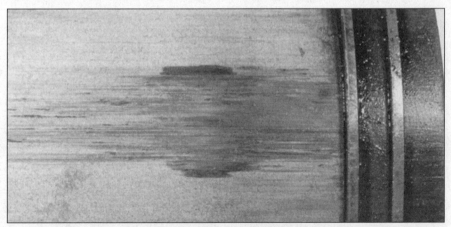

10.3 Scoring of the piston skirt is evidence of partial seizure. Light damage can be carefully filed smooth, although a new piston would be a more satisfactory repair. Establish the cause of the seizure before reassembly

10.5 This crankpin illustrates the effects of big-end seizure. The bearing has broken up, smearing metal around the pin

displaced piston pin circlip are typical causes, and are usually attributable to failure to check these areas during a previous rebuild, or to the re-use of old parts in the latter case. Bearing surfaces, too, can suffer seizure.

These include small-end bushes or bearings, especially on two-strokes where lubrication is less predictable in this area than is the case with four-stroke models.

5 The crankshaft big-end and main bearings may fail due to loss of lubrication, either because of oil starvation, or oil pressure loss from bearings that have become too worn **(see illustration)**.

6 On two-strokes, failure of the pumped supply may be the cause, or even reduced lubrication due to loss through worn main bearing seals.

7 In all of the above examples, the cause of the problem will require the engine to be stripped for examination before the exact reason for the failure becomes clear. In each case, seizure will be the final outcome of neglected services or the failure to notice a general deterioration of the engine condition in time.

8 When riding, the first signs of impending seizure are a slight increase in engine noise, accompanied by a loss of power. This will often seem puzzling at first, almost as if a brake has been applied.

9 If you spot the problem at this stage, declutch and stop the engine immediately, you may have acted in time to prevent the more serious total seizure. Even so, there is likely to be a certain amount of damage to the piston skirt at the very least, and the engine should be dismantled for examination.

10 The first thing to do is to try to establish the cause of the seizure. If this is something obvious, such as running out of oil on a two-stroke, allow the engine to cool and check whether it can still be turned over. If so, get the lubrication system working again, and then ride home very gently, stopping at once if you notice any further problems.

11 Where the cause of the problem is obscure, the engine is making unusual noises, or the seizure is total, it is preferable to have the machine recovered by trailer.

Chapter 11
Engine and transmission tasks

Contents

1 Introduction

Maintaining, overhauling and repairing faults on today's motorcycles is a relatively straightforward matter, requiring a reasonable toolkit, the necessary parts, a workshop manual and some common sense. Few detail components will require very much testing; it is more common now to make a few simple checks to see whether the part or assembly is working, and if not, to fit a new unit.

Keeping older machines running or restoring a motorcycle will require a greater level and range of workshop skills. An important skill is knowing when expert help is required.

With some items it is possible to obtain replacement parts, however the economics of modern motorcycle manufacture is tending to reduce the range of spares available.

In this Chapter we will be looking at some of the more usual problems which crop up when working on the average engine/transmission assembly. For detail information on dismantling and reassembly procedures, however, you will need to refer to the appropriate workshop manual, where you will find these areas covered in depth, together with the necessary specifications and clearances.

Restoration work on models for which information is scarce will also demand a back to basics engineering approach coupled with a study of similar machines.

2 Engine/transmission unit – dismantling and checking

1 To do this you will need some source of reference giving the dismantling and reassembly procedures and also the relevant specifications and torque wrench settings. A workshop manual for your machine will prove a necessity, but do not expect to find sufficient information in the owners handbook supplied with the machine; this does not cover overhaul or repair work.

2 The manual will show you what degree of dismantling is required for a particular job, and whether you need to remove the complete unit from the frame to allow access.

The extent of the dismantling work will also depend upon the nature of the fault. If, for example, an internal part has broken up in service, it would be risky not to strip the entire unit so that any residual debris can be cleaned out. If you fail to do this, metal particles may be dislodged at a later date, wrecking the engine again.

3 Be sure to clean the exterior of the engine/transmission unit thoroughly before dismantling commences. This will avoid road dirt getting inside the unit, and will make it a lot easier to work out exactly what went wrong. Look carefully at each part as it is removed, making an initial check for damage. Look out for pieces of metal or swarf which might give you a clue as to what has failed and why. The location of any such debris will be a key factor, so approach this methodically.

4 If you spot something which looks wrong, stop and work out whether this has any significance before proceeding; once you have removed it and forgotten its exact position it may be too late to make this sort of deduction.

5 The dismantled parts should be laid out in sequence on a clean bench top, small parts being placed in marked containers so that they can be refitted in their correct locations during reassembly. This is particularly important with items like valves, which will have bedded in to a corresponding guide and valve seat. A purpose built storage tray will be useful here.

6 If you have room, leave everything laid out in this way for now. Failing this, place groups of components in boxes and stack them to one side. Used cardboard cartons will provide useful temporary storage of this type, and can be thrown away when you have finished with them.

7 Before you start cleaning the individual parts, look at them closely for further signs of wear or damage, eg the build-up of carbon on pistons, plus any scorch marks or discoloration below the rings will give a good indication of the condition of the bores and rings without the need for direct measurement.

8 Check the sludge deposits which will have formed at the bottom of the crankcase. Is this just dirty oil, or does it contain metal particles? If so try to find out where they came from.

9 At the end of the dismantling process you should have formed a fairly clear picture of the condition of the engine, having noted any obvious failures and also the visible indications of normal wear.

10 The next step is to clean each part thoroughly to remove oil and dirt, placing each part on a clean surface after doing so. If parts are to be left for any length of time, put them in closed containers or cover them with clean cloth to prevent them from getting dirty again.

11 Sometimes it is necessary to apply heat to a part that needs to be dismantled or removed, more often than not when dissimilar metals are in direct contact with each other. Since each metal will have its own rate of expansion, when heat is applied one will expand more than the other, so that parts that were once a tight fit can be separated quite freely.

12 The manner in which the heat is applied requires careful consideration because if it is applied too locally as, for example, by a blowlamp or a welding torch, it is only too easy to cause the component to distort permanently, rendering it useless. The entire component should be heated by a flame, moving the heat source backwards and forwards, up and down, so that there are no hot spots.

13 Whenever possible, an oven should be used to bring the whole component to an even heat before any attempt is made to separate it into its component parts.

14 Special care is needed when heating alloys as too much heat will allow them to melt, with disastrous results. This also applies to large castings such as cylinder heads and crankcases, which will distort with ease unless adequate care is taken.

15 Remember to keep naked flames away from any fuels or similar combustible products and to take great care in handling the heated parts. To avoid the risk of serious burns, wear protective gloves or use some other form of protection to avoid contact with the hot surfaces.

16 When the dismantling work has been completed, allow the individual parts to cool slowly in the open atmosphere. Do not attempt to force cool them as this may cause distortion. If heat alone will not permit separation with gentle pressure, there is another reason why this will not occur, which must be investigated.

17 Never use a naked flame to separate components cast in Elektron, a mixture of magnesium and aluminium alloys sometimes used in an attempt to reduce weight on competition models. Magnesium burns very fiercely when it catches fire, and is very difficult to put out by some of the more common types of fire extinguisher.

18 Stubborn nuts and studs may be sprayed with releasing fluid and preferably allowed to soak for a few hours before attempting to undo them.

19 An impact driver is useful for releasing screws and bolts, but make sure the case or host component is supported properly before using the hammer.

20 Often a slight movement in the tightening direction will help break any corrosion and allow the nut or screw to be loosened.

21 If a nut or screw refuses to budge check that it does not have a left-hand thread.

22 If two components refuse to part, check that they are not held by some hidden bolt or clip.

Detailed checking

23 Using the specifications in the workshop manual in conjunction with the measuring equipment and methods described in Chapter 4, you can now set about making a detailed assessment of the engine's condition in readiness for any overhaul or reconditioning work.

24 Obvious wear or damage will make this unnecessary; eg a badly scored bore surface will mean that the engine will have to be rebored and new piston(s) fitted, so there would be little point checking the old pistons or rings.

25 It is a good idea to make a written note of any wear or damage found during this process. Later, you can sit down and consider the best course of action, and decide which aspects you can deal with at home and which require specialist help. The rest of this Chapter deals with the more common problem areas and suggests the best way to approach them.

3 Plain bearings and bushes

Plain bearings (shells)

1 Plain (shell) bearings and simple bushes and are to be found in many locations in the engine. They rely on a lubrication film between the bearing surface and the rotating part (journal) to provide support and prevent wear, the shaft being carried on a thin film of oil at fairly high pressure.

2 Metal bushes are usually of phosphor-bronze material. Rubber bushes are used in suspension mounting eyes. Fibre bushes have also been used in suspension pivots.

3 The bearing surface can be damaged by contaminants in the oil finding their way past the oil filter. In extreme cases the hardened surface of the shaft will also be damaged. The problem is often caused by neglected oil filter changes; the filter becomes choked with deposits, and to maintain circulation a pressure-sensitive bypass valve opens, allowing unfiltered oil to circulate. This is better than nothing, but the oil will get progressively dirtier, and damage to the bearing surfaces is almost inevitable if the situation continues for long.

4 With two-stroke transmissions, and those of many four-strokes, lubrication is by oil bath, the rotating parts flinging oil around the casing and onto the bushes and bearings. Again, neglecting regular oil changes allows the oil to become contaminated with particles and degraded by moisture.

5 General wear of plain bearing surfaces is difficult to assess in the average home workshop, even armed with the necessary clearance specifications. The tolerances required are very fine, and high-precision equipment would be needed to check them. It is, however, usually possible to gain some impression of the stage of wear by measurement, feel and visual assessment.

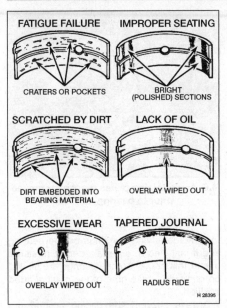

FATIGUE FAILURE

IMPROPER SEATING

CRATERS OR POCKETS

BRIGHT (POLISHED) SECTIONS

SCRATCHED BY DIRT

LACK OF OIL

DIRT EMBEDDED INTO BEARING MATERIAL

OVERLAY WIPED OUT

EXCESSIVE WEAR

TAPERED JOURNAL

OVERLAY WIPED OUT

RADIUS RIDE

H 28395

3.6 Typical plain (shell) bearing failures

6 Shell bearings will fail due to damage of their working surface, as a result of lack of lubrication, corrosion or abrasive particles in the oil **(see illustration)**. Small particles of dirt in the oil may embed in the bearing material whereas larger particles will score the bearing and shaft journal. If a number of short journeys are made, insufficient heat will be generated to drive off condensation which has built up on the bearings.

7 Applying a little sideways pressure to a shaft will reveal any movement which will generally indicate the need for renewal.

8 As bearings elsewhere in the engine (notably the crankshaft main and big-end bearings) become worn, eventually the capacity of the oil pump is outstripped by the rate of leakage around these bearings. This results in a loss of oil pressure and subsequent wear and possible failure of other bearing surfaces in the engine.

9 You will appreciate the need for fastidious maintenance, regular oil changes and above all, the need to resolve any unusual noise immediately.

10 If the shaft journal surface has become worn or damaged, you have a choice of either renewing it together with the bush, or getting the old one reconditioned. Again, this is a job for a professional engineering workshop. It may be possible to re-grind the bearing surface of the shaft if it is not too worn. A new undersized bush will then have to be made up to suit the new diameter.

11 Alternatively, the shaft end could be turned down to remove the damage, the surface then being built up by plating, or by a process called metal spraying. The reconditioned surface is then ground back to its original size and can be used with the standard bush. If you are faced with this sort of choice, first get a price for a new shaft and bush, then armed with this information, seek the advice of an engineering company, who will be able to advise you whether reconditioning would be cost-effective by comparison.

12 In cases where the machine is obsolete, or parts are unobtainable for some other reason, reconditioning may be the only option open to you.

13 In the case of plain bearing inserts used in main and big-end bearings on most four-strokes, you will be able to see quite easily where the bearing layer has worn through to the copper-coloured backing metal, and any discernible movement is usually a fair indication that the bearing has completed its useful life.

14 Renewal of split plain bearing inserts, which are normally used for crankshaft main and big-end bearings, is relatively straightforward. New bearing inserts are selected according to the manufacturer's specifications. Often the journals will be graded according to tolerance, and marked with a code letter or number. This is used to select the insert from a range of sizes to

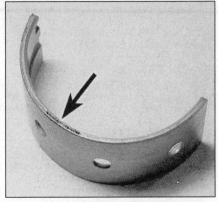

3.14 Shell bearings are either plain or grooved. They are generally identified by a colour code

obtain the required oil clearance. The inserts are usually identified by a dab of coloured paint **(see illustration)**.

15 If you detect freeplay after fitting new bearing inserts of the correct grade, and thus need to check journal wear, a product called Plastigauge will prove invaluable. Refer to Chapter 4 for details of how to use this product.

Removing and replacing bushes

16 Where a bearing or bush is set in the eye of a component, such as a suspension linkage arm or connecting rod small-end, removal by drift may damage the component. Furthermore, a rubber bushing in a shock absorber eye cannot successfully be driven out of position. If access is available to an engineering press, the task is straightforward. If not, a drawbolt can be fabricated to extract the bearing or bush.

17 To extract the bearing/bush you will need a long bolt with nut (or piece of threaded bar with two nuts), a piece of tubing which has an internal diameter larger than the bearing/bush, another piece of tubing which has an external diameter smaller than the bearing/bush, and a selection of washers **(see illustrations)**. Note that the pieces of tubing must be of the same length, or longer, than the bearing/bush. This assembly is known as a drawbolt and is described in Chapter 2, Section 14.

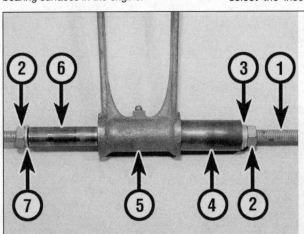

1 *Bolt or length of threaded bar*
2 *Nuts*
3 *Washer (external diameter greater than tubing internal diameter)*
4 *Tubing (internal diameter sufficient to accommodate bearing)*
5 *Suspension arm with bearing*
6 *Tubing (external diameter slightly smaller than bearing)*
7 *Washer (external diameter slightly smaller than bearing)*

3.17a Drawbolt components assembled to remove a bush from a suspension arm

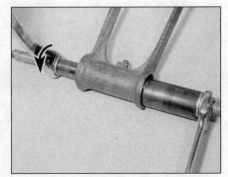

3.17b Drawing the bush out of the suspension arm

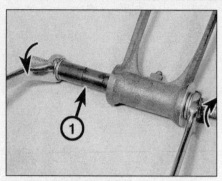

3.18 Installing a new bush (1) in the suspension arm

4.3 A typical ball bearing size marking

4.6 Any retaining plates must be removed prior to bearing removal

18 The same kit (without the pieces of tubing) can be used to draw the new bearing/bush back into place (see illustration). Where a bush is being replaced by a new item as a straight swap, the new bush can be used as the spacer. In pushing the old out you push in the new.

 One neat method for removing a bush in a blind hole is this. Turn a bar to a close sliding fit inside the bush. Three quarters fill the bush with grease. Insert the bar into the bush and give it a sharp tap with a hammer. The bush is hydraulically forced out of the hole.

4 Journal ball bearings

1 The most common type of bearing is the ball bearing journal. It can be supplied as a open type of bearing or shielded on one or both sides.

2 Open bearings are used in applications where lubrication is always present and sealed bearings are typically used in wheel hubs which are exposed to moisture and dirt.
3 Bearing manufacturers produce bearings to ISO size standards and stamp one face of the bearing outer race to indicate its internal and external diameter, load capacity and type (see illustration).
4 For example a bearing marked '6300RS' will have a bore of 17 mm, an outside diameter of 35 mm, and a width of 10 mm. The letters 'RS' indicate that it has a seal on one side only.

Removing ball bearings

Removal from a casing or housing

5 The bearing is meant to enter and leave its housing squarely. Any tapping at one side cocks the bearing and causes it to jam. Excessive force can easily damage both bearing and housing. Any force should be applied to the outer race of the bearing so as to avoid damage.
6 Before removing a bearing, always inspect the casing to see which way it must be driven out – some casings will have retaining plates or a cast step (see illustration). Also check

for any identifying markings on the bearing and if installed to a certain depth, measure this at this stage. Some bearings are sealed on one side – take note of the original fitted position.
7 Always support the casing around the bearing housing with wood blocks, otherwise there is a risk of fracture.
8 The method of removal depends on the location of the bearing and if the bearing is to be renewed. In a straight through bore, the old bearing can simply be driven out by using a drift and a hammer. The drift should bear on the outer race of the bearing, especially if the bearing it to be re-used (see illustration).
9 Unless access is severely restricted (as with wheel bearings), a pin-punch is not recommended unless it is moved around the bearing to keep it square in its housing as it emerges (see illustration).
10 Where a bearing locates in a blind hole in a casing, it cannot be driven out as described above. A slide-hammer with knife-edged bearing puller attachment will be required. The puller attachment passes through the bearing and when tightened expands to fit firmly behind the bearing. By operating the

4.8 A socket of the same diameter as the bearing outer race makes a good drift

4.9 Where assess is limited, a punch can be used to displace a bearing

4.10a The bearing puller is inserted into the bearing and expanded

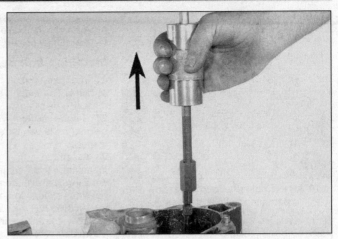

4.10b The slide-hammer is attached and the bearing withdrawn using a hammer action

slide-hammer part of the tool the bearing is jarred out of its housing **(see illustrations)**.

11 The expanding bolt described in Chapter 14 for removing wheel bearings can also be put to use here. The bearing can be withdrawn by using a tube and spacer to draw the bolt out using another nut on the bolt, or by improvising a slide-hammer.

Removal and installation can be made easier by warming the casing, as described overleaf.

Removal from a shaft

12 Where a bearing is pressed on a shaft, a puller will be required to extract it **(see illustration)**. Make sure that the puller clamp or legs fits securely behind the bearing and are unlikely to slip out.

13 If pulling a bearing off a gear shaft for example, you may have to locate the puller behind a gear pinion if there is no access to the back of the bearing **(see illustration)**.

14 Ensure that the puller's centre bolt locates securely against the end of the shaft and will not slip when pressure is applied. Also ensure

that the puller does not damage the shaft end. Operate the puller so that its centre bolt exerts pressure on the shaft end and draws the bearing off the shaft.

Checking for wear

15 Wear is generally associated with the balls themselves and as measurement is impossible an assessment of its condition will have to be made by feel and sound.

4.12 This puller clamps around the bearing and must be a tight fit

4.13 In this case the gear has to be removed because there is no access to the rear of the bearing

16 Before checking the condition, the bearing should be thoroughly cleaned by degreasing then washing with a high flash-point solvent or contact cleaner. Allow the bearing to dry.

17 The inner race of the bearing is then slowly rotated whilst holding the outer race stationary. The bearing should turn quietly and smoothly with no roughness in the movement. There should be no radial or axial play **(see illustrations)**.

4.17a Rotate the bearing through a complete revolution and listen and feel for any roughness

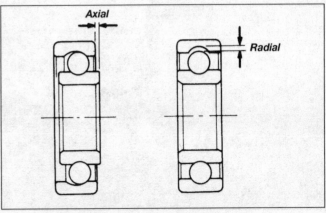

4.17b Play in any direction means a new bearing

4.18 An example of a journal bearing with damaged balls and cages

18 On seriously damaged bearings it may be possible to see pitting or imperfections of the rollers or balls, and in the bearing tracks of the races **(see illustration)**. Similarly there should be no traces of rust. Any such blemish means the bearing is no good.

19 Replace any damaged bearings.

20 If a bearing outer race has spun in its housing, the housing material will be damaged. The bore in the housing must be repaired before refitting the bearing. Alternatively you could consider using one of the proprietary bearing locking compounds.

Installing ball bearings

21 The bore or shaft must be clean and free of burrs. The mating surface of the bearing must also be clean.

22 Before assembly oil or grease the bearing balls as instructed in the workshop manual.

23 Assemble the bearing with the manufacturer's name and code facing outwards, away from the recess in the housing or locating shoulder on the shaft. If the bearing has a sealed face on one side, generally it is fitted with the sealed side facing outwards.

24 When drifting in a bearing, support the housing or shaft with wooden blocks.

25 Use a bearing driver, socket or tubular drift to install the bearing in its housing **(see illustrations)**. Force should only be applied to the outer race when drifting a bearing into a housing.

26 When installing a bearing on a shaft, use a tubular drift which bears only on the inner race of the bearing **(see illustration)**.

27 After assembly check that the bearing is seated correctly and rotates freely.

28 The bearing must not rotate in its housing, or on its shaft. Where there is a danger of this occurring, use one of the proprietary locking compounds designed for this application.

Using heat to help bearing removal and fitting

29 If the bearing's outer race is a tight fit in the casing, the aluminium casing can be heated to release its grip on the bearing. Aluminium will expand at a greater rate than the steel bearing outer race. There are several ways to do this, but avoid any localised extreme heat (such as a blow torch) – aluminium alloy has a low melting point.

30 Plastic components, such as the neutral switch, may suffer when the whole case is heated – remove them beforehand.

31 Approved methods of heating a casing are using a domestic oven (heated to 100°C) or immersing the casing in boiling water. Low temperature range localised heat sources

4.25a Bearing driver sets contain a variety of different diameter drivers

4.25b Using a bearing driver against the outer race of the bearing

4.25c A large socket being used as an improvised driver

4.26 The correct diameter drift used for installing this bearing onto its shaft

4.31a A casing can be immersed in a bowl of hot water

4.31b Using the heat from a hot air gun to provide localised heat

4.31c A domestic clothes iron being used to apply heat to a casing

4.32 Tapping the case down onto a wood surface may jar the bearing from the heated case

such as a paint stripper heat gun or clothes iron can also be used **(see illustrations)**. Alternatively, soak a rag in boiling water, wring it out and wrap it around the bearing housing.

 Warning: All of these methods require care in use to prevent scalding and burns to the hands. Wear protective gloves when handling hot components.

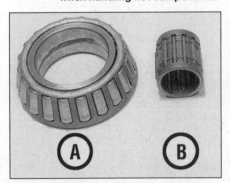

5.1 An illustration of a tapered roller bearing (A) and a needle roller bearing (B)

32 After heating, remove the bearing as described above. You may find that the expansion is sufficient for the bearing to fall out of the casing under its own weight or with a light tap on the driver or socket. If this method is attempted, first prepare a work surface which will enable the casing to be tapped face down to help dislodge the bearing – a wood surface is ideal since it will not damage the

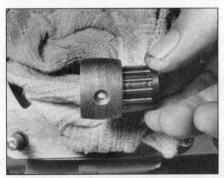

5.2 A typical application for a needle roller bearing is in the connecting rod of a two-stroke

casing's gasket surface **(see illustration)**. Wearing protective gloves, tap the heated casing several times against the work surface to dislodge the bearing under its own weight.
33 Allow the casing to cool down slowly to avoid the possibility of distortion.
34 Installation of bearings can be eased by placing them in a freezer the night before installation. The steel bearing will contract slightly, allowing easy insertion in its housing. This is often useful when installing steering head outer races in the frame.

5 Roller bearings

1 As the name suggests, needle roller bearings are similar to ball bearings except that the balls are replaced with rollers of very small diameter **(see illustration)**.
2 They are often used in two-stroke connecting rod small-ends, where they can survive the meagre lubrication available **(see illustration)**. When these break down you will

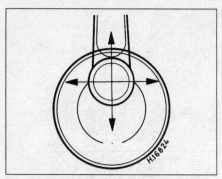

5.5 Any play in the directions shown means that the bearing will need to be replaced. Use a dial gauge for an accurate assessment

usually find cracked or damaged rollers, a broken cage, and in bad cases, indentation or pitting and scoring of the connecting rod small-end eye and the piston pin.

3 If only the bearing is damaged, it is permissible to renew this alone, though if the surfaces on which it runs are damaged, these too will need attention. In the case of small-end bearings, this may mean fitting a new crankshaft assembly.

4 Roller big-end bearings use larger diameter rollers of perhaps 6 mm. Again they may be found in two-stroke engines. The bearing assembly includes the crankpin, and this is usually in the form of a pressed-up assembly forming part of the crankshaft.

5 With this type of crankshaft assembly there should be a specific amount of axial (side-to-side) movement of the connecting rod between the flywheels, but no discernible radial (up-and-down) movement **(see illustration)**.

6 Axial play is normally measured with feeler gauges, whilst it is normally sufficient to check the radial play by feel. If you feel the need to measure this, set the crankshaft up on V-blocks and take a measurement using a dial test indicator (dial gauge). Be sure not to confuse any side play felt as being radial play.

7 If wear is discovered, some manufacturers offer an exchange crankshaft service for their models, though it is now increasingly common to simply purchase a new crankshaft outright. It is theoretically feasible to rebuild a roller big-end, but only if the replacement parts can be obtained.

8 Caged tapered roller bearings are found in many steering heads **(see illustration)**.

9 These may be removed and refitted using the methods described for ball bearings.

10 Inspection is perhaps limited to a visual check and to rotating the bearing and feeling for any roughness.

11 Examine the roller cage for signs of cracking and splits; any such damage means replacement of the bearing.

12 Do not re-use bearings once they have been removed.

13 It is possible to estimate the condition of the bearings by moving the front wheel from

5.8 Taper roller bearings are typically found in steering heads

side to side and feeling for any roughness or hesitation in movement. Adjust the steering head bearings to remove any play before doing this.

6 Oil seals

1 As the name suggests oil seals are used to prevent the escape of fluids. They are used to seal round rotating shafts and bearings. In two-stroke engines they also act as a pressure seal particularly for maintaining crankcase pressure. They also have a secondary function preventing contamination of bearings by moisture and dirt.

Oil seal removal and installation

2 Oil seals should be renewed every time a component is dismantled. This is because the seal lips will become set to the sealing surface and will not necessarily reseal.

3 Oil seals can be prised out of position using a large flat-bladed screwdriver **(see illustration)**. In the case of crankcase seals, check first that the seal is not lipped on the inside, preventing its removal with the crankcases joined.

4 New seals are usually installed with their marked face (containing the seal reference code) outwards and the spring side towards

6.3 An oil seal can be prised out of its location using a flat-bladed screwdriver

the fluid being retained. In certain cases, such as a two-stroke engine crankshaft seal, a double lipped seal may be used due to there being fluid or gas on each side of the joint.

5 Before installing a new seal, check that the shaft over which the seal is to be fitted, and the location in the housing are free from burrs which could damage the seal.

6 Smear grease over the seal lips before assembly.

7 Use a bearing driver or socket which bears only on the outer hard edge of the seal to install it in the casing – tapping on the inner edge will damage the sealing lip.

8 Oil seals will stiffen and dry up after long storage periods, leading to leakage. They should be renewed.

Oil seal types and markings

9 Oil seals are usually of the single-lipped type. Double-lipped seals are found where a liquid or gas is on both sides of the joint.

10 Oil seal manufacturers conform to the ISO markings for seal size – these are moulded into the outer face of the seal **(see illustration)**.

7 Crankshafts and camshafts

Crankshaft and camshaft reconditioning

1 If the engine manufacturer offers a range of undersized bearing inserts, renovation of a plain bearing crankshaft is, superficially, a simple matter of taking the crankshaft to an engine reconditioning specialist for grinding.

2 Check that the necessary undersize inserts are available before carrying out this work. Note that most Japanese manufacturers do not offer undersize bearings.

3 Many companies offer crankshaft reconditioning services. They usually specialise in one or two areas of reconditioning work, or on a particular model, and some will even undertake more major conversions, such as converting damaged cylinder heads to accept needle-roller camshaft bearings.

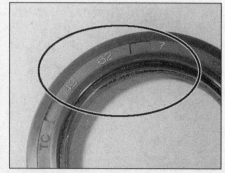

6.10 This seal marking indicates inside diameter, outside diameter and thickness in millimetres

4 The best way to reclaim a crankshaft with damaged journal surfaces would be to have the journal built up by plating or metal spraying and then ground back to the original size, as described above. Done properly, the crankshaft will be as good as new, and you will be able to use the original bearing inserts.
5 Metal spraying may sometimes allow a damaged small-end bearing surface to be reconditioned, though if there is enough metal around the eye, you could consider having the eye bored oversize and a bush fitted. Once again, the best course of action is to take the offending part to a specialist for evaluation.
6 Camshafts can be treated in a similar fashion to that described for crankshafts, and a good engineering company will be able to build up and re-machine both the bearing journals, and where necessary, the cam lobes **(see illustrations)**.
7 Camshaft lobe re-profiling is a fairly common procedure, and can also be used to alter the cam lift characteristics for a particular engine. This is useful where the engine is being tuned for competition purposes, but make sure you deal with someone who knows the engine concerned, particularly its limitations in racing applications.

Crankshaft balancing

8 This is a worthwhile operation on any engine especially one which has suffered failure. It is possible to balance the crankshaft by holding it between centres on the lathe, however this will only check the static balance condition.
9 For dynamic balancing specialist machinery is required – look for engineering firms advertising in the motorcycle press who can carry out this work.

8 Cylinder heads

Initial preparation

1 The amount of work involved in cylinder head reconditioning depends on the engine type; eg a single cylinder two-stroke being far easier to deal with than a dohc four-stroke four.
2 In the case of four-strokes, the valve and camshaft components must be removed before cleaning and inspection can begin. Remember that each valve assembly must be placed in a marked container, or storage tray, so that it is refitted in its original port and guide. Camshaft caps and any cam follower or rocker arm assembly should be stored in a similar manner, and for the same reason.
3 Once the head is stripped to the bare casting, cleaning work can begin. The object is to remove all traces of carbon deposits without causing damage to the soft aluminium alloy. If possible, it is best to have the

7.6a A damaged cam lobe requiring repair or renewal

deposits removed by dipping the head in a specially designed solvent cleaner. This is a commercial tank process using fairly strong chemicals and is not normally available for home use for safety reasons.
4 If you can find a local engineering company with this facility, however, it is worth paying to have the head cleaned in this way. It will save you a good deal of time and effort, and will remove deposits inside ports and other awkward areas. If you decide on this method and can arrange it locally, try to get the pistons and cylinder block cleaned at the same time. Note that the chemicals will probably remove any paint coating, and that all seals and any plastic parts must be removed or they too will be dissolved.
5 If the head casting is generally well-used, and especially where the outside surfaces are ingrained or corroded, consider having the casting bead blasted.
6 This method of cleaning is extremely efficient and well worth paying for. Before taking parts for blast cleaning, make sure that they are thoroughly degreased; dry carbon deposits are quite acceptable, but oil and grease will be received with little enthusiasm by the prospective blaster.
7 On ohc four-stroke models, or any machine with bearing surfaces on the head casting be sure to mask off these areas. Where camshafts are held by caps, cut a length of wooden dowel or plastic tubing to the same length as the camshafts and clamp this in place with the bearing caps. Cover valve guide bores and valve lifter bores by plugging them or by fitting plastic caps.
8 Be absolutely certain to specify glass bead or aqua-bead blasting only; on no account allow alloy castings to be abrasive blasted. After blast cleaning, **all** traces of residual dust and beads must be removed. Use a high pressure airline to blow through ports and oilways, and take care not to blow dust and other material into oilways from which it cannot be removed. Clean thoroughly in a degreasing solvent afterwards. Any small residual deposits of beads left unnoticed will invariably get dislodged after the engine is rebuilt, with disastrous consequences.
9 If you are unable to have the head cleaned chemically or by blast cleaning, you will have

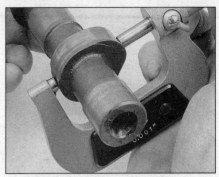

7.6b Measuring to check for wear on a cam lobe

to resort to the procedure of scraping off the carbon deposits. The success of this procedure is directly proportional to the amount of effort you are prepared to put into it. You will need various scraping tools, and these will have to be made up to suit. Choose materials which are slightly softer than the alloy to avoid accidental scoring of the surfaces (particularly the gasket faces), avoiding the temptation to use an old screwdriver or chisel.
10 Clean out the inlet and exhaust ports on four-stroke engines using steel wool.
11 Other useful equipment for this process includes small rotary brass wire brushes which can be used in the chuck of a power drill. Better still, purchase a flexible drive which can be fitted between the drill chuck and the brush. This will allow you to get into ports and other recessed areas otherwise inaccessible to a power tool.

Inspection of the bare cylinder head

12 When cleaning has been completed, the head casting can be checked for wear or damage. Normally, this consists of a careful visual check for cracks, and in the case of four-strokes, checking the condition and security of valve seats and guides.
13 If all this is in order, attention can be turned to checking for warpage of the gasket faces, and checks and measurements of all wear-prone areas such as valve guides, seats and bearing surfaces.
14 To carry out these checks refer to your workshop manual for the service specifications and wear limits.

Crack and leak detection

15 If you have reason to suspect other damage, it is a good idea to arrange to have the head crack detected. This again is a specialist engineering process, and one which may prove difficult to arrange locally.
16 Despite this, it is well worth having done if you are dubious about the condition of the head; there is little point spending money reconditioning a head which later turns out to have hairline cracks or other fundamental defects present.

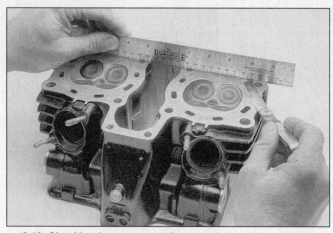

8.18 Checking for warpage using a straight-edge and feeler gauges

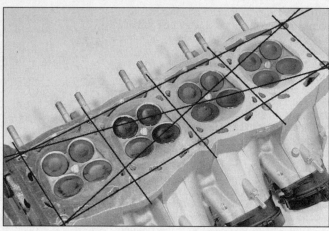

8.19 Showing the directions in which to check for warpage

Checking for warpage of gasket faces

17 Warpage of the gasket faces can occur due to incorrect tightening down of the head fasteners, or less commonly, through extreme conditions such as an overheated engine getting suddenly soaked in cold water. Most manufacturers prescribe warp limits for major engine components, and these should be referred to before making the check.

18 The easiest home method is to put a straight-edge across the machined face and check with feeler gauges if there is any gap between head and straight-edge **(see illustration)**.

19 Check across the diagonals and between mounting holes **(see illustration)**.

20 Alternately, place the casting, gasket face down on a clean surface plate. The one described in Chapter 4 can be used for this purpose, however take care not to accidentally mark the surface.

21 The gasket face is placed against the surface plate, making sure that both surfaces are completely clean – even a small piece of grit will give a false reading. Look for signs of daylight between the surfaces, and measure any discernible gap using feeler gauges. If the gap exceeds the manufacturer's warp limit (usually about 0.05 mm) it will be necessary to have the surface machined to correct the distortion.

22 Slight distortion can be corrected at home, using a sheet of abrasive paper taped to the surface plate or glass sheet. The gasket face is rubbed in a circular motion on the abrasive paper until the distortion is eliminated.

23 Lift the head regularly and check the appearance. High spots will show up as matt grey areas, and these will gradually get larger as the material is levelled. Eventually the surface should show an even matt appearance over its entire surface.

24 Note that where the surface is generally flat, with high spots around stud or bolt holes,

this indicates over-tightening of the cylinder head fasteners in the past.

25 Where the head is too big to fit on the abrasive sheet, or where the warpage is severe, it is better to have the mating surface machined **(see illustration)**.

26 On the lathe, small two-stroke heads can be mounted either on the faceplate, or on mandrel held in the three jaw self centring chuck. Take fine cuts across the face until the distortion is cut away. The head can then be rubbed on fine abrasive paper on the surface plate to finish it.

27 Alternatively, the larger heads can be mounted on the lathe cross slide and fly cut with the cutting tool located on the face plate or on a special tool holder screwed to the lathe spindle. A milling machine can also be set up to do this work.

28 There are specialist machine shops who can carry out this work; they will probably be found listed under car engine machinists.

29 Whichever method is used, it is essential that the minimum of metal is removed. Measurements must be taken to ensure that clearances are not reduced to dangerous limits.

> **HAYNES HiNT**
>
> *A rough appraisal of clearance can be made by reassembling the top half of the engine with a small layer of Plasticene or Blu-tack on the piston crown. Having turned the crankshaft through one complete cycle, the cylinder head can be removed, and the closeness of pistons to valves can be estimated.*

30 Excessive grinding or milling of the head surface will increase the compression ratio, and this in turn can cause pinking problems.

31 It is sometimes preferable for this reason to entrust the work to a specialist. This will allow the machine operator to take clearance measurements, and where necessary, carry out corrective machining to other parts.

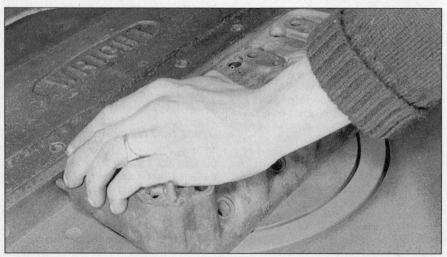

8.25 Most engine reconditoning specialists will undertake surface grinding to restore warped gasket faces

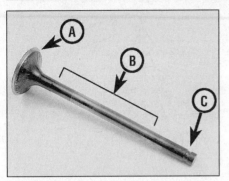

9.1 The main items to check for wear and damage; the valve face (A), the stem (B) and the collet groove (C)

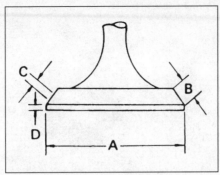

9.4 Measure the valve head diameter (A), face (B), seat contact (C) and head thickness (D)

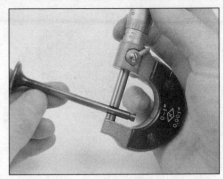

9.5a Measure the valve stem at two or three places

9 Valves, valve seats, guides and springs

Valves

1 The main areas to be checked are the valve face, stem and collet (keeper) groove **(see illustration)**, and the corresponding surface of the valve seat and guide, and the valve springs.

2 The first job is to clean off carbon deposits from the various components to allow close inspection and measurement. Clean off the accumulated carbon from the valves by scraping and with abrasive paper, taking care to avoid scratching or scoring the valve contact face or the stem.

3 One way to speed this process considerably is to clamp the valve stem in the chuck of a bench-mounted power drill or a lathe. A blunt scraper can then be applied very carefully to the valve to skim off the carbon. Take great care if you employ this method, both to avoid catching clothing or fingers in the rotating chuck or valve, and to avoid injury from flying debris – use grinding goggles to protect the eyes. A polished finish

can be achieved using progressively fine grades of abrasive paper.

4 Examine the valve face for wear or damage, particularly the seat contact area **(see illustration)**. Any indication of pitting or burning of the seat contact will require remedial work, or possibly renewal of the valve. Check also the condition of the valve seat in the cylinder head (see below). Use a vernier gauge to measure the head diameter and thickness, and the face and seat width.

5 The straightness and wear on the valve stem should be checked **(see illustrations)**. Valve stem wear will show up as a dull area on an otherwise highly polished surface.

6 Check the valve stem diameter in various

positions, comparing it at the most worn point with an unworn section.

7 Compare the readings with the wear limits given in the workshop manual. Renew valves which are outside the wear limits.

Valve guides

8 If the valve is within limits, check the fit of each valve in its guide. In many cases, the manufacturer will quote a maximum clearance figure, often assessed as the amount of 'wobble' found at the valve stem end. This can be checked using a dial gauge **(see illustrations)**.

9 Note that stem-to-guide clearance can be calculated by subtracting valve stem diameter from the guide bore diameter.

9.5b Check the valve runout at the stem (A) and head (B)

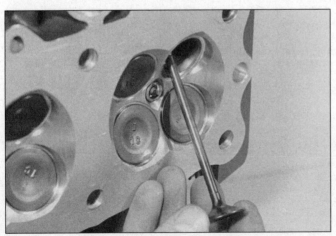

9.8a Insert the valve into its guide . . .

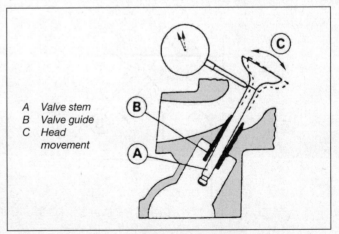

A Valve stem
B Valve guide
C Head movement

9.8b . . . and measure valve stem-to-guide clearance using the 'wobble' method

9.10a Insert a small hole gauge into the valve guide bore, expand it until it is a sliding fit, and lock it before withdrawing it

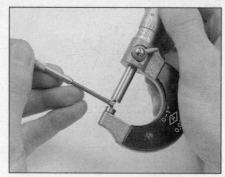

9.10b The locked gauge can then be measured with a micrometer

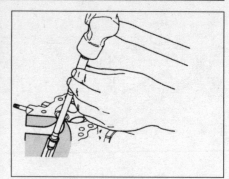

9.16 Driving a valve guide out of the cylinder head

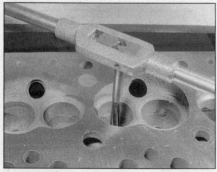

9.20 Reaming the newly inserted valve guide

10 Valve guide bore diameter can be measured using a small hole gauge **(see illustrations)**; take measurements at each end of the guide and in the middle.

11 Compare the readings with the specified wear limits, worn guides will have to be replaced.

12 In the home workshop, the removal and refitting work can be done, provided that you have or can make up special piloted drifts to support the guide during fitting, and have access to the necessary reamers to take the bore of the new guide to its finished size.

13 In most cases the cylinder head will have

to be heated in an oven to allow the guide to be removed and fitted without the risk of damage to the bore in which it sits. If this approach is specified in the workshop manual, it should not be ignored.

14 A normal domestic oven heated to 150°C, or even immersion in near boiling water will often suffice, but follow any directions regarding temperatures and heating methods carefully.

15 Do not use any form of heating with a flame; the localised nature of the heat may distort the head, and the relatively low and abrupt melting point of aluminium alloys can prove embarrassing at the very least!

16 The old guide is driven or pressed out of the head, and the new one fitted in its place **(see illustration)**.

17 Install the guide so that it seats on its cast step or wire clip.

18 Where the guide locating bore in the head has become loose, it may be necessary to have a guide with an oversize outside diameter made up and fitted. Do not knurl the outside diameter of the guide to increase its overall diameter.

19 Where there is insufficient material around the guide bore in the head, it may be necessary to build up the damaged hole by aluminium welding and then machine it back

to accept a standard size guide. The machining required will have to be of a high standard if the original valve angle is to be duplicated exactly.

20 The valve guide bore must now be reamed to the finished size to give the specified clearance **(see illustration)**.

21 When a new guide is fitted, the valve seat must be recut and a new valve fitted.

Valve seats and lapping (grinding)

22 The width of the valve seat can be measured using a vernier gauge or steel rule **(see illustration)**. Check that it is within the wear limits specified in the workshop manual.

23 If it is within limits the valve and seat can be lapped together to form a good seal. Lapping (grinding) involves rotating the valve whilst it is pressed against the seat.

24 A small quantity of grinding paste is smeared on the mating face before beginning the rotation **(see illustration)**. Small tins of paste containing both coarse and fine grades are available from motor accessory shops.

25 The common tool for this operation is a stick with a rubber sucker on the end which is stuck to the valve head. In practice this is not always satisfactory as the sucker tends to slip off. An alternative method is to use a piece of

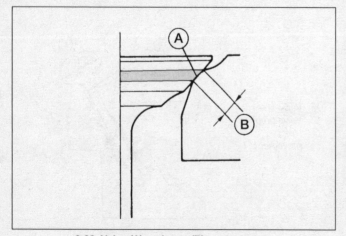

9.22 Valve (A) and seat (B) contact areas

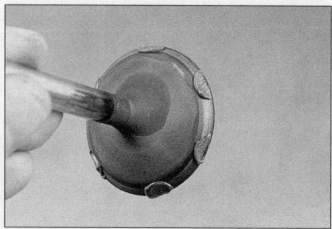

9.24 Apply the lapping compound very sparingly in small dabs, to the valve seating face only

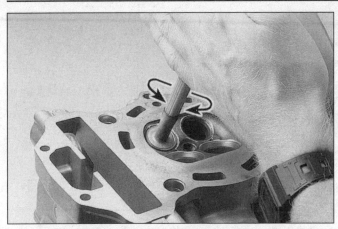

9.26a The tool is twisted to and fro between the palms of the hands

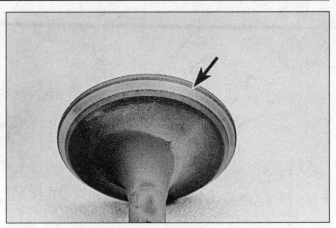

9.26b The valve face and seat should be the specified width and have a smooth unbroken appearance (arrowed)

rubber tube which is slipped over the valve stem after the valve has been inserted in the guide. With this method you pull instead of pushing as with the stick type grinding tool.

26 Continue the lapping operation by rolling the stick to and fro between the hands, until a smooth continuous line, the width of the seating face, appears on both valve and seat **(see illustrations)**.

27 If the seat width is out of limits, or a new valve guide has been fitted, a new seat must be cut **(see illustration)**. This is best done using a professional seat cutting machine.

28 If the valves are to be re-used, it is preferable to have them refaced to suit the reconditioned valve guides and seats. This will ensure that the contact surface is regular and of the correct width and angle. Another type of specialised grinder is used for this work.

29 Some reconditioning companies will carry out a pressure check of the finished work as a matter of course, as well as ensuring that the valve heights are correct for each assembly. This is vital, since if the valve sits too high or too low in its seat it may prove impossible to obtain the correct clearance adjustment on the assembled engine.

30 This last consideration applies equally where valves have been lapped in by hand on frequent occasions, using grinding paste. It should be kept in mind that each time this is done, some of the valve seat surface is ground away, and if done to excess, the valve will become recessed into the seat, or 'pocketed'.

31 Not only does this affect the height of the valve stem and thus the valve clearance adjustment range, but the pocketing effect makes the path that the incoming mixture and the outgoing exhaust gases must take tortuous and inefficient.

32 More seriously, it is not possible in some cases to renew a damaged valve seat, and so excessive valve lapping can effectively ruin the entire cylinder head. Check with a dealer whether replacement valve seats can be obtained for your engine.

33 For this reason, lapping valves in by hand must be done only occasionally and very gently, using a fine compound only, if pitting or burning of the faces has occurred, this should be corrected by machining as described above.

34 The problem of valve seat renewal is difficult to deal with where the manufacturer

does not recommend or supply parts to facilitate this procedure. The only choice, other than buying a new head, is to have a new seat made up specially and fitted into the existing head. Once again this is specialised and precision work, and is best left to a skilled professional.

35 Although most modern engines are suited to lead free petrol, older engines are dependant on the presence of lead in the fuel for keeping the valve seats in good order. As lead containing petrol is being phased out in the near future it may be wise during a rebuild to replace the valve seats with those made form materials suitable for lead free fuel where this is possible.

Valve springs

36 The valve springs are used to close each valve after it has been opened by the cam lobe. On most models, two concentric springs are fitted to each valve, the coils normally being wound in opposing directions. It is also common for the springs to be progressively wound, with tighter coils at one end than at the other **(see illustration)**.

37 This should be checked during dismantling and the correct direction of fitting

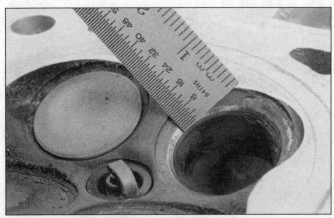

9.27 The width of the seat contact band is important. Some manufacturers specify a maximum figure beyond which re-cutting is prescribed

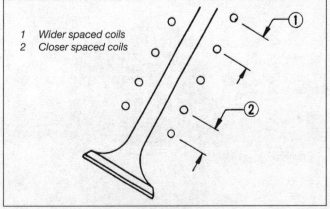

1 Wider spaced coils
2 Closer spaced coils

9.36 Valve springs are usually installed with their closer-wound coils towards the valve head

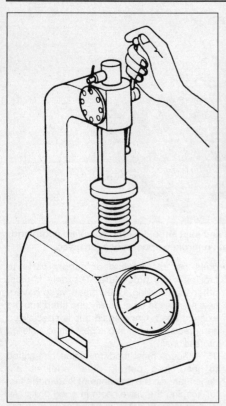

9.41 Valve spring pressure is checked on a test rig at a set length

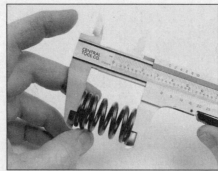

9.42 Measure the free length of each spring

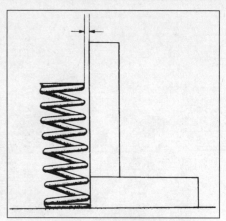

9.43 Check the valve spring for squareness

observed during assembly. This information usually appears in the workshop manual, but do not rely on it being available; always check this yourself during dismantling.

38 Initial checks should be made, looking for any indication of cracks at any point of the spring coils. Such defects will mean that the spring should be renewed as a matter of course, and common sense dictates that the remaining springs should be renewed as a precaution against their subsequent failure.

39 After a period of use, the effects of heat will begin to weaken the springs. This may not become apparent in normal use, but if the machine were to over-rev as the result of a missed gearchange, it is possible that the weakened springs might allow the valves to strike each other. When valves get tangled in this fashion, both are wedged open, and the next time the piston nears top dead centre, bent valves and a holed piston usually result.

40 Less dramatic symptoms include valve bounce, where maximum engine speed, and thus power, is restricted by the lazy response of the valves due to the weakened springs.

41 To avoid these occurrences, the springs should be checked during the overhaul. Many manufacturers specify the minimum pressure of each spring when it is compressed to a specified length. Whilst this is a good way to assess condition, it requires a special test rig to do so **(see illustration)**.

42 Other ways of specifying service limits on springs is to define a minimum free length, the spring being due for renewal if it has become permanently compressed to this limit. This is more easily checked by simple measurement, using a steel rule or a vernier gauge **(see illustration)**.

43 You should also check that the springs are still true, renewing them if distorted. This is easily checked with a set square **(see illustration)**, or by rolling the spring on the surface plate or any flat surface.

44 In the absence of the necessary service limits for the valve springs, it is worth renewing them as a precautionary measure on a high mileage engine. The relatively low cost is more than offset by the comparative cost of damage which could be caused by just one defective spring.

10 Camshafts, cam followers and rockers

1 The majority of four-stroke engine designs use a single overhead camshaft (sohc) or double overhead camshaft (dohc) layout.

2 Depending on the design, movement from the cam lobe is transmitted directly to the valve stem through a bucket-shaped cam follower, or indirectly through rockers.

3 Normally, dohc designs opt for the more efficient bucket-type cam follower **(see illustrations)**, though where more than two valves per cylinder are used it is necessary to use rockers to allow independent adjustment

10.3a The bucket-type cam followers contain shims to provide the correct valve clearance

10.3b The thickness of each shim is marked on the surface, although this may be checked using a micrometer

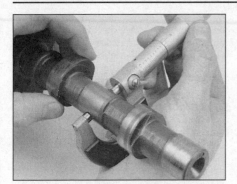

10.5a Measuring the cam bearing journal with a micrometer

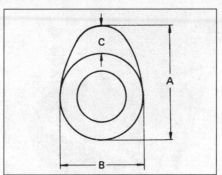

10.5b Camshaft lobe dimensions: A is the lobe height, B is the base circle diameter and C is the cam lift

of each valve clearance setting within the confines imposed by the valve layout.

4 In the case of pushrod-operated overhead valve (ohv) designs which are still in use on some models, notably Honda's CG125, the camshaft resides in the crankcase. Reciprocating motion is transmitted to rockers housed in the cylinder head by means of pushrods. Check that the pushrods are straight and the ends are undamaged.

5 The general check of the camshaft lobes and bearing surfaces have been discussed earlier in this Chapter, and reference should be made to this when assessing wear and damage. Most manufacturers specify service limits for bearing surfaces and lobe heights, and these can be measured using a micrometer **(see illustrations)**. This will give an accurate picture of the degree of wear of these areas, though in practice a visual check for scoring, scuffing and other damage to the surfaces is likely to be more revealing.

6 You will also need to check all other associated parts for wear or damage, as detailed in the workshop manual. Wear in cam followers, rocker mechanisms and the camshaft drive and tensioner can create a lot of mechanical noise, and it is as well to eliminate this at an early stage in the overhaul.

11 Cylinder bores

Cylinder bore examination

1 When examining the cylinder bore(s) and piston(s), attention should be focused on the condition of the bore surface before consideration is given to that of the piston. This is for the simple reason that if the bore is found to be worn or badly scored, you will have to have it rebored to suit an oversized piston, and it follows that further attention to the existing piston would be pointless. Note that certain bores cannot be rebored (see end of this Section).

2 After thorough cleaning, examine the bore surface closely, looking for signs of score marks or other damage **(see illustration)**. This will be made easier if a light source is shone through from the far end of the bore.

3 Towards the lower end of the bore you will find an unworn area denoting the extent of piston travel in this direction. You will need to use this part of the bore as a reference point for further inspection and any measurement.

4 Careful examination of the unworn part of

the bore will reveal a smooth machined surface, and you should be able to see a diagonal or diamond pattern formed by the fine honing marks left after the bore was originally finished; these fine scratch marks are intentional, and provide a good basis for comparing the rest of the bore surface.

5 As you move up the bore, the honing marks will become more faint, eventually being replaced by vertical marks where the piston has worn the bore surface down. These will be most evident on the parts of the bore corresponding to the piston thrust faces, at 90° to the piston pin bore.

6 At the upper limit of piston travel, a distinct wear line or ridge will be found, a few millimetres below the top of the bore, denoting the upper limit of travel of the top ring **(see illustration)**. With a few exceptions, bore wear will be greatest at this point, again at 90° to the piston pin axis.

7 Before checking for wear, satisfy yourself that the bore is in good general condition. Very light vertical lines are normal and acceptable, but any scoring deep enough to allow the loss of compression pressure means that reboring will be needed. Damage of this sort is almost invariably due to dirt getting into the engine either because the air filter has been omitted or used in a damaged condition, or in the case of four-strokes, because the oil has not been changed regularly.

8 Another cause is a blocked oil filter, which will have caused the bypass valve to open and let unfiltered oil circulate.

9 Whatever the cause of the contamination, the dirt inside the engine will have been trapped between the piston or rings and the cylinder walls, each particle acting as a cutting edge and wearing grooves into the wall. Where scoring is severe and deep on the thrust faces of the piston and on the corresponding area of the bore, partial seizure due to overheating or inadequate lubrication may have occurred. In such cases the piston skirt area will be badly scored, with areas of

11.2 If you find damage like this, put away the measuring tools. It is clear that a rebore and piston will be needed

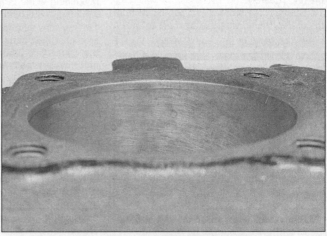

11.6 The wear ridge clearly shown

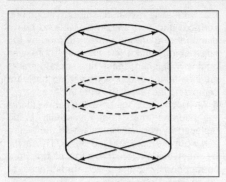

11.10a Bore measurement points. Make sure that you measure at right-angles to the bore

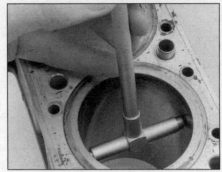

11.10b Use a telescoping bore gauge and read off the measurement with a micrometer

the skirt material smeared down the piston. Sometimes this will have caused the piston rings to become trapped in their grooves. Once again, if damage of this nature is evident, reboring will be needed.

10 Measure the bore **(see illustrations)** and compare the readings with the manufacturer's quoted service limits. Bore wear is usually in the region of 0.1 mm, though you should check the exact figure in the workshop manual. Accurate measurement will require checks of the bore diameter to be made at several places along the bore to find the area of maximum wear. From this is subtracted the diameter measured at the unworn area to give the amount of overall wear.

11 If you do not have the necessary equipment for this check to be made, use one of the piston compression rings to gain an approximate indication of the extent of wear as follows. Place the ring into the bottom of the bore, using the edge of the piston skirt to position it square in the bore.

12 Using feeler gauges, measure the end gap between the two ends of the ring **(see illustration)**, and make a note of the reading. Now repeat this procedure, this time with the ring positioned just below the wear ridge near the top of the bore; use a steel rule or the depth gauge on the vernier to help position the ring squarely.

13 Subtract the smaller end gap figure from the larger, then divide this by three to give a rough wear figure. If this exceeds the

11.12 Using piston ring end gap to determine bore wear

manufacturer's service limit for bore wear or taper, it is time for a rebore. Note that it is advisable to have your findings confirmed by an expert before taking further action.

14 Some manufacturers specify a figure for maximum ovality, or out-of-round. This requires several measurements to be made along the bore in each position taking one measurement in line with the piston pin axis and one at 90° to it. It is only feasible to make this type of measurement using direct and precise measuring equipment; the ring-and-feeler gauge method will not give an accurate indication.

Reboring and honing

Reboring

15 If wear or damage has been found it will be necessary to arrange a rebore.

16 Most dealers will have an arrangement with a local engine reconditioner or small engineering works for dealing with this type of machining, in which case you should make arrangements to deliver the cylinder barrel or block to the dealer, who will then supply the necessary pistons and get the work carried out.

17 If you intend dealing direct with an engineering company, or if you want any other machining work carried out, you should first work out exactly what you require to be done.

18 You may also have to supply pistons, or any other new parts which are to be fitted. If the chosen company deal specifically with motorcycle repair work they may have their own source of replacement parts, but often it will be quicker and easier if you supply these yourself. In the case of pistons, you will have to check the existing bore size, calculating from this the next oversize for the new pistons.

19 Make sure that the proposed rebore will remove all existing damage and order pistons accordingly, checking the available oversizes in the workshop manual.

20 As a general rule, piston oversizes are supplied in 0.50 mm increments, and there are usually two oversizes available; +0.50 mm and +1.00 mm. These steps are chosen so that normal wear or damage will be removed

by reboring to the next oversize, but you must be certain that this is the case before ordering. Note that oversizes in increment of +0.25 mm may be available for some engines – check with your dealer or an aftermarket piston supplier. Don't forget to order suitable rings for the new piston(s).

21 If, for example, the engine has a nominal bore size of 50 mm, and this is worn to 50.30 mm at the worst point, there is little point ordering +0.25 mm pistons; reboring to this size will not remove the damage, and you will have to go up two sizes to +0.50 mm. On multi-cylinder engines, the deciding factor will be the most worn bore, the remaining bores being taken out to the same size as this.

22 You must also take into account whether the engine has been rebored previously, and if so, whether further oversizes are available. This will be indicated after the bore(s) have been measured, though in some cases the oversize markings on the piston crown will be visible after cleaning.

23 If the engine has been bored to its maximum oversize on an earlier occasion, you may need to purchase a new cylinder barrel or block and start again with new standard pistons. On certain wet liner design engines you can renew the liners separately from the cylinder block. Decisions of this sort will require expert advice.

24 If you are arranging the work through a dealer, or if the engineering shop agree to take care of the whole process, you can leave them to make the required calculations. Do check whether they require specification information, and if required remember to supply this when you take the work in. In particular, provide details of the piston-to-bore clearances so that the bores can be finished to suit the new pistons.

25 Reboring may be done on the workshop lathe, although this is perhaps an adventurous project for amateur machinists.

Honing

26 Where you propose to fit new rings in an existing bore, it is well worth getting the bore honed, both to provide the cross-hatched surface needed to allow the rings to bed in normally, and to remove any wear ridge from the top of the bore.

Honing is carried out using a special tool comprising abrasive stones held in either a flexible or a fixed honing tool.

27 A flexible hone is spring-loaded and this ensures that the correct pressure is applied automatically to the stones as the tool rotates in the bore. This type of tool will remove the glaze from an existing bore, but is less good at removing the wear ridge.

28 Another popular type of tool for the removal of glaze is the *Flex-Hone* and similar devices. These look rather like large bottle brushes, the end of each bristle terminating in an abrasive tip.

29 Even when the cylinder and piston are within the service limits, honing the bore will

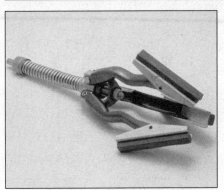

11.30a A simple flexible stone-type hone . . .

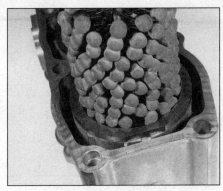

11.30b . . . and a bottle brush type hone

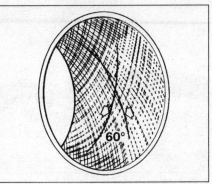

11.31 The bore should have a cross-hatch pattern, the lines intersecting at approximately 60°

remove the glaze caused by heated deposits left on the cylinder wall.

30 Honing can be done in the home workshop. You will need a flexible hone of the correct size fitted with fine stones **(see illustration)**, or a bottle brush type hone **(see illustration)**, plenty of light oil, ideally honing oil, clean rags and an electric drill motor set to run at a slow speed.

31 Hold the cylinder block in your vice using soft jaws so that the bores are horizontal or clamp the block to the work table of the pillar drill. The block can also be held to the bench top if it is too big for the vice or pillar drill. Mount the hone in the drill motor, compress the stones and insert the hone into the cylinder. Thoroughly lubricate the cylinder, then turn on the drill and move the hone up and down in the cylinder at a speed which produces a fine cross hatch pattern on the cylinder wall with the lines intersecting at approximately 60° **(see illustration)**.

32 Be sure to use plenty of oil and remove only sufficient material to give the desired effect.

33 When the cross hatching is seen, turn off the drill, but keep moving the hone until it stops revolving. The compress the stones and remove the hone.

34 Wipe the oil from the cylinder and repeat the procedure in the other bores of multi-cylinder engines.

35 At the end of all the honing operations wash the cylinders out with water to remove all traces of grit and swarf. Check that oil ways and stud holes are clean. After rinsing, apply a thin coat of light rust preventative oil to all the machined surfaces.

36 Honing will not remove the wear ridge. Ridge removal requires the use of a de-ridging tool prior to flexible honing, or the use of a fixed hone which is capable of removing the ridge as part of the honing process **(see illustration)**.

37 Although it might seem an insignificant process, the quality of the final honing has a lot to do with the success or failure of the whole reboring operation. Poor honing will cause excessive oil consumption, poor ring sealing or even abnormal ring wear.

External examination

38 Examine the outside of the block for broken fins, broken or damaged fasteners and threaded holes. Check that studs are not loose in their threaded holes.

39 Where heat is required as part of any repair procedure it is as well to carry out this work before work on the cylinder bores.

Special cases

40 Cylinders bores which have been treated with the Nicosil plating process can be reclaimed by specialist engine reconditioners, but cannot be rebored as described above.

41 New liners for two and four stroke engines and two-stroke porting can be carried out by specialist engine reconditioners. New liners may be required when several rebores have been carried out, or when extensive damage has occurred, and may be the only way to keep an old engine running. Note that new liners can be fitted to a liquid-cooled wet liner engine and renewal is the usual solution when the wear limit has been exceeded.

12 Pistons and rings

1 Before checking the pistons, first check the cylinder bore condition. If a rebore, new liners or a new cylinder block is required, new pistons will also be required.

2 If the pistons are still in place on the connecting rods, remove the circlips which retain the piston pin **(see illustrations)**, displacing the pin to free the piston from the connecting rod.

11.36 A fixed hone like this is required to remove an appreciable wear ridge

12.2a Wire circlips retain the piston pin on most engines and can be removed with long-nosed pliers

12.2b Where stamped circlips are fitted, use circlip pliers to remove them

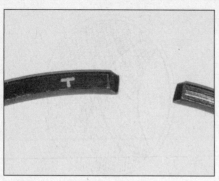

12.7 As each ring is removed, note any markings denoting the top surface of the ring

12.9a The luxury of a ring removal tool

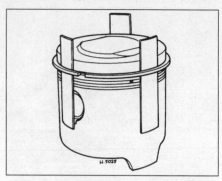

12.9b A cheap alternative is to use several thin steel blades, working them under the ring at equidistant points around its circumference

3 If this fails to allow removal, warm the piston with near-boiling water, taking care to avoid scalding your hands. The piston will expand with the heat and the pin should then push out easily.

4 As a last resort, use a pin removal tool or make up a drawbolt arrangement to remove the pin, but take care not to damage the piston's working surfaces.

5 Never resort to drifting the pin out or you risk damage to the connecting rod and bearings.

6 To prevent the circlip springing away or dropping into the crankcase, pass a screwdriver or rod, whose diameter is greater than the gap between the circlip ends,

through the piston pin. This will trap the circlip if it springs out. It is also a sensible precaution to cover the open mouth of the crankcase with a rag to prevent the pin disappearing into the case if it is accidentally dropped.

7 Continue preparation by removing the piston rings, taking care not to break them during removal. As each ring is removed, it should be checked for markings **(see illustration)**. Many rings have a letter or other marking near one end, and this normally indicates the upper face of the ring. It is important to fit rings in the correct groove and the right way up; some rings have a slight taper section.

8 To be on the safe side, mark each ring as it is removed to indicate its position and upper surface. A spirit-based felt marker is ideal for this.

9 It is possible to purchase ring removal tools which minimise the risk of breakage **(see illustration)**. A cheap alternative is to use several thin steel blades, working them under the ring at equidistant points around its circumference **(see illustration)**. With the ring lifted just clear of the ring groove in this way, it can be slid off the piston with ease.

10 The traditional method is to spread the ring ends with the thumbs and then slide the ring off the piston. Note that this requires a good deal of care if the ring is to be removed in one piece; piston rings are usually of cast construction and thus very brittle.

11 On occasions, two similar-looking rings will in fact differ minutely in section, or one may have a plated working face. All such factors should be noted, bearing in mind that you may not be reassembling the engine for some time if much work is needed, and it is very easy to forget such details **(see illustration 12.22)**.

12 Clean off all accumulated carbon from the piston crown using a blunt scraper and/or brass wire brushes.

13 The ring grooves must also be cleaned out, but great care must be taken to avoid enlarging them. You can buy abrasive string which is ideal for cleaning piston ring grooves. Otherwise patient and careful scraping is necessary, using whatever improvised tool you can find or make up. If you have a broken piston ring to hand, the end of this will make a good scraping tool. If you can get the pistons dipped in a carbon removing solvent tank, all the better.

14 Assuming that there is no obvious damage which would make further examination pointless, check the piston carefully for signs of cracking, especially around the bosses inside the skirt. Any hint of cracks will mean discarding the piston as a precaution against its complete disintegration later. If you have any doubts, have the pistons crack detected **(see illustrations)**.

15 Check the condition of the piston pin and the bores in the piston bosses **(see illustrations)**. Slip the piston pin back in place

12.14a This two-stroke piston has suffered when the rings welded themselves to the bore

12.14b Another two-stroke piston where the ring locating pin broke loose

12.14c The ring here has broken up and destroyed the piston

12.15a Measure the external diameter of the piston pin

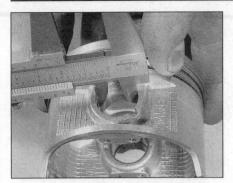

12.15b Measure the diameters of the piston pin bores in two or more places for each bore

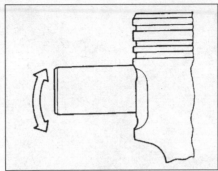

12.15c Slip the pin into the piston and try rocking it from side to side

12.17 Measure the piston at 90° to the piston pin bore

and try and rock it back and forth **(see illustration)**. If there is any play to be felt between the pin and the bores, or these have become worn or damaged through seizure, the piston and pin should be considered unserviceable. If you attempt to re-use the piston in this condition, the engine will be noisy, and the repeated impact allowed by the play can cause the bosses to fracture and break up.

16 The areas to be measured for wear will depend on the service information supplied by the manufacturer. Often a piston-to-bore figure is quoted, and this will have to be checked by direct measurement of both bore and piston. Subtract the piston diameter from the bore diameter to obtain the clearance figure.

17 It should be noted that pistons are usually slightly oval in section, the widest diameter being at the thrust faces, or at 90° to the piston pin axis. Wear will occur on the thrust faces, and is generally most significant near the base of the skirt due to the rocking action of the piston as it passes TDC and BDC, therefore measure the piston a short distance up from the bottom of the skirt **(see illustration)**. This distance may be specified in the manual.

18 Wear will also be evident in the rings and in the ring grooves. The ring groove widths should be examined and measured using a vernier gauge, or by checking with a new ring and feeler gauges **(see illustration)**. If the ring groove has become enlarged, there is little option to renewing the piston.

19 Wear of the working face of each ring where it bears upon the cylinder wall is fairly obvious, and this is usually checked by inserting the ring in the unworn area at the base of its bore and measuring the ring end

gap with feeler gauges **(see illustration)**. If the installed end gap service limit is reached or exceeded, renewal will be required. The free end gap, between ends of the ring may also be quoted in the specifications **(see illustration)**.

20 The end gap may be enlarged by clamping a file in the vice and filing the ring ends **(see illustration)**.

21 Less obviously, the ring top and bottom surfaces will become worn due to the continual reversal of thrust as the engine runs.

12.18 Checking the clearance in the groove using feeler gauges and a new ring

12.19a As when checking for bore wear, the ring is inserted in the bore to check the 'installed' end gap

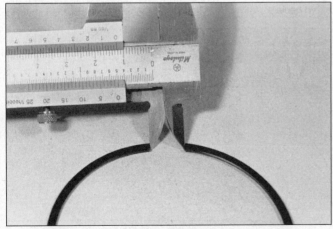

12.19b Using a vernier to check the 'free' end gap

12.20 Adjusting the end gap by filing

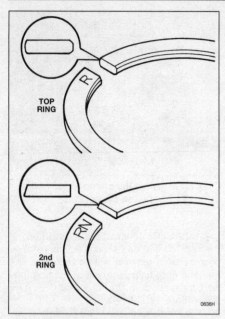

12.22 Typical differing ring markings and profiles for the compression rings

Most manufacturers quote a service limit for ring thickness, and this can be measured using a micrometer.

22 When installing rings do not confuse the top ring with the second; they may have different cross sectional shapes **(see illustration)**. The rings can be installed by hand or a ring installation tool can be used – do not expand the rings any more than is necessary to slip them over the piston. Always install the oil scraper ring on four-strokes by hand.

23 Fitting new rings would appear to be an easy and inexpensive way of getting more mileage from a part-worn engine, but in reality this practice is fraught with problems.

24 First of all, whilst the additional depth of a new ring may help locate it in an unworn section of the ring groove, the outer edge will lack proper support where ring groove wear has occurred. This can allow the ring to

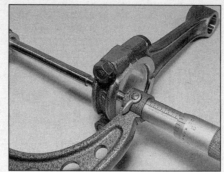

13.3a Measuring the width of the connecting rod

'flutter' in the groove and this will often cause rapid failure. The unworn area at the back of the ring groove can often be seen as a step in the sides of the groove.

25 Worst still is the problem of the wear ridge at the top of each bore. This is **always** present on a used engine, and the old rings will have worn to accommodate it.

26 If you fit new rings, the likelihood is that the top ring will strike this ridge and cause the ring to break up. This problem is avoided by removing the wear ridge.

27 When fitting an oversize piston make sure that the new rings are specified for that new size.

13 Connecting rods

1 Firstly check the connecting rod or rods for any obvious cracks or damage.

2 Check for any play between the small-end bearing and the piston pin as already described in Section 12 above.

3 At the big-end, measure the width of the crank pin and the width of the connecting rod **(see illustrations)**, and compare these with the specifications. Connecting rod sideplay be measured with feeler gauges **(see illustration)**.

13.3b Measuring the width between the crankshaft webs

13.3c Measuring connecting rod sideplay with feeler gauges

4 It is important that the connecting rod is not bend or twisted. This can be checked using the method described in paragraph 5 or 6.

5 Hold the connecting rod down on a parallel sided block on a surface plate. Use a dial gauge held in a stand and run the probe around the small-end boss. Any variation from side to side will indicate a twist in the rod. Turn the rod over and repeat the exercise. Any difference in reading from the first side will indicate that the rod is bent **(see illustration)**.

6 To check for bending, assemble the con-rod halves on a round bar which fits snugly in the big-end eye. Rest the bar in V-blocks and support the rod in an upright position **(see illustration)**. Fit another bar through the

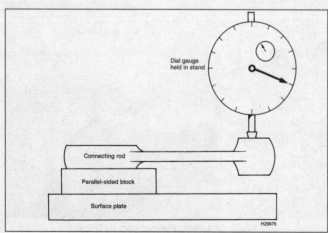

13.5 Checking the rod for twisting and bending

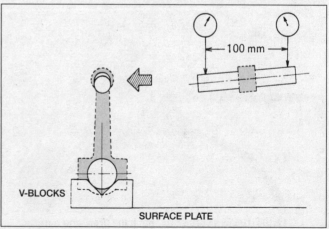

13.6a Checking the rod for bending

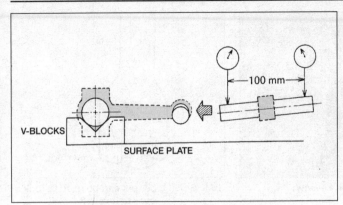

13.6b Checking the rod for twisting

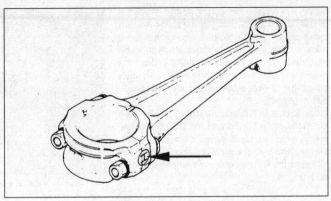

13.8 Typical connecting rod weight marking

small-end eye, positioning it centrally. At a point 50 mm from the centre of the small-end eye measure the distance from the bar to the surface, then do this 50 mm from the other side of the small-end. The distance should be identical on each side. You can alternatively mount a dial gauge above the bar and measure the depth to each point on the bar. To check for twisting of the rod, mount the big-end eye on V-blocks as described above and support the rod on its side **(see illustration)**. Again measure the distance from the bar to the work surface over a 100 mm length. Alternatively measure the depth from above with a dial gauge.

7 Do not attempt to straighten a bend connecting rod, replace it with a new one.

8 On any multi-cylinder engine, it is important that the connecting rods are of the same weight to minimise vibration. Rods are usually marked with a letter etched on one of their machined faces **(see illustration)**. Always replace the rod with one of the same weight group. Be careful not to confuse the weight marking on the rod with either the cylinder identification or bearing insert size code.

14 Damaged castings

1 The procedure for making effective repairs to casting damage will depend on the nature of the damage and its location. Impact damage to an unstressed outer cover, perhaps resulting from the machine being dropped, is annoying but relatively easy to deal with.

2 Internal fractures of the crankcase assembly due to stress or catastrophic failure of some internal engine part are an entirely different matter, and you will have to seek expert advice to find out whether repair would be viable. In many instances it will be easier and a lot safer to renew the damaged casting.

3 A collection of bits can be rebuilt, however the dimensional accuracy of the reconstructed part must be checked.

Welding

4 Castings can be repaired by expert welding. They can be difficult and unpredictable to weld, even in expert hands and using the best equipment. At best, the finished result is likely to be serviceable rather than cosmetically pleasing.

5 Any repair procedure involving heating, such as welding, will require careful consideration as to the long term effects on the internal structure and strength of the material. You must also consider whether the heating and cooling might cause any dimensional changes and misalignment problems. The latter would require corrective machining operations such as line boring and reaming of bearing housings which may be beyond the scope of the home workshop.

Epoxy fillers and putty

6 A range of steel or aluminium putties and fillers are available which can be treated as the parent metal when cured. They can be drilled and tapped and used to rebuild worn parts.

7 The cracked area must be absolutely clean and free from all traces of oil or grease. Apply the putty or filler according to the manufacturer's directions, trying to follow the final surface shape as closely as possible (the resin sets very hard and sanding it is no fun).

8 The finished repair can be disguised by refinishing.

Low temperature aluminium welding

9 For more information, refer to Chapter 7.

15 Engine seizure

1 In cases of total seizure you may have problems in getting the engine apart.

2 Applying penetrating oil around the top of the piston after the cylinder head has been removed may help to free it off, but often this will not work. In such cases, try dismantling

the engine around the cylinder barrel/piston assembly if you can. The crankshaft assembly and the cylinder barrel or block can then be taken as a unit to the bench for further attention. Where this is not possible, you will have to try to separate the piston from the bore in position.

3 With any serious seizure, you should accept that the piston at least is likely to be of little further use. The best that can be done at this stage is to try to avoid further damage to other engine parts. It may be possible to dislodge the piston by passing a length of timber down from the top of the bore and using this to drive the piston out. It will help if an assistant pulls upwards on the barrel or block.

4 In really extreme cases, you may have to demolish the piston so that the crankshaft can be freed, hopefully without damage to the crankshaft assembly. The exact method used will have to be decided according to individual circumstances, but will inevitably have to be fairly barbaric. Try to separate the crankshaft assembly from the crankcases if this is at all possible, leaving the crankshaft with the seized piston and barrel or block attached.

5 One possible approach is to chain drill around the piston crown to detach it from the seized skirt, remembering that the hardened steel piston pin will have to be avoided during this operation.

6 Once the crankshaft is freed in this way you will be left with the skirt area to be cut or chiselled out of the bore. This should be done with care, trying not to cause any more damage to the bore surface.

7 A less dramatic method is to have the seized piston pressed out of the bore, assuming that it is possible to gain access to allow this to be done. It is not easy to carry this out at home, and this job is probably best left to an engineering company.

8 Seized rings, where the ring land material has become smeared over the rings, trapping them in their grooves, will require careful freeing off, scraping away the smeared alloy until they can be removed and the grooves cleaned up properly.

9 Unless the seizure was only partial, the

piston will have been damaged too much for re-use. Very light scuffing of the skirt area can be rectified with judicious use of abrasive paper or fine files, but if material needs to be removed in this way it is unlikely that the piston will give the correct clearance. In such cases it is always more effective to renew the piston assembly.

10 In cases of full seizure, there will be little alternative to reboring and the fitting of a new oversize piston. In all cases of seizure, make certain that you establish and rectify the cause of the failure before the engine is rebuilt and run.

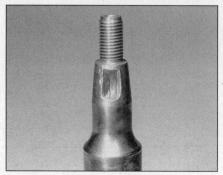

16.4 A worn keyway

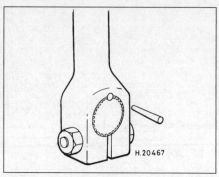

16.9 Small taper pin can be used to lock a lever to its shaft

16 Spline and keyway damage

1 Splines and keyways are frequently-used methods of locating parts on the ends of the various engine shafts, common uses ranging from alternator rotors, which are often keyed to the tapered end of the crankshaft, to components like the gearchange lever, which will normally be splined to the end of its shaft.
2 In general, the spline or key acts as a method of location, the component being secured in place with a nut or pinch bolt. In the case of the gearbox shafts, though, the gears are allowed a controlled amount of lateral movement for selection purposes, this being limited by circlips or shoulders machined into the shaft.
3 Where the component is fixed in position, wear is unlikely to take place unless it is not secured properly. If this happens, the component will chatter in relation to its spline or key, wearing both parts. A common example of this can be found on many kickstart levers; if not tightened securely, the splines of both the shaft and the lever will wear quite rapidly. If even slight wear is discovered it should be dealt with before it can become worse.
4 In the case of keyways, remove and examine the key. If it is worn, try fitting a new one, but check that this will prevent further

movement. If the keyway is worn **(see illustration)**, it is best to have the area built up with weld and a new keyway machined into the shaft end.
5 A suitable epoxy compound may also be used. If you do this, be sure to avoid getting the product on the taper surface, or you may never get the joint apart again!
6 Splines are less easy to deal with by welding, and in these cases it is preferable to use one of the epoxy based metal fillers to eliminate freeplay, provided that the spline supports a fixed component.
7 With worn kickstart or gearchange splines, check both parts for wear. If only the lever splines are worn, you may be able to resolve the problem by renewing the worn part. If the shaft splines are worn too, you can try using an epoxy compound to avoid the need to remove and renew the shaft to which it is attached.
8 Remember that you will have to allow for the need to remove the lever occasionally, so avoid any product which will produce a permanent joint.
9 A traditional method of repair, which avoids the need to renew the shaft, is to fit the lever in its normal position and then to drill a hole along the length of one spline, leaving a semi-circular slot in both parts. A hard steel taper pin, available from engineering suppliers, can then be tapped in place to locate the lever, and the pinch bolt tightened to secure it **(see illustration)**.

17 Clutch and gearbox – overhaul

Clutch

1 If the splined clutch centre becomes worn, the clutch plates will tend to chatter against it, causing indenting of either the splines or the slots in the outer drum. Damage of this type can often be responsible for erratic clutch operation, symptoms such as unreliable engagement or dragging occurring as the plates catch in the indentations **(see illustration)**.
2 In the case of the clutch outer drum, it is usually worth filing the drum slots flat and smooth, provided that the damage is not too severe **(see illustration)**. This will usually restore normal operation. In cases of heavy damage, however, the drum should be renewed.
3 The clutch centre is less likely to suffer, but should problems arise it is almost impossible to correct by filing **(see illustration)**. In such cases the clutch centre should be renewed, together with the plain and friction plates where these have become sloppy or badly worn.
4 Similar problems can occur in the case of wear between the clutch centre and the shaft to which it is attached **(see illustration 17.3)**, although this is normally prevented by the

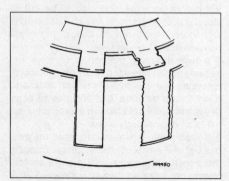

17.1 Comparison of unworn (left) and worn (right) friction plate and drum slots

17.2 Outer drum slots should be smooth and free of indentations – this example is worn

17.3 Check the clutch centre for wear from the plain plates (left arrow) and shaft splines (right arrow)

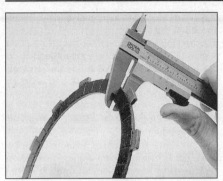

17.6a A vernier gauge is ideal for measuring . . .

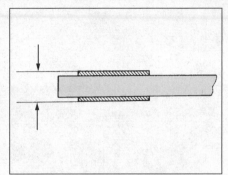

17.6b . . . clutch friction plate thickness

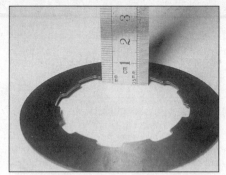

17.7 A steel rule can be used to measure diaphragm spring height

centre being secured in place by a retaining nut or circlip.

5 Inspect the plain plates for any sign of heating, which may have brought about a blueish colour change and check them for warpage on your surface plate **(see illustration 2.6 in Chapter 4)**.

6 Inspect the friction plates for signs of burning or glazing, measure the thickness with your vernier caliper **(see illustrations)**, and check for warpage. If they do not meet the specifications they must be replaced as a set.

7 Check the free length of the clutch springs and compare them with the specifications in the manual **(see illustration 9.42)**. The diaphragm springs can be checked by laying them on your surface plate and measuring the height of the inner edge using a ruler or the depth gauge on the vernier **(see illustration)**.

8 On hydraulically operated clutches check the master and slave cylinders, and pipework for leaks as you would for the braking system. Remember to carry out the correct procedure to bleed the system.

Gearbox

9 On gearbox shafts, or other instances where a sliding component is involved, wear will necessitate the renewal of the shaft and/or gear concerned; it is not possible to repair this sort of damage economically, and unless the shaft or gear is unobtainable, it is not worth having the damaged splines welded and re-machined.

10 Imprecise gear changes or the machine jumping out of gear are often indicative of worn dogs on the gear pinions. Check these for wear or damage, looking for rounded off or deformed leading edges **(see illustration)**. The best course of action in such cases is to renew the damaged parts, though it may be possible to have the dogs built up with weld and then filed and ground back to shape.

11 Erratic gear selection can also be attributed to worn or bent selector forks, worn grooves or worn selector drum tracks. These should be checked visually for obvious damage, and the fork and groove widths measured **(see illustrations)**, and compared with the specified dimensions. If wear of this type is discovered it is normally best to renew the gear(s) or the selector fork(s) as required.

12 Worn or chipped gear teeth will usually be obvious on inspection. This type of damage can occur as a result of general wear, abuse or neglected oil changes. The cost of building

17.10 Worn dogs like these will cause the machine to jump out of gear

up and recutting the gear teeth make repairs impractical; fit new gear pinions, preferably as pairs.

18 Gasket removal

1 All traces of old gasket material must be cleaned off jointing faces before they are reassembled with new gaskets or gasket compound.

17.11a Measure the width of the selector forks

17.11b Checking the amount of play between the groove and the fork. If this is excessive, gear selection problems may occur

18.2a Scrape off the gasket with a tool made from aluminium or brass

18.2b A knife blade will slice off paper gaskets

18.2c A household paint scraper will also do the job

18.2d A wire wool or plastic scourer will remove stubborn deposits and do a general clean up

2 Gaskets may be scraped off with a scraper tool made up from aluminium or brass, a knife blade, or a household paint scraper. A kitchen scourer may be useful in getting rid of stubborn deposits **(see illustrations)**.
3 The work has to be done carefully so as to avoid damage. Take care not to nick, or cut into the gasket face.
4 Before scraping areas where the gasket is firmly stuck, use one of the gasket removing products which are available from motor accessory shops.
5 Fine abrasive paper, wrapped round a flat file will clean up the gasket face **(see illustration)**.

Try and use it on opposite sides of the component mating face at the same time to ensure that it is held flat.

19 Runout checks

1 During most overhaul procedures it will be necessary to check the runout of one or more shafts against the service limits specified by the manufacturer, and this is even more important after a component failure which may have resulted in abnormal loadings being applied to the shaft.
2 An example would be after the failure of an engine or transmission component leading to the locking of the drive train; the sudden heavy torque loadings may have caused shaft damage, and this must be checked during the repair.
3 Refer to Chapter 4, Section 6 for runout checking equipment.
4 In principle any shaft or assembly can be checked for runout by holding it between centres or on vee blocks and rotating it with the probe of a dial gauge resting on it. Variations in the dial gauge reading give an indication of the straightness of the component about its axis **(see illustration)**. Note that manufacturers often specified a runout limit at a specified distance from the ends or centre of a shaft.
5 As a general rule it is not practical to attempt to straighten any machined part which has become bent in service. It will be almost impossible to get it true again, and even if you succeed, there is no guarantee that the stresses left in the metal will not lead to a fracture at a later date. In such cases it is always best to play safe and renew the damaged part.

20 End-float checks and shimming

1 Many of the shafts and other components on motorcycle engine/transmission units are assembled to fine tolerances to allow only a controlled amount of end-float. This ensures that meshing parts align correctly and keep to a minimum the noise and vibration which would occur if this play were excessive.
2 In many instances this free movement is governed by machining tolerances, and if the service limit figure is exceeded, renewal of the worn part(s) is indicated. Refer to Chapter 4, Section 6 for end-float checking equipment

18.5 Removing slight damage using fine grade abrasive paper wrapped around a flat file

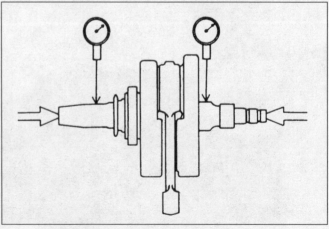

19.4 Checking runout on a crankshaft assembly

20.6a One or more shims can be found on shaft ends to control end-float

20.6b Shim size can be measured with a micrometer

3 Where shims are used to control end-float, it is essential that care is taken during dismantling to ensure that each shim is placed over the shaft to which it belongs, in the correct relative position. This is especially important in the case of some European models and failure to keep track of these shims during an overhaul may result in hours of meticulous checking, possibly requiring professional help.

4 Whatever the machine, never put all the various shims and washers together in one container.

5 In the case of certain plain bearing crankshafts, special semi-circular end-float shims are often found at one or more of the bearing caps. Like the bearing inserts, these must be checked and a new shim selected from the available range if endplay proves excessive.

6 In the case of the gearbox shafts, the position of one or more of the gear pinions will be controlled by plain round shims, rather like thin steel washers. Again, these can be obtained in varying thicknesses in most cases, allowing fine adjustment of end-float of the individual pinions **(see illustrations)**.

7 In roller bearing big-ends, end-float is allowed so that the connecting rod and piston can run true to the bore, a fairly generous allowance being made to compensate for machining tolerances. The play is controlled by thrust washers, and thus cannot be altered without pressing apart the big-end assembly.

8 On machines where pairs of bevel gears are used, typically those machines employing shaft final drive, shims are used to control the mesh depth of the gear teeth. This is a critical adjustment, and if too tight the gear teeth will wear rapidly, whilst excessive play will result in gear whine and backlash.

9 Shims may take the form of shim washers, or may be in the form of specially-shaped shims fitted to gasket faces of bevel drive housings. Exact details of the arrangements used will be found in the workshop manual.

10 In each of the above examples, measurement of end-float is made using either a dial gauge or by inserting feeler gauges at a specified point. Checking these clearances is an important stage of any overhaul, and can make a lot of difference to the smoothness and life of the rebuilt engine; do not overlook them. Additionally, it is

sometimes necessary to measure casing depth and perform a calculation to arrive at the correct shim thickness **(see illustration)**.

11 Another significant application of shimming will be found in the shim adjustment used in the valve clearance setting of many dohc four-stroke fours **(see illustration)**. Each of the tubular cam followers houses a shim selected from a range produced by the manufacturer for this purpose. Clearance adjustment by this method is inclined to be more lasting than screw-and-locknut arrangements, though less simple to correct. Many dealers keep a large range of these shims in stock, and may agree to allow you to exchange unwanted shims for those of the correct size.

21 Exhaust system

1 The exhaust system should be considered a semi-consumable item, its life depending upon the climate, the quality of the painted or plated finish of the system, road conditions

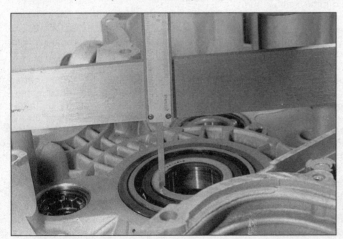

20.10 Shim size calculation using a depth gauge and a straight-edge placed across the crankcase surface

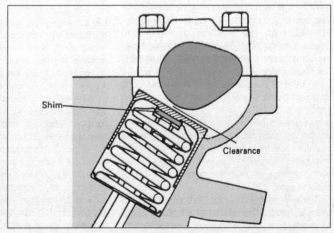

20.11 Different size shims are used to control valve clearance adjustment

Shim

Clearance

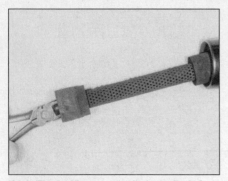

21.9 The baffle can usually be pulled clear after removing the retaining bolt

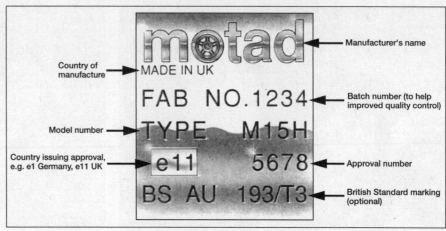

21.17 A stamp such as this ensures the purchaser that the equipment is fully compliant with current legislation

and usage of the machine. During use, the system passes the exhaust gases, including a certain amount of acidic compounds, and numerous short journeys and cool weather will allow some of this to condense on the inside of the system as it cools down. Longer runs and hot temperatures reduce the amount of acidic deposits, and tend to make the system last longer.

2 It is worth noting that many four-stroke systems will be found to have small drain holes at the lowest point of the system. These are meant to allow condensation to drain away, and it is worth checking and unblocking them regularly.

3 The exhaust gases from a two-stroke engine are more oily than those from a four-stroke because they can contain a much higher percentage of burnt or partially burnt oil that is expelled from the exhaust ports, along with some unburnt fuel. Note, however, that the use of unleaded fuel and modern two-stroke oils will result in a cleaner exhaust system.

Removal and installation considerations

4 The exhaust system will be held at the cylinder head (4-stroke engine) or cylinder barrel (2-stroke engine) by a flanged retainer held by nuts or bolts, and on some small machines a threaded ring may be used. Note that due to the exposed location of this fitting, the fasteners will most be corroded and covered in road dirt. Take time to clean them first and apply a penetrating fluid, preferably the night before. The exhaust system will be supported at the silencer end and most likely at a mid-point, where exhaust downpipe and silencer join.

5 It is usually best to slacken off all mounting points together, rather than remove them one at a time. On multi-cylinder exhaust systems it may be necessary to use jacks to support part of the system whilst removal or slackening is taking place.

6 Always renew the gasket rings at the cylinder head or barrel and where fitted, at the exhaust pipe-to-silencer join. Air leaks and poor running will result from a missing or broken up gasket.

7 On most systems, the silencer is rubber mounted at the rear of the machine. Check that the rubber mounting grommets are not worn or perished.

8 Always take care to fit mounting brackets, spacers and washers in their original order. Any misalignment in the mountings will create stress in the exhaust system and could lead to fracture. Make sure that all brackets and mounting bolts are in place before tightening them to the specified torque settings. It is good practice to smear the threads of exhaust system bolts will a copper-based grease prior to fitting; this will ease their removal the next time the system is removed. If the mounting bolts or nuts were found to be corroded on removal it is advisable to renew them due to the small cost involved.

Cleaning the system (two-strokes)

9 If the silencer has a detachable baffle pipe in its end, remove the baffle and scrub it clean using a solvent to dissolve the build-up of oily sludge **(see illustration)**.

10 If hard deposits have formed, which cannot be wire brushed off, they can be burnt off with a blow lamp or welding torch, which is played along the baffle. When it is cool the baffle can be tapped with a length of hard wood and wire brushed to dislodge and remove any remaining debris. Make sure that all the baffle holes are clear.

11 On more extreme cases the exhaust system can be divided by cutting through at a welded join. Each section is then dealt with in turn as described above, before welding the cleaned sections back together.

12 A particularly effective way in which to clean out a silencer and exhaust pipe internally is to fill the entire system with a solution of caustic soda, after having blocked off one end. This is somewhat drastic treatment and not recommended for the home workshop as caustic soda is a particularly nasty chemical for which adequate safety precautions must be observed.

Repairs

13 Repairs to the exhaust system are difficult to carry out successfully. You will find that rusting tends to come through from the inside in many cases, so that once visible on the outside there will be very little metal left under the chrome or paint. More importantly, the internal baffles will have been affected too, and will eventually break up, making the system illegally noisy. As a general rule, the silencer or complete system should be renewed as soon as serious rusting is evident.

14 It is possible to weld back brackets or lugs which break off through vibration, though in the case of chrome-plated systems this will damage the finish. On painted systems, the welding can be disguised with a fresh coat of heat-resistant exhaust paint.

15 In an emergency, you can effect a temporary repair to a holed exhaust using a proprietary repair paste, or in the case of splits or larger holes, an exhaust bandage. The emphasis here is on temporary; use this method to get you by while a new system is on order.

Fitting an aftermarket system

16 The original equipment parts are a safe choice, though prices tend to be exorbitant. There are many good quality aftermarket system available which offer better performance and are significantly cheaper. Note that stainless steel systems, although more expensive to buy, will last longer than a chrome-plated steel item.

17 In the UK there are legal requirements for any exhaust system for use on the road. These govern the noise of the system as well as the type approval. The quality of manufacture and any performance claims are also specified. Any exhaust system should carry an indelible stamp, usually embossed on the product, which shows that the silencer or system conforms with the regulations **(see illustration)**.

HAYNES HiNT *Before buying a new system, check if any modifications are required to the engine management systems, carburettor jetting etc. in order for the new system to function correctly. Check also if the fitting of the system invalidates any warranty on the machine and if your insurance company requires notification.*

22 Cooling system

1 Although this Section relates mainly to liquid cooling systems do not forget that engines relying on air cooling still require attention. The efficiency with which heat is lost to the air is dependent on the cooling fins on the cylinder barrel and head; if these fins become clogged with dirt, cooling will be impaired. This is especially true of machines used off-road.

2 The pressure cap can be situated on the top of the radiator, but is more often located on a filler neck sited above the radiator **(see illustration)**. Take care when removing the pressure cap when the engine and radiator are hot. Scalding hot coolant may be blown out under pressure. Wait until the engine is cool, then place a thick rag, like a towel, over the cap and turn the cap anticlockwise keeping downward pressure on the cap. Let any pressure escape before removing the cap. Note that system topping up should be done at the reservoir tank, not at the pressure cap.

Coolant

3 The coolant used is a mixture, usually in equal portions: 50% water and 50% antifreeze.

4 The antifreeze not only prevents the formation of ice in the system, but contains other chemicals which help reduce corrosion. Normally ethylene glycol is the base chemical for the antifreeze. Keep a supply of coolant mixture at hand for topping up purposes – never top up with water alone otherwise the antifreeze content of the system will be reduced. Note that antifreeze content can be checked with a coolant hydrometer **(see illustration)**.

5 Avoid using tap water in the cooling system. Tap water contains impurities, and will allow corrosion to take place more readily. Clean, filtered, rain water is preferable, and best of all is distilled or demineralised water, as supplied for topping up batteries.

6 The coolant will deteriorate with time and should be changed regularly according to the manufacturer's instructions. Drain the old coolant away and flush the system with water or a special flushing liquid. Refit any drain plugs and refill the system with the correct coolant mixture for your machine and the expected temperature conditions. Fill the radiator up the base of the filler neck and fill the reservoir tank up the upper level line.

HAYNES HiNT *When refilling the cooling system, use a funnel and length of hose (where necessary) and allow the coolant to flow slowly to prevent too much air entering the system.*

7 On certain systems air bleed pipes are fitted to disperse air in the coolant, on others you will have to bleed the system to remove any air. With the motorcycle upright on its centre stand and the transmission in neutral, start the engine and snap the throttle open three or four times to bleed any air from the cooling system (note that certain models have air bleed screws on the thermostat housing).

Stop the engine and top of the level to the base of the radiator filler neck. Fit the pressure cap securely and top up the reservoir tank if necessary.

8 Inspect the coolant regularly. If there is an indication of corrosion taking place the system should be flushed out and filled with fresh fluid. A strange smell to the fluid may indicate that combustion gases are contaminating the coolant.

9 A significant drop in coolant level indicates that there may be a leak in the system. Note that external leaks are usually highlighted by white-coloured deposits around the area adjoining the leak.

10 Do not allow antifreeze to come into contact with your skin or painted surfaces. Rinse off spills, and clear up any mess immediately.

Checking for leaks

11 Check the cooling system hoses which will age and break in time. These should be checked regularly and renewed as soon as there are signs of perishing and cracking visible. Do not forget that there may be small bore hoses taking coolant to the carburettors.

12 Cooling system leakage at the cylinder head to block joint can mean compression pressure getting into the cooling system, or coolant getting into the cylinder, and neither condition is desirable. If renewing the head gasket and any O-rings fails to solve the problem, or if it is a recurrent one, check the head and block faces for warping or corrosion, and have these skimmed where necessary.

13 On four-stroke engines make regular oil checks, and investigate immediate if you find traces of coolant in the engine oil. These may take the form of an oil/water emulsion; a thick white slimy deposit inside the crankcase and outer covers. Also check if coolant is leaking from the water pump seal **(see**

22.2 The pressure cap should be removed with care – note the warning on the cap

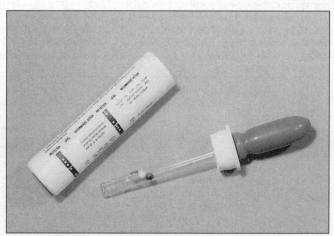

22.4 An hydrometer can be used to measure antifreeze strength

22.13 The water pump is usually fitted with a drainage hole on its underside. If the pump seal fails, coolant escapes through the hole rather than entering the engine's lubrication system

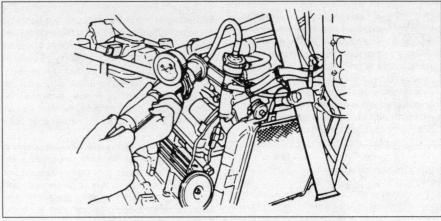

22.19 Cooling system pressure tester in operation

illustration). On two-stroke engines any coolant lost internally could be passing into the crankcase and the resultant running problems should alert attention.

14 Radiator leaks are sometimes difficult to diagnose, and the real answer is to find a garage with cooling system pressure test facilities. Where the matrix itself is split or holed through corrosion, the source of the leak may show up as beads of coolant escaping as the machine reaches normal operating temperature.

Overheating

15 Overheating problems may be due to the general accumulations of dead insects or autumnal debris around the core of the radiator, and this should be cleaned out regularly.

16 Sludge or corrosion deposits within the system will also prevent the correct flow of coolant. Use a proprietary flushing solution, following the maker's instructions carefully.

17 If the system seems clean internally and externally, the likely culprit is the thermostat. This is designed to regulate coolant circulation, the valve opening once the engine has reached a certain temperature. If the valve has stuck in the closed position, the coolant will be prevented from flowing through the radiator and the engine will overheat.

18 Most systems have an electric cooling fan mounted behind the radiator. Failure of the

temperature sensing fan switch or the fan motor will also cause overheating.

Testing the components in the system

Pressure testing

19 The cooling system can be pressurised to check for leaks. You will need a pump-operated pressure tester with a cap which fits the radiator filler neck and details of the test pressure for the engine. If these are not available, have the test carried out by a dealer – the system components can be damaged by applying too high a pressure. The system must be capable of holding the specified pressure for approx. six seconds (see illustration).

20 The pressure cap itself can be tested using the equipment described above (see illustration). You will need details of the cap test pressure and opening pressure. Note that the cap can fail due to damaged seals – check them carefully and renew the cap if in doubt about its condition (see illustration).

Thermostat

22 The thermostat can be checked by suspending the cap in a container of water (see illustration). The water is gradually heated, and the temperature monitored with a thermometer. The workshop manual will give details of the temperature at which the unit

should commence to open, and that at which it should reach its fully open position. It is quite easy to assess whether the thermostat is functioning correctly by this method.

Gauges and sensors

23 Temperature gauges are triggered by a sensor which varies its resistance as the temperature rises. The sensor can be checked in the same way as the thermostat, using a multimeter to check the resistance at specified temperatures.

Fan and pump

24 Check the condition of the fan blades and pump impeller and by grasping the fan/impeller trying and wiggle it to see if there is any play in the bearings.

25 Check the electrical soundness of the fan motor and fan switch.

Repairs

Radiator

26 Radiator repairs are difficult to carry out, as it is often difficult to establish the exact point of the leak.

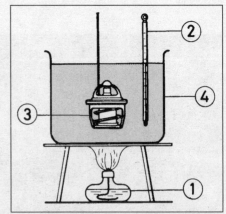

22.22 The method of checking the correct operation of the thermostat

1 Heat source
2 Thermometer
3 Thermostat
4 Heat-proof container

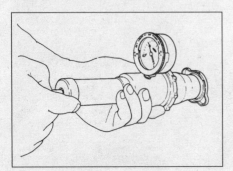

22.20a Checking the pressure cap with a pressure tester

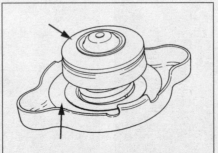

22.20b Pay attention to the seal condition (arrows) when checking the cap

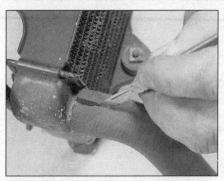

22.30 If the hose has hardened due to age and will not move, slit it with a sharp knife

27 Leaks in copper radiators may be soldered. The heat source must be fairly localised to avoid melting the joint further along. Epoxy resin putties can also be used, but take great care to get the surfaces chemically clean before adding the putty to the metal. The low temperature aluminium welding process may also be used.

28 The fins of the radiator should be gently straightened with pliers or a flat-bladed screwdriver if they are bent.

29 There are products available for sealing leaks in radiators, and the whole system. They do not interfere with the antifreeze or corrosion resistance of normal coolant, and may be used for a temporary repair.

Freeing and fitting hoses

30 Always make sure the hose clamp is moved well clear of the hose end. Grip the hose with your hand and rotate it whilst pulling it off the union. If the hose has hardened due to age and will not move, slit it with a sharp knife and peel its ends off the union **(see illustration)**.

31 Resist the temptation to use grease or soap on the unions to aid installation; although it helps the hose slip over the union it will equally aid the escape of fluid from the joint. It is preferable to soften the hose ends in hot water and wet the inside surface of the hose with water or a fluid which will evaporate.

32 Make sure the hose end is cut square, and push it all the way on to the stub. The clip

should be fitted on the plain section of the stub below the swaged collar.

33 Small bore hoses may be clamped in a similar manner to that described in the Section on brake hoses in the next Chapter.

Oil cooling

34 The lubricating oil is often used as an alternative means of cooling the engine, or it is necessary for the oil to be cooled in order to maintain the efficient working of the engine.

35 In either case the system will compose of a radiator, hoses and possibly, temperature sensors and even a thermostat.

23 Final drive chains and sprockets

Chain construction

1 Two types of chain are in common use: the simple roller chain, and the sealed O-ring chain **(see illustrations)**. The latter has an O-ring at each side between the side plates. The ring seals in a special lithium-based grease and also prevents dirt and moisture getting onto the rollers.

2 The X-ring type of chain is a development of the O-ring, which creates less friction in the link.

3 The chain may also be spilt or endless. The former is joined on the machine by a master or split link. To remove or fit the endless chain one of the rivets is pressed out and a soft rivet is then used to rejoin the chain.

Chain sizing

4 Chains are sized using a three digit number, followed by a suffix to denote the chain type **(see illustration)**. Chain type is either

standard or heavy duty (thicker sideplates), and also unsealed or O-ring/X-ring type.

5 The first digit of the number relates to the pitch of the chain, ie the distance from the centre of one pin to the centre of the next pin **(see illustration)**. Pitch is expressed in eighths of an inch, thus:

● Sizes commencing with a 4 (eg 428) have a pitch of 1/2 inch (12.7 mm)
● Sizes commencing with a 5 (eg 520) have a pitch of 5/8 inch (15.9 mm)
● Sizes commencing with a 6 (eg 630) have a pitch of 3/4 inch (19.1 mm)

6 The second and third digits of the chain size relate to the width of the rollers, again in imperial units, eg the 525 shown has 5/16 inch (7.94 mm) rollers **(see illustration 23.4)**.

Breaking and joining chains

Master/split link chains

7 Find the position of the split link in the chain and position it at a convenient place on the rear sprocket **(see illustration)**. Use a pair of blunt nose pliers to push the spring clip so that the open end of the clip is free of the pin. Wiggle the clip so that the wider part split can be pulled off the other pin.

8 Remove the link sideplate and withdraw the link from the other side of the sprocket.

9 Use a new master/split link suitable for the size of the chain.

10 Pull the ends of the chain onto adjacent teeth on the rear sprocket, lubricate the pins with grease and push the link through the open rollers from the wheel side of the chain. Put the sideplate over the pins and refit the spring clip by pushing the clip over the leading roller and then slide it back and clip the trailing roller by using the blunt nose pliers. The clip

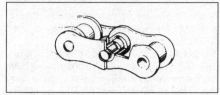

23.1a The standard unsealed chain link

23.1b The O-ring chain link

23.4 A typical chain size code stamped on a side plate

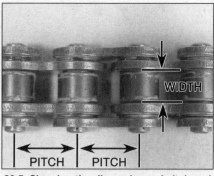

23.5 Showing the dimensions of pitch and width of rollers

23.7 The split link positioned on the sprocket to ease removal and refitting

23.10 The closed end of the spring clip should face the normal direction of wheel travel

23.12a For altering chain length, a chain splitting tool is required

23.12b The tool is used as shown to drive out the chain rivets, allowing the chain to be separated at the required point

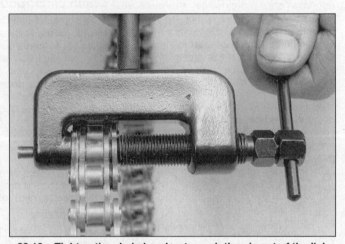

23.16a Tighten the chain breaker to push the pin out of the link

should locate in the grooves on each pin and the closed end of the clip should face the direction of travel **(see illustration)**.

11 Do not join old and new lengths of chain, nor use more than one master/split link per length of chain.

12 A chain splitting tool like the one illustrated can be used for removing links to shorten the chain length **(see illustrations)**.

Endless chains

13 Drive chains for all but small bikes are continuous and for safety reasons do not have a clip-type connecting link. The chain must be broken using a chain breaker tool and the new chain securely riveted together using a new soft rivet-type link. Never use a clip-type connecting link instead of a rivet-type link. Various chain breaking and riveting tools are available, either as separate tools or combined as illustrated in the accompanying photographs – read the instructions supplied with the tool carefully.

14 To avoid splitting the chain, the swinging arm assembly must be removed.

15 The need to rivet the new link pins

correctly cannot be overstressed – loss of control of the motorcycle is very likely to result if the chain breaks in use.

16 Rotate the chain and look for the soft link. The soft link pins look like they have been deeply centre-punched instead of peened over like all the other pins, and its sideplate may be a different colour. Position the soft link midway between the sprockets and assemble the chain breaker tool over one of the soft link pins

23.16b Withdraw the pin and remove the tool

(see illustration). Operate the tool to push the pin out through the chain **(see illustration)**.

17 On an O-ring chain, remove the O-rings and carry out the same procedure on the other soft link pin and separate the link **(see illustration)**.

18 Certain soft link pins (particularly on the larger chains) may require their ends being filed or ground off before they can be pressed out using the tool.

23.17 Separate the chain link

23.20a Insert the new chain link with O-rings through the chain

23.20b Fit the O-rings over the pin ends

23.20c Slip the sideplate over the pins

23.22 Using a clamp to press on the sideplate

23.23a Assemble the chain tool, now for assembly not for braking, position over one pin and tighten it fully. Repeat for the other pin

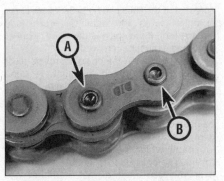

23.23b An unriveted pin end is shown at (B) and a correctly riveted pin end at (A)

19 Check that you have the correct size and strength (standard or heavy duty) new soft link – do not reuse the old link. Look for the size marking on the chain sideplates **(see illustration 23.4)**.

20 On an O-ring chain, install a new O-ring over each pin of the link and insert the link through the two chain ends **(see illustration)**. Install a new O-ring over the end of each pin, followed by the sideplate (with the chain manufacturer's marking facing outwards) **(see illustrations)**. If installing an X-ring chain, check that the rubber X-rings are positioned the correct way around as following the instructions supplied with the chain.

21 On an unsealed chain, insert the link through the two chain ends, then install the sideplate with the chain manufacturer's marking facing outwards.

22 Note that it may not be possible to install the sideplate using finger pressure alone. If

using a joining tool, assemble it so that the plates of the tool clamp the link and press the sideplate over the pins **(see illustration)**. Otherwise, use two small sockets placed over the rivet ends and two pieces of the wood between a G-clamp. Operate the clamp to press the sideplate over the pins.

23 Assemble the joining tool over one pin (following the maker's instructions) and tighten the tool down to spread the pin end securely **(see illustrations)**. Do the same on the other pin.

24 Check that the pin ends are secure and that there is no danger of the sideplate coming loose. If the pin ends are cracked the soft link must be renewed.

Inspection and maintenance

Standard unsealed chains

Note: *If you decide to fit a sealed chain instead of the standard unsealed type, check*

that its roller width is suitable for the sprockets and that its external size will not foul on the chain guard or other components.

25 Regular lubrication is essential. Use one of the aerosol chain lubricants or a heavy motor oil, such as SAE80.

26 To clean and inspect the chain for wear, remove it from the machine. Wash off dirt and old lubricant with a degreasing solvent or paraffin (kerosene) and allow the chain to dry. Do not use high pressure washers which will force water and dirt into the rollers.

27 Check the chain for damage, and check that each link pivots freely. Chain stretch is usually expressed as a measurement over a specified number of links and will be detailed in the workshop manual **(see illustration)**. Stretch is measured at several places on the chain because the chain rarely wears evenly. A quick check of chain wear can be made by pulling the chain backwards off the rear

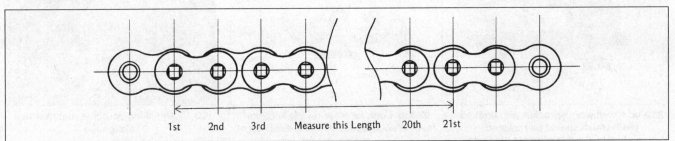

23.27a Chain stretch is often expressed as a measurement over 21 pins with all slack taken up

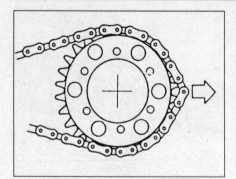

23.27b A quick check of chain wear

23.28 The hot immersion lubrication is the best method for unsealed chains

Sprocket examination and alignment

33 Check the condition of the teeth on the sprocket. Any chipped or hooked teeth mean a new sprocket is required **(see illustration)**. Inspect the sprocket teeth for wear, noting that wear will occur on one side of the teeth depending on whether it is the front (driving) sprocket or rear (driven) sprocket **(see illustration)**.

34 Rotate the rear wheel with the bike on its centre stand and the rear wheel off the ground and see if there are any tight spots in the chain. Mark the position of the front and rear sprockets and rotate the wheel a few more times and see if the tight spot occurs at the same place. If it does, then it is likely that the sprockets are worn rather than the chain.

35 The runout of each sprocket can also be checked by mounting your dial gauge on a firm stand with the plunger running on a diameter just inside the teeth **(see illustration)**. An investigation into the condition of the drive assembly, or a replacement sprocket is required if the runout exceeds the service limit.

36 The sprockets should be in the same plane, that is in the same line as each other and the chain. This can be roughly checked by eye by sighting along the chain from the rear of the machine. Where space permits, a steel rule or straight-edge can be used in a similar way to checking the wheel alignment. There is a small alignment tool available which locates on the sprocket and has a pointer which should align with the chain.

37 Misalignment can be caused by poor wheel alignment due to uneven chain adjustment, wear in the swinging arm bushes and rear hub assembly, or frame damage. Note that poor chain alignment can cause the chain to break or jump the sprockets at high speed.

sprocket; if the links can be pulled clear of the sprocket teeth the chain is worn **(see illustration)**. If the chain is damaged, worn or stretched if must be renewed.

28 Having cleaned the chain, its rollers must be packed with fresh lubricant. A good method of lubrication is to use a hot-immersion lubricant **(see illustration)**. This is supplied in a large metal container, and can be heated up over a gas burner or on a stove until it melts. The chain is placed in the hot lubricant, which penetrates the links and rollers. The chain is then removed and hung over the can until excess lubricant has drained off, and the remainder has set to a waxy consistency inside each bush. Lubrication by this method will extend the life of the chain considerably.

29 The correct amount of chain freeplay is essential and is usually measured midway between the sprockets, on the bottom run of the chain **(see illustration)**. If too slack, the

chain will snatch when taking up drive and there is a danger of the chain jumping off the sprockets. If too tight, the chain will wear quickly and may even break, place high loading on the gearbox and rear wheel bearings and absorb a surprising amount of power. Note that chains do not wear evenly and it is important that freeplay measurement is taken with the tightest point of the chain at the midway position. Refer to the freeplay figure specified in the workshop manual and take note whether adjustment is made with the machine on its centre stand or on the side stand.

Sealed chains (O-ring/X-ring)

30 Although lubricant is sealed into the chain rollers by the O-rings (or X-rings) the external surface of the rollers requires regular lubrication. Use a heavy motor oil, such as SAE80, or an aerosol chain lubricant which is marked as being suitable for O-ring chains.

31 The sealed chain can be cleaned with paraffin (kerosene) or an aerosol type chain cleaner which is specially formulated for O-ring chains and approved by the chain manufacturer. Volatile solvents and petrol (gasoline) should not be used as they will damage the seals, as will a coarse bristled brush.

32 Refer to the information for standard chains for chain stretch and adjustment information.

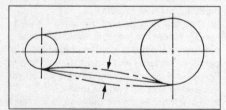

23.29 Chain freeplay is measured midway between the sprockets on the bottom run

> **HAYNES HiNT** *If the sprockets require renewal, fit new sprockets and a new chain at the same time. The running together of old and new components will result in an increased rate of wear*

23.33a A well worn sprocket with hooked teeth which should be replaced immediately. On this example the teeth have also begun to break up at the ends

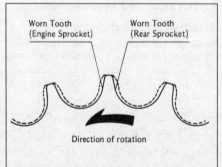

Worn Tooth (Engine Sprocket) Worn Tooth (Rear Sprocket)

Direction of rotation

23.33b Look for wear on the sprocket teeth in accordance with the direction of chain rotation

23.35 Checking sprocket runout with a dial gauge

Chapter 12
Frame, suspension and brake tasks

Contents

1 Introduction

1 In this Chapter we will be looking at the frame and suspension components, together with some of the more common operations relating to these areas.
2 In many respects, the frame, suspension and brakes are the major safety-related areas of a motorcycle, and you will need to be particularly aware of this when dealing with the maintenance and repair of these parts; always remember that if you make a mistake during an engine rebuild, the engine might break down on you – a similar mistake with the brakes could kill you.

2 Frame inspection

1 Check the frame and swingarm for cracks, splitting, and rust damage particularly around the welded areas. A thorough inspection usually means a complete stripdown of the bike.
2 Poor wheel alignment and handling may be attributed to problems with the frame.
3 Check that the bolts holding subframes such as the seat and rear mudguard assembly are tight. Check that engine mounting bolt holes are not worn oval, and that any engine mounting brackets are in good condition.
4 The frame can be checked for straightness by specialist firms who have the necessary equipment to do this to the accuracy required. These firms may also have the facility for straightening a bent frame. A rough assessment can be made in the workshop by checking the wheels for vertical alignment as described in Chapter 14.
5 If the frame has been damaged in an accident, it may be advisable to renew the frame rather than straightening it. It is not easy to detect what stresses have been introduced into the structure or metal of the frame by the accident or by the straightening forces.

3 Front suspension

1 The exact cause of suspension faults can be difficult to assess at times, and very often what feels like a fork problem may turn out to be play in the rear suspension. For this reason, whenever you are faced with some sort of steering or suspension fault it is best to check right through the front and rear suspension systems and also the steering head assembly.
2 Poor damping can be caused by using the wrong grade or amount of oil, or by having different amounts in each leg. Check this by draining the old oil completely.
3 Weak fork springs and wear in bushes and bearings will allow vague or imprecise fork action, and it is advisable to check for wear during oil checks or changes.
4 Adjustments incorrect. If the forks fitted have air-assistance, adjustable preload or adjustable rebound or compression damping, check that the setting is the same for each fork and that it suits the set-up of the rear shock absorber. Where anti-dive is fitted, again make sure that the setting suits your riding style.

4 Front suspension – telescopic forks

Problems

1 Stiff fork operation can result from a number of faults, but most commonly this is due to the forks becoming twisted in the fork yokes. This can be rectified by slackening the wheel axle nut and lower yoke pinch bolts, and then bouncing the forks repeatedly to allow them to settle in the correct position. The wheel axle and pinch bolts should then be tightened to the specified torque figure.
2 Erratic fork action could be due to damage to the fork tubes as a result of impact, causing the forks to stiffen or stick at a particular

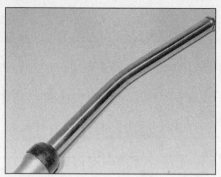

4.3a This stanchion has gone past the point of repair

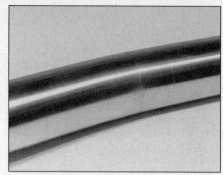

4.3b This stanchion is slightly creased at the bend and would not be safe to repair

4.5 If the fork tube protrudes above the top yoke, measure the height of the fork tube above the top yoke

point. This may not be easily visible, and to check it you will have to dismantle the forks so that the tubes can be tested for runout (see paragraph 21 below).

3 Slight bending of a fork tube can be corrected using a press to straighten it. This method may work if damage is minimal, but carries the risk of invisible fatigue areas which could result in the tube breaking at a later date. Other drawbacks include cracking or flaking of the hard chrome surface **(see illustrations)**. As a general rule it is always safer to fit new fork tubes.

4 Other causes of erratic damping include contamination by dirt or water, which entails dismantling and cleaning the internal parts of each leg. A failed fork oil seal will allow oil to be expelled from the fork and the ingress of water.

Dismantling

5 Before removing the forks, measure and record any alignment or height difference between the top of the fork tube and the yoke so that they can be replaced correctly **(see illustration)**. If the forks have preload adjusters, take note of their setting at this stage.

6 The wall thickness of the threaded end of the tube is thin and it is easy to damage the internal threads. Slackening the top yoke clamp bolts helps take pressure off the threads and makes the fork top bolt easier to unscrew. The fork top bolt is also under pressure from the fork spring and may fly off on its release. Keep some downward pressure on it and release it slowly. Eye protection is advised. Note that it is much easier to slacken the top bolt whilst the fork is held in the yokes than if the fork has already been removed from the machine.

7 Drain the fork oil from the top of the fork or via the drain plug at the bottom of the fork. Pump the fork to expel as much oil as possible.

8 Dismantle one fork completely and store its components in a marked box or tray.

9 Telescopic forks are of very similar construction, and a common problem during dismantling is releasing the damper rod bolt so that the fork tube and slider can be separated. What normally happens is that the damper rod rotates inside the tube, making removal of the bolt virtually impossible, though if you are lucky the pressure from the fork spring may exert enough friction to hold it still.

10 The manufacturer can usually supply a holding tool which is passed down inside the stanchion to engage with the damper rod head. This allows the rod to be immobilised while the bolt is released. For the home workshop, an alternative method may be used to prevent the rotation of the damper rod.

11 Most damper rods have a recess in the head, and it will be necessary to find something which will locate in this. The first problem is finding out the shape and size of the recess. It is difficult to get enough light into the fork tube to be able to see the damper rod, and it is helpful to be able to measure the recess when making up a holding tool. This can be done by sticking a piece of modelling clay to the end of a length of wooden dowel. If this is then pressed against the damper rod, you will be able to take an accurate impression of the recess.

12 On forks which have a hexagonal recess, you can make up a tool using a bolt with the appropriate size of hexagon attached to a length of steel tube **(see illustration)**. The bolt should be slid into the tube and either welded in place or drilled and pinned or riveted. At the upper end, drill a hole through the tube walls to allow a tommy bar to be used. An alternative method is to use a socket and a long extension **(see illustrations)**.

13 The solution is less easy where a round recess is used. The most generally useful improvised tool that we have discovered is a piece of square bar, the ends of which have been ground to a blunt point. This can be pressed into the recess, the edges on the point providing enough 'bite' to hold the

4.12a A bolt welded to a long bar (left) which will locate in the damper rod head (right)

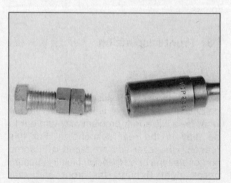

4.12b Select a bolt to fit the damper rod head, fit a couple of nuts on the bolt threads and fit a deep socket over the nuts . . .

4.12c . . . wrap tape around the bolt threads and socket to hold the two together

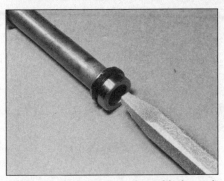

4.13a A length of square bar with the end ground to a blunt point can be used to hold a damper rod with a round recess . . .

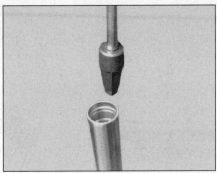

4.13b . . . and is similar to the design of this manufacturer's service tool

4.13c Alternatively a tapered wooden dowel can be pressed into the damper rod head

damper still **(see illustrations)**. An alternative to this is to use a length of wooden doweling, again with the end tapered **(see illustration)**.

14 Make a note of which way up the spring is fitted. There may be a difference in the coil spacing at one end of the spring.

Bearing surfaces, seals and bushes

15 The fork tube and slider of a telescopic fork are machined to close tolerances during manufacture, the bearing surface being formed by the machined surface of the slider, or by renewable bushes.

16 Lubrication is provided by the damping oil, and the assembly is closed by a seal pressed into the top of the slider. Where bushes are fitted, these are often coated with Teflon to reduce friction, and thus improve the action of the fork.

17 The oil seal in the top of the lower leg is in an exposed position, and vulnerable to damage from road dirt. To minimise this problem, a dust seal is usually fitted to prevent dirt from entering the seal and causing damage. In the case of off-road models fork gaiters exclude all dirt from the fork tube surface.

18 Once the oil seal lip becomes damaged by dirt, wear of the seal, fork tube and bush surfaces is rapid, and it is worth checking these areas regularly for signs of deterioration; damage can be difficult and costly to rectify.

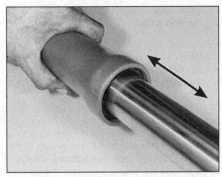

4.19a The slide-hammer action of fork separation . . .

19 In bushed forks, it is normal practice to separate the fork tube and slider by pulling them sharply apart in a slide-hammer action **(see illustration)**. Because the bottom bush cannot pass through the top bush, this action serves to displace the top bush as the two components are separated. The fork oil seal and its backing washer will be displaced from the fork slider at the same time **(see illustration)**.

20 In an unbushed fork arrangement, the fork tube and slider and easily separated, leaving the seal components in place in the slider. Use a large flat-bladed screwdriver to prise out the dust seal and oil seal from the fork slider **(see illustration)**, noting that the oil seal will be retained by a stamped or wire circlip.

4.19b . . . will free the oil seal (1), washer (2), upper bush (3) and lower bush (4)

21 On unbushed forks, wear between the fork tube and slider will allow play between them, giving rise to poor fork action and juddering under braking. It is normally necessary to renew the fork slider (and possibly the fork tube) to resolve the problem, repair being impractical.

22 With bushed forks, renewal of the bushes can restore fork action and precision. The upper bush, housed in the top of the slider will be displaced along with the oil seal (see paragraph 19) and can be slid off the fork tube. The lower bush resides on the end of the fork tube and can be gently sprung apart with a large flat-bladed screwdriver to enable it to be slipped off the fork tube end **(see illustration)**.

4.20 Use a large flat-bladed screwdriver to prise the oil seal out of the slider

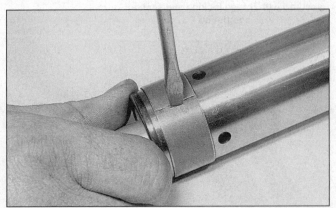

4.22 Gently spring open the split to allow the lower bush to be slipped off the fork tube

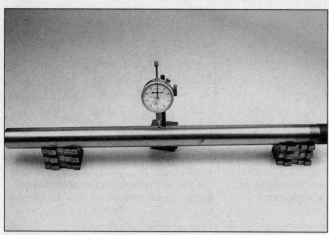

4.26 Fork tube runout is checked with vee-blocks and a dial gauge

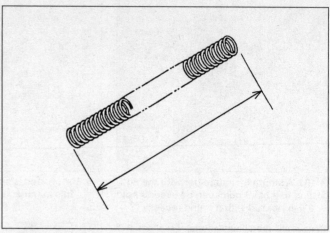

4.27 Free length is the total length of the fork spring when it is not compressed

Cleaning and inspection

23 Clean all old damping oil off the fork components and make sure that the oilways in the damper assembly are clear.

24 Inspect the tubes for scratches, corrosion and pitting, especially in the area which passes through the seals. Excessive or abnormal wear in one area indicates that the tube may be bent.

25 Check the seal seating for damage. Any nicks or scratches will give rise to leaks.

26 Check the fork tube for runout. This is best done with the tube supported on

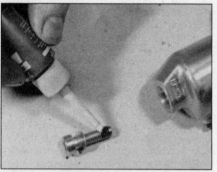

4.29 The damper rod Allen bolt should be secured with thread locking and sealing compound

4.30 Use a calibrated measuring cylinder to add the fork oil

V-blocks, using a dial gauge **(see illustration)**. Failing this, a good indication can be given by rolling the stanchion across a dead flat surface like a sheet of glass.

27 If the fork springs have sagged, their length will be reduced. Check the free length of the springs using a long steel rule and compare with the service limit specified in the workshop manual **(see illustration)**. Replace both springs if either are beyond the service limits – never renew one spring on its own.

28 Wear of the fork bushes is best checked with the fork assembled and will be felt as movement between the fork tube and slider. Visually inspect the bushes for wear of their working surfaces. If their surface coating has worn through or they are scored or otherwise damaged, renew both bushes in each fork.

Reassembly

29 Follow the instructions in the manual. Remember cleanliness is very important to avoid damaging new seals and blocking

oilways. When installing the damper rod Allen bolt, clean its threads and apply or drop or two of thread locking and sealing compound to the first few threads **(see illustration)**; make sure that the sealing washer is in place under the Allen bolt head.

30 Fill the fork with the correct amount of the recommended oil. A measuring jug or cylinder is required for this job **(see illustration)**. Note that calibrated large syringes can be obtained for measuring and injecting the oil into the fork. Fill the fork slowly to avoid introducing air bubbles into the oil.

31 After adding the oil, **slowly** pump the tube and slider to evenly distribute the oil and expel any air. Leave the fork in an upright position for five minutes to allow the oil level to settle and any oil bubbles to come to the surface.

32 Usually a fork oil level will be specified from the top of the oil to the top of the tube. Use a steel rule or the depth gauge on your vernier to check the oil level **(see illustration)**.

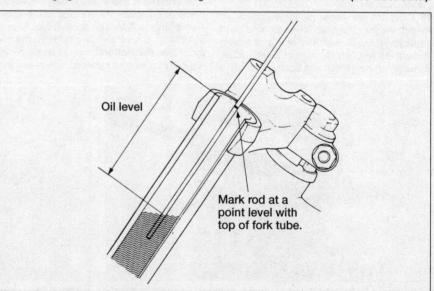

Oil level

Mark rod at a point level with top of fork tube.

4.32 A length of welding rod can be used to measure fork oil level

Note that you could also use the fork oil level gauge described in Section 6. Before measuring oil level, check whether the manufacturer specifies that it be checked with the spring removed and fork tube fully compressing into the slider – this is normally the case.

33 Add or remove oil until the oil level is correct.

34 Both forks should have the same oil level otherwise uneven damping will result.

35 When fitting the fork top bolt, you may find that it is difficult to start its threads whilst pressing down on the fork spring and/or spacer, and there is a danger of damaging the threads if care is not taken. Make sure that the fork leg is fully extended and clamp the fork tube in the fork yokes to ease the task. Keep a steady downward pressure whilst tightening – a ratchet wrench is useful for this operation **(see illustration)**.

36 Always check that the forks operate smoothly after rebuild and each fork tube extends through the top yoke by the same amount.

Repairing damage to fork tubes

37 The most common problem is rust pitting of the fork tubes, although scratches and scoring may also be present **(see illustration)**. This causes oil leakage as the lips of the oil seals are torn by the sharp edges of the pitting. In some cases, normal fork action effectively pumps the damping oil out of the forks.

38 Excessive damage will mean replacement with new items, however it is possible to reclaim tubes by re-chroming and finishing to the correct size **(see illustration)**. Specialist firms advertise this service.

39 In an emergency, you could try the well-known dodge of filling the rust pits with epoxy putty, such as Araldite. The fork tube must first be degreased, preferably with solvent, so that no trace of grease or oil remains. Apply a layer of epoxy putty to the pits, and allow it to harden. The putty can now be sanded back to

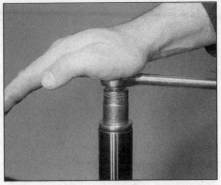

4.35 A socket and ratchet handle used to tighten the fork top bolt. Apply even downward pressure until the threads are engaged

the level of the surrounding plating, leaving as smooth a surface as possible. This repair method will certainly improve matters, and if the degreasing was thorough, should last for some time. It is doubtful whether it would be reliable in the case of air-assisted forks though.

40 Future damage of this type can be prevented by fitting fork gaiters over the exposed area of the fork tubes. You should be able to find suitable gaiters at most motorcycle dealers, but if you have problems, try an off-road motorcycle specialist.

Fork oils

41 Refer to Chapter 17 for information on fork damping oils.

---

5 Front suspension – air assisted forks

1 The information given in Section 4 can be applied, plus the following considerations.

2 Before starting to remove the forks, release the air pressure. Remove the cap from the air valve and depress the valve core to release air

pressure in the forks – the pressure gauge may well have an attachment for this.

3 Air leaks from air-assisted forks will prevent the forks operating normally, this will be masked to some extent by the fork springs. The most common cause is a worn or damaged seal. These seals have to withstand fork air pressure in addition to retaining oil, so a little damage to a seal lip will inevitably cause loss of pressure.

4 Note that most seals must be fitted facing in a particular direction, or they will not be able to withstand air pressure.

5 Do not forget that a leaking air valve may be responsible for the problem; check this first because the valve is easier to renew than the seals.

6 Fork air pressure should be checked regularly. This is of particular significance where the two fork legs are not interconnected, because imbalance between them can result in handling problems.

7 You should use a syringe-type fork air pump, and also a suspension-type pressure gauge when carrying out checks and adjustments; those produced for use on tyres are not sufficiently accurate for this work.

8 **Never** use a garage air-line to inflate the forks; you will probably destroy the seals in the attempt. Where the fork legs are not interconnected, take great care to make sure that the pressure in each leg is the same. This is of more importance than the exact pressure setting. Never exceed the maximum air pressure specified by the manufacturer; quite apart from the high preload which will result, the oil seals are likely to blow out under the pressure.

---

6 Front suspension – cartridge type forks

1 With cartridge type forks, the damping action is contained in a separate container (the cartridge) inside the fork tube.

4.37 This badly rusted fork tube has destroyed the oil seal. A replacement seal would soon go the same way

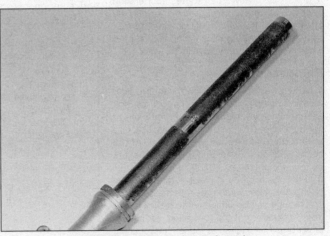

4.38 This fork tube is beyond repair

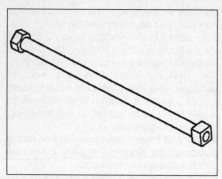

6.5a This Kawasaki service tool passes over the damping adjuster rod . . .

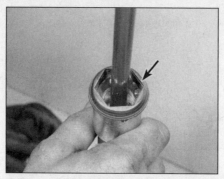

6.5b . . . and engages the hex in the top of the cartridge

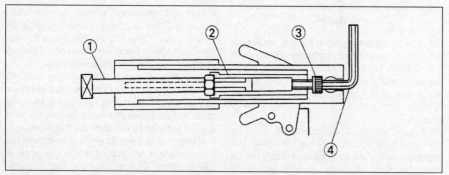

6.5c With the cartridge (2) held with the tool (1), the retaining bolt (3) can be unscrewed with an Allen key (4)

2 Advantages over conventional forks are in better control of the suspension by using wide bearing surfaces with Teflon impregnated bushes, plus improved control of the oil flow. The disadvantage is that they wear out quickly. This is due to the contamination of the oil by particles of aluminium, steel and Teflon which are rubbed off the contacting surfaces. Apart from the increase in clearance between the parts, the contaminated oil does not retain its ability to transmit loads. Both conditions affect the damping characteristics of the assembly.

3 It is the view of some suspension specialists, that cartridge forks should be cleaned and the oil changed after the first forty hours of riding. It is in this first period when most dirt accumulates in the forks.

Removal

4 Note the spring preload setting and rebound damping setting on the fork top bolt assembly before dismantling. In the case of spring preload, if necessary measure and record the distance between the top of the spring preload adjuster and the top of the fork bolt.

5 Leave the top bolt in place, it maintains the spring pressure which prevents the cartridge unit turning as you unscrew the retaining bolt from the bottom of the fork slider. An impact driver may be required to loosen the retaining bolt. Note that there are service tools to hold the cartridge unit whilst the retaining bolt is

unscrewed **(see illustrations)**, although the fork top bolt must first be removed.

6 Unscrew the fork top bolt from the fork tube, noting that some means must be devised for holding the spring compressed whilst the top bolt preload/damping adjuster is separated from the cartridge piston rod. Withdraw the cartridge unit from the fork tube.

Disassembly and cleaning

7 For those cartridges which can be taken apart you will need the manufacturer's instructions and special tools. The cartridge and components can be cleaned using a

mineral-based solvent. Do not use detergent of petrol (gasoline).

8 Submerge the bottom of the cartridge in a container of cleaner and gently pump the piston rod to flush the solvent through the valves to flush out any dirt. Wear eye protection in case of accidental squirts of fluid. Gloves should also be worn.

9 Clean the inside of the fork tubes and let the parts dry naturally.

10 The fork seals and bushes can be dealt with as described for the conventional fork in Section 4.

Assembly, oil filling and air bleeding

11 Install the cartridge unit in the fork and install the retaining bolt. Apply a drop or two of thread locking and sealing compound to the retaining bolt threads.

12 Fill the fork with the specified quantity of the correct oil for cartridge type forks.

13 Extend the fork assembly and gently compress it to allow any air to escape. Repeat this process about ten times, then pump the piston rod gently to expel all the air from the cartridge unit. All the air has been expelled if the rod moves with some resistance throughout its travel on compression or extension. Let the fork stand upright for five minutes to allow the oil level to settle and any air bubbles to rise to the top of the oil.

14 The manufacturer specifies the oil level within the fork. This can be checked using the ruler or vernier as above, however it is more accurate to use a special kit, which comprises a syringe and levelling device **(see illustration)**. The level is usually specified with the spring removed and the fork fully compressed.

15 Set the gauge to the oil level specified in the workshop manual. Insert the scale end into the fork tube until the stop butts against the top of the tube. Draw fluid up into the syringe until the flow ceases and air is drawn into the syringe. If no oil was drawn into the gauge, there is not enough oil in the fork; add oil and repeat the level check.

16 Repeat the process for the other fork. It is **essential** that the levels are the same.

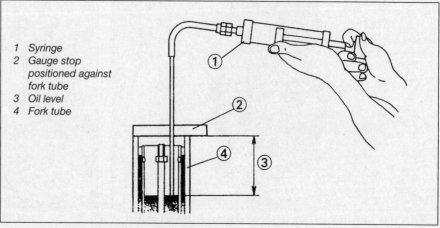

1 Syringe
2 Gauge stop positioned against fork tube
3 Oil level
4 Fork tube

6.14 A fork oil level gauge

7 Front suspension –
other types

Leading or trailing link

1 With this sort of system, there is a mechanical linkage, controlled by damped or undamped suspension units. Maintenance is confined to checking for play in bushes and bearings, and regular lubrication of these pivot points.

2 Most suspension problems will be traced to excessive play in the pivots, usually requiring the renewal of the various bushes or bearings, and possibly the pins upon which they bear.

3 The structural parts of the assembly should be checked for cracks and damage as you would for other frame parts.

4 The shock absorber units should be checked for leaks and corrosion.

Swinging arm type

5 These take the form of the single arm, or an 'A' frame. Steering is still located conventionally using yokes and ball or roller bearings.

6 The comments regarding inspection and maintenance on conventional forks apply to the forks used on this type of suspension.

7 The swinging arm assembly contains many more bushes and seals than the conventional front fork, and these need examination and inspection as instructed in the manual. The advice on bearing and bush removal and refitting given in this manual will be appropriate.

8 This type of suspension incorporates tapered swivel joints which are not found on conventional suspension systems. The use of heat, or special tools are required to separate this type of joint.

9 The swivel joints and pivot points may require greasing at specified intervals.

10 The damper should be inspected for leaks and damage.

Hub centre steering

11 As the name implies the front wheel is pivoted at the hub and is steered via a linkage from the handlebars.

12 This type of suspension and steering utilises bearings and swivel joints which should be treated with the same methods of inspection and maintenance as outlined in the manufacturer's and this manual.

13 The structural parts of the assembly and shock absorbers should be inspected for cracks and damage as you would other frame parts.

14 The swivel joints and pivot points may require greasing at specified intervals.

8 Steering dampers

1 These devices are fitted to some bikes as standard or can be fitted as an aftermarket accessory to improve the steering.

2 Check the unit for signs of leaks and corrosion on the damper rod.

3 Check that the mounting points allow the correct amount of movement.

9 Steering head bearings

1 Most machines use either a taper-roller or caged ball bearing arrangement to support the steering head assembly in the frame. The uncaged ball bearing arrangement (cup and cone bearing) is still used on a number of small-capacity machines.

2 In all cases, hardened steel outer races are pressed into the steering head. The lower inner race is pressed onto the steering stem and the upper inner race is located under the top yoke. The bearing balls or rollers reside between the inner and outer races. Caged balls or rollers are usually integral with the bearing inner race, whereas the uncaged type require individual positioning between the races when assembling the steering head. In all cases, an adjuster and locknut arrangement allows the freeplay to be taken up without applying significant pressure to the bearing assemblies.

3 After a period of time the grease in the bearings will have hardened and need renewing if the bearings are to be maintained in good condition.

4 In time, and if periodic re-greasing of the bearing has been neglected, their condition will deteriorate, the races eventually becoming pitted or indented, making the steering feel stiff and notchy. This may not be immediately obvious in normal riding, but can cause the machine to feel vague and tend to wander. The remedy is to renew both bearing assemblies.

 HAYNES HINT *If using a pressure washer to clean the machine, take care to direct its jet away from the steering head assembly. It is easy to wash vital grease out of the steering head bearings if care is not taken.*

Checking for wear and correct freeplay

5 With the machine on its centre stand, block or jack up the frame to lift the front wheel off the ground, or get an assistant to hold down the rear of the machine.

6 Starting in the straight-ahead position, turn the bars slowly in each direction and feel for any roughness or stiffness.

7 Gauge the effort to turn the bars in each direction. The bars should turn smoothly both ways.

8 Grasp the forks and try to move them backward and forward. Any movement shows that there is a slackness in the bearings **(see illustration)**. If a steering damper is fitted, disconnect it to check for play in the bearings. Note that play in the fork bushes may be misinterpreted as play in the steering bearings – take care not to confuse the two.

9 You will now be able to gauge whether the bearings need tightening, or if any roughness or stiffness is present, whether the bearings need greasing or replacing.

10 Follow the procedure in your workshop manual for setting freeplay. Note that the objective is to eliminate freeplay in the bearings – adjust so that the bearings are under a very light loading, just enough to remove any freeplay. Overtightening will cause premature bearing failure.

9.8 Checking for play in the steering head bearings

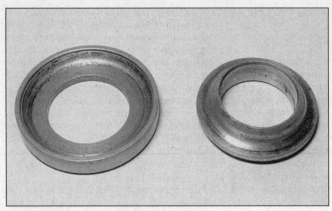

9.12a Examine the bearing races carefully – these are pitted and must be renewed

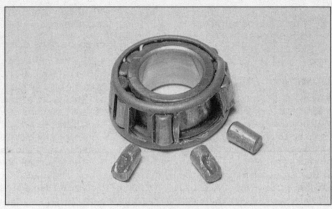

9.12b Damage to this degree is unlikely, but check the rollers and cage carefully

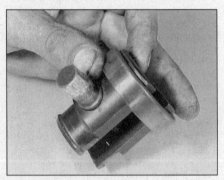

9.13a This tool can be expanded to fit the outer race exactly . . .

Bearing removal

11 Separate the steering head from the frame following the procedure in your workshop manual.
12 Clean all old grease off the bearings and races. Examine the bearing outer races in the frame. If they are pitted, scratched or worn they must be renewed **(see illustration)**. Similarly inspect the balls or rollers and the bearing inner races. If in any doubt

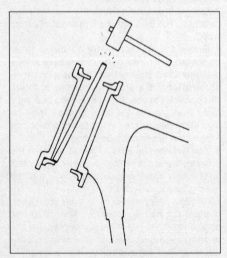

9.13d . . . can be used to drive out the races

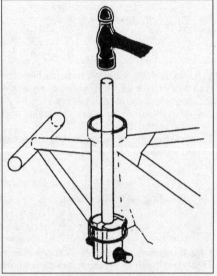

9.13b . . . and used with a drift to drive the race from the frame

13 The outer races can be withdrawn using a universal slide-hammer type bearing extractor, or driven out of the frame using a long drift **(see illustrations)**. If using the drift method tap firmly and evenly around the race to ensure that it drives out squarely. It may

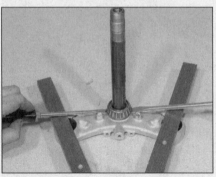

9.14a The lower inner race can be levered off the steering stem . . .

9.13c A long pin punch passed down through the frame . . .

prove advantageous to curve the end of the drift slightly to improve access.
14 The lower inner race will be pressed over the steering stem, and can usually be prised off the lower yoke by tapping wedges below it; screwdriver blades are useful for levering it off the steering stem **(see illustration)**. If the bearing proves stubborn, assemble a bearing puller with an appropriate attachment to seat under the lip of the bearing, and operate the puller to draw the bearing off the stem **(see illustration)**.

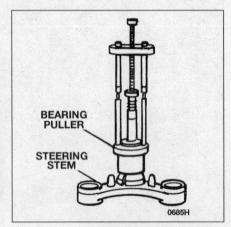

BEARING
PULLER

STEERING
STEM

0685H

9.14b . . . or pulled off with an extractor

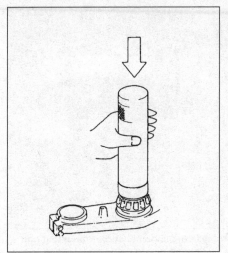

9.15 When fitting the new inner race, the drift must only bear on the inner edge of the race

Bearing installation

15 When refitting the lower inner race on the steering stem, use a length of tubing with a slightly larger diameter than the steering stem to drive the bearing home. Take great care that the tubing does not contact the actual working surface of the bearing, or in the case of caged tapered-roller or caged-ball bearings, the cage or rollers/balls **(see illustration)**. There is usually a seal fitted between the inner race and the lower yoke to protect the bearing from road dirt and water ingress.

16 New outer races can be installed in the frame using a fabricated drawbolt tool **(see illustration)** or a piece of tubing (or large socket), but ensure that the working surface of the races is not damaged by contact from the installing tool. It may be helpful to leave the new races in a freezer overnight to contract them slightly and ease installation.

17 Apply grease to the working surface of the races and the rollers or balls **(see illustration)**. In the case of uncaged ball

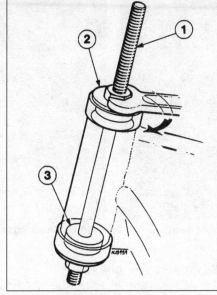

9.16 A drawbolt tool can be made up to install the outer races

Illustrated for lower race installation, the threaded bar (1) has a thick washer (2) positioned against the top of the frame and a guide (3) which locates against the surface of the new lower race

bearings, note that the grease is essential to keep the balls in place as the steering stem is installed in the frame. Also on uncaged bearings, note that there should be some space between the balls; do not be tempted to add an extra ball as this will prevent the balls rolling correctly **(see illustration)**.

18 Assemble the steering stem and top yoke on the frame together with the new upper bearing inner race and any dust seals fitted. Carry out normal bearing adjustment as detailed in your workshop manual, noting that it is normal practice to preload new bearings so that they settle in, and then set normal freeplay.

10 Rear suspension

1 Most rear suspension faults result from wear in the bearings and linkages used, or from deterioration of the shock absorber(s).

2 The wide variety of suspension designs make it impossible to generalise adequately on overhaul techniques, for which you will need the specific procedures described in your workshop manual.

3 It is worth making the point that regular cleaning and maintenance will pay off, especially where a suspension linkage is concerned. Most of these employ large numbers of tiny needle roller bearings, most of which are positioned to take full advantage of the grit and water thrown off by the rear tyre. The seals used to protect them are easily damaged in these conditions, and if they are not renewed immediately, the bearing will soon follow suit.

Shock absorbers

4 Shock absorbers are usually of sealed construction, and replacement parts are not usually available. It is however, worth seeking the advice of a suspension specialist, especially if the unit is an aftermarket shock absorber. Suspension unit mounting bushes **(see illustration)** can be renewed and are usually pressed from the eye of the unit using a drawbolt tool (see Chapter 2, Section 14).

5 Aftermarket shock absorbers are usually of better quality than those fitted to the bike as original equipment. In some cases the handling characteristics can be transformed simply by fitting a good quality shock absorber. Seek advice from a reputable suspension specialist and make sure that the spring and damper rate characteristics are suited to your bike, and that the mounting centres are correctly sized and spaced.

6 For air-assisted units you should use a syringe-type air pump, and also a suspension-type pressure gauge when

9.17a Pack the bearings with grease prior to assembly of the steering head

9.17b Grease is essential to stick the balls in place on an uncaged ball arrangement

10.4 Rubber bushes in shock absorber mountings will usually resist all attempts at driving them out – use a drawbolt tool

10.9 Checking for play in the swingarm pivot bearings

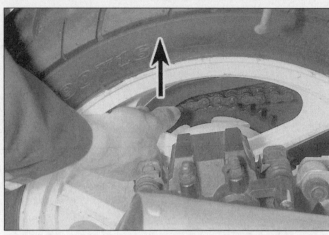

10.10 Checking for play in the shock absorber mounting and linkage pivots

carrying out checks and adjustments; those produced for use on tyres are not sufficiently accurate for this work. **Never** use a garage air-line to inflate the units; you will probably destroy the seals in the attempt. Where the units are not linked, take great care to make sure that the pressure in each is the same.

7 Care should be taken when disposing of gas-assisted shock absorbers. Unless you have full details of how to do this, take the shock absorber to a motorcycle dealer or seek advice from a suspension specialist.

Swingarm and linkage

8 Wear can occur in the swingarm pivot bearings, the shock absorber mountings and on models with a suspension, linkage (single shock) also in the linkage pivots. When checking for wear, set the bike on its stand so that the rear wheel is off the ground, and thus all weight is off the rear suspension. Note that performing the checks with the rear wheel removed and drive chain disconnected will make any problems more obvious.

9 Grasp each end of the swingarm and feel

for any side-to-side play in the swingarm pivot **(see illustration)**. On single shock models, disconnect the shock and linkage arms from the swingarm, and on twin shock models, disconnect both shock absorbers from the swingarm, then repeat the test.

10 Grasp the rear wheel at the top and attempt to pull it up **(see illustration)**. There should be no play before the suspension begins to compress. Any play felt will be in the shock absorbers mountings, or on single shock systems, in the linkage pivots.

11 Swingarm or linkage pivot bearings are usually of the needle roller or ball bearing type and are a press fit in their housings. First slide out any inner sleeves and prise out the grease seals from each side of the housing **(see illustrations)**. Accepting that the bearings will be renewed, a pin punch can be used to tap them out of position **(see illustration)**. Tap evenly around the bearing to ensure that it leaves its housing squarely.

12 When installing new bearings care must be taken to ensure they are not damaged by the installation tool. A piece of tubing or a socket can be used, but it must bear only on the outer race and not the rollers **(see illustration)**. It is preferable to make up a drawbolt tool (see Chapter 2, Section 14) to press the new bearing into position.

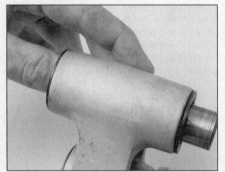

10.11a Slide the inner sleeves out . . .

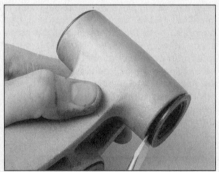

10.11b . . . and prise out the grease seals

10.11c A pin punch can be used to drive out old bearings

10.12 Installing drift must fit just inside the bore of the housing and against the bearing outer race only

11 Disc brakes

 Warning: The dust created by the braking system may contain asbestos, which is harmful to your health. Never blow it out with compressed air and don't inhale any of it. An approved filtering mask should be worn when working on the brakes.

1 Regular maintenance and checks of the braking system are of obvious importance to the safety of the rider and other road users.

11.7 Smear copper grease on the pad backing plate

11.10 Dial gauge mounting arrangement for checking disc runout

2 Reference to the owner's handbook supplied with the machine will give details of the checks and adjustments which are needed on a particular model, whilst the workshop manual will provide more detailed information on maintenance and overhaul of the system.

3 Routine servicing of braking system will eliminate most failures and problems, but the additional points mentioned here may help in some cases.

Disc brake squeal

4 This is a common problem on many models and may be due to a number of factors. Always check the caliper carefully, removing the pads for close inspection and cleaning. Oil or grease contamination may provoke squealing, as can worn pads.

5 In some cases, renewing the pads just before they reach the wear limit mark or line may help.

6 If new pads or a thorough cleaning of the caliper fail to solve the problem, the noise may be due to high frequency chattering between the pads and the pistons. Try removing the pad and cleaning its metal backing metal. Note where the pad backing metal is marked where it is in contact with the piston.

7 Apply a thin film of copper grease to the back of the pads **(see illustration)**. **On no account use other types of grease** – these will melt and contaminate the friction material when the pad gets hot. Assemble the pads, taking care not to get any copper grease on the friction surface.

8 Where the disc surface is drilled or slotted, it is not unknown for strange noises to be produced during braking. If the disc is in good condition, you may have to live with the noise, but if the disc is part-worn, you can try putting a slight chamfer on the edges of the holes or slots. If this fails, a new disc may be the only answer.

Disc brake judder

9 Judder can often be attributed to a warped disc, or one on which the surface has worn unevenly.

10 Check the disc runout with the specified limits, using a dial gauge mounted on the fork leg or swingarm **(see illustration)**.

11 Measure the disc thickness, and check carefully for low spots, or scored areas **(see illustration)**. Compare the measurement with the service limit specified in your workshop manual. Often the minimum disc thickness is stamped in the disc itself **(see illustration)**.

12 Where plain cast iron discs are used the inevitable rust patch which marks the outline of the pads when the machine has been left unused for a time may cause the brake to grab at this point, but this should wear off as the disc is scrubbed clean by the pads and is thus only a temporary problem.

13 Where drilled or slotted discs are fitted, check that the holes are unobstructed; as well as reducing unsprung weight, these holes allow dust and dirt to be removed from the disc surface.

14 If the disc is damaged in any of the ways mentioned, or worn below its service limit, fit a new one, together with new pads. On twin

11.11a Use a micrometer to measure disc thickness

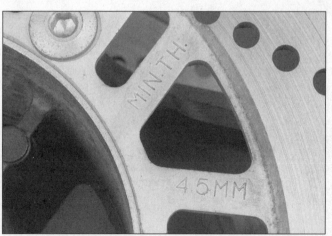

11.11b Minimum thickness is often stamped in the disc

11.25a Flexible hoses can be clamped with a brake hose clamp . . .

11.25b . . . or a wingnut type clamp

disc front brakes, replace both discs at the same time.

Disc brake fade

15 Fade under braking can be due to pads of the wrong grade being fitted; make sure that any replacement pads are recommended for your machine.

16 Even high-quality pads will cause fading when they are worn. This need not be because there is no friction material left; it is important to note that the friction material also functions as a thermal insulator between the disc and the caliper, and this is why the wear limit mark is reached while there is still a good thickness of material left. Ignore this reminder to renew the pads at your peril.

17 Once the heat insulation becomes ineffective, heat can transfer to the caliper, and thus to the hydraulic system. This can boil the fluid under heavy braking, causing unexpected and serious fading.

Poor braking effect or feel

18 This may be due to the type of system in use (some are better than others in this respect) or to general wear and tear. Points to look for are seized caliper pistons, or in the case of sliding calipers, seizure of the slider pins **(see illustration 11.27b)**. Note that in countries where salt is used on the roads this

will contribute to caliper sticking problems. The caliper should be stripped and overhauled and all traces of corrosion removed.

19 Deterioration of the flexible brake pipes can also cause this effect.

20 On machines which employ a braking-linked anti-dive system, remember that problems in this area can affect brake performance too.

21 Old or aerated brake fluid will reduce the boiling point of the fluid, and produce brake fade. Ensure that the fluid is renewed at the interval recommended by the motorcycle manufacturer; this is usually every one to two years. Bleed the brake system or air.

Brake lines

22 If an overhaul of a normally good system does not improve it, check the brake lines.

23 These should be renewed at intervals specified by the manufacturer, irrespective of their apparent condition. The inner reinforcing will gradually weaken in use, allowing the line to swell slightly under pressure. Even marginal swelling, probably imperceptible to the eye, can cause the brake to feel vague and spongy.

24 If you fit new brake lines, and intend keeping the bike for some time, consider fitting braided stainless Teflon lines instead of

the standard type. These are thinner overall, but considerably tougher, but a good investment if you are looking for optimum safety and performance. They also look good!

25 It is often necessary to clamp a flexible hose in order to carry out some work further down the line. Any clamping method must not cause permanent distortion to the hose nor cause any damage **(see illustrations)**. Do not clamp braided steel hoses.

Caliper and master cylinder wear

26 Wear can cause all sorts of braking system problems. Due to its exposed position, the caliper is more vulnerable to the effects of road dirt than the master cylinder.

27 Sliding calipers (with the piston(s) on one side only) can suffer from seized or sticking slider pins. Separate the caliper body from the mounting bracket to access the slider pins. Clean all old grease off the pins and inspect the dust boots for splitting **(see illustration)**. Smear the pins with a silicone grease and check that they slide easily in the caliper **(see illustration)**.

28 Opposed-piston calipers do not pivot, and thus do not suffer the problems described above, but all calipers are prone to pistons sticking or seizing in their bores. Usually this is due to seal failure allowing moisture to get between the exposed end of the piston and the caliper bore.

29 Note that neglected fluid changes will have allowed the fluid in the system to absorb moisture, and this in turn will have promoted corrosion between the caliper bore and piston.

30 Master cylinders are less likely to suffer problems than the calipers, but problems do occur. These can range from corrosion and blocked ports, to general wear and seal failure. Unlike calipers, seal failure is not always obvious; air can be drawn back into the system without external signs of leakage.

31 In the case of any suspected fault in the hydraulic system, it is vital that it should be

11.27a Check that dust boots are not cracked or split

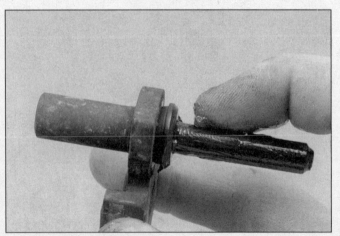

11.27b Smear silicone grease over the slider pins

investigated promptly, before the brake fails in service. The large variety of calipers and master cylinders precludes coverage here, so for specific information, refer to the workshop manual for your machine. Always check the availability of seal kits for calipers and master cylinders before dismantling – new seals must be used when overhauling hydraulic components.

32 Certain manufacturers specify caliper bore and piston service limits to enable these items to be checked for wear. You will need a micrometer and vernier gauge or small hole gauge to measure these components. Similar information is often specified for master cylinder bore and piston diameters.

 HAYNES HINT *Although all seals are renewed when overhauling a caliper or master cylinder, always take careful note of the fitted position of the original seals as the components are dismantled. Seals are often chamfered on one edge and must always be fitted the correct way around.*

Brake fluid

33 See Chapter 17 for information on brake fluids.

34 Always renew fluid at the specified intervals. Old fluid is dangerous because it is hygroscopic, absorbing water vapour from the air. Normal braking temperatures can then cause boiling, and the resulting air will make the brake fade in use. Regular changes of the fluid will remove this moisture, which if left will cause corrosion of the system.

35 The usual hydraulic fluids are mineral based. The master cylinder reservoir cap is marked with the fluid type and you should always stick with this recommendation. Synthetic fluids are used by some motorcycle manufacturers and again the reservoir cap will be marked accordingly. Note that you cannot

mix mineral and synthetic fluids. Note that different seals are used in synthetic fluid systems so do not be tempted to switch fluid types without seeking professional advice first.

Bleeding

Caution: Hydraulic fluid will mark or damage paintwork and many plastic finishes. Keep the fluid well away from these areas, and protect vulnerable parts like the fuel tank by covering it with clean cloth before working on the system.

36 It will be of no surprise that air, even in small amounts, will seriously affect the operation of the brakes. If you suspect that air is present, the system must be bled to expel it.

37 Whilst the procedure for bleeding brake systems varies from machine to machine, and is dependent on the exact arrangement used, the principle is to pump fluid from the master cylinder, through the pipes to the caliper. Here, the fluid is allowed to emerge through a bleed valve provided for this purpose and is caught in a suitable container. The bleed valve is usually positioned at the highest point on the caliper.

38 Special brake bleeding tubes can be purchased, and these help prevent air working back into the caliper by utilising a one-way valve. This also means that the job can be more easily carried out by one person **(see illustration)**.

39 The normal bleeding procedure for most models is as follows, but check your workshop manual for any special procedures which might apply to your machine, such as if the caliper has two bleed valves.

a) *Remove the rubber cap from the bleed valve and attach a length of tubing or a special bleed tube to it; make sure that the tube fits snugly and there are no air leaks. Place the other end in the container which is to catch the fluid, submerging the end in hydraulic fluid* **(see illustration)**.

b) *Remove the master cylinder reservoir and top up to the maximum level, using only*

the recommended type and grade of new hydraulic fluid.

c) *If the system is empty, open the bleed valve and pump the brake lever or pedal rapidly until fluid appears at the bleed tube, then check and top up the reservoir. Loosely refit the reservoir cap or cover to exclude dirt and to prevent spouts of fluid being expelled during the bleeding operation.*

d) *With the bleed valve closed, pump the lever or pedal until resistance can be felt. Keep the pedal or lever depressed, then open the valve slightly until the flow of fluid slows to a near standstill. Close the valve, then release the pedal or lever.*

e) *Check the level of fluid in the reservoir, and top it up where required.*

f) *Repeat steps d) and e) until air bubbles no longer emerge with the expelled fluid, then tighten the valve fully and check brake operation.*

g) *Remove the bleed tube and refit the bleed valve dust cap, wipe up any fluid spills, being particularly careful to remove fluid spots from the paintwork (see below). Dispose of the used fluid safely.*

40 On motorcycles which have a brake-linked front suspension anti-dive system, check if bleed valves are fitted in the anti-dive unit or connecting unions. If so, they must be bled of air in accordance with the front brake system.

41 If you are changing the brake fluid as part of the routine maintenance interval, connect up the brake bleeding equipment as described above and expel all old fluid from the system. As the fluid nears the bottom of the reservoir, top up with new fluid and continue the bleeding operation until the new fluid has passed down through the hydraulic lines and is expelled into the container.

 HAYNES HINT *Old brake fluid is invariably much darker in colour than new fluid, making it easier to see when old fluid has been expelled from the system.*

11.38 A one-man brake bleeding kit

11.39 Conventional brake bleeding equipment

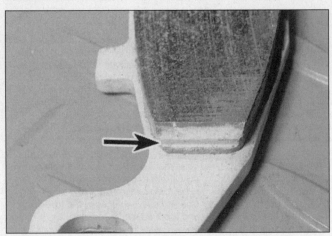

11.47a On this pad the wear limit is indicated by a step in the friction material

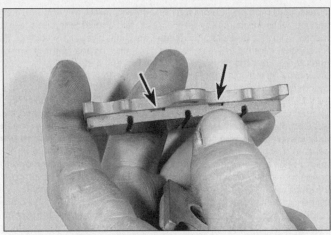

11.47b When this pad wears down to the limit, the grooves in its friction face with disappear and the cutouts (arrowed) will be exposed

42 Never keep old fluid for re-use – it will be dirty and will also have absorbed moisture, lowering its safe working temperature. Dispose of old brake fluid safely.

43 If it proves difficult to bleed the brakes, the system may be aerated (air bubbles trapped in the hydraulic lines). Let the system stabilise for a few hours to allow the air bubbles to settle out, then repeat the operation.

Anti-lock and linked braking systems

44 On these systems, there will be many more hydraulic lines than on a conventional front or rear brake system. Those lines which run along the frame are likely to be small-bore metal pipes and it can be very difficult to bleed air from these pipes using conventional equipment and the hand-operated method described above. In such cases a pressure bleeding kit is often advised which attaches to the fluid reservoir. Alternatively, there are kits available which operate by sucking fluid through the system using a vacuum pump.

45 On ABS and linked systems there are usually additional bleed valves located on the pressure modulators and control valves. On linked systems, note that it is usual to bleed the system components in a particular order – refer to your workshop manual for details.

46 Note that the amount of fluid required to bleed or fill an ABS or linked system will be greater than for a conventional system.

Brake pads

47 Brake pads have a groove, step or cutout in their friction material to denote their wear limit **(see illustrations)**. Additionally, some manufacturers also specified a minimum thickness for the amount of friction material remaining; 1.5 mm being a typical amount. Depending on the caliper design, the amount of friction material remaining on the pads can be seen without removing them from the caliper.

48 When brake pads are renewed, always replace both pads in the caliper at the same time, and also renew the pads in the other caliper on dual front brakes.

49 New brake pads need a bedding down period of about 200 miles before they will operate effectively.

12 Drum brakes

1 Other than regular maintenance and adjustment, details of which will be found in the Service and Repair Manual for the machine concerned, there is little to go wrong with a drum brake arrangement. Faults will occur as the machine gets older, however, and this will be more likely if maintenance has been neglected. The more common problems are described below.

Binding or dragging brakes

2 This may be due to corrosion in the operating mechanism causing seizure. With cable-operated systems, check that the cable works smoothly and freely after disconnecting it at the brake plate.

3 If necessary, lubricate the cable to restore normal operation.

4 Sometimes a cable will begin to fray at the upper end, this normally being caused by the nipple seizing in the handlebar lever or pedal. The frayed strands of the inner will tend to catch in the outer cable, holding the brake partially on. This is a dangerous situation, and the cable must be renewed at once. See Chapter 7 for repairing and replacing cable nipples.

5 Another likely spot for problems is the brake cam, which may become stiff in its bore due to old, dried out grease or corrosion. To prevent this, remove the brake shoes and operating arm and push out the cam for cleaning and lubrication. If this is attended to

regularly, the risk of seizure will be eliminated.

6 Be careful not to apply an excessive amount of grease to the working faces of the cam, or the surplus grease may find its way on to the shoes.

Brake judder

7 Judder may be due to localised rusting or damage to the drum surface.

8 Check the drum surface for runout. This can sometimes be caused by the drum being pulled oval due to irregular spoke tension, where the wheel is of the wire spoked type.

9 The best thing to do if you discover this problem is to have the wheel dealt with by a wheel builder. It may be possible to pull the drum back to the correct shape by adjusting the spoke tension correctly.

10 Any remaining ovality can be corrected by skimming the drum, provided that this does not take the drum diameter beyond its service limit. To do this you can use a lathe providing it has a large enough capacity to swing the diameter of the drum.

Weak or ineffective brakes

11 Inefficiency can be caused by a number of problems, and you should check the obvious areas first, such as the condition of the shoes.

12 If the lining material has become contaminated with oil or grease, new shoes should be fitted, having first degreased the brake parts and repaired the cause of the contamination.

13 If there is no sign of grease on the linings, check for glazing of the friction surface. This can be caused by overheating the linings under heavy braking, or because of brake drag.

14 The linings can be restored by roughening the surface with abrasive paper. Do this outside, and wear a particle mask to avoid inhalation of asbestos dust.

15 Temporary problems can be experienced if water gets into the brake, and this will tend to take some time to dry out naturally. To

12.17a The pointer will show when brake wear is within the working range

12.17b Drum brake shoes wear more on the leading edge

13.3a A pressure cable lubricator for use with aerosol cable lubricant

speed up this process, try riding for a while with the brake held lightly on; the friction will produce enough heat to help evaporate the water. Do not overdo this procedure; excessive heat will result in glazing (see above).

16 Mechanical problems include a loss of leverage at the operating arm. Ideally, the cable or operating rod should pull on the arm at an angle of approximately 90°. If the arm is positioned incorrectly, or if the shoes have worn down to the service limit, this angle may have altered, and less braking effort will be produced by a given amount of pressure at the lever or pedal.

17 Check for shoe wear first; there is often a pointer on the brake cam which will show when the linings are worn to the point where

renewal is advisable **(see illustrations)**. If the brake arm angle still seems wrong, check that it is fitted in the correct position on the splines of the cam. On many brakes, a dot or line on the end of the cam should align with the split or dot in the arm.

18 A few machines may be encountered where twin leading shoes (tls) brakes are fitted. With this type of brake there is normally an adjuster in the link between the two cams, and it is important to make sure that this is set so that the two brake shoes operate in unison.

13 Cable lubrication

1 Disconnect the cable at its upper end.

2 Check the cable for damage, and replace if necessary.

3 Lubricate the cable using a pressure cable lubricator **(see illustrations)**.

4 An improvised set-up can be just as effective **(see illustration)**.

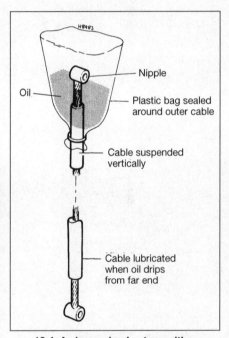

13.4 An improvised set-up with a makeshift funnel and motor oil

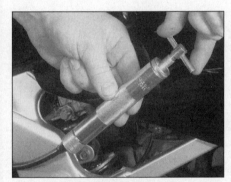

13.3b This type of cable lubricator is filled with light oil and operated . . .

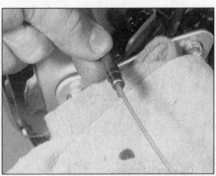

13.3c . . . until oil emerges from the other end of the cable

Notes

Chapter 13
Electrical and ignition tasks

Contents

1 Introduction and general requirements for electrical work

1 This Chapter describes the more general repairs and test methods for electrical and ignition components. For obvious reasons, it is not model specific, and any procedures must be accompanied by test data specific to the model being worked on. Equally, you will need a wiring diagram specifically for your bike.

2 The electrical system seems to cause more owners problems than any other aspect of their machine, and this is probably mostly a result of the generally intangible nature of electricity; you simply cannot see how it works. For much of the time you can deal with the normal type of electrical faults without any great understanding of electrical theory, and this Chapter was written with this approach in mind.

3 Those wishing to investigate the theoretical aspects of motorcycle electrics in greater depth should refer to the Haynes *Motorcycle Electrical Manual TechBook*.

4 Electrical work is largely a self-contained area within the general subject of workshop practice, and as such requires a few specialised tools and safety considerations. Before we look at examples of actual workshop jobs, the notes below should be considered.

Safety considerations

5 There is generally more risk of damage to the electrical system than to you, should you make a mistake while working on the machine. Nevertheless there are a few simple precautions which can virtually eliminate this possibility.

6 Unless the system actually needs to be live, disconnect and remove the battery. The battery negative (–ve) earth (ground) lead should always be disconnected first, and re-connected last.

7 On most machines a negative (–ve) earth system is employed, so as a rule of thumb, disconnect the negative lead first. No matter how careful you are, it is easy to accidentally short circuit the system when connecting or disconnecting components and leads. Note that the voltages produced by the ignition system can be dangerous.

8 The battery contains sulphuric acid and gives off an explosive gas when being charged. Therefore take care to handle the battery safely and avoid any naked heat sources and provide a well ventilated area when the battery is being charged.

Special tools and equipment

9 The basic tools outlined earlier in Chapters 2 and 5 will be required for electrical work, as well as mechanical work. In addition, there are a few extra pieces of equipment which you will need.

10 A selection of terminals will be needed to replace any which are broken or corroded. These can be bought in kits as required from vehicle electrical specialists.

11 An assortment of colour-coded insulated wire will be needed for repairs and alterations to the system. It is obviously preferable that the new wires match the colour coding of the original. You can either buy this new, in reels or cut to length, or as a cheap alternative, try a local motorcycle breaker for the wiring harness from a scrapped machine.

12 Whether you obtain new or used wire, it should be noted that its current-carrying capacity is determined by the effective diameter of the conductor. The conductor area of any replacement wire must be at least equal to that of the original. If it is smaller, the circuit concerned may not receive sufficient power, and the risk of an electrical fire is increased due to the conductor becoming hot in use.

13 PVC insulating tape is useful for repairing breaks in the wiring insulation and covering repairs. You can also use it to tape extra wires neatly to the existing harness, and in emergencies only, to tape up bare wire ends or wires which have been twisted together to make a temporary connection. Keep a roll in the toolkit carried on the machine.

14 Nylon cable ties are invaluable for tidying up the harness and strapping wires (or control cables) to the frame. You will find them a useful replacement for the original metal ties when these break off. Again, it is worth carrying a few of these on the machine, taped to the frame below the seat, for emergency repairs of all sorts.

15 Consumable materials include such things as aerosol contact cleaner, WD40, abrasive paper and fine files, small nuts and bolts, fibre or nylon washers and silicone grease.

2 Basic circuit testing methods

1 In the event of most electrical faults, the first problem to be faced is tracking down the cause. In many instances the fault will be due to a simple mechanical failure such as a broken wire, or a loose or corroded connection.

Basic testing procedures

Checking for continuity

2 The term continuity describes the uninterrupted flow of electricity through an electrical circuit.

3 Continuity can be checked by measuring circuit resistance using a simple multimeter, battery-operated continuity tester, or an ohmmeter. With the tester probes touched together, check that the meter reading is zero or the continuity tester sounds or illuminates. If necessary, adjust the meter to set the reading to zero.

4 Along the connecting wires there should obviously be very little resistance if any is detectable at all, and switches should present no resistance when switched to the ON position and infinite resistance when switched OFF **(see illustration)**.

5 For the purposes of simple continuity checks or resistance measurements, disconnect the machine's battery to avoid the risk of the battery voltage damaging the tester or meter.

6 Using the machine's wiring diagram, locate the suspect wiring run, using the wiring colour-coding to guide you. Check the continuity between each end of a wiring run, moving through the circuit until the break is located **(see illustration)**.

7 When dealing with combination switches or blocks with multiple connectors, check the wiring diagram to make sure that you are connecting across the right pair of wires.

8 Continuity can also be checked by passing a small current through the system and having a light bulb or buzzer activated when the circuit is closed. This method uses the traditional home-made battery and bulb test kit described in Chapter 5.

Checking for voltage

9 Using the voltage applied from the bike battery, continuity can also be checked by measuring that the battery voltage is present throughout the circuit.

10 A multimeter is the instrument for this test. With one probe connected to the earth or ground terminal of the battery or to some clean contact on the frame, the other probe is placed in the circuit **(see illustration)**. The battery voltage should be read on the meter.

11 Where you need to check for voltage on a circuit, leave the battery connected, and set the meter to the appropriate volts range (this will normally be 0 – 10 volts dc in the case of 6 volt machines, and 0 – 20 volts dc on 12 volt systems). Without disconnecting any of the wiring, connect the correct meter probe to a sound earth (ground) point on the frame. On negative (–ve) earth machines this means the black meter probe.

12 Connect the remaining probe to the connector terminal to be tested, pushing it into the back of the connector. Switch on the ignition, and where necessary, the circuit under test, and note whether battery voltage is shown. If you do not get a reading, make similar checks back along the wiring harness until the break is located.

13 Taking an actual reading will give you an

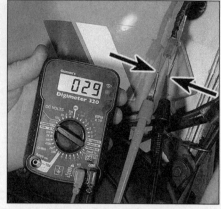

2.4 A front brake light switch being checked for continuity at the wiring sub-harness connector

indication of the condition of connectors and switches etc. because you will be able to see a voltage drop across a poorly connected component or wire. This indicates an internal problem with the component.

14 On machines where direct lighting is used, the power to the headlamp is fed direct from the flywheel generator, rather than from the battery. It follows that you will need to run the engine to check for power on the affected circuits. Note also that direct lighting current is unrectified, or ac. This means that you must set the meter to the **ac volts** range for this type of check. This is also the case on larger machines where voltage checks are made on the alternator output; this too is ac before it passes through the rectifier – refer to your workshop manual for the exact test procedure and test meter setting.

> ⚠ **Warning: In the case of ignition system components, especially those used in electronic systems, very high voltages are present. These can be unpleasant or even dangerous if care is not taken to avoid shocks, and no testing is normally done with these systems under power.**

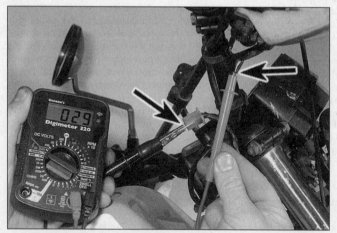

2.6 Checking the continuity between each end of the wiring sub-harness

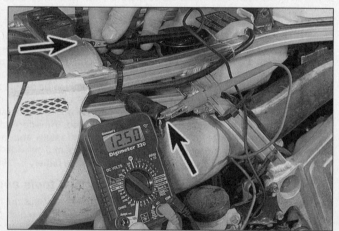

2.10 dc voltmeter shows battery voltage when connected across the load and frame earth (arrows)

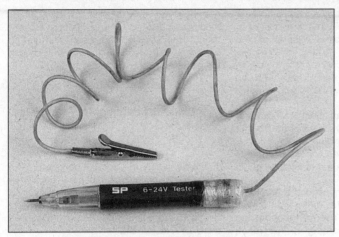

2.15a A simple test light for checking voltage

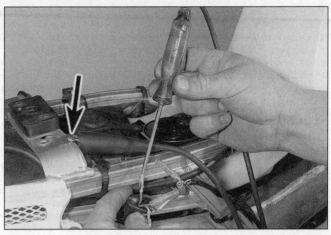

2.15b The test light earth is connected to the frame (arrow) and its positive probe into the circuit

15 A test light or buzzer can be substituted for the voltmeter **(see illustration)**. Connect the instrument's negative (–ve) probe to the battery negative terminal or a sound earth on the frame, then connect the positive probe into the circuit being tested **(see illustration)**. With the ignition ON, the light should illuminate or buzzer sound to indicate that voltage is present.

What to look for

16 Although it is impossible to list all the areas where faults will occur, there are certain areas which are more likely than others to cause problems, and it is always best to check these first. You should also refer to any fault diagnosis information in your workshop manual.

17 Loose or corroded connections are the single most common cause of electrical faults, and may be responsible for a number of symptoms. Common problems are intermittent or erratic operation of lighting circuits, and turn signal systems are especially prone to this sort of fault. The cure is to work through each connection in the circuit, separating all connectors and checking for looseness, corrosion or the presence of water.

18 Clean the connection carefully, or if badly corroded, renew it and pack the connector with silicone grease to prevent water getting into it in the future.

19 This applies equally to earth (ground) connections, which can disrupt the circuit just as easily. Areas especially prone to earthing faults include turn signal and stop/tail lamps, where it often causes erratic operation and can result in frequently blown bulbs. If the ground connection is corroded, clean all the contact surfaces back to bare metal. Check the security of the main earth lead from the battery to the frame and the earth lead from the engine unit to the frame.

20 Bulb failure may be due to old age, vibration, loose or damaged wiring (see above) or fluctuations in the supply. If the bulb

envelope is clean and a section of the filament is damaged, vibration is the most likely cause. Check the mounting of the lamp and where necessary remount it using rubber washers to damp the vibration.

21 Blown bulbs can be due to current surge or other supply problems, in which case the bulb envelope will normally have become blackened, or will have a silvery appearance. If the fault keeps recurring, check the charging system voltage – you could have a faulty voltage regulator or rectifier.

22 On direct lighting machines, make sure that the bulbs are all of the correct wattage. If one bulb is of the wrong rating, excess current may blow it or other bulbs. A resistor unit is often used to shunt excess current to earth. If this fails, or if it becomes partially or fully disconnected from the circuit, repeated bulb failure is likely.

23 Overcharging or undercharging of the battery may be due to a failure of the voltage regulator or rectifier unit, and this should be removed and tested using the test details in the workshop manual. A defective battery, with a dead cell may provoke this sort of charging problem.

24 Turn signal system faults are usually caused by a blown or out-of-circuit bulb. If this happens, the remaining lamp on that side will flash rapidly and dimly. Check and renew or refit the bulb as required.

3 Wiring harness

Repairs

1 Damaged wires or connectors require careful soldering of the new terminals, after cutting off the old ones with side cutters. The spade terminals used in multi-pin connectors are held in place by a small tang, and the terminal can usually be freed after this has

been displaced with a small screwdriver blade.

2 Remember to fit the wire through the connector housing before crimping or soldering the new terminal to it.

3 If a section of wire has become damaged, cut through the insulation at the damaged point and strip back a few millimetres of insulation on each end. Tin the exposed wire, then overlap the ends and solder them together.

4 For details of soldering techniques, refer to Chapter 7. Wrap the repair after it has cooled off, using PVC tape.

5 In some instances, especially on older machines, it may be necessary to renew a whole section of wiring. If you can, try to get a spare wiring harness from a similar model at a breaker, and just swap sections of wiring as required.

6 If you have to make up your own section of harness from scratch, try to match wiring colours as far as possible, and be sure that the conductor gauge of the new wire is at least equal to that of the old one.

7 If the damage is extensive or general to the whole system, it may be worth fitting a new harness. This is a long involved process, but not beyond the capabilities of most owners if approached systematically. Again, get a good used harness if you can; it will be cheaper and easier than buying it new or making up your own.

8 Points to watch out for are extra wires, which will be found on most models. These are for circuits applicable to other markets, and are present simply because it is easier for the manufacturer to make a single universal harness than many variations of it. Occasionally, these 'spare' wires can be used to replace a damaged one in the harness, but check its connections and diameter carefully first.

9 The bullet or prong connectors can come apart underneath the plastic protectors and not be noticed. When doing a continuity check, wiggle the connectors to see if there is an intermittent fault.

10 Occasionally a wire may break in the middle of a run. A continuity check with the multimeter at both ends of the wire in turn should identify which piece of wire is faulty. Breaks may be detected by gently stretching the wire until the insulation gives at the fault point.

Routing

11 Group wires together and run them through PVC sleeving for protection, remembering to fit this before any connections are soldered into place.

12 Check that the wiring harness or cable is not twisted or kinked.

13 Try and route cables to keep then away from sharp edges. If this is not possible protect the wires with electrical tape or tube.

14 Avoid laying the harness near the projecting ends of bolts and screws and maintain sufficient clearance so that spanners do not snag.

15 Keep the wiring away from exhaust pipes and other hot parts.

16 Check that any grommets through which the wiring passes are seated properly in their fixing hole.

17 Check that the wiring harness nor any single cable is fixed with excessive slack or pulled too tight.

18 The wiring should not be routed in a place where it might be pinched by a moving part.

19 Wiring to handlebars controls should be checked over the range of movement of the bars to make sure that it is not stretched or trapped, nor interferes with the smooth movement of the steering.

Installing new wiring

20 On custom specials or restoration work you may have to build a new wiring harness from scratch or modify an existing one. If possible, choose a wiring harness from the same model as the engine, which will include the generator/alternator, regulator, and ignition system wiring.

21 Although you may be aiming for a very simple direct system, the lighting system may demand that certain ancillaries such as a battery are fitted in the system.

22 Before beginning to lay out the wiring, install all the required components, switches, lights etc. to check that wiring connections can be made easily and safely.

4 Electrical cable sizes and ratings

1 The conductor is almost invariably made from copper, and is composed of a number of thin strands rather than a single thick one, to allow the cable to bend easily without risk of the conductor breaking. The conductor is twisted into a gentle spiral bundle, and the

whole is then protected by a plastic insulator layer, normally available in a wide range of colours to permit colour-coding of the electrical system.

2 The cable size is shown as the number of strands and the diameter of each one, eg 14/0.30 would denote 14 strands. each of 0.30 mm diameter.

3 The size rating of an electrical cable is expressed in terms of the area of the copper conductor, and this indicates its current-carrying capacity and its voltage drop (loss due to electrical resistance) over a given length.

4 Electrical cable is produced in both metric and Imperial sizes. The manufacturer will select the cable sizes used throughout the electrical system according to the loads expected in a given circuit. The cable must be able to carry the appropriate current without overheating or excessive volt-drop, both of which are affected by the conductor area.

5 A summary of the commonly-available metric and imperial cables sizes is shown below.

Size	Metric cables current rating (A)	Volt drop (V/m/A)
16/0.20	4.25	0.0371
9/0.30	5.5	0.02935
14/0.25	6.0	0.02715
14/0.30	8.5	0.01884
21/0.30	12.75	0.01257
28/0.30	17.0	0.00942
35/0.30	21.0	0.00754
44/0.30	25.5	0.006
65/0.30	31.0	0.00406
84/0.30	41.5	0.00374
97/0.30	48.0	0.00272
120/0.30	55.5	0.0022
80/0.40	70.0	0.00182

Size	Inch cables current rating (A)	Volt drop (V/ft/A)
23/0.0076	5.75	0.00836
9/0.012	5.75	0.00840
14/0.010	6.00	0.00778
36/0.0076	8.75	0.00534
14/0.012	8.75	0.00540
28/0.012	17.5	0.00770
35/0.012	21.75	0.00216
44/0.012	27.5	0.00172
65/0.012	35	0.00116
97/0.012	50	0.0008
120/0.012	60	0.00064
60/0.018	70	0.00057

6 It should be noted that various factors will have an effect on the cable's capacity. It is especially important to consider the rate at which heat can be dissipated from the cable; a single exposed cable being much better than cables bunched together in a wiring loom in this respect.

7 Where the cable is included in a loom and thus less able to shed unwanted heat, reduce the effective current rating to 60% of that shown in the above table. A good rule-of-

thumb is to use a size or two larger than that indicated by the expected current rating; this will obviate any overheating problems, and will ensure minimal volt-drop in the circuit.

5 Electrical connectors

1 A wide variety of electrical connectors are in use on motor vehicles in general, though on most motorcycles you will encounter only a few of these. Irrespective of the type of terminal used, a sound electrical connection is the main requirement.

2 It is preferable to use soldered joints. Done properly, these ensure a good electrical and mechanical connection between the conductor and its terminal, and will not give rise to problems later.

3 Soldering techniques are discussed in some detail in Chapter 7 of this manual, and if you are not familiar with the process it is worth using a few terminals for practice before any real repairs or alterations are undertaken.

4 Crimped joints are more common than soldered joints these days, the former being much quicker and easier to carry out. If done carefully, and assuming that the wire end and terminal are clean prior to assembly, this type of connection is nearly as good as a soldered joint, though there remains the possibility of corrosion occurring in the joint unless it is well protected.

5 Crimping is fairly straightforward to carry out, requiring the cable insulation to be stripped back by the specified amount before the terminal is crimped in place using special pliers. With most crimp-fitting terminals, two crimped joints are made, one to secure the conductor, and a second to hold the insulation.

6 It is possible to purchase terminal kits which include a selection of terminals and a crimping tool in a partitioned box. This is a good idea as an initial purchase; you can add extra terminals later if you find that you need them.

7 Look for corrosion and inspect each connector for slackness and damage to the insulation. Unless serious corrosion has taken place, it is not normally necessary to renew these connectors.

Flat-blade connectors

8 These are commonly-used connectors also known as spade terminals, and are either crimped or soldered to the end of a cable. Available in a range of sizes, these connectors are produced in male and female patterns, allowing cables to be connected together or to electrical components having the corresponding connector half. In most cases, the terminal will be insulated with a plastic sleeve which slides over the exposed metal part to prevent short-circuits.

Bullet connectors

9 Bullet connectors are an alternative type to the flat-blade connectors and are cylindrical in shape. They will often be encountered on motorcycles other than where multi-pin connectors are used, as the female can be multi-socket. The 'bullet' terminal is fitted by soldering or crimping it to the bared cable end, the connection being made by pushing it into an insulated tubular connector.

Eyelet and forked terminals

10 These will be found where components or cables from the harness need to be connected to earth (ground). The terminal is crimped or soldered to the wire end, and then secured by a bolt or screw to a sound earth point.
11 Often a shakeproof washer will be found under the fastener head; this bites into the component paintwork, thus improving electrical contact.

Multi-pin connectors

12 Most connections to the main harness are made using multi-pin connector blocks, and

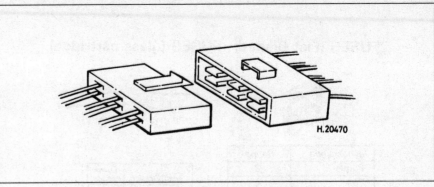

5.14 A multi-pin connector with security latch

these are usually moulded in such a way that it is impossible to fit the two halves incorrectly. Each connector will carry two or more wires relating to a certain circuit or component. On certain machines, the connector blocks are colour-coded.
13 Inside the plastic connector halves will be found a number of flat-blade or bullet-type connectors.
14 These are frequently held in place with a small sprung peg or tang, and close examination of the connector will usually reveal exactly how the terminal is secured. It is normally possible to depress the tang or peg to allow the terminal to be withdrawn from the connector half, and this can be

invaluable where it is necessary to remove corrosion **(see illustration)**.
15 It is a good idea to pack the inside of each connector half with silicone grease. This excludes moisture and air, preventing subsequent electrical faults, and is especially useful on off-road machines.
16 Multi-pin connectors are normally sold complete with the switch or component to which they are wired, and it is unlikely that you will be able to locate a supplier of the connectors or terminals. The usual method of dealing with this type of problem is to remove the affected wires from the connector block and to fit a single bullet-type connector to bypass the damaged terminals.

Self-stripping connector

17 This type of connector is very useful when adding extra wiring to the circuit. Closing the connector over the wiring splits the insulation and joins the new wire to the bared original wire **(see illustration)**.

6 Fuses

1 Just about every machine uses at least one fuse to protect the electrical equipment from damage in the event of a fault such as a short circuit. The fuse acts as an intentional 'weak link' and is designed to fail well before damage can be caused to the circuit concerned.
2 On small machines and mopeds, a single main fuse is usually all that is fitted, whilst on larger models, individual circuits are normally fused separately.
3 The fuses are plugged into a fusebox or holder which is normally located within easy reach behind a bodypanel or below the seat. On many larger machines provision is made in the fusebox for the fitting of additional circuits for electrical accessories.
4 There are four types of fuse currently used on motorcycles **(see illustration)**.

Glass cartridge fuse

5 Glass cartridge fuses are used on many machines and comprise a short length of

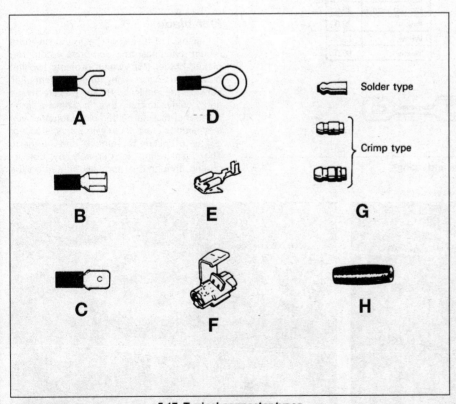

5.17 Typical connector types

A Fork	D Eyelet	G Bullet connector male
B Flat-blade female	E Flat-blade piggy back	H Bullet connector female
C Flat-blade male	F Self-stripping connector	(can be single or multiple)

FUSES (Flat Bladed) FUSES (glass cartridge)

cone end

flat end

Identification	Rating
Purple	3
Pink	4
Orange	5
Brown	7.5
Red	10
Blue	15
Yellow	20
White	25
Green	30

Identification	Lucas Ratings
Length 25.4mm (1")	
Cone end	AMP
Blue	3
Yellow	4.5
Nut Brown	8.0
Red on Green	10.0
White	35.0
Length 29.4mm (1⁵/₃₂")	
Flat end	
Red on Blue	2.0
Red	5.0
Blue on Green	8.0
Black on Blue	10.0
Light Brown	15.0
Blue on Yellow	20.0
Pink	25.0
White	35.0
Yellow	50.0

FUSES (ceramic type)

Identification	BSS Ratings
Length 25mm	AMP
Yellow	5
White	8
Red	16
Blue	25

FUSIBLE LINK (ribbon fuse)

6.4 Fuse types and ratings

glass tubing inside which a fuse wire of the required rating is connected between metal end caps **(see illustration)**. The fuse is either fitted in an individual fuse holder, or more commonly, clipped between terminals in a fuse box.

6 This type of fuse can sometimes be difficult to identify as having failed if its wire has broken or blown near the metal end caps; check by substitution, or carry out a continuity test if you are in any doubt. Note that there are two basic types of glass cartridge fuse; cone end types which are 25.4 mm (1.00 in) long, and flat end types which are 29.4 mm (1.16 in) long. Make sure that you purchase the correct length for your machine!

Ceramic fuse

7 Ceramic fuses are most often found on older European machines where they take the place of the glass cartridge type **(see illustration)**. The coloured ceramic body supports the one-piece fuse element and end caps, the whole assembly being clipped between terminals.

8 Note that glass fuses are normally rated at the fusible value whilst ceramic fuses are rated at the maximum continuous current that they can carry, which is half of the fusing value.

Flat-blade

9 Flat-bladed fuses will be found on more recent machines, and comprise a coloured plastic holder from which projects two flat blade terminals. The fuse element lies between the terminals. These fuses are simple and positive in use, though where a large number of fuses are fitted close together you may need to grasp them with a special tool or a pair of pliers to remove and fit them. The fuse rating is denoted by colour-coding, though it is normally printed on the

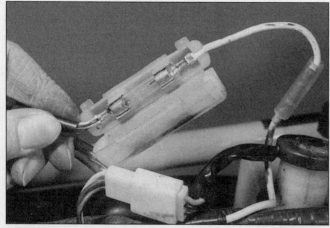

6.5 A break in a glass cartridge fuse can be easily seen through its glass body

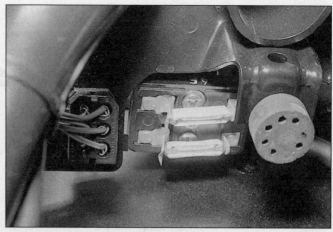

6.7 On the ceramic type fuse metal strips run each side of the ceramic body

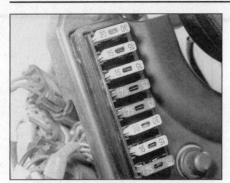

6.9a Flat-blade fuses are a plug-in fitting . . .

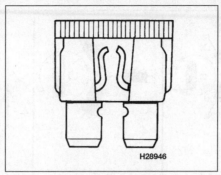

6.9b . . . and a break can easily be seen through its plastic case

6.11 This type of circuit breaker can be reset by pushing the button back in

end of the plastic holder as well **(see illustrations)**.

Ribbon/ fusible link

10 Ribbon fuses are less likely to be encountered than the more common types described above. but may be found on a few models. The fuse element consists of a flat metal strip. usually secured at each end by a small screw. When fitting a new fuse of this type be sure to handle them carefully – the soft element is easily torn or broken if twisted.

Circuit breakers

11 Circuit breakers are occasionally used in place of a main fuse, and have the advantage that they may be reset after a fault has occurred **(see illustration)**. Most types consist of contacts operated by a bi-metal strip, and are designed to break the circuit if the current exceeds the rated figure.

12 The unit has a reset button mounted on the case, and this can be used to reset the circuit after the fault has been resolved and the unit allowed to cool down.

13 The circuit breaker is a sealed unit, and if it develops an internal fault it must be renewed.

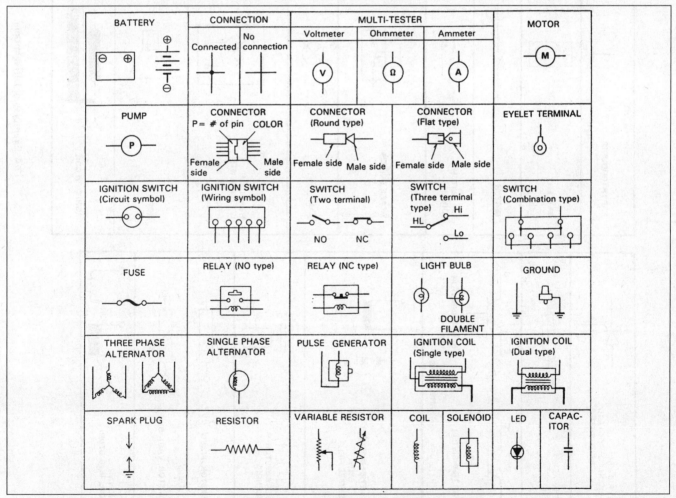

7.3 Examples of the symbols used by Honda

Abbreviations used: NO = Normally open, switch is open at rest   NC = Normally closed, switch is closed at rest   # = Number

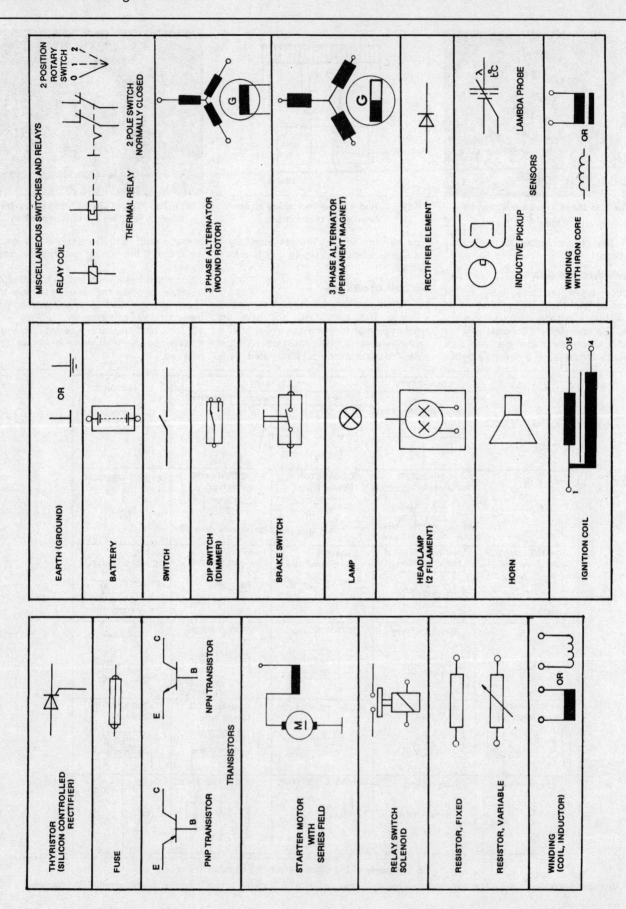

7.4 Examples of DIN symbols

7 Wiring diagrams

1 An understanding of circuit diagrams is important for trouble shooting in a motorcycle electrical system, and when you wish to add on electrical accessories.

2 The wiring is colour-coded and a legend is usually given on the diagram, however it is also necessary to recognise components from the symbols represented on the diagram. Unfortunately this has not been standardised.

3 Japanese wiring diagrams use pictorial symbols and in addition may have the component name printed alongside **(see illustration)**.

4 On European motorcycles, the German DIN standards will be met, and on these diagrams the meaning of the symbols is not so clear **(see illustration)**.

5 The DIN system also uses standard codes which identify the terminal and component, making wire tracing easier.

6 The layout of the typical wiring diagram can appear confusing, but do not be daunted by them. Essentially each individual item breaks down into a supply wire coming from, or to, the battery, then to the load/component item concerned. The circuit is completed by returning through the bike frame directly, or through a short connecting wire.

7 All separate circuits are in parallel and the currents taken by each add up to the total load current, which should not exceed that provided by the alternator.

8 If you are wiring a bike from scratch, it is worth drawing out the various sub-circuits such as ignition, brake lights, lighting and so on, as separate layouts.

8 Batteries

Safety

1 Batteries contain sulphuric acid and give off explosive gases when being charged.

2 Wear eye protection whenever working with a battery, especially when topping-up or charging. If any acid is spilt on your skin wash it off immediately with cold water and seek medical attention.

3 Do not smoke or create any sparks whilst working on the battery.

4 Before disconnecting a battery, turn the ignition main switch OFF.

5 Disconnect the earth or ground connection first. On all except a few older machines, this will be the negative (–ve) side of the battery.

6 When refitting the battery to the machine, make sure that the battery breather pipe is unrestricted and vents into clear space below the machine. Note that there will be no breather pipe on MF (Maintenance Free) batteries.

7 Clear up any acid spills immediately.

8 Dispose of an old battery by taking it to an approved recycling or disposal facility.

General maintenance

9 Many charging system faults can be attributed to a defective battery – always check and recharge the battery before looking elsewhere.

10 In most cases, motorcycle batteries can be expected to last for about three years. If you maintain the battery carefully, this life can be extended somewhat, and equally, neglect will tend to shorten its working life.

11 Keep the outside of the battery clean and dry. Remember that dirt on and around the battery will have a certain amount of acid in it, so take care.

12 The terminals should be taken apart for cleaning from time to time, and coated in petroleum jelly, or non-metallic grease, to inhibit further corrosion.

13 The level of the electrolyte must be checked regularly, and if necessary topped up, using distilled or demineralised water. You should not need to add acid to the battery once it has been filled initially; the only fluid loss is water which will evaporate. Maintenance-free batteries do not require topping up.

HAYNES HiNT *In cases where frequent topping up is required, the charging system output is too high. This will most likely be due to a faulty regulator/rectifier.*

14 As the battery ages, and under the effects of vibration, there will be a gradual accumulation of lead sulphate around the plates in the battery cells. This will tend to accumulate around the bottom of each cell, and where the battery has a clear or translucent case you may be able to see these deposits. As the sediment builds up, it will eventually cause the cell(s) affected to short out internally, and this indicates the imminent failure of the battery.

Terminal number	Wire leading from	To
1	Ignition coil	Contact breaker or ignition control unit
2	Magneto	Ignition switch (shorting switch)
4	Ignition coil HT	Spark plug
15	Ignition switch	Ignition coil
15a	CDI pulse coil	CDI trigger terminal
15/54	Main switch or ignition switch	Coil, warning light, fuse for daylight current consumers (brake lights, horn, turn signals, etc)
30	Battery +	Starter, ignition switch
31	Battery -	Earth (ground)
31b	Switch	Earth (ground)
49	Ignition switch	Flasher unit
49a	Flasher unit	Turn signal switch
50	Starter button switch	Starter relay (solenoid)
51	Alternator or generator regulator	Battery, starter button or main switch
54	See 15/54	-
L54	Turn signal switch	Left turn signal light
R54	Turn signal switch	Right turn signal light
56	Lighting switch	Dip (dimmer) switch
56a	Dip (dimmer) switch	Headlight main beam and warning light
56b	Dip (dimmer) switch	Headlight dipped beam
57	Lighting switch	Parking light
58	Lighting switch	Tail light, licence plate light, side light (side car)
59	Charging coil of flywheel magneto	Rectifier
61	Alternator or generator regulator	Charge warning light
B+	Battery positive	-
B-	Battery negative	-
D+	Alternator +	Regulator
DF	Alternator exciter winding	Regulator
L	Turn signal switch	Left turn signal light
R	Turn signal switch	Right turn signal light
UVW	Individual phase terminals	3-phase rectifier pack

8.16 The electrolyte level must be between the two level marks in each cell

8.17 Remove the cell caps to top up electrolyte level

8.18 On some models an electrolyte level sensor is connected to a warning light on the instrument panel

Checking battery condition

Electrolyte level (except MF batteries)

15 The outside of the battery case is marked to show the minimum and maximum levels.
16 Each cell should be within the specified range (see illustration).
17 To top up, unscrew or pull off the cell caps and top up with distilled water – do not use tap water for topping up (see illustration).
18 Some batteries are fitted with a sensor which checks the fluid level. Check that this is operating correctly (see illustration).

Open-circuit voltage

19 A quick check can be made by measuring the voltage across the terminals using a dc voltmeter or a multimeter set to the dc volts function; set the meter to the 0 to 20 volts dc range. Remove the battery from the motorcycle and connect the meter positive (+ve) probe to the battery positive terminal and its negative (–ve) probe to the battery negative terminal (see illustration).
20 A sound fully charged 12 volt battery should produce between 12.3 and 12.6 volts across its terminals (12.8 volts for an MF battery). On machines with a 6 volt battery, voltage should be between 6.1 and 6.3 volts.

21 If battery voltage is low (below 10 volts on a 12 volt battery or below 4 volts on a 6 volt battery), charge the battery and test the voltage again. If the battery repeatedly goes flat, investigate the motorcycle's charging system.

Electrolyte specific gravity (except MF batteries)

22 An hydrometer, which measures the specific gravity of the electrolyte solution can also be used to asses the state of charge of the battery as the specific gravity is related to the proportion of water to acid in the battery. On a fully charged battery the reading in each cell should be between 1.260 and 1.280. If it is less than 1.200; the battery requires charging.
23 The specific gravity will vary with temperature; it should be measured at 20°C (68°F). Add 0.007 to the reading for every 10°C above 20°C and subtract 0.007 for every 10°C below 20°C. Add 0.004 to the reading for every 10°F above 68°F, and subtract 0.004 for every 10°F below 68°F.
24 To check the SG, remove the battery and then take off one of the cell caps and suck up a little of the electrolyte solution. Take the reading (see illustration), then return the solution to the cell. Repeat for all the other

cells. After checking, rinse the hydrometer thoroughly with clean water.
25 The scale of the hydrometer may actually be calculated in volts or there may be a conversion chart provided.
26 The cells on a serviceable battery should all have a similar specific gravity.
27 Ensure that you purchase a battery hydrometer which is suitable for motorcycle applications. These will have a smaller bore hose for insertion into the filler holes in the battery and accept a smaller volume of electrolyte than automotive type hydrometers.

On-load testing

28 Motorcycle manufacturers usually specify a voltage test with the battery in-circuit and a load applied. The test meter is connected as described above in the open-circuit test and the engine started; sometimes the manufacturer specifies that the headlight is turned ON.
29 Refer to the workshop manual for your motorcycle for the exact test procedure and expected results.

Battery charging – conventional batteries

30 The battery on most machines will require occasional recharging off the machine,

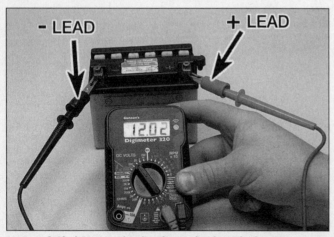

8.19 An open-circuit voltage check on the battery

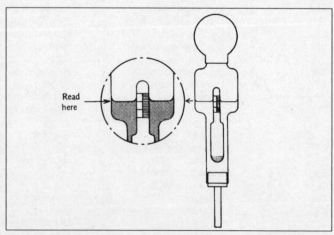

8.24 Take the reading on the hydrometer scale at the point shown

especially when a lot of short night-time trips are done, and the charging system cannot keep up with demand.

31 The battery will also need charging at approximately 6 weekly intervals whilst the vehicles is not being used.

32 The rate at which the battery can safely be charged is dependent on its capacity, which is expressed in units of ampere-hours, or Ah, this figure being marked on the battery case. As an example, a small two-stroke model with direct lighting will usually have a battery rated at about 6 volts, 4Ah. On larger models the battery capacity will be around 12 volts, 14Ah.

33 The maximum safe charging rate is 1/10 of the rated amp/hour capacity, which means in the case of the two examples given, a maximum of 0.4 amps and 1.4 amps respectively.

34 This poses something of a problem when using normal DIY battery chargers, because these are designed for use on the much heavier automotive batteries. These chargers are current controlled, which means in practice that they will charge at whatever rate the battery will accept, normally around 2 – 4 amps.

35 This is much too high for motorcycle batteries and can seriously damage them. In the case of small batteries, the current from an automotive battery charger is probably enough to destroy the battery, possibly causing it to explode.

36 The answer is to use a special charger designed for use on motorcycle batteries. These have a much lower output, and are often constant current types, producing about 1/2 amp output. Whilst it would take some time to recharge a 14Ah battery at this low rate, it is safe to use on all motorcycle batteries.

37 These chargers can be bought through motorcycle dealers, and you should either check that you get the correct output voltage for your machine (6 or 12 volt) or get a dual voltage version.

38 When using any type of charger, always check that the voltage setting is right for the battery, that the charger leads are connected round the right way (positive red to battery positive (+ve), and negative black to battery negative (–ve) terminal), and that the battery vent pipe (conventional batteries) is clear. Slacken the cell caps to ensure that there is no risk of excess pressure building up inside the battery. After charging, remember to tighten the caps before refitting the battery.

39 Allow the battery to cool down before refitting it to the bike.

Battery charging – maintenance-free batteries

40 The alternator will normally charge the battery at the required rate at a regulated voltage of between 14 – 16 volts.

41 A non-regulated charger should **not** be used for charging maintenance-free batteries as it will destroy the battery by over-charging it.

42 A constant current charger is required for charging MF batteries. The charge current is set according to the battery rating, ie 1/10 of its amp/hour capacity and should take into account whether the battery is slightly discharged or completely flat.

43 The charger should be used with a timer or a voltage sensor to avoid over charging.

44 The battery should not be charged on the bike or damage will occur to other electrical equipment.

Fitting a new battery

45 Select a make and specification of battery which matches that required by your motorcycle. Not only is its electrical capacity important, but it must be of the correct dimensions to fit the battery carrier.

46 The battery may be available already filled or with a separate container of acid.

47 It is safer to purchase a filled battery, but if you have to fill it yourself follow the instructions supplied carefully, and wear protective goggles and gloves.

48 If the battery is supplied filled, make sure that it is also fully charged. To charge a new battery, charge it at the correct rate for 3 to 4 hours (see above).

49 Check that the terminals and cable connectors are clean. Tighten the connectors making sure that they will not get bent and/or foul the frame when the battery is pushed into its position.

50 Replace any terminal protection covers, and on conventional batteries check that the breather pipe is correctly routed; there is often a breather pipe routing diagram attached to the battery carrier.

Causes of battery problems

Battery dead or weak

51 The battery itself may be faulty due to damaged or corroded terminals, sulphated plates, or sediment build-up.

52 The cables may be making poor contact.

53 The load may be excessive due to the addition of high wattage lights or other accessories.

54 The ignition switch may be defective by either failing to make internal contact or by shorting to earth/ground.

55 The regulator/rectifier may have failed.

56 The alternator stator coil may have an open or short circuit.

57 The wiring may be faulty with loose connections or wiring earthed/grounded.

These faults may occur anywhere in the electrical system.

Battery overcharged

58 Overcharging is noticed when the battery gets excessively warm and required topping up frequently.

59 This can be caused by a defective battery, or one which is of the wrong specification.

60 A faulty regulator may cause overcharging.

9 Switches

1 With very few exceptions, electrical switches on motorcycles are sealed assemblies, and are thus difficult to repair in the event of failure.

2 You should start by deciding what exactly the problem is; if it is a simple case of water contamination, you can try spraying WD40 or a similar silicone-based product into the switch mechanism. This will displace any water inside it, and will often solve the problem without the need for further dismantling. It follows that the better your access to the switch, the more likely you are to succeed, but even spraying the fluid through the extension straw supplied will usually reach the internal parts quite well.

3 Where the switch in question serves only a single function and is relatively inexpensive, it is rarely worth spending too much time on it; it will be quicker and probably more successful to renew items like brake light or sidestand switches.

4 With more complex switch assemblies, like the handlebar clusters, the cost of a new assembly makes further investigation worthwhile. Trace back the switch wiring to the block connector and disconnect it.

 Warning: Always disconnect the battery negative (–ve) lead as a safety precaution before disconnecting switch wiring – this is particularly important in the case of the ignition (main) switch.

5 You can check which contacts are faulty at this stage, using a multimeter or a continuity tester. The wiring diagram normally includes smaller block diagrams of the switch contacts connected in each position, and you can check each of these in turn until the fault is located **(see illustration)**.

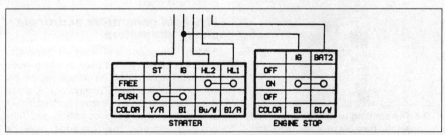

	ST	IG	HL2	HL1
FREE			O—O	
PUSH	O—O			
COLOR	Y/R	Bl	Bu/W	Bl/R

STARTER

		IG	BAT2
OFF			
ON		O—O	
OFF			
COLOR		Bl	Bl/W

ENGINE STOP

9.5 Typical switch connection tables found in most wiring diagrams

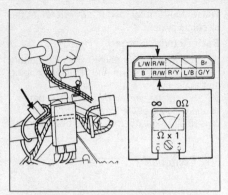

9.6 Simple continuity checks can often save unnecessary dismantling and identify a problem

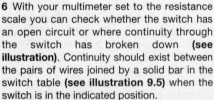

9.7a A typical handlebar switch assembly in two sections – note the locating pin and hole in handlebar (arrows)

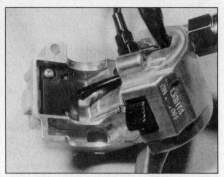

9.7b It is often possible to remove the internals either as sub-assemblies, or in component form. The switch contacts may now be accessible for cleaning

6 With your multimeter set to the resistance scale you can check whether the switch has an open circuit or where continuity through the switch has broken down **(see illustration)**. Continuity should exist between the pairs of wires joined by a solid bar in the switch table **(see illustration 9.5)** when the switch is in the indicated position.

7 Further dismantling may or may not be possible, depending on the type and make of the switch used. In some cases, the switch halves serve to locate individual switches, and these are easily unscrewed for separate inspection **(see illustrations)**.

8 In other designs, the switch mechanisms are housed direct in the outer casing, and with these you will have to actually dismantle the mechanism **(see illustration)**. Only you can decide if it is worth risking this operation; there is a good chance that it will be difficult to get it all back together again, even if you can get it apart in the first place.

9 If the switch is useless as it stands, there is no real loss in attempting a repair, and the worst that can happen is that the attempt fails. The method of dismantling the switch is entirely dependent on the type concerned, and you will have to figure this out as you progress. It is a good idea to work on a clean surface so that any escaping parts can be recovered easily, and to make a sketch of the switch internals as a guide during assembly.

9.8 Dismantling to this level is usually possible. Beware of loose balls and springs which may escape

10 Remember that you will not be able to buy new parts for the switches; any repairs are entirely down to your own ingenuity. If the repair attempt fails, it will have been an interesting undertaking anyway.

11 Before you order a new assembly, check the local breakers to see if they have a suitable used replacement in stock.

10 Generators and alternators

1 Most machines use ac (alternating current) generators of some description. These can take the form of simple flywheel generators such as those used on lightweight two-strokes, mopeds and similar models where direct lighting is used, or single or three-phase alternators as used on modern more sophisticated machines.

2 There is great variety in the types and designs in current use, and if you develop generator problems it is essential to refer to your workshop manual for the specific test procedures and specifications.

DC generators

3 DC generators (dynamos) are generally only found on older motorcycles. If you encounter a dynamo-equipped model, the appropriate test details will be found in the workshop manual for the machine.

4 There are a few specialists who can offer reconditioning services for these devices and who advertise regularly in the classic motorcycle press.

Flywheel generators and single phase alternators

5 Many alternator and flywheel generator problems can be traced back to wiring faults or defects in rectifiers and voltage regulators, where these are fitted. Always check these areas first, and where a battery is fitted, make sure that it is in good condition and fully charged, or any test readings may be erroneous.

6 Simple resistance tests will reveal faults such as open circuits or shorted windings, and if this is the problem, the stator assembly and/or rotor may need to be renewed.

7 Test by measuring the resistance between any pair of output wires. The resistance should be the same for each pair. An ammeter place in series in the charging circuit will check the output of the generator.

8 On permanent magnet (single phase) alternators and flywheel generators, it is possible for the rotor to become demagnetised, and this will reduce the output of the generator significantly. An auto-electrical specialist may be able to re-magnetise the rotor for you, the other option being to buy a new one.

9 Causes of demagnetisation include reversed wiring connections and impact to the rotor, so avoid this happening when working on machines so equipped. This is one reason why a rotor must never be struck to jar it free during removal.

Three-phase alternators

10 The three-phase alternator is either mounted on one end of the crankshaft and has a separate regulator/rectifier unit mounted on the frame, or is belt or chain driven off an auxiliary shaft in the engine and contains integral regulator and rectifier units; the latter is generally known as an automotive-type alternator.

11 Always check the brushes and the slip rings (where applicable) if poor output is a problem. If the brushes are worn or the slip rings dirty, the output will drop markedly over a period of time. Fit new brushes, and burnish the slip rings with fine abrasive paper or an ink eraser to give a bright finish.

12 If the slip rings are very dirty, skim and polish the surface on the lathe yourself or take the rotor to an auto-electrical specialist.

13 Where the output drops suddenly, the cause may be an open-circuit in one of the windings. A resistance test can be carried out to check the windings for continuity.

14 If the battery goes flat, but the charging rate is correct, then the rectifier may be leaking current. Insert an ammeter between the battery negative terminal and the disconnected negative battery cable and check if any current is passing. A new rectifier is required if any current is detected. Note that tests can be made on the rectifier diodes to confirm that the rectifier is faulty.

Generator and alternator repairs

15 Motorcycle manufacturers do not always supply individual replacement parts for these assemblies. Note that a local auto electrical specialist may be able to assist with replacement parts, and be able to rewind the existing part for you, which could cost less than buying a new assembly.

16 Motorcycle breakers are a good source of second-hand generators and alternators, but take along your old unit to make sure that the proposed replacement will fit and if of the correct rating. Take note of any output markings or model numbers on the old unit as a guide.

11 Starter motor and circuit

1 The starter motor circuit comprises the starter motor, a relay, a switch and the battery. On some models this system is interlocked with other switches to prevent the starter motor operating unless the transmission is in neutral, the clutch lever pulled in or the sidestand retracted. Refer to the wiring diagram for the actual model to determine which components make up the starter circuit.

Initial system checks

2 The starter motor draws a very heavy current while it is turning the engine over, and this is why the motor is switched indirectly through a relay (solenoid). If the motor was controlled by the handlebar switch contacts they would be burnt out in no time under the heavy current passed through the circuit. This should always be kept in mind if a starter fault develops.

3 Many problems will eventually be traced to a partly discharged battery, or one with a weak cell. During normal riding the battery may be perfectly adequate for the loads imposed upon it, but when the starter operates, the current demands may just prove too much. Check that the battery is fully charged before proceeding with further checks.

4 With the ignition switched on, check that the kill switch is set to 'RUN' and the gearbox is in neutral. Press the starter button and listen for a response from the relay; this should click into engagement. Repeat this check, this time with the headlamp switched on. Normally, the headlamp will dim as the starter motor turns. If the motor fails to run, but the headlamp goes out completely, it is a

good indication of a discharged or faulty battery.

5 Check the main fuse (often located on or near the starter relay) and if fitted, the starter circuit fuse.

Checking the starter relay (solenoid)

6 The starter relay is a heavy-duty switch which is controlled remotely from the handlebar switch. When this is pressed, power is fed to the relay, a low current being used to close the main contacts electromagnetically. When closed, these connect the heavy starter motor cable direct to the battery.

7 A quick check of the relay operation is to disconnect the heavy duty cable between it and the battery, making sure that the cable end is kept clear of any earth (ground) point. Connect a multimeter or continuity test circuit to the two large terminals on the relay. (One of these will be the battery terminal which was just disconnected, the other holds the heavy lead to the motor.)

8 Switch on the ignition and press the starter button. You should hear a click as the relay contacts close, and the meter should indicate zero ohms. When the button is released, the contacts should open again and the meter indicate high resistance. Switch the ignition OFF.

9 If there is no response from the relay, make sure that there is battery voltage at the thin lead from the starter button to the solenoid when the button is depressed. If no voltage is shown here, the fault lies in the switch circuit (ie the power supply from the battery to the ignition switch and from the ignition switch to the starter switch). Note that on most motorcycles, the starter circuit will only operate if the engine kill switch is in the RUN position.

10 If you read battery voltage when conducting the test described in Step 8, the relay has failed and must be repaired or renewed. If you can get the unit apart, you can attempt a repair.

11 Check that the solenoid plunger is free to move, and clean up the heavy-duty switch contacts with fine abrasive paper. Where the

unit is of sealed construction, or the solenoid windings have failed, renewal will be your only option.

12 Sometimes the above test may show that the relay is working normally, even though the motor will not run. This can be caused by burnt contacts in the relay; they may handle the test current without difficulty, but be incapable if carrying the heavier motor current. It is difficult to devise a test for this, and if you cannot dismantle the unit for examination, the best option here is to substitute a sound relay and see whether this resolves the fault.

Overhauling the starter motor

13 If the above checks have indicated a motor fault, you should first make enquiries at a dealer to see whether you can get parts for the motor used on your model. In some cases, a good range of repair parts is available, though in others the motor must be renewed as a unit in the event of a fault.

14 The workshop manual will give details of the procedure for removing the motor and dismantling it for examination.

15 The first area to check is the brushes and the copper-coloured commutator on which they bear.

16 Make a note of the brush connections, then disconnect the brush leads and remove the brushes. Worn or sticking brushes can cause the motor to fail or turn abnormally slowly.

17 Measure the brush lengths, and renew them if worn down to the service limit (see illustration). If your motor is not supported by spare parts backup, take the worn brushes to an auto-electrical specialist and get hold of the nearest size and type you can. The new brushes can then be filed to shape to fit the brush holders. Clean the brushholder unit using electrical contact cleaner, removing all accumulated dust and dirt.

18 Clean the commutator. The surface of the commutator should be examined closely for scoring and general wear, and check the condition of the commutator slots (see illustration). If it is only lightly scored, use a strip of fine abrasive paper to smooth the surface down, removing no more of the soft

11.17 A vernier gauge or ruler can be used to measure brush length

11.18a The darkened area of the commutator shows the place of greatest wear

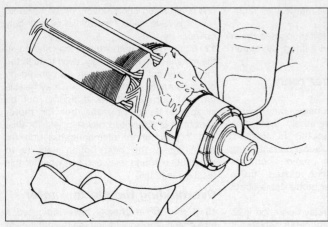

11.18b Cleaning up the commutator surface

11.19 Commutator must not be skimmed beyond the service limit

copper material than is essential to restore the surface **(see illustration)**. Remove any grit which may have become embedded in the commutator grooves.

19 Where damage is severe, the surface of the commutator is cleaned up by taking a fine cut across it while the armature is turning at high speed in a lathe. Do not go below the specified service limit for commutator diameter **(see illustration)**.

20 After any resurfacing work, check the depth of the slots between the commutator segments, and if necessary cut them back to the specified depth (usually around 0.5 – 1.0 mm, or 0.002 – 0.004 in) **(see illustration)**.

21 A tool for carrying out this work can be made up from an old hacksaw blade. Grind the sides of the teeth until they are exactly the same width as the grooves, then bind the other end with PVC tape to form a handle. The grooves can then be cut back to the correct depth, making sure that the sides are parallel and the bottom of the groove is kept square.

22 If the above methods fail to get the motor to work, you will have to check the armature and field coil windings for open or short circuits **(see illustrations)**.

23 Look closely around the armature where the windings are soldered to the commutator segments; blobs of solder here indicate overloading of the windings, the melted solder having been flung off. This will produce 'dead' pairs of segments, which will result in the motor not operating if it previously came to rest with these segments in contact with the brushes, a common cause of intermittent motor failures.

24 If you can get to the wire ends easily, you could try soldering them back into place. Where this is impossible, you will have to buy a new armature assembly, or get the old one rewound professionally.

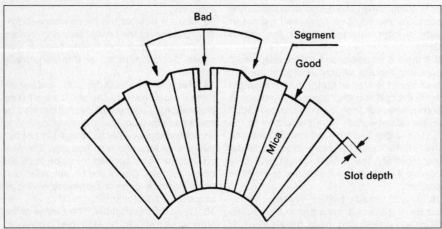

11.20 Good and bad conditions for the commutator slots

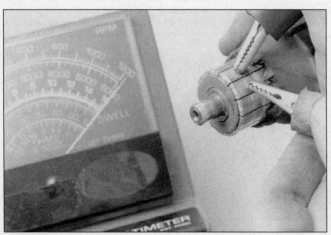

11.22a Continuity should exist between the commutator bars

11.22b There should be no continuity between the commutator bars and armature shaft

12 Spark plugs

1 Spark plugs are produced in a wide range of sizes and grades to suit various applications, and it should be noted that only one of these is likely to be suitable for a particular engine.

2 The correct type will be recommended by the motorcycle manufacturer, and this information will be found in the owner's handbook supplied with the machine or workshop manual. The spark plug recommendation can also be found in the plug manufacturer's catalogue.

3 Changes of plug grade are only normally needed where the machine is used in unusual climatic conditions, or where the type of use the machine is subject to indicates that a change might be appropriate. One exception to this rule is where the motorcycle manufacturer lists alternative grades of plug for normal riding and sustained high speed use, or for frequent short journeys.

Identification

4 Each spark plug manufacturer employs a combination of letters and numbers to denote the thread diameter, reach, type and heat range of their plugs, as well as any special characteristics of a given plug.

5 This can be useful where the make of spark plug recommended by the motorcycle manufacturer cannot be obtained locally, though as a rule it is best to adhere to the original specification.

Size

6 Motorcycle engines use plugs with a 14 mm thread/20.6 mm hexagon or 12 mm thread/18 mm hexagon. A few four-stroke moped engines employ the smaller 10 mm thread/16 mm hexagon type, where fitting space is limited.

7 The reach (thread length) of plugs varies considerably, and it is important that the

12.13a Measuring the electrode gap using the wire gauge

correct type is chosen; too short a plug will result in masking of the electrodes, carbon build-up in the exposed threads in the cylinder head and possible misfiring. Too long a plug may result in it contacting the piston, with consequent engine damage.

Heat range

8 The heat range of the plug is not obvious from examination, but is of great importance in use. The heat range is chosen to suit the operating temperature range of a specific engine. In most applications, the electrode area of the plug should be kept at around 450° – 950°C (840° – 1740°F).

9 If the plug runs too cool, carbon and oil fouling of the electrodes will occur, whilst at higher temperatures there is the risk of oxide fouling, burnt electrodes and pre-ignition damage.

10 The plug electrode temperature can be controlled by regulating the rate at which the plug can shed engine heat, and in practice this is accomplished by altering the effective length of the ceramic insulator nose inside the plug body.

11 The series of colour photographs on the inside rear cover of this manual illustrate the main problems likely to be suffered by spark plugs, and this can form a useful basis for diagnosing running faults. Note that if the condition of the plug taken from your engine

12.13b Adjusting the gap using the ramped tag on the same gauge

indicates that the plug grade is incorrect, check this carefully before considering a change of grade. It is more usual that abnormal plug condition is reflecting some and ignition of fuel/air mixture problem.

Plug maintenance

13 The gap between the electrodes should be checked using feeler gauges and reset if not at the specified distance **(see illustration)**. The spark plug gap will be given in your owners manual, workshop manual or specified by the spark plug manufacturer. Do not lever on the centre electrode to alter the gap, always bend the outer (earth) electrode using the proper tool **(see illustration)**. Feeler gauges can be used for gap measurement, although the wire type gauges are preferred **(see illustration)**.

14 Where multi earth electrode plugs are fitted, note that the use of a wire type gauge is essential for gap measurement due to their curved profile **(see illustration)**. Plug manufacturers usually advise that multi-electrode plugs are renewed if the gap becomes too large.

15 Spark plugs can be cleaned with a fine wire brush and then wiped with a solvent cleaner to prevent spark tracking paths developing.

16 The plug should be refitted by hand to ensure that the cylinder head threads are not

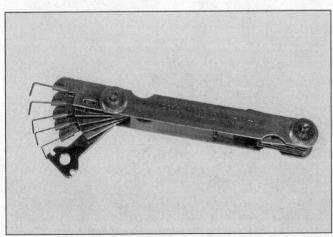

12.13c Wire type gauges are also available as keys

12.14 Triple-earth type spark plug design

damaged by cross threading and then tightened to the specified torque. The threads can be smeared with a graphite or copper-based grease to aid future removal. If no torque setting is specified, refer to the following guide. Above all, take care not to overtighten the plugs.

17 For flat seated plugs, use a plug spanner until the first resistance is felt, then turn a new plug a further 90°. Used plugs need only be turned through 30° as the seal will have been compressed **(see illustration)**.

18 For new and used conical seal plugs, turn by only 15° after the first resistance is felt **(see illustration 12.17)**.

 HAYNES HiNT *Damaged spark plug threads in the cylinder head can be repaired using a thread insert (see Chapter 6 for details).*

13 Ignition systems – checking

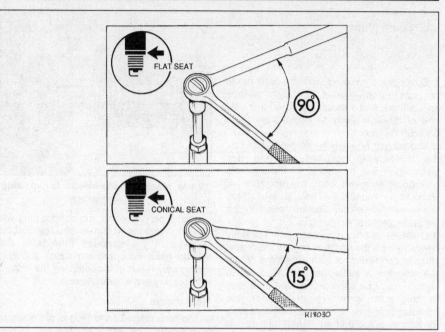

12.17 The correct angle torque to be used when tightening plugs

1 The ignition systems used on most current machines are fairly reliable, many requiring no attention other than checking, cleaning or renewal of the spark plug(s).

2 Note also that it is essential to ensure that the plug is of the correct type for your machine; use of a plug of the wrong heat range or reach will often cause ignition problems.

3 The method of checking the system in the event of a fault will depend upon the arrangement used, and you should refer to your workshop manual for detailed information.

Checking for a spark

4 In all cases, the first thing to check is whether there is a spark at the plug electrodes. Disconnect one of the plug leads and connect the lead to a spare spark plug

and lay the plug on the engine so that its metal body is in contact with the bare metal **(see illustration)**.

 Warning: Don't remove one of the spark plugs from the engine to perform this check – atomised fuel being pumped out of the open spark plug hole could ignite, causing injury!

5 Note that in the case of electronic systems, it is essential that the plug body is earthed; if the HT circuit remains open, the ignition control unit may be damaged.

6 Check that neutral is selected and that the engine kill switch is set to the 'RUN' position. Switch on the ignition and crank the engine using the kickstart lever or electric starter, observing the plug electrodes.

7 The plug should produce a fat and regular

blue spark. If the spark looks weak or yellowish, this indicates partial failure of the system, whilst no spark at all speaks for itself. Refit the HT lead and perform the check on the other plug(s).

8 It is always worth trying new plugs at this stage; eliminating them as a source of trouble may save much unnecessary work.

9 The plug cap may also be a source of trouble. Most caps incorporate a resistor, the purpose of which is to suppress radio and television interference. Occasionally these may break down, presenting an excessive resistance to the HT pulse and thus preventing normal sparking. As with spark plugs, the best way of checking for this fault is by fitting a new plug cap although their resistance can be measured if the manufacturer has supplied a specific resistance figure **(see illustration)**. In

13.4 Ensure that the spark plug body makes good contact with the engine – if necessary hold with insulated pliers

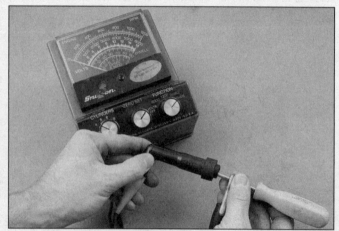

13.9 Measuring the suppresser cap resistance

the case of multi-cylinder machines try swapping plug caps from one HT lead to another; if the weak spark moves with the cap, then it can be assumed to be at fault.

10 Note that the HT lead rather than the suppresser cap could be at fault. Check that the lead is making good contact at the HT coil (you can unscrew the HT lead knurled retainer on certain models) and at the suppresser cap end. Using a multimeter or continuity tester, check for continuity from one end of the lead to the other. There will be a certain amount of resistance in the HT lead, but infinite resistance (no continuity) indicates an internal break in the lead.

11 Before checking individual ignition system components, you should check through the ignition system wiring, using the wiring diagram in the workshop manual for reference. Look out for loose, corroded or waterlogged connections or damaged leads. Faults of this type must be checked and eliminated before moving on to a detailed check of the system components.

Checking the spark gap

12 If the engine starts but misfires, make the following checks before deciding that the ignition system is at fault.

13 Most ignition systems should be able to produce a spark across a six or seven millimeter (1/4 in) gap (minimum). A simple test fixture **(see illustration)** can be constructed to make sure the minimum spark gap can be jumped. Make sure the fixture electrodes are positioned seven millimeters apart.

14 Connect one of the spark plug leads to the protruding test fixture electrode, then attach the fixture's alligator clip to a good earth on the engine **(see illustration)**.

15 Crank the engine over (it will probably start and run on the remaining cylinders) and see if well-defined, blue sparks occur between the test fixture electrodes. If the minimum spark gap test is positive, the ignition coil for that cylinder (and its companion cylinder, where applicable) is functioning properly. On a two coil arrangement, repeat the check on one of the spark plug leads that is connected to the

13.13 A simple spark gap tester can be made from a block of wood, two nails, a large crocodile clip, a screw and a piece of wire

other coil. If the spark will not jump the gap during either test, or if it is weak (orange colored) check the HT coil resistances.

14 Flywheel generator ignition systems

1 These devices normally employ an ignition source coil which powers the system. This forms part of the generator stator assembly, the remaining coils being used to power the lighting and charging circuits.

2 The ignition timing is often fixed, and uses contact breakers housed inside the generator to control sparking. Although at one time used extensively on mopeds and small capacity motorcycles, the flywheel generator system has now been superseded by electronic systems.

3 Note that the battery, where one is fitted, plays no part in powering the ignition circuit.

4 With this type of system, the condition of the contacts and their gap setting are of vital importance, and any burning or pitting of the contact surfaces or inaccuracy of the gap setting will affect the operation of the system to a marked extent **(see illustration 15.4)**. Always check and clean (or better still, renew) the contacts, and check and adjust the gap before looking at other aspects of the system. Badly burned contact faces indicate a faulty

13.14 Connect the tester – when the engine is cranked, sparks should jump the gap between the nails

capacitor (condenser), which will allow excessive arcing across the contacts.

5 The contact breaker assembly should be renewed if it is badly burnt, but you should also fit a new capacitor at the same time. These are not easy to test without elaborate equipment, but they are cheap enough to warrant renewal as a precautionary measure **(see illustration)**.

6 Light burning or pitting of the contact faces can be corrected by restoring the surfaces with a fine Swiss file or with fine abrasive paper. Try to leave the contact faces as smooth as possible and slightly convex in shape. Note that if too much material is removed, it may prove impossible to obtain the correct gap setting.

7 In view of the need to remove the flywheel rotor to gain access to the contact breakers, it is normally preferable to fit a new contact breaker set, rather than spend time and effort trying to rectify damaged contact faces.

8 Other possible causes of ignition faults are damaged source coil windings, a demagnetised rotor, or a faulty ignition HT coil, HT lead or plug cap. These should be checked and eliminated systematically.

9 On a few models, the ignition timing is variable by moving the position of the stator assembly, and details will be found in the workshop manual about checking and resetting the timing, where this is possible.

10 In many cases, no ignition timing adjustment is possible, but slight alterations can be made by varying the contact breaker gap within the specified range **(see illustration)**. Again, the workshop manual will give details of this.

11 Note that under normal circumstances, the timing setting should not require attention, and this is unlikely to be the true cause of the problem. To check the timing you will need to refer to the relevant specifications, which in the case of most small two-strokes will give the setting as a piston position (usually in millimetres) before top dead centre (BTDC).

12 The firing position is normally shown as a mark on the edge of the flywheel rotor, and the contact breaker points should be at the point of separation when this mark aligns with

14.5 Take care not to apply too much heat when soldering the leads onto a new condenser

14.10 Ignition timing is adjusted by opening and closing the points gap on many models

15.4 Checking the contact breaker point gap

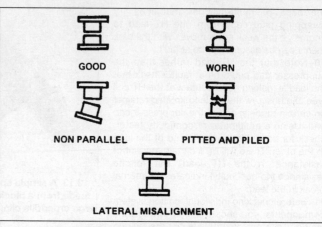

GOOD   WORN

NON PARALLEL   PITTED AND PILED

LATERAL MISALIGNMENT

15.5 Contact breaker point condition

a fixed index mark on the crankcase. It is not normally necessary to verify the accuracy of the timing marks, but if you have reason to suspect that they may be incorrect, note that this can only be checked accurately using a dial gauge and a spark plug thread adapter (refer to Chapter 4).

15 Coil and contact breaker ignition systems

1 These are similar to the arrangement described in Section 14, but derive their power from the battery.
2 In addition to the checks described above, make sure that battery voltage is being supplied to the ignition coil(s), checking back through the wiring and engine kill switch to the ignition switch. The workshop manual will provide details on contact breaker gap and ignition timing procedures, and also resistance tests on the ignition coil(s).
3 With coil and contact breaker systems, the ignition timing is usually advanced automatically, using a mechanical automatic

timing unit (ATU). Check that the ATU weights move smoothly and freely, without signs of sticking. Apply a drop of light machine oil to each pivot, and to the cam support spindle.

Setting the points gap

4 The correct setting of the gap between the contact breaker points should be checked regularly and reset if necessary according to the instructions in the manual for the machine **(see illustration)**. Always check the gap when the points are fully open.
5 Examine the condition of the points. They should be flat and smooth and the faces of the fixed and moving contact should be parallel when they meet **(see illustration)**. It is often easier to carry out this check with the points assembly removed.
6 Another method of checking the gap is to measure the amount of time, or more correctly the amount of angular rotation during which the points are closed.
7 A tester called a dwell meter is used for this check. The electrodes of the meter are connected across the points and will give a reading in degrees or percentage dwell. This figure can be checked against the specification in the manual.

8 The contact breaker gap is adjusted to give the correct amount of dwell.

Ignition timing

9 The ignition timing should be checked following the instructions in your workshop manual.
10 On most machines there are timing marks which give the position at which the points should open. Static timing can be checked using these marks **(see illustration)**. The timing mark on the backplate is usually signified by the letter F, which should align exactly with the fixed mark on the crankcase when the points are beginning to open. Adjustment is normally carried out by unclamping the backplate on which the points are mounted and rotating the plate to the required position. The backplate clamping screws must then be retightened.
11 Dynamic timing, that is with the engine running, can be done with a stroboscope, preferably of the xenon type. The stroboscope is connected as directed by the manufacturer and the light shone at the timing marks with the engine running at idling speed. The moving marks will appear 'frozen' and can be compared to the set marks **(see illustration)**.

15.10 Timing F mark shown aligned with the fixed mark on the crankcase

15.11 A stroboscope in operation checking dynamic timing

If the marks do not align, stop the engine and make any adjustments, then start the engine and repeat the test until the marks accurately coincide.

12 One advantage of the dynamic method of checking is that the ignition advance can be checked. By running the engine at approximately 3500 rpm the full advance mark on the backplate (usually two scribed lines II) should come into alignment with the fixed mark. If they do not, then the ATU is faulty.

16 Electronic ignition systems

 Warning: Be aware that electronic ignition systems can produce very high voltages which can be dangerous.

1 Electronic system components are generally reliable and will usually last the life of the motorcycle. Where faults do occur, always check the wiring and connectors before suspecting failure of the main components. Check that the battery is fully charged and that you have a good spark at the plug(s) (see Section 13).

Caution: If checking for a spark as described in Section 13, note that it is essential that the spark plug body or spark gap tester makes a good earth contact with the cylinder head, otherwise the ignition system could be damaged.

2 Ignition faults are best located in a logical manner. Refer to the wiring diagram for your bike and identify the ignition system circuit components. If you are working on a multi-cylinder engine you will be able to determine whether the fault only occurs on a particular pair of cylinders or whether it affects the complete system.

3 The ignition HT coil primary and secondary resistances can be checked with a multimeter set to the ohms function, referring to your workshop manual for the exact test connections and expected values. Don't forget to check the HT leads and suppresser caps as well.

4 The ignition pickup coil(s) (or pulse coil as it is sometimes known) is triggered by a rotor mounted on the end of the crankshaft. Resistance values for the pickup coil are specified in the workshop manual and this can be checked by taking a reading across the wiring sub-harness from the engine. There will be a measurable resistance across the pickup coil, but very high resistance indicates an open-circuit condition. Always check the wiring sub-harness and connectors before assuming that the pickup coil is at fault.

5 Test values for the ignition control unit are sometimes provided by the motorcycle manufacturer and are usually an out-of-circuit test of the unit's resistances. It should be noted that the actual resistance figures specified can often only be obtained using a particular test meter and discrepancies have been discovered when testing on other meters. In view of the replacement cost of ignition control units, it is stressed that any results you obtain are verified by a motorcycle dealer before purchasing a new unit.

17 Engine management systems

1 Engine management systems control fuelling and ignition to achieve optimum performance and clean emissions. At the heart of the system is an electronic control unit into which is fed input signals from sensors which measure throttle position, fuel pressure, air pressure and temperature, engine speed and exhaust oxygen content. The control unit compares the values received to performance maps to produce the correct output signals for ignition timing and fuel control.

2 There is very little that the DIY mechanic can do to test an engine management system. The manufacturer will often specify a particular test instrument or fault code reader to obtain information from the system and it follows that the test values they provide can only be obtained with this equipment.

3 Where testing is possible using home workshop equipment, be very careful that the connections are make correctly. Because of their sensitive nature, the electronic components may be permanently damaged by excess current and voltage, which may be applied accidentally whilst checking.

Notes

Chapter 14
Wheels and tyres

Contents

1 Introduction

1 Wheels are either wire spoked, cast alloy or of composite construction. Although the majority of bikes now use cast alloy wheels, wire-spoked wheels still have a place on trail and competition bikes, and for cosmetic reasons on retro-styled road bikes. Wheel repair (where possible), bearing replacement, alignment and balancing are covered in this chapter.

2 Tyre sidewall markings are explained and information provided on tyre safety, renewal and repair.

2 Wheels –
checks and overhaul

1 The traditional wire spoked wheel has largely become displaced by the cast wheel, though ironically some recent factory custom and retro models have made wire spoked wheels a design feature. With one or two exceptions where the spokes join the wheel rim outboard of the tyre, tubed tyres only are used.

2 The cast alloy wheel lends itself well to mass production, the machining of the basic casting being a far less complex process wire wheel building. The technique allows new castings with various spoke designs to be produced as a styling feature, and permit the use of tubeless tyres.

3 The composite wheel uses an extruded aluminium alloy or steel rim riveted to pressed steel or aluminium spokes and a cast and machined centre hub. Again, tubeless tyres can be used.

Checking and servicing wire spoked wheels

4 Wire spoked wheels are unique in that they can be taken apart and rebuilt should the need arise, the big catch being that to do so requires time, patience and skill.

5 The advantage is that you can repair minor damage, fit new parts where needed, and even alter the rim size should you find a need to do so, though the more complex jobs are best left to a professional wheel builder.

6 Routine checks on wire spoked wheels comprise spoke tension, rim runout and bearing freeplay.

7 A quick way of identifying loose spokes is to tap each one in turn with a screwdriver. A sound spoke will be under tension, and will produce a fairly musical note as it is struck. A loose spoke will make a dull sound and may rattle or buzz. It is important to keep the spokes under tension; leaving them loose for any length of time will result in spoke breakage.

8 The spokes are tightened by turning the threaded nipple using a special spoke key **(see illustration)**. At a push you could use a small self-locking wrench, but the correct tool is preferable **(see illustration)**.

9 In almost every case, the nipple is fitted through holes in the rim (though a few wire spoked wheels may be found which use tubeless tyres. In these cases a solid rim is used, the spokes being inverted with the nipple at the hub end).

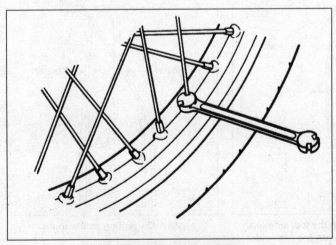

2.8a Adjusting spoke tension

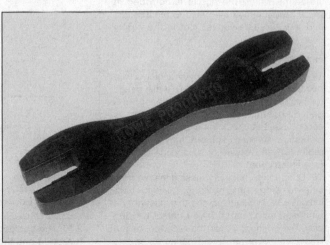

2.8b A spoke key

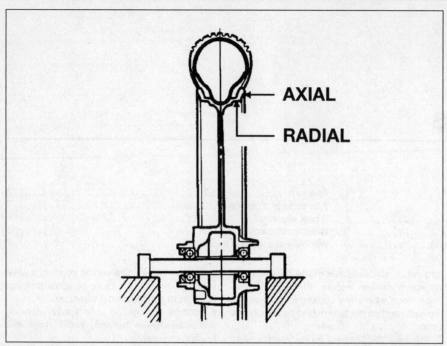

2.14 Radial (out of round) runout and axial (side to side) runout measurement points

10 As the nipple is turned, the spoke is tightened, and in normal circumstances you need only bring the loose spoke up to a similar tension to the others.

11 Be sure to remove any dirt from the spoke end before adjusting it, and apply a little oil or maintenance spray to help it turn easily. It is important that the nipple is turned just enough to restore tension; excessive tightening will pull the rim out of true.

12 If the spoke is really loose, requiring several turns to tension it correctly, you will need to remove the tyre and the rim tape so that the inside of the nipple can be checked. Any protruding spoke ends must be filed smooth and flush with the nipple head so that there is no risk of their puncturing the inner tube.

13 You may also need to remove the tyre in situations where the nipple is corroded in place. Apply penetrating fluid to the threads, and use the screwdriver slot in the nipple head to turn it.

Rim runout

14 Rim runout is checked by arranging a wire pointer close to the rim edge, or a dial gauge for preference, and turning the wheel. As a general rule, about 1 mm or so of runout is acceptable, but check the exact figure in your workshop manual. Runout may be either radial (up-and-down) or axial (side-to-side) **(see illustration)**.

15 During this check, try rocking the rim from side to side. Any obvious freeplay here indicates worn bearings, and this must not be confused with runout. If you detect bearing play, the bearing(s) must be renewed, or the wheel will never run true. Bearing renewal is discussed later in this Section.

16 If you find radial (up and down) runout, the wheel can be trued by slackening several of the spokes on the low side of the wheel, and then tightening the opposing spokes by a similar amount to pull the rim into shape **(see illustration)**. Slacken the spokes at the lowest point by two or three turns, then slacken the adjacent spokes by progressively less turns to ensure that the rim is not pulled out of shape. Care must be taken to ensure that spokes from each side of the hub are slackened or tightened by a similar amount, or you will find that you have introduced axial play to add to your problems!

17 Axial play, or side-to-side wobble, will require that two or three spokes on the tight side of the hub are slackened, and the opposing spokes tightened to pull the rim sideways and into line **(see illustration)**.

18 As you will appreciate, anything other than minor adjustments will tend to become complicated, with one alteration tending to cause distortion elsewhere. This is where the experience of the professional wheel builder will pay off, since he will be able to allow for this effect during adjustment. Most wheel builders will undertake truing at reasonable cost, and in practice it may be quicker and easier to have this work done for you.

19 If the distortion is significant following impact damage, it is preferable to have the wheel examined properly in case there are signs of splits or deformation in the rim.

20 If you ignore loose spokes they will eventually break, leading to excessive stress and subsequent breakage of others. It is vital that any broken, bent or corroded spokes are renewed promptly, or you will end up having to have a complete wheel rebuild.

21 Re-spoking requires the removal of the tyre, inner tube and rim tape to gain access to the nipple heads. You can order a new spoke and nipple from the local dealer for your model, though this may take time to arrange.

22 A local wheel builder, on the other hand, should be able to make up a spoke of the correct length to pattern, and this is probably a better way of getting a replacement. If just one or two spokes are to be renewed, you can do this at home, threading the new spoke into position, fitting the nipple and truing the wheel as described above.

23 Where a number of spokes are broken, bent or rusted, it will be quicker to have the wheel checked and the work done by an expert. It may be advisable to have a complete new set of spokes.

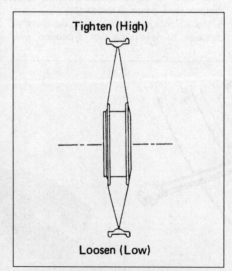

2.16 The spokes on the low side are loosened and those on the high side tightened to correct radial runout

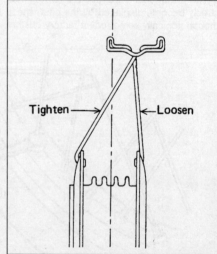

2.17 Correcting axial runout

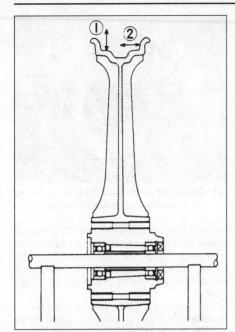

2.30 Check wheel radial (1) and axial (2) runout on a cast wheel with the tyre removed and the gauge tip against the inner machined face of the wheel

24 When the work is complete, check that all spoke ends are ground or filed smooth, and do not omit to fit the rim tape or band before the tyre and tube are refitted.

25 Significant damage which has resulted in a buckled rim, or just general old age and corrosion, will mean that the wheel will need complete rebuilding. This is likely to be a job for the expert; you can try it at home if you wish, but be warned that you will spend many hours trying to get the rim true, possibly without success. See the Section on wheel building below.

26 Take the complete wheel to the builder so that the offset (the position of the rim centre in relation to that of the hub) can be measured before the old spokes are cut away. Take the wheel axle with you so that it can be used to support the wheel during the truing operation.

27 You should also check the wheel bearings and renew these if worn, or it may prove difficult to true the wheel.

28 You may wish to get the hub blasted and polished or painted while the spokes are out of the way, in which case tell the wheel builder of your intentions. The bearings must be removed from the hub during any refinishing work.

29 Bear in mind that you are not limited to the original rim type. Where a chrome plated steel rim was fitted, you may prefer to specify a replacement in alloy, which is a little lighter and easier to maintain. Similarly you could use stainless steel spokes in place of plated ones.

Checking cast alloy wheels

30 It is comparatively easy to check cast wheels, simply because there is little that can be done to correct any discrepancy found. Start by checking for bearing freeplay (see Section 4), and rim runout as described above for wire spoked wheels **(see illustration)**.

31 Worn bearings should, of course, be renewed (see below). Rim runout will be a problem to deal with. If this exceeds the limits set by the manufacturer, or if there is a distinct wobble caused by a deformed rim, the complete wheel must be renewed. There is no satisfactory way to straighten a twisted or bent wheel, and no attempt should be made to do so. Remember that the forces which caused the damage may well have set up potential fracture sites in the casting.

32 Corrosion of cast wheels is a common problem, but not a serious one unless it becomes extensive **(see illustration)**. Small chips or patches of damaged lacquer should be repaired by sanding and polishing the corroded area to match the original, and then touching in the lacquer coat to protect the metal.

33 More extensive damage is best dealt with by removing the tyre, and also the tube, where fitted. Remove the wheel bearings and have the whole wheel cleaned up by bead blasting. The surface finish can be either left matt, or can be buffed up to a bright finish. Protect the cleaned metal by coating it with a proprietary clear wheel lacquer, which can be bought in aerosol cans from most car accessory shops.

Checking composite wheels

34 At first sight, a composite wheel would appear to be a good prospect for rebuilding, but in reality few of them are. Any damage usually means replacement.

35 You should make the usual checks for runout, damage and wheel bearing freeplay as described for cast wheels.

36 In the case of wheels using steel spokes and alloy rims, check carefully for signs of corrosion where the rim meets the spokes; corrosion here is likely to be caused by electrolytic action between the two metals, and can seriously weaken the wheel structure.

37 The rivets holding rim to spoke can be hidden by plastic protectors. The centre nuts are locked by drilling and pinning and cannot be tightened if they work loose **(see illustration)**.

38 The only alternative to buying a new wheel is to check the dealers and the motorcycle press for companies willing to undertake reconditioning work.

3 Rebuilding a wheel

Before dismantling the wheel

1 Sketch or photograph the wheel to record the spoke pattern.

2 Measure the length of spokes; this is important if the hub is conical or has flanges of different diameters.

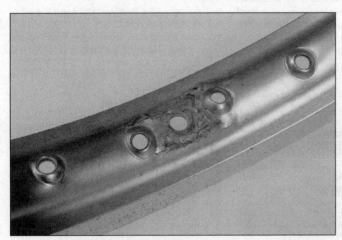

2.32 Corrosion has set into this cast alloy wheel with disastrous results

2.37 A Comstar composite wheel. Note that the hub to spoke fixing nuts are drilled and pinned axially and cannot be adjusted

3 Lay a straight-edge across the rim and measure the distance between the hub flange and the rim; this is called the off-set.

A wheel building/checking jig

4 A suitable jig can be made up from an old swingarm provided it has enough clearance for the wheel to rotate. A wooden mounting block can be fixed to the bridge or a plate welded to this in order that the arm can be bolted vertically to a bench or held in a vice.
5 The chain adjusters can be used to position the axle horizontally.
6 You will need spacers to prevent the wheel moving sideways along the axle.

Wheel building

7 Collect the right number of each length of spoke required with sufficient nipples. Inner and outer spokes are angled differently.
8 Beginning at the valve hole, fit the spokes on one side of the wheel with the spokes leaving the hub on the inside of the hub flange. Follow the pattern you recorded. You may be able to follow the rubbing marks made by the old spokes.
9 Then lace the spokes leaving the outside of the hub on the same side.
10 Tighten the nipples finger-tight and be prepared to slacken some in order to fit the later spokes.
11 When all the spokes are fitted, put the wheel in the jig and then tighten the spokes gradually whilst checking that the off-set is maintained and the runout, both axially and side-to-side is within limits.
12 The runout will be large at first and will be reduced as you work round the wheel. Begin by checking side-to-side runout with a pencil held by a rubber band on a block. A straight-edge can be used first of all to check axial

differences, and when the rim is not parallel with the wheel axle.
13 A dial gauge set in a stand should be used for final checking.
14 Tighten spokes in groups of four, preferably using a proper spoke spanner, although a small open-ender or adjustable will do.
15 There is no set tension quoted for the spokes, although some motorcycle manufacturers specify a torque setting. The rim must be held firmly with no movement relative to the hub and all the spokes must be at the same tension. Check by spinning the wheel with a screwdriver across the spokes and listen for an even tone.
16 When you have finished (a process which may take a long time) carefully angle-grind or file off any bits of spoke which stick up proud of the nipple, and fit a new rim tape.

4 Renewing wheel bearings

1 A common arrangement for the wheel bearings on many machines is two ball bearings pressed into the central bore of the wheel hub. The bearings are located internally by either a tubular spacer or by shoulders machined into the hub. The assembly is generally protected by one or more grease seals.
2 In the case of the rear wheel on a chain drive machine, there is often a third bearing carried in a detachable sprocket carrier and cush drive unit.
3 The above arrangement will be found on a large number of Japanese machines, where wheel bearing arrangements have become almost standardised. It is not possible to list all the various systems in detail in this book, and it follows that the appropriate workshop manual should be consulted to see which arrangement applies to your model.
4 Most shaft drive models use a similar method of attaching the rear wheel, the shaft and bearings forming part of the bevel drive assembly.
5 When checking wheel bearing play, first

4.5 Check for wheel bearing play by trying to move the wheel about the axle

support the motorcycle so that the wheel is raised off the ground. Grasp the wheel in two diametrically opposite places and attempt to move it about the wheel axle **(see illustration)**. Any play will be immediately obvious.
6 Occasionally, you may encounter a threaded bearing retainer at this stage. These require a special pin spanner to remove them, though in the absence of the correct tool you can often make up an improvised version from steel strip, drilling holes to correspond with those in the retainer and fitting small bolts to act as the locating pins. The accompanying line drawing shows an example of this type of tool **(see illustration)**. Always check the threads on the retainer before attempting removal; you may find that those on the right-hand side are left-handed.
7 As a rule, the wheel is removed and any separate grease seals removed from the hub using a large flat-bladed screwdriver **(see illustration)**. Place the wheel on wood blocks so that the hub is supported and the disc or sprocket is protected
8 The first bearing can be driven out after levering the spacer to one side, using a thin drift with a parallel tip, and working around the bearing inner race **(see illustrations)**. This will drive out the bearing and the spacer will drop free.
9 Turn the wheel over and drive out the other bearing using the drift.
10 Note that the removal of the bearings will place great stress on the balls and races; it is

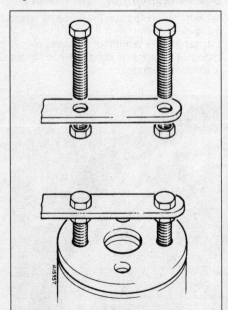

4.6 An improved peg spanner for removing threaded retainers

4.7 Removing the oil seal by levering gently

4.8a Using a drift to knock out the bearings

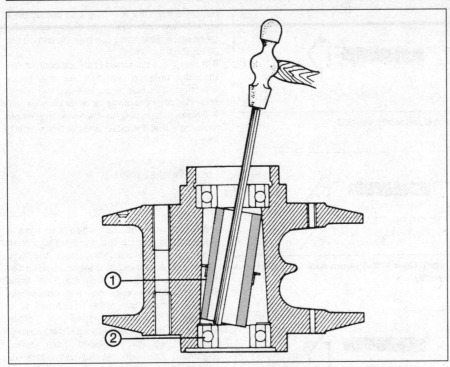

4.8b Knock the spacer (1) to one side so that the drift bears on the bearing (2)

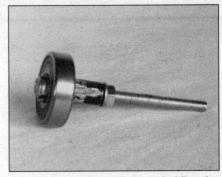

4.11 An expanding bolt shown holding the inside bore of the bearing

not advisable to refit bearings once removed from the hub.

11 If you cannot gain access to the back of the bearing through the hub, a knife-edged bearing puller can be used with a slide-hammer to pull the bearings from the hub. The author has also used an expanding bolt of the type used to anchor bolts into concrete floors to good effect; pass the bolt down through the bearing and tighten its nut to expand the cone shape to grip the inside of the bearing, then strike the end of the bolt from the opposite side of the hub **(see illustration)**.

12 If new bearings are to be fitted, these can be ordered from the relevant dealer, though if you take the old bearings to a motor factor it may be possible to obtain standard replacements at a lower cost. The bearings can usually be matched from the part number stamped or etched on them, or by direct measurement **(see illustration)**.

13 Unless sealed on both sides, the new bearings should be packed with high-melting point grease before installation.

14 Prior to installing the bearings, make sure that the bearing housing in the wheel hub is clean and undamaged. If the old bearing had spun in the housing, the new bearing will most likely be a loose fit; a bearing locking compound can be used between the housing and bearing outer race to secure it, but if damage is severe the wheel must be renewed.

15 Place the wheel on wood blocks so that the hub is supported and the disc or sprocket is protected. Place the bearing in position so that its sealed side faces outwards, or so that the manufacturer's marking faces outwards. Tap the bearing squarely into the hub using a drift which bears only on the bearing's outer race **(see illustration)**. Special tools are available for this purpose, but a socket of the correct size makes a useful alternative.

16 Refit any seals. Lightly tap the seal in place using a drift which bears on the outer edge of the seal, not the lips.

5 Wheel balancing

1 The front wheel should be statically balanced, complete with tyre and dust cap on valve. An out of balance wheel can produce dangerous wobbling at high speed.

2 Some tyres have a balance mark on the sidewall. This must be positioned adjacent to the valve. Even so, the wheel still requires balancing.

4.12 The bearing manufacturer's marking will appear on the outer race – this denotes the type and size of bearing

4.15 This bearing is being driven into place using a socket. Note the drift which fits into the square drive to avoid hammering directly on the socket

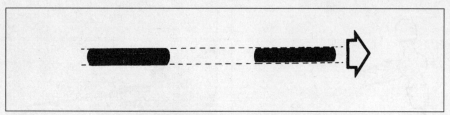

6.1a The front and rear wheel correctly aligned

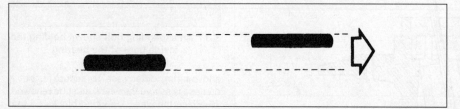

6.1b The rear wheel is offset in relation to the front. Check that wheel spacers have been refitted correctly

6.1c The rear wheel at an angle to the front usually indicates that the wheel is out of alignment in the swingarm. Check the adjusters before looking for frame damage

3 With the front wheel clear of the ground, spin the wheel several times. Each time, it will probably come to rest in the same position. Balance weights should be attached diametrically opposite the heavy spot, until the wheel will not come to rest in any set position, when spun. Various types of weight are fitted to wheels. Those with wire spokes often use cylindrical weights with a slot to allow them to be fitted around a spoke. The weight is then slid down over the nipple to locate it. In the case of cast alloy wheels, the weights may be clamped to the rim edge, or stuck to the rim flange. In some cases, weights must be affixed in certain positions in relation to the spokes.

4 It makes sense to have the wheel properly balanced at a tyre fitting specialist when a new tyre is fitted.

5 Although the rear wheel is more tolerant to out-of-balance forces than is the front wheel, ideally this too should be balanced if a new tyre is fitted. Because of the drag of the final drive components the wheel must be removed from the machine and placed on a suitable free-running spindle before balancing takes place. Balancing can then be carried out as for the front wheel.

6 If the bike is damaged in an accident, check that the balance weights are still firmly attached. It is also wise to have the wheel balanced after checking for other damage.

7 Before beginning to balance the wheel make sure that it is clean and the tyre properly fitted.

6 Wheel alignment

1 Alignment of the rear wheel can have a significant effect on the handling and road holding of a motorcycle, with the tyre continually scrubbing at a slight angle to the axis (centreline) of the machine **(see illustrations)**. The main cause of poor wheel alignment on chain drive machines is a cocked rear wheel, where the chain tensioners have not been adjusted evenly. However, on all machines poor wheel alignment can be caused by frame or suspension components being distorted, often as a result of accident damage.

2 Machines which use shaft final drive have no requirement for adjustment of the rear wheel position, and so the problem of alignment through maladjustment never arises. Similarly, certain chain drive models, especially those with single-sided swingarms, employ a form of chain adjustment using an eccentric pivot which prevents misalignment of the wheel.

3 Most machines have a set of alignment marks on the ends of the swinging arm, and these provide a useful check of the accuracy of the wheel position **(see illustrations)**.

4 For an infallible test of the alignment however use a straight-edge gauge, string gauge or sprocket alignment gauge as described in Chapter 5. Allowance must be made when the tyres are of different widths. Note that an uneven wheel offset is

6.3a Conventional chain adjuster markings on the swingarm

6.3b Eccentric cam type chain adjuster markings

acceptable on some shaft drive machines –
check with your workshop manual or a dealer
for details.

5 If the check shows that the rear wheel is
cocked **(see illustration 6.1c)**, use the drive
chain adjusters to bring it back into line; this
will obviously not apply to shaft drive
machines. Once the wheels are correctly
aligned, you can then check whether the
manufacturer's alignment marks on the
swingarm ends are reliable.

6 If the check shows that the wheels are out
of line (offset from centre) **(see illustration
6.1b)**, check that there is no freeplay in the
swingarm bearings and front/rear wheel
bearings, also check that the wheel bearings
are not worn. If you don't know the history of
the machine, check also that all wheel
spacers are fitted in their correct positions.
Note that an uneven wheel offset is
acceptable on some shaft drive machines –
check with your workshop manual or a dealer
for details.

**Regular inspection of the
tyre wear pattern will also
give you an indication when
alignment problems may be
present.**

7 Tyre sizes and markings

1 The manufacturer will specify the size and
type of tyre to be used on a particular model,
this information being given in the owner's
handbook, workshop manual, and also on a
label attached to the bike's chainguard or
mudguard/fender **(see illustration)**.

2 Any replacement tyre should conform to the
size, composition and speed rating specified
by the motorcycle manufacturer.

Tyre sizes

3 The tyre size, speed rating and load index
are moulded into the tyre sidewall **(see
illustration)**. In the example shown, this part
of the sidewall marking shows: 180/55 ZR 17,
which can be interpreted as follows.

4 The overall width of the tyre is shown first,
and in this example is given in millimetres.
This is followed by a slash mark, then a
second figure indicating the aspect ratio of
the tyre section. In the example this is 55, and
indicates that the height of the tyre section is
55% of the width, thus 99 mm.

5 The letter Z which follows is the speed
rating; this tyre is safe for use above 150 mph

7.1 A typical tyre information label

(240 kmh). A second letter indicates that the
tyre is of bias-belted or radial construction, as
opposed to a cross-ply, eg this tyre is a radial
construction. Next comes the rim diameter of
17 inches.

6 Some tyres also show a load index number
followed by the tyre speed rating again, eg
130/90 H 17 **68**H. This may be omitted on
modern tyres where the maximum load is also
written on the tyre wall.

7 On some tyres, the size is given in
inches, rather than in millimetres, the latter
sizing relating to modern low-profile tyres. A
list of the older imperial sizes, together with

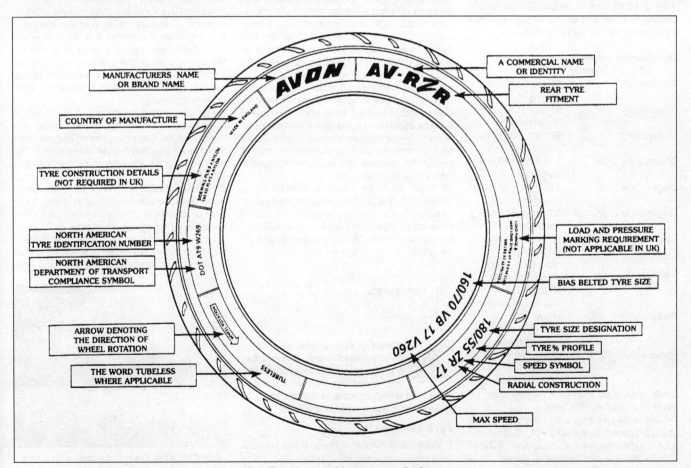
7.3 Standard markings on a typical tyre

the nearest metric equivalents is shown below.

Old sizes Imperial	Low-profile equivalents Imperial	Metric
2.50/2.75	3.10	80/90
3.00/3.25	3.60	90/90
3.50	4.10	100/90
4.00	4.25/85	110/90
4.25	4.70	120/90
4.50/5.00	5.10	130/90

Speed ratings

8 The table shown below relates to the system of speed rating markings adopted by the European Tyre Manufacturers, though in practice most of the markings will be found on tyres from outside Europe.

9 Note that the speed rating denotes the theoretical top speed of the machine, not the speed at which it is normally used. The speed rating system relates more to the level of stress likely to be imposed by a class of motorcycle over a broad range of speeds, rather than to its actual top speed. This is why a motorcycle manufacturer may stipulate a V-rated tyre for a machine which is perhaps limited to a top speed of 115 mph.

10 On no account be tempted to fit an S-rated or H-rated tyre to save money when a V or Z rated tyre is required; you will be placing yourself and others at risk, and may be breaking the law by doing so.

Construction	Speed symbol	Speed
Diagonal ply	L	75 mph (120 kmh) maximum
Diagonal ply	M	81 mph (130 kmh) maximum
Diagonal ply	P	93 mph (150 kmh) maximum
Diagonal ply	S	113 mph (180 kmh) maximum
Diagonal ply	T	118 mph (190 kmh) maximum
Diagonal ply	H	130 mph (210 kmh) maximum
Diagonal ply	V	above 130 mph (210 kmh) at reduced loadings*
Bias-belted ply	VB	above 130 mph (210 kmh) at reduced loadings*
Radial ply	VR	above 130 mph (210 kmh) at reduced loadings*
Radial ply	ZR**	above 150 mph (240 kmh) at reduced loadings*

*Note maximum approved speed may be marked on tyre, eg V260 kmh
**A ZR rated tyre may also carry a W speed rating preceded by a load index and followed by a maximum speed. For example, a ZR17 (73W) V280 tyre can be used at speeds up to 280 kmh (174 mph).

Load index

11 The load index number denotes the maximum load that a tyre can carry at the speed indicated by its Speed Symbol. and under the service conditions specified by the manufacturers. The numbers and their load capacities are as follows.

LI	Kg	LI	Kg	LI	Kg
32	112	48	180	64	280
33	115	49	185	65	290
34	118	50	190	66	300
35	121	51	195	67	307
36	125	52	200	68	315
37	128	53	206	69	325
38	132	54	212	70	335
39	136	55	218	71	345
40	140	56	224	72	355
41	145	57	230	73	365
42	150	58	236	74	375
43	155	59	243	75	387
44	160	60	250	76	400
45	165	61	257	77	412
46	170	62	265	78	425
47	175	63	272	79	437
				80	450

Radial and bias-belted tyres

12 The terms 'radial' and 'bias-belted', relate to the way in which the casing plies are configured; those of the radial and bias belted versions offering a lighter and more flexible construction to the traditional diagonal (cross-ply) tyres. This in turn ensures that the tyre tread is kept in better contact with the road surface. Offering improved grip and reduced wear rates, albeit at greater initial cost.

13 Not all machines are suitable for use with radial or bias belted tyres; the wheels must be able to accept tubeless tyres, and the degree of success depends to some extent on suspension design. Unless the machine was fitted with this type of tyre as original equipment, always consult the machine manufacturer or importer before making the change.

14 Note that the tyre construction is indicated by the speed symbol. In the case of cross-ply tyres, a single letter is used, whilst on radial or bias-belted tyres, this is indicated by a second letter, 'B' for bias-belted and 'R' for radial.

---

8 Tyre safety

 Warning: Your safety, and that of other road users, depends to a great extent on tyre condition and suitability. You should not use a tyre which can cause danger to yourself or anyone else on the road.

Tyre choice

1 Make sure that the tyres fitted to your machine are of the type and size recommended by the motorcycle manufacturer, paying particular attention to speed ratings. The use of the wrong type or size of tyre is dangerous, and may be illegal.

2 Tubeless tyres may only be used on wheels designed for this type of tyre. If you wish to use tubeless tyres on other wheels, check whether this is permissible with the manufacturer or importer. Note that tubeless tyres cannot normally be used on wire-spoked wheels (except where the spokes join the rim outside of the tyre seating), and that some cast alloy wheels may be unsuitable due to their rim seating.

3 Don't run front tyres on the rear wheel and vice versa. Don't have a radial or bias belted front on the same bike as a crossply rear, or a radial front with a bias belted rear.

4 Dual purpose trail tyres can be used on and off road, however the more effective they are off-road the less effective they are on tarmac. Motocross tyres marked NOT FOR ROAD USE, or COMPETITION USE ONLY should not be used on the road.

Regular checks

5 Check tyre condition regularly, looking for wear or damage. In the UK, it is illegal to use a tyre on which the tread depth is less than 1 mm. The tread must be visible over three quarters of the tyre width and all the way round with no bald patches. In fact a tread depth of 2 mm is a more realistic figure to preserve good road holding **(see illustration)**.

6 In the case of damage, it is illegal to use a tyre which has a cut deep enough to expose the casing plies or cords, or one which shows signs of bulges or other indications of the separation of the sidewall or tread from the underlying casing.

7 Remove stones or pieces of metal which have become embedded in the treads, and check that the underlying casing has not been damaged. Note that foreign objects left in the treads can gradually work in deeper, causing punctures.

8 Remove any oil or grease from the tyres. Apart from the obvious risk of skidding, oil or grease anywhere on the tyre will attack the rubber if left for any length of time.

9 Check tyre pressures regularly, preferably each day before the machine is ridden, and at least once a week. Riding a machine with

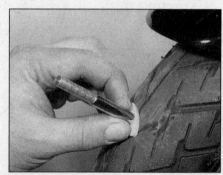

8.5 Checking the tread depth with a tyre gauge

incorrect tyre pressures is illegal and dangerous, and will shorten tyre life considerably **(see illustrations)**.

10 Pressures must be checked when the tyre is cold – never after the machine has been ridden. Tyres warm up in use, and the air pressure will rise accordingly. The specified pressures apply to a tyre at atmospheric temperature.

11 Use an accurate pocket gauge to check pressures (see Chapter 5); do not rely on filling station forecourt gauges, which may be inaccurate.

Tyre renewal

12 In the case of tubed tyres, the inner tube should be renewed each time a new tyre is fitted, and whenever there have been more than two or three puncture repairs. Make sure that the inner tube is the correct size.

13 In the case of tubeless tyres, fit a new valve assembly each time the tyre is renewed.

14 Keep the valve clean, and always refit the dust cap to exclude dirt and to provide a secondary seal in case of valve failure.

15 Wheel balance should be checked each time a new tyre is fitted, or whenever imbalance is felt.

Puncture repair – tubed tyres

16 It is advisable to fit a new inner tube, however punctured tubes can be repaired using a kit. If the tube already has several patches, or the tube is torn or split, renew it.

17 Don't forget to remove the item that caused the puncture from the tyre.

Puncture repair – tubeless tyres

18 In the event of punctures, note that in the case of tubeless tyres the tyre must be removed from the rim and a headed plug fitted from the **inside**. Repairs made using a plain plug fitted from the outside are illegal. Tubeless tyres should be renewed if a second puncture occurs. Note that repairs to tyres with a speed rating higher than V (ie Z or W rated tyres) are not advised by the tyre manufacturers.

19 In the event of an emergency, the only recommended 'get-you-home' repair is to fit a standard inner tube of the correct size. If this

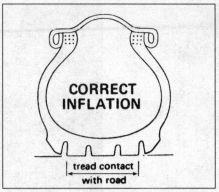

8.9a A correctly inflated tyre will keep its designed contour thereby giving maximum road holding and wear

8.9b Under-inflated tyre will reduce tread contact and handling, and increase risk of damage to tyre casing

course of action is adopted, care should be taken to ensure that the cause of the puncture has been removed before the inner tube is fitted. It will be found that the valve in the rim is considerably larger than the diameter of the inner tube valve stem. To prevent the ingress of road dirt, and to help support the valve, a spacer should be fitted over the valve.

9 Tubed tyres – removal, puncture repair and fitting

1 To the inexperienced, tyre changing represents a formidable task, yet if a few simple rules are observed and the technique learned the whole operation is surprisingly simple.

2 To remove the tyre from either wheel, first detach the wheel from the machine.

Removal

3 Deflate the tyre by removing the valve insert and when it is fully deflated, push the bead from the tyre away from the wheel rim on both sides so that the bead enters the centre well of the rim. Remove the locking cap and push the tyre valve into the tyre itself.

4 Insert a tyre lever close to the valve and lever the edge of the tyre over the outside of

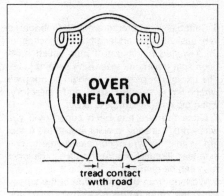

8.9c An over-inflated tyre will wear faster and also increases the risk of damage

the wheel rim **(see illustration)**. Very little force should be necessary; if resistance is encountered it is probably due to the fact that the tyre beads have not entered the well of the wheel rim all the way round the tyre.

5 Note that where the machine is fitted with cast alloy wheels, the risk of damage to the wheel rim can be minimised by the use of proprietary plastic rim protectors placed over the rim flange at the point where the tyre levers are inserted **(see illustration)**.

9.4 Deflate the inner tube and insert the tyre lever next to the valve

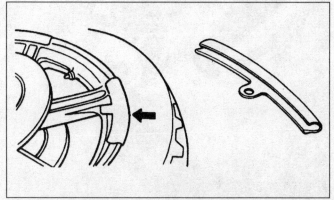

9.5 Plastic rim protectors can be easily fabricated to protect the rim at the point where the tyre levers are to be inserted

9.7 Use two levers to work the first bead over the edge of the rim

9.8 Removing the second bead from the wheel rim

6 Suitable rim protectors may be fabricated very easily from short lengths (4 – 6 inches) of thick-walled nylon petrol pipe which have been split down one side using a sharp knife. The use of rim protectors should be adopted whenever levers are used and, therefore, when the risk of damage is likely.

7 Once the tyre has been edged over the wheel rim, it is easy to work around the wheel rim so that the tyre is completely free to one side **(see illustration)**. At this stage, the inner tube can be removed.

8 Working from the other side of the wheel, ease the other edge of the tyre over the outside of the wheel rim that is furthest away **(see illustration)**. Continue to work around the rim until the tyre is free completely from the rim.

Puncture repair

9 If a puncture has necessitated the removal of the tyre, reinflate the inner tube and immerse it in a bowl of water to trace the source of the leak. Mark its position and deflate the tube. Dry the tube and clean the area around the puncture with a solvent-

soaked rag. When the surface has dried, apply rubber solution and allow this to dry before removing the backing from the patch and applying the patch to the surface.

10 It is best to use a patch of self-vulcanising type, which will form a very permanent repair.

11 Note that it may be necessary to remove a protective covering from the top surface of the patch, after it has sealed into position. Inner tubes made from synthetic rubber may require a special type of patch and adhesive, if a satisfactory bond is to be achieved.

12 Before refitting the tyre, check the inside to make sure that the object which caused the puncture is not trapped.

13 Check the outside of the tyre, particularly the tread area, to make sure nothing is trapped that may cause a further puncture.

14 If the inner tube has been patched on a number of past occasions, or if there is a tear or large hole, it is preferable to discard it and fit a new one. Sudden deflation may cause an accident, particularly if it occurs with the front wheel.

15 Clean the wheel to remove any old bits of rubber, sealant, tyre or chain lubrication. On

wire-spoked wheels, check that the rim tape is in position over the spoke ends; if any of the spoke ends protrude through the nipples, they should be filed back.

Fitting

16 To fit the tyre, inflate the inner tube sufficiently for it to assume a circular shape but only just. Then push it into the tyre so that it is enclosed completely **(see illustration)**. If the tyre has a balance mark (usually a spot of coloured paint), this must be positioned alongside the valve. The arrow indicating direction of tyre rotation must face the right way.

17 Lay the tyre on the wheel at an angle and insert the valve through the rim tape and the hole in the wheel rim **(see illustration)**. Attach the locking cap on the first few threads, sufficient to hold the valve captive in its correct location.

18 Starting at the point furthest from the valve, push the tyre bead over the edge of the wheel rim until it is located in the central well. Continue to work around the tyre in this fashion until the whole of one side of the tyre

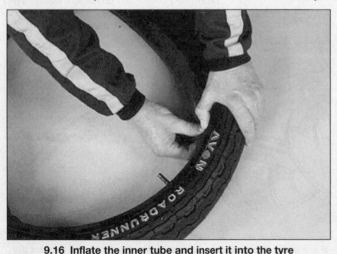

9.16 Inflate the inner tube and insert it into the tyre

9.17 Lay the tyre on the rim and feed the valve through the hole in the rim

9.18 Work the first bead of the tyre over the wheel rim

9.19 Finish easing the second bead over the rim at the tyre valve point

9.20 Push the valve up into the tyre as the last section is fitted to avoid trapping the inner tube

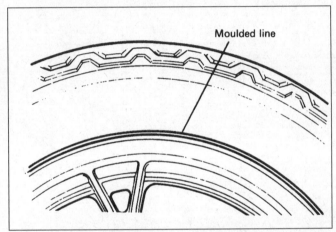

Moulded line

9.21 The moulded line should be equidistant from the wheel rim all the way round the wheel

is on the rim **(see illustration)**. It may be necessary to use a tyre lever during the final stages.

19 Make sure that there is no pull on the tyre valve and again commencing with the area furthest from the valve, ease the other bead of the tyre over the edge of the rim **(see illustration)**.

20 Finish with the area close to the valve, pushing the valve up into the tyre until the locking cap touches the rim **(see illustration)**. This will ensure the inner tube is not trapped when the last section of the bead is edged over the rim with a tyre lever.

21 Check that the inner tube is not trapped at any point. Reinflate the inner tube, and check that the tyre is seating correctly around the wheel rim. There should be a thin rib moulded around the wall of the tyre on both sides, which should be equidistant from the wheel rim at all points **(see illustration)**. If the tyre is unevenly located on the rim, try bouncing the wheel when the tyre is at the recommended

pressure. It is probable that one of the beads has not pulled clear of the centre well.

22 Adjust the tyre pressure to that specified by the manufacturer and fit the dust cap.

23 Tyre replacement is aided by dusting the side walls particularly in the vicinity of the beads, with a liberal coating of French chalk. Washing-up liquid can also be used to good effect, but this has the disadvantage (where steel rims are used) of causing the inner surfaces of the wheel rim to corrode.

Caution: Do not be over generous in the application of lubricant or tyre creep may occur.

10 Tubeless tyres – removal, puncture repair and fitting

1 Removal, repair and fitting of tubeless tyres

should be left to a professional motorcycle tyre specialist, rather than attempted in the home workshop for the following reasons.

2 The force required to break the seal between the wheel rim and tyre bead is considerable and requires a bead breaking tool. It is highly likely that you could damage the wheel rims by attempting this without the proper tool and skill.

3 Puncture repair of tubeless tyres must be carried out by a professional (see Section 8). Note that repairs to tyres with a speed rating higher than V (ie Z or W rated tyres) are not advised by the tyre manufacturers.

4 The initial inflation of tubeless tyres require a high pressure airline to seat the beads against the wheel rim.

5 Tyre changing specialists will fit a new tyre valve and also balance the wheel afterwards.

6 Note that some saving can be made by removing the wheel yourself.

Notes

Chapter 15
Machine tools

Contents

1 Introduction

1 Recent years have seen a big increase in the availability of reasonably priced machine tools of good quality. This has meant that anyone wishing to carry out a restoration project, major repair work or the construction of a 'special' can equip the workshop with the necessary facilities.

2 The detailed use of these machines is beyond the scope of this manual, however this Chapter will summarise the use of the most common equipment.

3 All the machine tools in this Section require an electrical supply. Check that the existing supply will be able to cope with the additional load and that any wiring complies with the relevant safety standards (see Chapter 1).

Safety

4 The use of machine tools and any powered hand tool brings a greater safety risk. In industry, many machines may only be used by people who have been on an approved training course, and have been awarded a certificate to show that they have completed the course successfully.

5 It may be necessary for you as an individual to go on training courses run by industry, the local further education centres, or by equipment suppliers. This will help improve your skill as well as show you the safe way to work.

6 In addition to the basic safety rules outlined in Chapter 1 the following points are particularly relevant to machine tools.

● Ensure that the electrical supply is capable of providing the extra power needed, and that the fuses and circuit breaker are of an appropriate rating. It is advisable to consult a qualified electrician.

● Ensure that ON-OFF switches are clearly marked and easily accessible.

● Always turn the power off before making any adjustments or settings.

● Completely isolate the power supply before carrying out any repairs to machine tools.

● Always allow moving parts to stop before touching them. This is particularly important in the case of revolving parts such as drill and lathe chucks.

● Take care that revolving wheels on angle grinders and drill chucks have stopped before setting them down.

● Note that using machine tools and being able to work in a more professional way is great fun, but be aware that it means you must be more vigilant about safety.

● Being unexpectedly distracted does not help your concentration when you are measuring or at a crucial point when setting up your carburettors. An unexpected distraction when using a power tool can be very dangerous – you must encourage safe working practice to all visitors to the workshop.

2 Drilling machine

1 These machines are referred to as pillar drills, or drill presses, and are available with columns of different heights which obviously allow for a greater variety in the size of work,

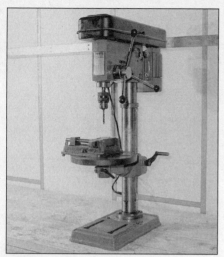

2.1 Probably the first machine tool to be bought for the workshop. Ideally all holes should be drilled on a machine like this

but also means that the drill can be mounted on a bench, or on a stand on the floor **(see illustration)**.

2 The main advantages of drilling by machine are as follows **(see illustrations)**:

a) *The work can be held safely by bolting to the drilling table, or clamped in a machine vice which itself is bolted to the table.*

b) *Drilling is more accurate for both position and angle to the material surface being drilled.*

c) *The speed of rotation and feed into the work can be more easily controlled.*

3 For maximum use in the workshop the drilling machine should have a table which rotates and tilts, a depth stop which will not allow you to drill deeper than a set

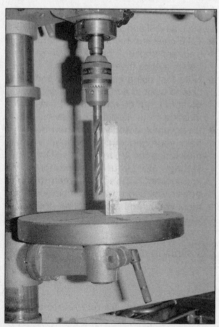

2.7 It is important that the drill and table are at right-angles

2.2a A drill press in use. Note the guard around the drill chuck

amount, and a range of five speeds from 250 to 3000 rpm or so.

Installation

4 Bolt the drill to the floor or the bench securely.

5 Check that the column is vertical and that the bolts are tightened equally.

6 Ensure that the electrical cable is securely out of the way and will not interfere with drilling operations.

7 With the machine in place, fit a drill, which you have checked is straight, in the chuck and use your set square to check that the table and the drill are at right-angles **(see illustration)**. Check from the side and the front, and make any minor adjustments until the drill is perpendicular to the table from all sides. This is a wise move every now and then, and certainly each time after the table has been tilted.

The drilling operation

8 Fix the work, which has been marked out and centre popped as usual, to the work table, or in a machine vice which is clamped to the work table **(see illustration)**.

9 If you are drilling through the work piece make sure that the drill will go into the centre hole of the work table and not into the table itself.

10 The drill bit is set in the chuck and an appropriate speed selected.

 Warning: Always remove the chuck key immediately after tightening the chuck. It should never be left in the chuck or on the table where it may be swept away at high speed.

2.8 A machine vice made from castings in the workshop. Vices are available from tool shops

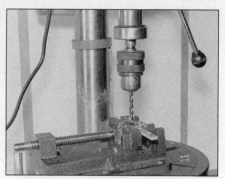

2.2b Using a bench drill to make a group of accurately aligned holes

11 Adjust the height of the table and clamp it. Always approach the correct height from the bottom of the column to avoid any problems with slack in the winding gear.

12 Set the depth control if required.

13 Position the guard. The guard will prevent swarf or particles from being thrown in your eyes, but it will also prevent swarf, lubricant, and broken drill bits from being spread around the drilling area where they may cause a hazard.

14 Switch on the motor and feed the drill bit into the work at a steady rate. Stop drilling if the drill bit shows signs of overheating or generates a lot of noise. Both conditions are a sign that something is amiss – you may be drilling too fast for the material or the drill may be blunt.

15 When the drilling is done, switch off the machine before attempting to remove the work or change the drill bit.

16 Tapping can be done by gripping the tap in the chuck which is rotated by hand with gentle pressure applied by the feed handle. The removable side handle from your hand electric drill clamped around the chuck may help in rotating the chuck **(see illustration)**.

2.16 Using this old drill handle around the chuck makes tapping easier

2.19 The table is tilted to allow a hole to be drilled at an angle to the centre line of the work piece

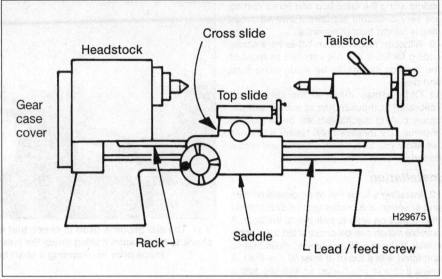

3.3 The basic parts of the lathe

Remember the turn and reverse method of tapping (see Chapter 2).

17 If you have to drill a hole in the same position in more than one component, use the machine vice without moving it, or bolt some locating blocks to the table using the first component as a model. This will save marking out each component individually.

18 The depth stop is also used to set the depth of any counter bores and counter sinking.

19 The table may be tilted to drill holes at angles to the surface of the work piece (see illustration).

20 Within limits the drilling machine can also be used for small scale polishing and wire

brushing. Whilst acceptable for occasional use, this is not recommended, especially on the smaller machines.

3 Lathe

1 The lathe is the basic machine tool. In addition to its turning and thread cutting facilities, it can be used as a drilling, a milling, or grinding machine. By using the two centres, the lathe can also be used for checking the alignment, static balancing, and runout of shafts and various rotating assemblies.

2 Basically, the lathe allows you to cut metal accurately to shape by using prepared cutting tools. Normally the workpiece is firmly located and revolved in a chuck, and a cutting tool is made to cut the workpiece in a series of controllable movements.

3 Familiarise yourself with the basic parts of the lathe (see illustration).

4 The size of a lathe is usually described by giving the centre height and the maximum distance between headstock and tailstock. The dimension for the centre height may be replaced by one which quotes the 'swing', or the maximum diameter of component which the lathe can rotate.

5 For a motorcycle workshop, a lathe which will accommodate a component of 250 mm (10 in) diameter, and has 450 mm (18 in) in length between its centres will be able to tackle most jobs (see illustration). Note that it is not often that a component of 250 mm diameter is to be machined, so a smaller lathe at a reasonable price should not overlooked.

Construction and accessories

6 The range of spindle speeds should be approximately between 50 rpm and 1500 rpm in a series of not less than 6 steps.

7 The lathe should be provided with a tool post, for mounting your cutting tools, a three-jawed self centring chuck, a four jaw chuck on which each jaw can be moved independently to allow odd shaped pieces to be held. A face plate, which screws to the headstock spindle and allows things to be bolted to it for machining, and two lathe centres, one for the headstock and the other for the tailstock.

8 Graduated dials to the handwheels on the saddle slides are essential. The graduations show 0.02 mm or 0.001 in of movement.

9 Other useful items would include a pumping system for cutting fluid and a four way tool post. Powered movement of the

3.5 A typical small workshop lathe. The gearing can be changed by removing the gear case cover

saddle along the lathe bed and screw cutting are very desirable features. Powered cross feed is handy, but not essential.

10 Although most modern lathes have screw cutting facilities it is not essential as most of the threads can easily be made using taps and dies.

11 Older lathes made in the UK will be calibrated in thousandths of inches and the screw cutting mechanism will be for cutting imperial size threads only. Newer machines will allow you to cut both imperial and metric threads.

Installation

12 Installing a lathe has to be done with care and attention. If it comes with its own cabinet then it may be wise to bolt this to the floor. A suitable bench can be constructed from angle iron or 100 mm x 75 mm timber, cross braced and fitted with a top of at least 50 mm thick. It helps if this is positioned so that the top is level in all directions. The lathe is then positioned on the cabinet or bench. If your machine doesn't come with a tray then it is advisable to make or buy one. This sits on the bench with the lathe on top.

13 Lathes are heavy and you will require assistance to lift and position the lathe safely.

14 Chose a site in your workshop which will allow you access for maintenance and cleaning and for work. Don't forget that you may need access to the headstock end for changing gears and feeding material through the spindle.

3.17 The dial gauge is used to check that the lathe centres are in line. This is the sort of check to make when bolting down the lathe, however in this instance the check is being made prior to mounting a shaft between centres to check for runout

15 Follow the makers instructions for levelling and final bolting down.

16 The lathe is usually provided with adjusting screws for setting the level. The level can be checked by placing a spirit level along and across the lathe bed.

17 As the holding bolts are tightened the lathe bed will twist slightly. A tip is to hold a long piece of bar about 25 mm diameter between centre point at the spindle and the tailstock. Then a pointer is mounted in the tool holder and closed onto the bar so that it just touches. Make a note of the reading at several places along the bar. They should be the same. A dial gauge indicator could be used for this job **(see illustration)**.

18 Tighten the lathe holding down screws and make any adjustments to the adjustable feet until the lathe is held firmly and the readings on the bar are as they were before. The lathe should now be firmly located and without any stresses.

19 Make sure any wiring cable, switches etc are fixed out of the way, and protected against spillage of lubricant.

Cutting tools

20 Cutting tools are made of high speed steel, often abbreviated to HSS. You can buy cutting tools from tool suppliers and they may come with the ends ground to the correct shape. A useful range of shapes for cutting tools are shown in illustration 3.21b.

21 The shape varies according to the material, and the type of work being done. In all cases however the tool must cut without rubbing, and therefore the clearance angles are important. The top rake also assists with clearing away the swarf **(see illustrations)**.

22 It is almost impossible to grind the tools to the theoretically correct shapes by hand, but experience has shown that slight variations make little of no difference in practice.

23 You can grind your own tools using a bench grinder, and some means of preparing tools is essential. Attachments are available for the electric hand drill, but a bench grinder is preferable.

Lathe work

24 The skills and knowledge to produce work accurately and to a good finish take a little while to acquire. You will gain these things with experience, however, it is essential that you seek advice from an expert , or enrol on a suitable training course, in order to learn the basics.

25 Lathes can be used to produce a whole range of items, and carry out repair and

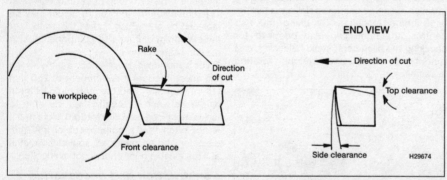

3.21a A sketch of typical clearance angles on a knife-edged tool for cutting steel

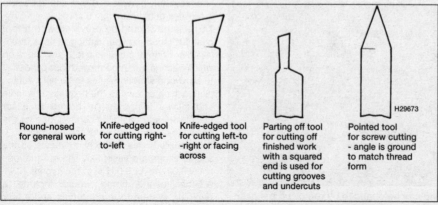

3.21b A selection of the most common tool shapes in plan view

renovation work. All manner of bolts, spacers, axles, nipples, etc can be produced; brake drums can be skimmed and flywheels lightened. Access to a lathe means that the manufacture of special extractors, flywheel pullers, bearing removers, drifts and peg spanners can all be made to measure.

26 The lathe can be used as a drilling machine, milling machine and for grinding, although the latter is not to be encouraged as the lathe is not well enough protected to keep out the very small particles of grit and swarf which will damage slides and screw threads.

27 Although primarily for metal work, a lathe will allow you to turn wood, and a range of plastics and manufactured materials.

28 Typical examples of lathe work are shown in Chapter 7.

4 Milling machine

1 There are basically two types of milling machine: a horizontal miller in which the cutting tool is rotated on a horizontal axis, and a vertical miller which looks like a pillar drill in that the cutting tool is revolved about a vertical axis. The milling machine has a work table which can be moved accurately by means of screw threads in the same way as the cross slide of the lathe.

2 For motorcycle work the vertical mill is the most useful.

3 The milling machine is used for cutting flat surfaces, hexagon and square sides, keyways, gears, etc. In most instances the milling job can be done on the lathe, although this is generally slower, or by sawing and filing by hand.

4 The milling machine can also be used as a pillar drill, with the advantage of accurate hole positioning, but the disadvantage of reduced distance between chuck and work table.

5 Bench grinder

1 The bench grinder is invaluable for shaping and sharpening lathe tools, resharpening drill bits as well as putting an edge on a chisel, reforming screwdriver blades, and deburring.

2 Usually they are supplied with two wheels: a coarse grit wheel for general shaping, and a fine grit wheel for the final sharpening **(see illustration)**.

3 The grinder should be equipped with eye shields, which should be in place during any grinding operation, and tool rests on which the tool being ground can be positioned. The tool rest should be set with a minimum clearance between the edge of the rest and the wheel **(see illustration)**.

4 Mount the grinder on a suitable bench or table top, or on a wall-mounted bracket. Keep it away from other machine tools and engine assembly areas; the small particles flung off the wheel can do damage as they will act like grinding paste.

5 It is important to have a good source of light so fix an overhead lamp near by.

6 Tool and drill bits need to be held firmly, but not forced against the wheel. This will allow you to move the tool or bit across the wheel to grind the correct angles.

7 The grinding process generates a lot of heat which may be sufficient to alter the temper and hardness at the tool point. Do not let the tool point start to change from its natural colour. Keep dipping the tool in a small container of water placed nearby to keep it cool.

8 Do your grinding against the circumference of the wheel. Avoid using the side of the wheel; it is not designed to cope with side forces.

9 Take care when changing wheels to follow the manufacturer's instructions especially as to the position of spacers between the wheel and the clamping nuts.

10 Many grinders come with attachments for fitting a wire brush and a polishing mop **(see illustration)**. These can be very useful for de-scaling old metal and putting a good finish on a restored part.

11 Drill grinding jigs can also be fitted to grinders to help in the drill bit grinding process.

6 Compressed air equipment

1 Although paint spraying is the most common reason for considering compressed air equipment, in the home workshop, there are a variety of uses for compressed air. These include air tools, grit and bead blasting, high pressure cleaning, and of course tyre inflation.

2 Compressors are classified by how much pressure, measured in pounds per square inch (psi) or bars, they can develop and how much air, cubic feet per minute (cfm), which they can provide. For workshop use they are generally powered by an electric motor.

5.2 A typical small grinder suitable for the motorcyclist's workshop

KEEP THE GAP HERE SMALL

5.3 Keep the tool rest correctly positioned close to the wheel and use the guards provided

5.10 A more robust grinder fitted with a polishing mop

6.4 Buy a compressor which can handle the demands of your largest air tool

3 At the small and cheaper end of the scale are the compressors which do not have an air receiver tank. These are fine for jobs which you can do in short bursts and are capable of spraying paint when coupled to a suitable spray gun.

4 A suitable compressor for workshop use would provide up to 80 psi at a minimum rate of 3.5 cfm and have a 240 volt motor rated at least at 1.5 hp. This compressor coupled with a receiver tank will carry out most workshop tasks **(see illustration)**.

5 Ideally the compressor should have an air filter for the compressor intake, a pressure gauge showing the working pressure, and a moisture/oil filter on the output line. The air container or receiver should also have a safety relief valve.

6 Use good quality air line with quick release fittings.

7 A compressed air line is useful for drying components after cleaning and for cleaning carburettor passages, but make sure that the air from the pump is filtered and unlubricated. Take care not to blow muck and metal into oilways and other places where damage may be caused by firmly embedded foreign matter which is impossible to remove.

8 If you are considering buying the grit blasting guns which are available, check that the compressor will provide the correct pressure; blasting requires a higher pressure output than spraying.

9 Never allow an air jet to contact your skin.

Spraying accessories

10 The area of paint on motorcycles is relatively small and a small finishing spray gun will probably fulfil all that is required.

11 For touching up damaged paintwork and for custom work a basic air brush is a useful addition.

12 Painting is a messy business and ideally areas should be set aside for preparation work, the actual painting, for drying, and for cleaning the spray equipment.

13 Remember that the chemicals used for painting and cleaning constitute a fire hazard. Refer to the safety notes in Chapter 1.

14 The majority of motorcycle components are not too large and it is worth building a small booth out of hardboard fitted with a simple revolving table and a cross bar on which to hang things.

Grit and bead blasting

15 A special gun which fires prepared beads or grit from its own reservoir is used to clean off old paint, corrosion, and loose rust particles. The surface of a bead blasted component provides a good key for paint, and bead blasted aluminium parts look very smart.

16 The grit is provided in sacks and is recyclable if you can catch it. Construct a box with one side open big enough to take a fuel tank for example and use this as a blasting chamber.

17 Use eye protection and a face mask to prevent the inhalation of dust, grit and paint particles.

Air tools

18 Hand held drills, screwdrivers, socket drivers can all be powered by air. They are usually lighter and faster than their electrical counterparts, however they are obviously not so transportable.

19 Mechanics who have to clean off-road machinery can make use of pressure washers.

20 Kits with a variety of air tools including spray guns, tyre inflators and air blowers are a cheap way of providing the most useful accessories. However, it is better to buy what you need as you want it, and choose the best quality you can afford relative to the type and amount of use planned.

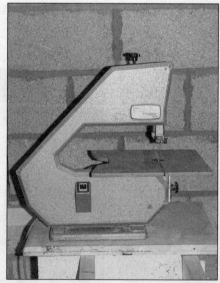

8.1 A properly set up bandsaw will cope with wood, aluminium, plastics and steel in straight lines and on corners

7 Welding equipment

1 A description of welding process and the choice of equipment is included in Chapter 7. Here is just a reminder that any electrical mains requirement will have to be considered when planning the supply to the workshop.

2 It is worth collecting a set of clamps and side cutters just for use as welding accessories as they will tend to get spattered and spoiled during welding.

3 As the welding process generates heat and sparks, the installation and area in which welding takes place must be free of flammable material.

8 Bandsaw

1 This machine is a bit of a luxury if used only for motorcycle work. A typical small, basic machine has a 100 mm depth of cut, is able to take work pieces up to 300 mm long and is powered by an electric motor of 400 watts **(see illustration)**. Blades are available from 6 mm wide with metal and wood cutting teeth. The narrower blades allow the cutting of curves.

2 The saw can be used for cutting steel stock up to 4 mm thick, or aluminium up to 10 mm with suitable metal cutting blades.

3 Typical bandsaw work is cutting out engine plates, and material for brackets etc. Thicker wood sections can be sawn and this makes the job of pattern making and general model making easier than by hand.

4 Usually saws are provided with attachments which make it easier to produce multiple pieces to the same length or at a set angle.

5 An alternative and most useful tool is the hand held jig saw for which metal cutting blades are also available.

9 Angle grinder

1 This is a hand held electric tool fitted with a grinding wheel. The most common size for the small workshop would have a 115 mm diameter wheel.

2 It is used for putting vee grooves and chamfered edges on steel in preparation for welding, trimming away damaged fasteners, and cleaning away rusted areas.

3 The grinder can also be fitted with metal cutting discs, wire brushes and sanding discs, and thus is a very versatile tool to have in the workshop **(see illustration)**.

10 Buying machine tools

New equipment

1 In recent years there has been a big increase in the number of makes and suppliers of machine tools. The cost of machinery has correspondingly reduced so that drilling machines, lathes and welding equipment are now well within the range of the DIY mechanic.

2 Good advice is to treat the purchase of a machine tool as you would a motorcycle. For new equipment, get copies of the technical leaflets from all the suppliers and compare the specifications.

3 Discuss your needs with the suppliers and don't be afraid to ask for discounts or for an accessory to be included in the price. A supplier with a friendly, knowledgeable and reliable service is preferred.

4 You should also ask if delivery and installation is included in the price; lathes can be heavy items.

Second-hand equipment

5 Buying privately caries the same risks as when buying a motorcycle, therefore treat the purchase as if you were buying a second-hand bike. Examine a used machine for signs of abuse in the form of scars on the working surfaces, rounded nuts and broken handles etc. Check the condition of the electrical wiring and switch gear. Run the machine and listen for signs of harshness when you operate all the handwheels and controls.

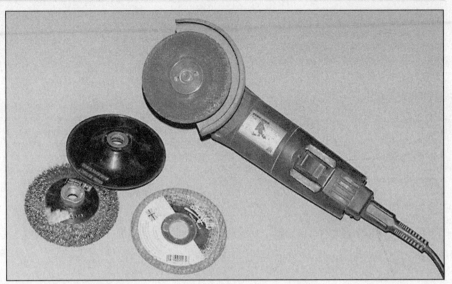

9.3 An angle grinder with a 115 mm diameter dished grinding wheel and a range of accessories

6 Ask what equipment will come with the machine and if it is included in the price.

7 Do not be afraid to do some work on the machine and check the accuracy and reliability. Check the amount of backlash or slack in the screw threads of the slides. Whilst small amounts of adjustment are acceptable there is nothing worse than a machine tool with unreliable accuracy.

8 Reputable dealers will offer a guarantee and will often be able to supply spares.

9 Lathes and milling machines particularly will last for many years if maintained and used properly. It is therefore worth being choosy about the equipment you buy.

11 Other useful and home-made tools

1 There are a variety of other powered tools which you might consider depending on your particular interests. Included in this list might be a polishing machine, a belt sanding/finishing machine, a powered hacksaw, folding machine, and a bearing press.

2 Having bought the basic tools, you will find that you now have the means of making the most of the other sundry equipment which you may require.

Chapter 16
Chemicals, cleaners and sealants

Contents

1 Introduction

1 It is amazing how many chemicals turn up in workshops; from cleaning fluids to epoxy resins. For any one job there is often a bewildering choice of product.

2 The chemical manufacturers generally have catalogues which give a brief guide to the properties of each item and more detailed information should be available on a product information sheet. This information will list any special features and other information about safety, storage, limitations to use etc.

2 Cleaning products

1 General purpose cleaners include detergents, wax and shine additives, wax polish and colour restoring compounds. Detergent sprays and liquids are used for engine cleaning and removing general road dirt and grime.

2 Carburettor cleaner is used for removing the carbon and gum deposits from carburettor parts. A cheap alternative is cellulose paint thinner, which is fairly effective on carburettor bodies. Beware of using it on plastic parts, since these may be damaged.

3 Brake system cleaner is another specialised cleaning product for use on hydraulic brake parts. In the absence of this product, parts can be cleaned in clean brake fluid, or in some cases, denatured alcohol. You should never use petrol (gasoline) or similar solvents on brake parts, or the seals will be damaged.

4 Electrical contact cleaner is a highly volatile trichloroethane-based solvent for cleaning electrical contacts and switches, which it leaves completely free of grease or residue. It is also very useful for cleaning other parts which need to be absolutely free of grease.

5 Maintenance sprays such as WD40 and similar silicone-based products are invaluable general-purpose lubricants and water repellents. They provide a very light, penetrating lubrication, and will displace water from switches and electrical connectors. Never be without this one.

6 Economies can be made by buying in bulk, for example detergent in 5 litre containers, however bear in mind the problems of storage, and the rate at which you use the product.

3 Contact cleaner

1 This is a solvent cleaner, normally based on trichloroethane and is used for cleaning electrical switches, contacts and connections. It is a highly volatile product which washes out dirt or grease and then evaporates rapidly to leave a dry surface with no residual grease film.

2 Although primarily intended for use on electrical parts, it is very useful for any application where a part must be completely grease-free. A good example would be preparation of two surfaces to be glued together.

3 Care must be taken when using this type of product on or near plastic surfaces, some of which may be damaged by it. It should only be used in a well-ventilated area, and care should be taken to avoid inhaling the vapour.

4 Sealants and jointing compounds

1 Gaskets are used to seal the mating surfaces between components and keep lubricants, fluids, vacuum or pressure contained within an assembly.
2 Sealants and jointing compounds are materials which can be used to replace a conventional paper or metal gasket, or to assist the gasket in making a seal.

Jointing compounds

3 These include a range of compounds which are used with a conventional gasket. They assist in making a good seal and in holding the gasket in position during assembly.
4 The range of jointing compounds can be summarised as follows:
 a) Set hard for use on permanent assemblies.
 b) Semi-hardening for long working life, but easy separation of the components.
 c) Non-hardening for use as for general sealing duties, and with a gasket where there is metal-to-metal contact.
5 There is a particular type called an anaerobic gasket which can be used in the assembly of engine and gearbox structural components. This type of compound does not need contact with air in order to cure and hence will set when 'boxed in'.

Room Temperature Vulcanising (RTV) sealants

6 Silicone rubber 'Instant Gasket' products are effectively a room temperature vulcanising (RTV) silicone compound which sets to a flexible rubber-like consistency. They form an in-place gasket which can be applied to both horizontal and vertical joints.

When to use an RTV type sealant

7 RTVs have an operating temperature of -50 to 250°C which makes them suitable candidates for most jobs on a motorcycle engine, except cylinder head and exhaust header gaskets.
8 They have good resistance to most oils, water, transmission fluids and antifreeze.
9 Give best results on joints where the pressure squeeze is low, eg a cylinder head cover.
10 When the surfaces contain small irregularities, the RTV can fill the gaps to provide a seal.
11 Can be used to replace paper, cork, felt and rubber gaskets.

When not to use an RTV type sealant

12 When the working temperature is outside the range for the sealer, eg combustion chamber area.
13 When the joint requires closing by torquing down to high pressures.
14 When the gasket provides a set clearance between the mating surfaces.
15 When there is likely contamination by petrol (gasoline), and paraffin (kerosene).

Using RTV type sealants

16 It is good practice to make sure that the jointing surfaces are clean, free of grease, dry and reasonably flat.
17 Squeeze a bead of the sealant around the mating surfaces and leave for about ten minutes until the bead forms a tacky skin. Do not use too much sealant as there is a the danger of sealant breaking off inside the assembly and blocking oilways. Note that RTV gives off acetic acid when curing and you will detect a vinegar like smell – this can cause slight irritation.
18 Assemble the joint while the RTV is in this tacky stage and tighten the fasteners.
19 Any excess sealant can be trimmed off the outside with a sharp pointed knife blade.
20 Although a range of sealants are provided for the motor vehicle industry, your local builders merchants or DIY store will have identical products which are sold as sealants for baths and aquariums. They often require a squeeze gun to operate, but are cheaper to buy.
21 Sealers, especially those sold for use in the home, come in different colours. The clear drying type are useful for sealing loose instrument lenses and can even stick and seal headlamp reflectors to their lenses.
22 RTVs withstand vibration and can be used to prevent chaffing between bike parts which are likely to rub, fairing and frame fittings for example.
23 Good results can be obtained by using RTV to waterproof electrical connectors, and similar techniques can be employed for projects such as converting an inexpensive car dashboard clock for use on a motorcycle by sealing the face of the LCD display to the case.

Removing gasket sealants

24 There are several products now available which are designed to remove both jointing compounds and RTV sealants.
25 The gasket remover contains a solvent which softens the old compound and is mildly abrasive so that careful rubbing will remove carbon and burnt oil residues thus preparing the surface for a new joint.
26 When using products of this type, be careful to follow the manufacturer's directions closely.

Exhaust system sealants

27 Exhaust sealant is useful for preventing leakage from joints in the exhaust system. Sealants are available which can withstand the very high temperatures and prevent the leakage of carbon monoxide.
28 Repairs to exhaust systems can be made using either a repair putty or a bandage which is impregnated with an epoxy resin which sets on heating. Repairs of this type must be considered temporary solutions, but they are worth considering if it is necessary to order a replacement silencer.

Choosing the correct sealant

29 Refer to your workshop manual or the sealant manufacturer's specification sheet for guidance on the type and strength of sealant required.
30 Sometimes the manufacturer will specify a particular product for a given application, in which case you will need to purchase this through a dealer.

5 Adhesives

1 The range of glues available is very large and includes glues that will stick almost anything to anything, glues designed to be waterproof, and glues designed for specific applications.
2 A tin of impact adhesives and a PVA (polyvinyl acetate) glue are useful products to keep in the workshop. They can be used for a variety of jobs such as sticking trim or fixing seat covers to bases.
3 You may have reason to require one of a number of adhesives during repair or overhaul work on motorcycles. A motor accessory shop will probably stock whatever you need, however the manufacturer's catalogue will give you a comprehensive guide.

'Super' glues

 Warning: Do not allow 'Super glues' to contact your skin. This type of glue sets in a matter of seconds and care should be taken not to stick your fingers together or stick your skin to a component.

4 These are extremely strong and transparent adhesives which will stick to almost anything within seconds. They are useful where small amounts are required. Usually just a few drops of the glue are required. Effectively they are impact adhesives.
5 Super glues are useful for joining O-rings. This can be handy if you find yourself in need of a certain size of O-ring in an emergency. The technique involves selecting a slightly larger O-ring than the one you need, and carefully cutting out a section using a scalpel or craft knife to give clean ends. These can then be secured with a drop of 'super' glue.
6 This practice is well proven, and you can even buy 'custom' O-ring kits, if required. Be wary of using shortened O-rings where sealing is vital, such as oilways, where loss of pressure could cause serious damage.
7 Avoid getting the glue on other parts which should not be stuck and don't allow the glue to set without contacting another surface. The fast setting time means that wiping clean must be done immediately.

8 A useful addition to keep in the glue stock is a glue remover. These products will remove stains and excess glue, and even work on 'super' glues.

Epoxy resins

9 Epoxy resin adhesives are two-pack products which are mixed together to form a sticky paste. There is a large range of adhesives, fillers and putties available; a solution for nearly every problem.

10 The two parts, the body and the hardener, are mixed in set proportions before applying as a glue or as a filler. The proportions are not usually critical, and will affect the setting time. The mixture can be prepared on a piece of cardboard using the plastic spreader which comes with the product, a spatula, or even a stiff piece of cardboard. The cardboard can be thrown away at the end.

11 A development of the epoxy adhesive are epoxy putties, which allow damaged metal to be built up. The hardened putty can be treated much like metal, and can be drilled and tapped, if necessary. Repairs made using this method are strong, but do not rely on them for structural repairs to engine or frame parts. They are, however, ideal for repairing cracks in engine covers or similar damage.

12 As with all gluing operations, it is important to ensure that the surfaces to be joined are as clean as possible.

13 For application details refer to the instructions which come with the product or the manufacturer's information sheet.

 Warning: During the mixing and setting time fumes may be given off. As epoxy compounds can also harm your skin, wear thin plastic gloves.

6 Locking compounds

1 These products are generally anaerobic type adhesives which cure in the absence of air.

Thread locking

2 There are a number of types of thread locking compound on the market. These products are used to ensure that fasteners cannot loosen in service, and are often employed in place of lock washers or spring washers.

3 In some instances, the manufacturer of a particular machine may specify the grade of locking compound to be used on specific fasteners, but for general use there are three basic types.

a) *A low strength compound will be needed for small nuts and screws. If a medium or high strength type is used it may prove impossible to release the fastener later.*

b) *A medium-strength compound is normally used for general purposes. This gives good resistance to loosening, whilst permitting easy dismantling later.*

c) *A high-strength compound is used in specific applications, such as anchoring studs into casings. This will make a semi-permanent fitting, and may prove difficult to shift at a later date, and so should never be used on ordinary nuts and bolts.*

4 All of these locking products require the thread to be completely clean and free of grease. It is well worth using aerosol contact cleaner to ensure this. One or two drops of the compound are applied to the cleaned thread, and the fastener can then be fitted and tightened.

5 The compound will begin to harden after it loses contact with air, sealing the threads together. An added advantage is that corrosion is effectively prevented once the fasteners have been assembled.

6 It is important that all traces of old thread locking compound should be removed during subsequent overhauls.

Bearing fixing

7 This type of compound is used for securing bearings. It will increase the strength of the normal press fit.

8 Where the bearing is a loose fit, perhaps because the bearing has been spinning, then the sealant will hold the bearing in place.

7 Special paints

1 In addition to the range of cellulose and oil-based paints there are number of specialist paints for use on engines and ancillary equipment.

2 These include engine lacquers which give corrosion resistance as well as improve appearance, and temperature resistant and dispersant paints for exhaust systems. These may require special thinners and cleaning materials.

3 Tyre paint and coloured marking pens can be used to smarten up bike tyres.

8 Rust inhibitors

1 Rust inhibiting paints can be applied as a primer to bare metal surfaces. As with any painting operation the surface must be free of loose material and clean. Make sure that the whole of the surface is coated and there are no pin head size spots which have not been coated.

2 Rust killing solutions can be used on bare metal which has rusted or on painted surfaces which have rust blemishes. Again make sure that all the affected area is covered. It may be necessary to strip some of the paint adjacent to the rusty area to check the limit of the rusted area.

3 Follow the manufacturer's instructions as to the preparation of the surface for further painting or finishing.

4 Paints may require special thinning and cleaning materials. Usually the rust killing solutions and brushes can be cleaned with water.

 Warning: Rust inhibitors contain acids and chemicals which can cause irritation.

Notes

Chapter 17
Fuels, fluids and lubricants

Contents

1 Introduction

1 This Chapter looks at the various fuels, oils and fluids which are available. Where appropriate, the methods of grading the products are explained.

2 The oil manufacturers generally have catalogues which give a brief guide to the properties of each item and more detailed information should be available on a product information sheet. This information will list any special features and other information about safety, storage, limitations to use etc.

2 Fuels

1 Gasoline, which is normally called petrol or motor spirit in the UK, is a complex product. The subject of the production of gasoline and other products from simple crude oil could easily fill a book, and it is not proposed to delve too deeply into it here.

2 Suffice it to say that the product sold as 'petrol' or 'gasoline' in the filling station can be described as a mixture of volatile hydrocarbons and various additives designed to be burnt as a fuel in a wide variety of internal combustion engines.

Octane rating

3 The octane rating of petrol (gasoline) describes its resistance to 'knocking', by which is meant the inclination of the petrol (gasoline) to explode violently, rather than to burn in a rapid but controlled manner.

4 The higher the octane number, the greater the resistance to this undesirable behaviour. The standard method of describing octane rating is by the 'Research Octane Number'

(RON), which describes the degree of knock resistance under normal driving conditions. A second standard, the 'Motor Octane Number' (MON, sometimes known as MM) is considered more representative of fuel behaviour at higher speeds, and both ratings are sometimes quoted. Note that in the US fuel is often expressed in terms of its Antiknock Index; this represents an average of the research octane number (RON) and the motor octane number (MON) and may be posted on service station pumps.

5 At the time of writing the research octane numbers of pump petrol on sale in the UK should conform to the following ratings:

Leaded 4-star	*97 RON minimum*
Premium unleaded	*95 RON minimum*
Super unleaded	*98 RON minimum*

Leaded 2-star (90 RON) and 3-star (93 RON) are no longer available in the UK

Additives

6 The common additives used in pump petrol sold in the UK are summarised below. Note that the proportions of these additives vary, particularly in the case of anti-icing additives, which must be balanced against the proportion of high-volatility fractions in the fuel to suit seasonal weather conditions. Different additives may therefore be used in fuel sold in other countries.

Unleaded petrol (gasoline)

7 There is a well-justified move to reduce the levels of lead in pump petrol sold in the UK, and the current leaded grades have had restricted lead levels (a maximum of 0.15 grammes per litre) since 1st January 1986, since when pump petrol has been termed 'low-lead'. Prior to this the accepted level was 0.40 grammes per litre.

8 Unleaded petrol is defined as containing less than 0.013 grammes of lead per litre, and the term 'unleaded' means that no lead is added to the fuel. Note that it is not lead-free. Premium unleaded and super unleaded are available in the UK, their octane ratings being shown above. Note that regular unleaded (91 RON) may be found in other countries.

9 It is anticipated that leaded petrol will be phased out within the foreseeable future, and this may cause problems for older machines which have not been designed to run on this type of fuel. It is anticipated that there may be additives made available, and there are already conversion kits using alternative materials, in order that older engines may use unleaded fuel.

10 It should be noted that unleaded petrol can be used only in engines designed to operate with this type of fuel. If used in unsuitable engines, it will normally lead to

Additive	Function	Effect
Anti-oxidant	Stabilises fuel	Prevents gum formation
Lead	Boosts octane	Reduces knocking
Detergent	Reduces deposits	Keeps engine in tune and clean
Anti-icing	Lowers freezing point of moisture	Prevents carburettor icing in cold weather
Anti-corrosion	Reduces corrosion	Increases engine life

problems of knocking and possible damage to the valves and valve seats.

Warnings and safety

 Warning: Petrol (gasoline) is extremely flammable, so take extra precautions when you work on any part of the fuel system. Don't smoke or allow open flames or bare light bulbs near the work area, and don't work in a garage where a natural gas-type appliance is present. If you spill any fuel on your skin, rinse it off immediately with soap and water. When you perform any kind of work on the fuel system, wear safety glasses and have a fire extinguisher suitable for a class B type fire (flammable liquids) on hand.

11 Make sure that you use a petrol (gasoline) or the minimum octane rating or higher. Use of a lower octane fuel can lead to pinking and engine damage. If your engine is designed for use with unleaded fuel, always use it in preference to leaded; quite apart from the environmental benefits, unleaded fuel will produce less spark plug and engine deposits and extend exhaust system life.

12 Do not add oil to the petrol (gasoline) of a four-stroke engine. On a two-stroke engine without an oil-injection system, select an oil which is designed for pre-mix systems and use it in the ratio advised by the motorcycle manufacturer.

13 Do not use old or stale petrol (gasoline) in the engine. If the motorcycle has not been used for some time, drain all fuel from its tank and carburettors and take it to a fuel station or motorcycle dealer for disposal – do not pour fuel into the household drainage system or onto the ground. Any fuel should be transported in a container marked as being suitable for holding petrol (gasoline). Note that it is good practice to drain the fuel tank and carburettors of fuel before putting a motorcycle into storage.

3 Engine oil

1 Motorcycle manufacturers invariably list one or more grades of motor oil for use in the engine/transmission unit (four-strokes) or in the gearbox (two-strokes).

2 Motor oils are classified according to their viscosity and performance classification.

3 Viscosity is denoted by the SAE number of the oil. This is based on a viscosity standard set by the Society of Automotive Engineers (SAE) and relates to the time taken for a given volume of oil to flow through a calibrated capillary tube at specified test temperatures. The higher the number, the greater the viscosity (thickness) of the oil.

4 Monograde oils are classified by a single number, with the SAE prefix. In the case of four of these grades, the SAE rating applies to viscosity at 100°C, the four grades being SAE 20, SAE 30, SAE 40 and SAE 50.

5 A further six grades of oil are rated according to tests at temperatures between -5°C and 30°C, and have a W suffix to denote this. The six grades are SAE 0W, SAE 5W, SAE 10W, SAE 15W, SAE 20W and SAE 25W.

6 Few motorcycle manufacturers recommend a monograde oil, and this is because current engines are designed and built with modern multigrade types in mind. Monograde oils still have an application in older engine designs, particularly those where ball and roller bearings are used throughout, especially in the case of the big-end assembly. In these applications, an SAE 30 or SAE 40 grade is normally recommended for winter use, with a change to an SAE 50 grade for summer.

7 Multigrade oils, the type specified for use in most modern engines, are based on a monograde to which has been added polymers and other additives to allow it to meet a range of viscosity requirements. At low temperatures, the oil is relatively thin, providing good performance when the engine is first started. As engine temperature rises, the additives reduce thinning, allowing a higher viscosity rating to be achieved. These characteristics are particularly well suited to engines in which plain bearings are used extensively.

8 Many motorcycle manufacturers specify an SAE 10W/40 motor oil. In this example, the oil behaves as an SAE 10W oil at low temperatures, but remains sufficiently viscous at high temperatures to retain SAE 40 characteristics.

9 Additives are included in most motor oils to reduce oxidation and improve the load-carrying capabilities. In addition, dispersants are added to keep carbon, metal particles and water in suspension. These prevent the formation of sludge deposits, the contaminants being removed when the oil is changed.

10 Oil performance is indicated by a suffix, based on standards formulated by the American Petroleum Institute (API) and the Society of Automotive Engineers (SAE). For petrol (spark ignition) engines, this suffix begins with an 'S', followed by a second letter, currently ranging from 'A' (lowest quality) through to 'J' (highest quality). A suffix which commences with the letter C relates to compression ignition engines (diesels).

11 Most motorcycle manufacturers specify an SG or SH quality oil, and lower grade products should be avoided to prevent premature engine wear. Bear in mind that motorcycle engines put great pressures on their lubricants; the use of inexpensive but low quality lubricants is a false economy.

12 Two-stroke engines are lubricated by a total-loss system in which oil is fed to the engine either mixed with the incoming fuel, or by direct injection using a pump. Any excess oil is burnt along with the fuel, and so the oil need not have the dispersal additives normally associated with four-stroke motor oils.

13 Most two-stroke oils are monograde types of around SAE 30 or SAE 40, and

include additives to reduce carbon build-up and plug fouling. Nowadays separate types are produced for pump injection, tank-mixing and pre-mixing. The distinction between the last two types is significant; tank-mixing types can be added direct to the fuel tank in the recommended proportions, whilst pre-mix types require the fuel and oil to be mixed together before adding to the machine's fuel tank. With the exception of a few mopeds and off-road two-strokes, almost all current road-going two-strokes use a pump fed arrangement, tank-mix and pre-mix systems being favoured for competition use where weight and complexity can be reduced by omitting the tank, pump and oil pipes.

Synthetic oils

14 Synthetics are becoming increasingly popular choices for motorcycle engine lubrication. Originally formulated for racing, these advanced-specification lubricants are now widely available for road use. Claimed advantages are higher performance than equivalent conventional mineral-based oils, and suitability for use in demanding situations such as turbocharged engines. The only disadvantage is the relatively high cost of these lubricants.

15 Synthetic two-stroke oils are becoming increasingly popular, despite the higher cost. All-synthetic two-stroke oils must not be used with conventional mineral-based types, and generally require the mixture ratio to be reduced. They are primarily intended for high performance machines.

16 Part-synthetics can normally be used on road machines, including pump-fed engines, without alterations to the mixture ratio. Like the all-synthetic types, part-synthetics claim to deliver higher lubrication performance and to reduce smoke emission from the exhaust.

Castor based oils

17 Castor-based oils were often used in racing engines, and have no application for modern engines. These vegetable-based oils offer exceptional lubrication performance, but must be changed much more frequently than mineral oils. All castor-cased oils are more expensive than equivalent mineral oils.

18 Under no circumstances should castor and mineral oils be mixed, or a thick sludge will be formed in the engine oilways. possibly resulting in the failure of the lubrication system. Where an engine has been run on a castor-based oil, all traces of the old oil must be removed before switching to a mineral oil, ideally by stripping and cleaning all engine parts.

Choosing the correct oil

19 Choosing an oil can prove less straightforward than it might seem. The motorcycle manufacturer will normally include in the owner's handbook a list of oil brands and grades which they endorse, and it is generally safe to assume that these are well suited to a particular model.

Four-stroke multigrade oils

20 The major oil companies all produce oils of equivalent viscosity and quality, and where the SAE number and API suffix is shown on the packaging, the choice of an alternative brand of the correct grade is easy enough. Unfortunately, there are one or two oil companies who omit to give viscosity information on the cans or bottles in which the oil is sold.

21 As a general rule, most modern road-going machines will require a high API class (SG or SH) multigrade mineral oil with a viscosity of around SAE 10W/40. Any reputable brand of oil meeting these requirements should be safe to use in your machine, but do check the manufacturer's recommendations before choosing an oil.

Two-stroke oils

22 For most road-going two-strokes, a conventional good quality two-stroke oil is all that is required, and many of these can be used in pump or tank-mixed applications. Engine oil costs add appreciably to the cost of running a two-stroke machine, and there is little to be gained by using an expensive synthetic racing oil in the average restricted moped.

23 In the case of high-performance two-strokes, a part-synthetic oil may be justifiable, though the cost consideration will apply here as well.

24 Only in the case of pure competition machines is a fully synthetic oil worth consideration. Given the relatively low mileage covered by (most) competition bikes, the extra expense can be warranted by the greater protection and cleaner running offered by these oils.

25 Similar to the API rating used to denote multigrade engine oil performance, you may encounter the Japanese JASO standard on two-stroke oil containers.

4 Gear oils

1 A few machines will require a gear oil for use in a separate gearbox, though the vast majority of four-strokes employ a shared motor oil supply for the engine and the transmission components. Exceptions are four-strokes which have a separate reservoir of oil for the gearbox, the final drive on a shaft-driven motorcycle, and the gearbox on a two-stroke engine.

2 Gear oils are traditionally mineral-based monograde oils, containing high-pressure additives to deal with the high loadings imposed by meshed gear teeth. More modern derivatives offer limited multigrade ranges.

3 Ironically, few motorcycle gearboxes actually use gear oil. This is because the gearboxes on four-stroke models are normally built in unit with the engine, and so must share the same lubrication supply. This in turn means that the

gearbox assembly must be designed to operate with engine oil, rather than gear oil. Another reason for the use of engine oils in the transmission system is the use of wet clutches; because the clutch runs in oil, it must be of low viscosity or clutch slip and drag would occur. This applies equally to two-stroke models.

4 Gear oils are normally found on shaft-drive models, where the bevel gears in the final drive system demand a lubricant capable of withstanding the high pressures and shear loads generated by the gear teeth. Gear oils are generally heavier than motor oils, typically around SAE 80 or SAE 90. Hypoid gear oils are often specified for shaft drive applications.

5 The variety of gear oils is less easily summarised than equivalent motor oil grades, and the best advice here is to check carefully the exact specification stipulated by the manufacturer, and to use an oil conforming to this. If there is any doubt as to the requirements of your machine, seek the advice of a reputable dealer, who will be able to recommend a suitable product.

5 Fork oils

1 Fork oil is a special light oil grade specially designed for use in telescopic forks. They are monograde lubricants containing additives to make them better suited to this type of application. Amongst these are additives to reduce oxidation and to minimise corrosion of the suspension components. Most important are the anti-foaming additives. As the name suggests, these prevent the formation of air bubbles, as the damping oil is forced through the damping orifices at high speed and pressure. Where foaming is allowed to occur, cavitation of the oil, and consequently erratic damping performance will result.

2 Most manufacturers specify a particular grade of fork oil, and these usually range from SAE 5W to SAE 20W. Whilst some oil manufacturers are able to offer a range of fork oils in varying grades, others are more vague and may not even mention the oil viscosity on the container.

3 Make sure that the correct grade is used, since this can have an appreciable effect on the damping characteristics of the fork. In some cases, especially on off-road models, altering the grade of fork oil can be used as an easy method of fine-tuning fork performance.

4 Some companies produce oils in a wide range of viscosities, which may be mixed together. This allows the damping effect to be tailored to personal preference, and is of obvious use in racing applications, where fine-tuning of the suspension may have some bearing on the competitiveness of the machine. It is also of great use for road machines, allowing the owner to change the damping performance to suit his or her own riding style.

5 Some manufacturers specify automatic transmission fluid (ATF) for use in their forks.

6 Suspension fluids can be added to the range of fork oils, and are similar products designed for use in both telescopic front forks and in rebuildable or refillable rear shock absorbers. Like conventional fork oils, these are available in a range of viscosities, and these can be mixed to obtain the required damping effect. Mainly intended for racing machines, these products can be used for road-going machines where the damping oil in the rear shock(s) can be changed; for obvious reasons, they are of little use where the damper unit is of sealed construction.

6 Air filter oils

1 These are specially-formulated oils designed for use with foam element air filters. This type of oil has additives to make it 'tacky' and is thus able to trap dust and moisture more effectively than conventional lubricating oils. Originally designed for off-road use, these products can usefully be used on road going machines which use this type of air filter.

7 Greases

1 Greases are an alternative to oil for lubrication purposes in applications where a liquid lubricant would be inappropriate. Most general-purpose greases combine a mineral oil with a lithium soap base to produce a general purpose high melting-point grease suitable for general lubrication of wheel and steering head bearings and suspension pivots.

2 Multi-purpose high melting-point grease is used for numerous greasing applications on various parts of the motorcycle. These lithium-based greases will withstand fairly high temperatures, such as those generated in the wheel hubs, without melting, and are usually chosen for use in wheel bearings for this reason. This grade of grease should be kept in the grease gun for regular maintenance purposes.

Molybdenum disulphide and graphite grease

3 Molybdenum disulphide grease is sometimes specified for assembly use, where it provides initial lubrication to protect engine bearing surfaces in the first few vital seconds of running before full oil circulation is restored. It is also useful for some general lubrication applications, providing a degree of dry lubrication where a conventional grease would fail. Molybdenum disulphide pastes are also available and these contain a much higher percentage of molybdenum disulphide.

4 Graphite grease is used in similar applications to molybdenum disulphide grease, and for the same reasons. The graphite content maintains lubrication after the grease has hardened with age or burnt off with heat.

5 Molybdenum and graphite greases are also useful in areas like spark plug threads, where the graphite or molybdenum is left behind to provide lubrication after the grease base has burnt off.

Silicone greases

6 Silicone grease is a useful product for the wet-weather or off-road rider. Packed into wiring connectors and switches, it is extremely effective at excluding water, and a machine protected in this way will often work quite happily even if half submerged in water. Silicone grease is often specified for the the slider pins of a sliding type brake caliper. It is usually sold in small tubes and can be purchased from motorcycle dealers.

7 It is also of use as a lubricant with many plastic parts, and may be obtainable from builders' merchants where it is used to lubricate plastic drainage systems during assembly

8 Heat sink grease is a special silicone-based product designed for use in some electronic components, and may be found packed around temperature sensors on some machines with automatic cold-start systems. As its name suggests, this grease is designed to help conduct heat away from the component which it is packed around. Like silicone grease, it may prove difficult to locate a source of supply. An electronics shop may be the best place to try.

Copper grease

9 This is a high-temperature product able to provide lubrication on engine and brake parts which reach very high temperatures. Copper grease is an anti-seize and anti-squeal product. It can be applied to the backing metal of brake pads to reduce squealing, and is useful on fastener threads during assembly to prevent seizing. It is especially good on fasteners subject to high temperature, such as exhaust mounting nuts and studs. Like graphite and molybdenum greases, it is ideal for use on spark plug threads.

Brake greases

10 These are specially-formulated products designed for use on hydraulic brake components. Conventional greases must never be used in braking system applications; the grease would attack and damage the brake seals.

8 Chain lubricants

1 Chain lubricants are available in aerosol spray form and also hot immersion products.
2 In the case of the former, the lubricant is

applied in dilute form along with a solvent. This mixture is designed to penetrate the chain rollers and bushes, the solvent evaporating to leave the lubricant film as a sticky residue. Some of these products incorporate polymers and other non-fling additives to help them adhere to the chain.

3 Immersion-type chain lubricants are usually sold in round containers designed so that the chain can be cleaned and then coiled up and placed in the container. The lubricant is then heated until it melts, the chain sinking into the lubricant which penetrates the rollers and bushes. The chain is then removed and hung up to allow residual lubricant to drain off. Once cooled, the bushes will be filled with the waxy lubricant.

4 Of the two types, aerosol sprays are far quicker and easier to use, and a lot less messy. Immersion lubricants probably provide better protection for the chain, but only if the process is carried out regularly.

5 In the case of O-ring or X-ring (sealed) chains, use either a compatible aerosol product, or gear oil, because the hot immersion type will be unable to penetrate the rollers and bushes and will damage the O-rings.

6 O-ring and X-ring (sealed) chains should only be lubricated with a product which is marked to indicate that it is safe for use on these chains or the O-rings may be destroyed.

9 Penetrating fluids

1 Penetrating fluids are invaluable for helping in the task of freeing seized or rusted fasteners. The product should be applied to the affected fastener and allowed to work for as long as possible.

2 Where the location and position of the seized fastener permits, the fluid can be contained around a fastener by forming a funnel from modelling clay around the area. Fill the funnel with the penetrating fluid and allow it to stand overnight if possible.

3 If you can move the fastener even fractionally, penetration will be speeded up considerably.

4 Water dispersing and spray lubricant aerosol products like WD40 will act as a penetrating fluid to some extent, though Plus Gas and similar products are specifically designed for this job and usually work better.

10 Hydraulic fluids

1 Hydraulic fluids are used in the hydraulic systems used on disc brakes (and some clutches). Available in various grades and specifications, it is important that the fluid used is as specified by the manufacturer.

2 Using non-specified fluids or other oils can cause rapid seal failure, a potentially lethal condition.

3 A peculiarity of most hydraulic fluids is that they are hygroscopic, which means that they absorb moisture from the air. This leads to a lowering of the boiling point of the fluid, which may cause the fluid to boil under heavy braking, causing rapid and unexpected brake fade.

4 The moisture can also lead to internal corrosion of the braking system components.

5 Fluid should be changed every 1 to 2 years to avoid these problems.

6 Note also that hydraulic fluid will mark or damage paint and plastic surfaces.

Fluid specification

Glycol-based fluids

7 Fluids are catalogued according to SAE standards, or more commonly by the American DOT system. Where a DOT code is not shown, compare the dry boiling point specifications.

8 Most fluids are based on the chemical called glycol and are graded partly in relation to their boiling points; the higher the DOT rating, the higher the boiling point. The wet boiling point, after absorbing moisture, and the viscosity are also important considerations when grading the fluid.

9 Typical glycol based fluids are DOT 3, DOT 4, and DOT 5.1. A silicone based fluid is available with the code DOT 5 (see below).

10 A mineral based hydraulic fluid is also available for high performance applications. It has a dry boiling point in excess of 300°C, which is higher than the glycol- and silicone-based fluids.

11 Fluids which are based on different base chemicals should not be mixed. As a rule stick to using one manufacturer's fluid and make sure it always conforms to the correct grade. Because the fluid is hygroscopic, always seal the container when not in use.

12 A fluid of an inferior DOT grade should not be used in a system which requires a higher grade, eg don't use DOT 3 fluid in a system which requires DOT 4. Note that you can use DOT 4 in a DOT 3 system, providing all old fluid is fully drained and the system refilled with new fluid.

Silicone-based fluid (DOT 5)

13 Silicone hydraulic fluid avoids the main drawback of conventional fluid in that it does not absorb water, and so the problems of corrosion and reduced boiling points do not occur.

14 The fluid does provide a more spongy feel, but does not attack paintwork.

15 It may be possible to convert to a synthetic fluid, but note that this will normally require a complete overhaul of the system first as seals etc. may not be compatible with the new fluid. Before attempting the conversion, consult an authorised dealer for the machine concerned to check whether the conversion is advisable.

Chapter 18
Dealing with damage

Contents

1 Introduction

1 Repairing an accident damaged machine at home can be a complicated business, and can also be dangerous unless you are very painstaking in your assessment of the extent of the damage. On the other hand, provided that the damage is not too great, it can be well worth doing.

2 Where it is of a minor or cosmetic nature, like that caused if the machine is dropped while stationary, for example, you may not even need to bother with an insurance claim. In many instances you would have to pay an excess which would make this an expensive option anyway.

3 Insurance companies will often write off a machine with seemingly superficial damage, simply because the cost of the necessary replacement parts is so high.

4 Another factor taken into account is the cost of labour involved when a damaged frame has to be renewed. In both areas the private owner is at an advantage.

5 Firstly, you may be prepared to accept some of the cosmetic damage which would normally have to be put right under an insurance claim, and you may be able to locate used parts from a local breaker rather than buying new parts at full price.

6 Secondly, you have the advantage of not having to pay labour charges, which makes a labour-intensive job like frame replacement viable.

7 If you are unfortunate enough to be involved in an accident, try to keep in close touch with the bike during any subsequent insurance claim assessment. In all probability, the bike will be taken to the local dealer who will prepare an estimate for the repairs. Often a claims adjuster will visit the dealer to verify the extent of damage and to see if the estimate is realistic.

8 If the insurance company decides that the machine is not worth repairing and writes it off, you should consider negotiating to purchase the damaged machine back from them and organising the repair work yourself. The machine may still be yours even though the insurance company declares it a 'write off'. Before you do this be absolutely certain of the extent of any damage, and talk to the dealer about this.

9 The term 'write off' may mean that a commercial repair is possible but not economical, or that the machine is physically too damaged to be repaired safely. Check which condition refers to your bike.

10 Where you need to buy second-hand parts, check that they will fit your machine before you buy them. Remember that detail changes are often made at random throughout production runs. If possible take patterns with you so you can make comparisons.

11 Even when buying second-hand from a dealer or breaker, check what warranty arrangements are on offer. Often there is a time limit after which the breaker will not refund your money. If buying a complete engine (or just the crankcases) or a frame, note that you will need to inform the licensing authorities of the new engine/frame serial number so that it can be correctly documented. Make sure that you purchase these parts from a reputable source; it is easy to unwittingly purchase second-hand parts which originate from a motorcycle which has been recorded as stolen.

2 Front-end damage

1 This is the most common area of accident damage where another vehicle is involved, and the usual result is bent forks, a damaged front mudguard, wheel and tyre and probably damage to the headlamp, turn signals, instrument and fairing **(see illustration)**. This will not be cheap to repair, and since most of the machines in the local breaker will have been scrapped after similar accidents, the chances of finding a good set of forks and a front wheel are slim.

2 If you can find these parts second-hand, all well and good, but be absolutely certain that they are undamaged. If the only option is new parts, check the prices very carefully before undertaking the repair.

3 Another significant risk is that the frame will have been damaged. This will usually be evident around the steering head region, but may not be easily visible. **Do not take chances with frame damage;** have the frame checked on a jig by a suitably equipped dealer. Light damage may be repairable, again requiring jig work. Heavier damage means a new frame.

3 Handlebars, controls and switchgear damage

1 Handlebars are easily damaged in an accident, even where the machine is simply dropped at a standstill or at low speed. Normal chrome-plated tubular steel bars are

Following front end damage, check that the lock stops on the steering lower yoke and frame headstock are undamaged. The lock stops should prevent the handlebars contacting the fuel tank (and thus trapping your hands) on the full lock positions – note that this is usually scrutinised at the MOT test.

2.1 The result of a slide down the road – bent forks, smashed turn signals and headlight

not worth straightening, either from the point of view of cost or the risk of subsequent failure of a damaged set. Buy some new bars, and transfer the switches and controls to them.

2 If you are considering fitting non-original bars, make sure that they do not foul on the tank (see *Haynes Hint*), or fairing (where fitted). It is also important that the existing cables, wiring and hydraulic hoses will reach; if these need to be renewed to suit the new handlebar, it could become an expensive and complicated prospect.

3 On machines fitted with separate steel or cast alloy handlebars, the situation is different; it is unlikely that you will have much choice in replacement assemblies, and so you will have to settle for the original type on most models.

4 If you can find them, complete control lever assemblies together with the associated switches, are a good prospect for second-hand purchase. If the only damage is to the lever blade, however, it makes sense to buy this new. Switch clusters in particular are expensive new, and a safe second-hand purchase.

5 Where the lever assembly includes a brake or clutch master cylinder, by all means look for a second-hand replacement, but be wary of acquiring a worn-out unit, or one which looks similar, but has a different master cylinder bore or stroke dimension.

4 Footrests and pedals damage

Steel components

1 Depending on the arrangement used, it may be possible to straighten footrests, and also brake and gearchange pedals. If the footrests are of the folding type commonly used as pillion footrests, and sometimes for the rider's footrests, it is unlikely that repair would be cost effective, and new ones should be fitted. On machines with fixed footrest bars, as in the case of many mopeds and commuter models, these can be straightened unless very badly deformed.

2 The assembly should be removed from the machine for straightening. Heat the footrest using a blowlamp, or by pushing it into hot coals in a fire or boiler, until it glows a cherry red colour. This will soften the metal, allowing it to be straightened without risk of fracturing. Taking care to avoid burns, remove the footrest from the heat source and hammer it back into shape, using an anvil or a similar large piece of steel and a hammer.

3 Once the footrest has been allowed to cool, rub it down with progressively finer grades of abrasive paper until the surface is bright and smooth. Prime the bare metal as soon as possible to prevent corrosion, and then refinish to match the original paint coat. On items like footrests it is often easier and more economical to use a brushing enamel in preference to aerosol paints.

4 A similar technique can be used to straighten control pedals, but note that where these are chromium plated, the surface finish will be destroyed. You will either have to accept a painted finish on the repaired lever, or buy a new replacement.

Aluminium components

5 It is almost impossible to straighten aluminium alloy components. Grazes and scratches from road contact can be filled smooth and finished with emery paper, but distorted or fractured footrests and levers must be renewed.

5 Fuel tank, seat and fairing/bodywork damage

1 These are all worth buying second-hand, the main problem being that they will be amongst the first things to be sold when a bike gets to the breakers.

2 Tanks, fairings and bodywork may need to be refinished to match the paint scheme on your machine, so budget for this, plus the cost of any decals. Despite this, a second-hand replacement is usually a more economical solution than repairing a dented tank. Note that repair kits are available for

ABS plastic fairings and materials can be purchased for repairs to glass fibre fairings (see Chapter 8); if the repair is beyond your capabilities seek the advice of one of the specialist bodywork repair companies who advertise in the motorcycling press – it is surprising how a shattered fairing can be pieced back together and refinished. If the fairing has suffered considerable damage, don't forget to check the condition and alignment of the mounting brackets.

 HAYNES HINT *Original equipment fairings and bodywork are expensive. It is possible to buy replica panels for many current models, although check the alignment of mountings and decals/colours with adjoining original bodywork.*

3 Removing dents from metal fuel tanks is a difficult process, often requiring the bottom of the tank to be cut out to allow access. Shallow dents and similar damage can be dealt with by using body filler, but remember that you must also budget for the cost of repainting the tank and applying new decals.
4 Seats can be refurbished by fitting a new cover if required. You can either buy a cover and fit it yourself, or send the seat for recovering to any one of a number of specialists in this work. Alternatively, a local coach trimmer or upholsterer may be able to do the work for you.

6 Exhaust system damage

1 Second-hand exhausts are fine if they are in nearly new condition, otherwise it is better to buy new.
2 One problem is that once a system has been used on a machine, it may prove reluctant to line up with the mounting points on another.
3 Where the silencer is separate from the exhaust pipes, a second-hand replacement silencer could be considered, otherwise it is generally preferable to fit a new system, particularly on multi-cylinder models.

7 Frame and forks damage

1 Again, these are good value second-hand, but only if you can be sure that they are not damaged. It is worth having the frame alignment checked professionally before you use it.
2 On no account buy a frame which has had its serial number defaced or altered – it is probably stolen and will create difficulties with re-registration even if the question of theft has been resolved.

3 Fork assemblies are also worth looking for, but the problem of accident damage applies here too. Only if you can be certain that no front-end damage has been suffered should you consider second-hand forks. Check that the forks move smoothly and evenly, and reject them if there are any signs of damage or if tight spots can be felt.
4 Frame and fork repairs are beyond the scope of most home workshops, and really require specialist alignment jigs to check properly. Slight damage can be repaired, but this will probably mean professional help. In some cases it may prove impossible to correct the damage economically, and a reputable dealer will be able to assess with some accuracy whether repair or replacement is the best choice.

8 Engine/transmission unit damage

1 These are well worth buying if your own engine is extensively damaged. Note however that you will be taking a chance on its condition, and you may have trouble obtaining a unit for a popular model.
2 As with frames, defaced engine numbers almost always mean a stolen bike. Despite these reservations, this is very often an economical way to get the machine on the road again.
3 Where accident damage has been sustained, you may be able to replace the damaged parts, usually the crankcase outer covers, with new or used items. In such instances, remember to check first that more serious but less obvious damage has not occurred; there would be little point in buying a new outer cover if it later transpires that the crankshaft is bent or the crankcases cracked.
4 The cast alloy parts of engine/transmission units are easily damaged. In some cases, the resulting cracks can be repaired by aluminium welding, or by home repairs using epoxy resins or low temperature aluminium welding. These techniques are discussed in Chapters 7 and 9. The success or failure of such repairs is dependent on the extent of the damage, the type of alloy, and the skill of the repairer, but good results can often be obtained on small cracks or holes. If it is not possible to achieve a good cosmetic finish to the repair, consider disguising the area by spraying the cover with heat-resistant matt black paint, after filing and sanding the weld flat.
5 Welding the more important castings, such as the crankcases, is a job best left to an expert. In many instances, the problem of bearing surface alignment and the risk of distortion may render the proposed repair impractical, and if this is the case it will be safer to buy a new pair of crankcases.
6 Similar problems may be encountered when attempting to weld cylinder heads; it may be possible to repair a crack, but the

resulting distortion may make the head unusable. For this reason, always seek professional advice.

9 Electrical and ancillary component damage

1 These are almost always worth buying second-hand, there being little risk to your safety if the replacement later proves to be defective. Lamp units, instrument panels and the various electrical parts like turn signal relays, alternators, regulator/rectifiers and ignition control units are very expensive to buy new, and likely to be in good condition if taken from a scrapped machine. If possible, ride your own machine to the breakers, and fit the part there and then to check that it works. Ensure that electronic components are exactly the same as the defective part you are replacing – even if the wiring connections and mounting match the original, the fitting of the wrong component could result in further damage to other electronic components in that circuit.
2 Repairs to a cracked turn signal or tail lamp lens can be made by sticking the broken pieces back together, but extensive damage will require renewal of the lens.
3 Beware of the sensitive nature of engine management units or ABS control units; if part of the circuit is disturbed or a component fails, their fault memory may require resetting although the faulty component has been replaced; this is a task for the appropriate dealer.

10 Buying complete machines

1 Buying a complete accident-damaged, vandalised or stolen-recovered machine from a breaker can be a good basis for an accident rebuild, or even for building up a bike from scratch.
2 Stolen/recovered machines or those which have been vandalised are obviously preferable to accident damaged ones. Most of these machines reach the breaker having been written off by the insurance companies as uneconomic to repair for various reasons. Most breakers will take considerable trouble to avoid stolen machines. Even so, always check all documentation, and ask the police to make sure that the machine has not been reported stolen before you part with money. To this end, remember to note down engine and frame numbers when checking the machine.
3 Buying parts this way is usually more cost-effective than buying piecemeal as the need arises, provided that you have the space and time to dismantle the bike yourself. You may even be able to offset some of the cost by selling off surplus parts.

Notes

Length (distance)

Inches (in)	x 25.4 = Millimetres (mm)	x 0.0394 = Inches (in)
Feet (ft)	x 0.305 = Metres (m)	x 3.281 = Feet (ft)
Miles	x 1.609 = Kilometres (km)	x 0.621 = Miles

Volume (capacity)

Cubic inches (cu in; in³)	x 16.387 = Cubic centimetres (cc; cm³)	x 0.061 = Cubic inches (cu in; in³)
Imperial pints (Imp pt)	x 0.568 = Litres (l)	x 1.76 = Imperial pints (Imp pt)
Imperial quarts (Imp qt)	x 1.137 = Litres (l)	x 0.88 = Imperial quarts (Imp qt)
Imperial quarts (Imp qt)	x 1.201 = US quarts (US qt)	x 0.833 = Imperial quarts (Imp qt)
US quarts (US qt)	x 0.946 = Litres (l)	x 1.057 = US quarts (US qt)
Imperial gallons (Imp gal)	x 4.546 = Litres (l)	x 0.22 = Imperial gallons (Imp gal)
Imperial gallons (Imp gal)	x 1.201 = US gallons (US gal)	x 0.833 = Imperial gallons (Imp gal)
US gallons (US gal)	x 3.785 = Litres (l)	x 0.264 = US gallons (US gal)

Mass (weight)

Ounces (oz)	x 28.35 = Grams (g)	x 0.035 = Ounces (oz)
Pounds (lb)	x 0.454 = Kilograms (kg)	x 2.205 = Pounds (lb)

Force

Ounces-force (ozf; oz)	x 0.278 = Newtons (N)	x 3.6 = Ounces-force (ozf; oz)
Pounds-force (lbf; lb)	x 4.448 = Newtons (N)	x 0.225 = Pounds-force (lbf; lb)
Newtons (N)	x 0.1 = Kilograms-force (kgf; kg)	x 9.81 = Newtons (N)

Pressure

Pounds-force per square inch (psi; lbf/in²; lb/in²)	x 0.070 = Kilograms-force per square centimetre (kgf/cm²; kg/cm²)	x 14.223 = Pounds-force per square inch (psi; lbf/in²; lb/in²)
Pounds-force per square inch (psi; lbf/in²; lb/in²)	x 0.068 = Atmospheres (atm)	x 14.696 = Pounds-force per square inch (psi; lbf/in²; lb/in²)
Pounds-force per square inch (psi; lbf/in²; lb/in²)	x 0.069 = Bars	x 14.5 = Pounds-force per square inch (psi; lbf/in²; lb/in²)
Pounds-force per square inch (psi; lbf/in²; lb/in²)	x 6.895 = Kilopascals (kPa)	x 0.145 = Pounds-force per square inch (psi; lbf/in²; lb/in²)
Kilopascals (kPa)	x 0.01 = Kilograms-force per square centimetre (kgf/cm²; kg/cm²)	x 98.1 = Kilopascals (kPa)
Millibar (mbar)	x 100 = Pascals (Pa)	x 0.01 = Millibar (mbar)
Millibar (mbar)	x 0.0145 = Pounds-force per square inch (psi; lbf/in²; lb/in²)	x 68.947 = Millibar (mbar)
Millibar (mbar)	x 0.75 = Millimetres of mercury (mmHg)	x 1.333 = Millibar (mbar)
Millibar (mbar)	x 0.401 = Inches of water (inH₂O)	x 2.491 = Millibar (mbar)
Millimetres of mercury (mmHg)	x 0.535 = Inches of water (inH₂O)	x 1.868 = Millimetres of mercury (mmHg)
Inches of water (inH₂O)	x 0.036 = Pounds-force per square inch (psi; lbf/in²; lb/in²)	x 27.68 = Inches of water (inH₂O)

Torque (moment of force)

Pounds-force inches (lbf in; lb in)	x 1.152 = Kilograms-force centimetre (kgf cm; kg cm)	x 0.868 = Pounds-force inches (lbf in; lb in)
Pounds-force inches (lbf in; lb in)	x 0.113 = Newton metres (Nm)	x 8.85 = Pounds-force inches (lbf in; lb in)
Pounds-force inches (lbf in; lb in)	x 0.083 = Pounds-force feet (lbf ft; lb ft)	x 12 = Pounds-force inches (lbf in; lb in)
Pounds-force feet (lbf ft; lb ft)	x 0.138 = Kilograms-force metres (kgf m; kg m)	x 7.233 = Pounds-force feet (lbf ft; lb ft)
Pounds-force feet (lbf ft; lb ft)	x 1.356 = Newton metres (Nm)	x 0.738 = Pounds-force feet (lbf ft; lb ft)
Newton metres (Nm)	x 0.102 = Kilograms-force metres (kgf m; kg m)	x 9.804 = Newton metres (Nm)

Power

Horsepower (hp)	x 745.7 = Watts (W)	x 0.0013 = Horsepower (hp)

Velocity (speed)

Miles per hour (miles/hr; mph)	x 1.609 = Kilometres per hour (km/hr; kph)	x 0.621 = Miles per hour (miles/hr; mph)

Fuel consumption*

Miles per gallon (mpg)	x 0.354 = Kilometres per litre (km/l)	x 2.825 = Miles per gallon (mpg)

Temperature

Degrees Fahrenheit = ($°C$ x 1.8) + 32   Degrees Celsius (Degrees Centigrade; $°C$) = ($°F$ - 32) x 0.56

* It is common practice to convert from miles per gallon (mpg) to litres/100 kilometres (l/100km), where mpg x l/100 km = 282

A

ABS (Anti-lock braking system) A system, usually electronically controlled, that senses incipient wheel lockup during braking and relieves hydraulic pressure at wheel which is about to skid.

Aftermarket Components suitable for the motorcycle, but not produced by the motorcycle manufacturer.

Allen key A hexagonal wrench which fits into a recessed hexagonal hole.

Alternating current (ac) Current produced by an alternator. Requires converting to direct current by a rectifier for charging purposes.

Alternator Converts mechanical energy from the engine into electrical energy to charge the battery and power the electrical system.

Ampere (amp) A unit of measurement for the flow of electrical current. Current = Volts ÷ Ohms.

Ampere-hour (Ah) Measure of battery capacity.

Angle-tightening A torque expressed in degrees. Often follows a conventional tightening torque for cylinder head or main bearing fasteners.

Antifreeze A substance (usually ethylene glycol) mixed with water, and added to the cooling system, to prevent freezing of the coolant in winter. Antifreeze also contains chemicals to inhibit corrosion and the formation of rust and other deposits that would tend to clog the radiator and coolant passages and reduce cooling efficiency.

Anti-dive System attached to the fork lower leg (slider) to prevent fork dive when braking hard.

Anti-seize compound A coating that reduces the risk of seizing on fasteners that are subjected to high temperatures, such as exhaust clamp bolts and nuts.

API American Petroleum Institute. A quality standard for 4-stroke motor oils.

Armature The part of an electrical motor or solenoid which comprises the electrical windings in which a current flow or a magnetic field is generated or excited.

Asbestos A natural fibrous mineral with great heat resistance, commonly used in the composition of brake friction materials. Asbestos is a health hazard and the dust created by brake systems should never be inhaled or ingested.

ATF Automatic Transmission Fluid. Often used in front forks.

ATU Automatic Timing Unit. Mechanical device for advancing the ignition timing on early engines.

ATV All Terrain Vehicle. Often called a Quad.

Axial play Side-to-side movement.

Axle A shaft on which a wheel revolves. Also known as a spindle.

B

Backlash The amount of movement between meshed components when one component is held still. Usually applies to gear teeth.

Ball bearing A bearing consisting of a hardened inner and outer race with hardened steel balls between the two races.

Bearings Used between two working surfaces to prevent wear of the components and a build-up of heat. Four types of bearing are commonly used on motorcycles: plain shell bearings, ball bearings, tapered roller bearings and needle roller bearings.

Bevel gears Used to turn the drive through 90°. Typical applications are shaft final drive and camshaft drive.

BHP Brake Horsepower. The British measurement for engine power output. Power output is now usually expressed in kilowatts (kW).

Bias-belted tyre Similar construction to radial tyre, but with outer belt running at an angle to the wheel rim.

Big-end bearing The bearing in the end of the connecting rod that's attached to the crankshaft.

Bleeding The process of removing air from an hydraulic system via a bleed nipple or bleed screw.

Bore The diameter of a cylinder or often the cylinder itself. Can also refer to the surface of a hole. To machine a hole using the lathe.

Boss The raised area on a component, the thickness being provided for more strength.

Bottom-end A description of an engine's crankcase components and all components contained there-in.

BTDC Before Top Dead Centre in terms of piston position. Ignition timing is often expressed in terms of degrees or millimetres BTDC.

Bush A cylindrical metal or rubber component used between two moving parts.

Burr Rough edge left on a component after machining or as a result of excessive wear.

C

Caliper The component carrying the piston(s) and brake pads.

Calipers Leg-like measuring instrument, hinged in the middle and used to gauge gaps, bores or external sizes.

Cam chain The chain which takes drive from the crankshaft to the camshaft(s).

Canister The main component in an evaporative emission control system (California market only); contains activated charcoal granules to trap vapours from the fuel system rather than allowing them to vent to the atmosphere.

Castellated Resembling the parapets along the top of a castle wall. For example, a castellated wheel axle or spindle nut.

Catalytic converter A device in the exhaust system of some machines which converts certain pollutants in the exhaust gases into less harmful substances.

Centrifugal The force to throw components outwards, away from the centre.

Charging system Description of the components which charge the battery, ie the alternator, rectifier and regulator.

Circlip A ring-shaped clip used to prevent endwise movement of cylindrical parts and shafts. An internal circlip is installed in a groove in a housing; an external circlip fits into a groove on the outside of a cylindrical piece such as a shaft. Also known as a snap-ring.

Clearance The amount of space between two parts. For example, between a piston and a cylinder, between a bearing and a journal, etc.

Coil spring A spiral of elastic steel found in various sizes throughout a vehicle, for example as a springing medium in the suspension and in the valve train.

Compression Reduction in volume, and increase in pressure and temperature, of a gas, caused by squeezing it into a smaller space.

Compression damping Controls the speed the suspension compresses when hitting a bump.

Compression ratio The relationship between cylinder volume when the piston is at top dead centre and cylinder volume when the piston is at bottom dead centre.

Concentric Having a common centre line.

Constant rate When each increment in load on a coil spring produces an equal change in length.

Continuity The uninterrupted path in the flow of electricity. Little or no measurable resistance.

Continuity tester Self-powered bleeper or test light which indicates continuity.

Cp Candlepower. Bulb rating commonly found on US motorcycles.

Crossply tyre Tyre plies arranged in a criss-cross pattern. Usually four or six plies used, hence 4PR or 6PR in tyre size codes.

Cush drive Rubber damper segments fitted between the rear wheel and final drive sprocket to absorb transmission shocks.

D

Decarbonisation The process of removing carbon deposits - typically from the combustion chamber, valves and exhaust port/system.

Degree disc Calibrated disc for measuring piston position. Expressed in degrees.

Detonation Destructive and damaging explosion of fuel/air mixture in combustion chamber instead of controlled burning.

Dial gauge Clock-type gauge with adapters for measuring runout and piston position. Expressed in mm or inches.

Diaphragm The rubber membrane in a master cylinder or carburettor which seals the upper chamber.

Diaphragm spring A single sprung plate often used in clutches.

Diode An electrical valve which only allows current to flow in one direction. Commonly used in rectifiers and starter interlock systems.

Direct current (dc) Current produced by a dc generator.

Disc valve (or rotary valve) A induction system used on some two-stroke engines.

Dog A projection from a moving part, mating with another dog or a slot on another part, so that the two components may be locked together or left free of each other. Used in gearboxes to connect pinions together.

Double-overhead camshaft (DOHC) An engine that uses two overhead camshafts, one for the intake valves and one for the exhaust valves.

Drivebelt A toothed belt used to transmit drive to the rear wheel on some motorcycles. A drivebelt has also been used to drive the camshafts. Drivebelts are usually made of Kevlar.

Driveshaft Any shaft used to transmit motion. Commonly used when referring to the final driveshaft on shaft drive motorcycles.

Dwell That period of rotation of a valve or contact-breaker cam in which events, as it were, stand still.

E

Earth return The return path of an electrical circuit, utilising the motorcycle's frame.

Eccentric Not central. An offset cam used to drive or be driven. Also used in chain adjustment.

ECU (Electronic Control Unit) A computer which controls (for instance) an ignition system, or an anti-lock braking system.

EGO Exhaust Gas Oxygen sensor. Sometimes called a Lambda sensor.

Elastic The condition in which any material will stretch or deform and return to its original shape.

Electrolyte The fluid in a lead-acid battery.

EMS (Engine Management System) A computer controlled system which manages the fuel injection and the ignition systems in an integrated fashion.

Endfloat The amount of lengthways movement between two parts. As applied to a crankshaft, the distance that the crankshaft can move side-to-side in the crankcase.

Endless chain A chain having no joining link. Common use for cam chains and final drive chains.

EP (Extreme Pressure) Oil type used in locations where high loads are applied, such as between gear teeth.

Evaporative emission control system Describes a charcoal filled canister which stores fuel vapours from the tank rather than allowing them to vent to the atmosphere. Usually only fitted to California models and referred to as an EVAP system.

Expansion chamber Section of two-stroke engine exhaust system so designed to improve engine efficiency and boost power.

F

Fatigue The weakness caused in materials by repeated bending, vibration, or shock loading.

Feeler blade or gauge A thin strip or blade of hardened steel, ground to an exact thickness, used to check or measure clearances between parts.

Ferrous A material made from iron.

Final drive Description of the drive from the transmission to the rear wheel. Usually by chain or shaft, but sometimes by belt.

Firing order The order in which the engine cylinders fire, or deliver their power strokes, beginning with the number one cylinder.

Flooding Term used to describe a high fuel level in the carburettor float chambers, leading to fuel overflow. Also refers to excess fuel in the combustion chamber due to incorrect starting technique.

Free length The no-load state of a component when measured. Clutch, valve and fork spring lengths are measured at rest, without any preload.

Freeplay The amount of travel before any action takes place. The looseness in a linkage, or an assembly of parts, between the initial application of force and actual movement. For example, the distance the rear brake pedal moves before the rear brake is actuated.

Friction The resistance preventing two bodies in contact moving relative to each other.

Fuel injection The fuel/air mixture is metered electronically and directed into the engine intake ports (indirect injection) or into the cylinders (direct injection). Sensors supply information on engine speed and conditions.

Fuel/air mixture The charge of fuel and air going into the engine. See **Stoichiometric ratio**.

Fuse An electrical device which protects a circuit against accidental overload. The typical fuse contains a soft piece of metal which is calibrated to melt at a predetermined current flow (expressed as amps) and break the circuit.

G

Gap The distance the spark must travel in jumping from the centre electrode to the side electrode in a spark plug. Also refers to the distance between the ignition rotor and the pickup coil in an electronic ignition system.

Gasket Any thin, soft material - usually cork, cardboard, asbestos or soft metal - installed between two metal surfaces to ensure a good seal. For instance, the cylinder head gasket seals the joint between the block and the cylinder head.

Gauge An instrument panel display used to monitor engine conditions. A gauge with a movable pointer on a dial or a fixed scale is an analogue gauge. A gauge with a numerical readout is called a digital gauge.

Gear ratios The drive ratio of a pair of gears in a gearbox, calculated on their number of teeth.

Glaze-busting see **Honing**

Grinding Process for renovating the valve face and valve seat contact area in the cylinder head.

Gudgeon pin The shaft which connects the connecting rod small-end with the piston. Often called a piston pin or wrist pin.

H

Helical gears Gear teeth are slightly curved and produce less gear noise that straight-cut gears. Often used for primary drives.

Helicoil A thread insert repair system. Commonly used as a repair for stripped spark plug threads.

High tensile A tough material of high tensile (or 'stretch') strength.

Honing A process used to break down the glaze on a cylinder bore (also called glaze-busting). Can also be carried out to roughen a rebored cylinder to aid ring bedding-in.

HT High Tension Description of the electrical circuit from the secondary winding of the ignition coil to the spark plug.

Hydraulic A liquid filled system used to transmit pressure from one component to another. Common uses on motorcycles are brakes and clutches.

Hydrocarbon Hydrogen and carbon compound forming the basis of all lubricants and oils formed from crude oil.

Hydrometer An instrument for measuring the specific gravity of a lead-acid battery.

Hygroscopic Water absorbing. In motorcycle applications, braking efficiency will be reduced if DOT 3, 4 or 5.1 hydraulic fluid absorbs water from the air - care must be taken to keep new brake fluid in tightly sealed containers.

I

lbf ft Pounds-force feet. An imperial unit of torque. Sometimes written as ft-lbs.

lbf in Pound-force inch. An imperial unit of torque, applied to components where a very low torque is required. Sometimes written as in-lbs.

IC Abbreviation for Integrated Circuit. A single component which incorporates many different electronic components in one unit.

Ignition advance Means of increasing the timing of the spark at higher engine speeds. Done by mechanical means (ATU) on early engines or electronically by the ignition control unit on later engines.

Ignition timing The moment at which the spark plug fires, expressed in the number of crankshaft degrees before the piston reaches the top of its stroke, or in the number of millimetres before the piston reaches the top of its stroke.

Infinity (∞) Description of an open-circuit electrical state, where no continuity exists.

Inverted forks (upside down forks) The sliders or lower legs are held in the yokes and the fork tubes or stanchions are connected to the wheel axle (spindle). Less unsprung weight and stiffer construction than conventional forks.

ISO Abbreviation for International Standards Organisation.

J

JASO Quality standard for 2-stroke oils.

Joule The unit of electrical energy.

Journal The bearing surface of a shaft.

K

Kickstart Mechanical means of turning the engine over for starting purposes. Only usually fitted to mopeds, small capacity motorcycles and off-road motorcycles.

Kill switch Handebar-mounted switch for emergency ignition cut-out. Cuts the ignition circuit on all models, and additionally prevent starter motor operation on others.

km Symbol for kilometre.

kmh Abbreviation for kilometres per hour.

L

Lambda (λ) sensor A sensor fitted in the exhaust system to measure the exhaust gas oxygen content (excess air factor).

Lapping see **Grinding**.

LCD Abbreviation for Liquid Crystal Display.

LED Abbreviation for Light Emitting Diode.

Liner A steel cylinder liner inserted in a aluminium alloy cylinder block.

Locknut A nut used to lock an adjustment nut, or other threaded component, in place.

Lockstops The lugs on the lower triple clamp (yoke) which abut those on the frame, preventing handlebar-to-fuel tank contact.

Lockwasher A form of washer designed to prevent an attaching nut from working loose.

LT Low Tension Description of the electrical circuit from the power supply to the primary winding of the ignition coil.

M

Main bearings The bearings between the crankshaft and crankcase.

Maintenance-free (MF) battery A sealed battery which cannot be topped up.

Manometer Calibrated tubes used to measure intake tract vacuum. Used to synchronise carburettors on multi-cylinder engines.

Micrometer A precision measuring instrument that measures component outside diameters.

MON (Motor Octane Number) A measure of a fuel's resistance to knock.

Monograde oil An oil with a single viscosity, eg SAE80W.

Monoshock A single suspension unit linking the swingarm or suspension linkage to the frame.

mph Abbreviation for miles per hour.

Multigrade oil Having a wide viscosity range (eg 10W40). The W stands for Winter, thus the viscosity ranges from SAE10 when cold to SAE40 when hot.

Multimeter An electrical test instrument with the capability to measure voltage, current and resistance. Some meters also incorporate a continuity tester and buzzer.

N

Needle roller bearing Inner race of caged needle rollers and hardened outer race. Examples of uncaged needle rollers can be found on some engines. Commonly used in rear suspension applications and in two-stroke engines.

Nm Newton metres.

NOx Oxides of Nitrogen. A common toxic pollutant emitted by petrol engines at higher temperatures.

Non-ferrous A metal material which is not made from iron.

O

Octane The measure of a fuel's resistance to knock.

OE (Original Equipment) Relates to components fitted to a motorcycle as standard or replacement parts supplied by the motorcycle manufacturer.

Ohm The unit of electrical resistance. Ohms = Volts ÷ Current.

Ohmmeter An instrument for measuring electrical resistance.

Oil cooler System for diverting engine oil outside of the engine to a radiator for cooling purposes.

Oil injection A system of two-stroke engine lubrication where oil is pump-fed to the engine in accordance with throttle position.

Open-circuit An electrical condition where there is a break in the flow of electricity - no continuity (high resistance).

O-ring A type of sealing ring made of a special rubber-like material; in use, the O-ring is compressed into a groove to provide the sealing action.

Oversize (OS) Term used for piston and ring size options fitted to a rebored cylinder.

Overhead cam (sohc) engine An engine with single camshaft located on top of the cylinder head.

Overhead valve (ohv) engine An engine with the valves located in the cylinder head, but with the camshaft located in the engine block or crankcase.

Oxygen sensor A device installed in the exhaust system which senses the oxygen content in the exhaust and converts this information into an electric current. Also called a Lambda sensor.

P

Periphery The distance round the outside, or circumference.

Pitch The distance between two specified points such as gear teeth, screw threads or chain rollers.

Plastic A type of material made from long chains of molecules, usually with a central chain of carbon.

Plastigauge A thin strip of plastic thread, available in different sizes, used for measuring clearances. For example, a strip of Plastigauge is laid across a bearing journal. The parts are assembled and dismantled; the width of the crushed strip indicates the clearance between journal and bearing.

Pneumatic Containing or operating with air or another gas.

Polarity Either negative or positive earth (ground), determined by which battery lead is connected to the frame (earth return). Modern motorcycles are usually negative earth.

Pre-ignition A situation where the fuel/air mixture ignites before the spark plug fires. Often due to a hot spot in the combustion chamber caused by carbon build-up. Engine has a tendency to 'run-on'.

Pre-load (suspension) The amount a spring is compressed when in the unloaded state. Preload can be applied by gas, spacer or mechanical adjuster.

Premix The method of engine lubrication on older two-stroke engines. Engine oil is mixed with the petrol in the fuel tank in a specific ratio. The fuel/oil mix is sometimes referred to as "petroil".

Pressure The exertion of force by one body on the surface of another. Expressed in bars or psi.

Primary drive Description of the drive from the crankshaft to the clutch. Usually by gear or chain.

Printed circuit board (PCB) A sheet of insulating material on which a circuit is printed or etched, and on which can have components or integrated circuits can be mounted.

PS Pfedestärke - a German interpretation of BHP.

PSI Pounds-force per square inch. Imperial measurement of tyre pressure and cylinder pressure measurement.

PTFE Polytetrafluroethylene. A low friction substance.

Pulse secondary air injection system A process of promoting the burning of excess fuel present in the exhaust gases by routing fresh air into the exhaust ports.

Q

Quartz halogen bulb Tungsten filament surrounded by a halogen gas. Typically used for the headlight.

R

Rack-and-pinion A pinion gear on the end of a shaft that mates with a rack (think of a geared wheel opened up and laid flat). Sometimes used in clutch operating systems.

Radial play Up and down movement about a shaft.

Radial ply tyres Tyre plies run across the tyre (from bead to bead) and around the circumference of the tyre. Less resistant to tread distortion than other tyre types.

Radiator A liquid-to-air heat transfer device designed to reduce the temperature of the coolant in a liquid cooled engine.

Rake A feature of steering geometry - the angle of the steering head in relation to the vertical.

Ratio The proportion of one thing to another, in terms of quantity. Often reduced to a comparison against unity (one) as a base figure.

Rebore Providing a new working surface to the cylinder bore by boring out the old surface. Necessitates the use of oversize piston and rings.

Rebound damping A means of controlling the oscillation of a suspension unit spring after it has been compressed. Resists the spring's natural tendency to bounce back after being compressed.

Rectifier Device for converting the ac output of an alternator into dc for battery charging.

Reed valve An induction system commonly used on two-stroke engines.

Regulator Device for maintaining the charging voltage from the generator or alternator within a specified range.

Relay A electrical device used to switch heavy current on and off by using a low current auxiliary circuit.

Resistance Measured in ohms. An electrical component's ability to pass electrical current.

RON (Research Octane Number) A measure of a fuel's resistance to knock.

rpm revolutions per minute.

Runout The amount of wobble (in-and-out movement) of a wheel or shaft as it's rotated. The amount a shaft rotates 'out-of-true'. The out-of-round condition of a rotating part.

S

SAE (Society of Automotive Engineers) A standard for the viscosity of a fluid.

Sealant A liquid or paste used to prevent leakage at a joint. Sometimes used in conjunction with a gasket.

Service limit Term for the point where a component is no longer useable and must be renewed.

Shaft drive A method of transmitting drive from the transmission to the rear wheel.

Shell bearings Plain bearings consisting of two shell halves. Most often used as big-end and main bearings in a four-stroke engine. Often called bearing inserts.

Shim Thin spacer, commonly used to adjust the clearance or relative positions between two parts. For example, shims inserted into or under tappets or followers to control valve clearances. Clearance is adjusted by changing the thickness of the shim.

Short-circuit An electrical condition where current shorts to earth (ground) bypassing the circuit components.

Skimming Process to correct warpage or repair a damaged surface, eg on brake discs or drums.

Slide-hammer A special puller that screws into or hooks onto a component such as a shaft or bearing; a heavy sliding handle on the shaft bottoms against the end of the shaft to knock the component free.

Small-end bearing The bearing in the upper end of the connecting rod at its joint with the gudgeon pin.

Spalling Damage to camshaft lobes or bearing journals shown as pitting of the working surface.

Specific gravity (SG) The state of charge of the electrolyte in a lead-acid battery. A measure of the electrolyte's density compared with water.

Straight-cut gears Common type gear used on gearbox shafts and for oil pump and water pump drives.

Stainless steel A tough durable steel that does not rust and is highly stain resistant. Usually incorporates at least 25% of the alloying metal, chromium.

Stanchion The inner sliding part of the front forks, held by the yokes. Often called a fork tube.

Stoichiometric ratio The optimum chemical air/fuel ratio for a petrol engine, said to be 14.7 parts of air to 1 part of fuel.

Sulphuric acid The liquid (electrolyte) used in a lead-acid battery. Poisonous and extremely corrosive.

Surface grinding (lapping) Process to correct a warped gasket face, commonly used on cylinder heads.

T

Tapered-roller bearing Tapered inner race of caged needle rollers and separate tapered outer race. Examples of taper roller bearings can be found on steering heads.

Tappet A cylindrical component which transmits motion from the cam to the valve stem, either directly or via a pushrod and rocker arm. Also called a cam follower.

TCS Traction Control System. An electronically-controlled system which senses wheel spin and reduces engine speed accordingly.

TDC Top Dead Centre denotes that the piston is at its highest point in the cylinder.

Tensile strength The strength of a material when it is stretched.

Thread-locking compound Solution applied to fastener threads to prevent slackening. Select type to suit application.

Thrust face A working surface of a piston, bearing, shim etc, which takes the thrust and any rubbing action.

Thrust washer A washer positioned between two moving components on a shaft. For example, between gear pinions on gearshaft.

Timing chain See **Cam Chain.**

Timing light Stroboscopic lamp for carrying out ignition timing checks with the engine running.

Top-end A description of an engine's cylinder block, head and valve gear components.

Torque Turning or twisting force about a shaft.

Torque setting A prescribed tightness specified by the motorcycle manufacturer to ensure that the bolt or nut is secured correctly. Undertightening can result in the bolt or nut coming loose or a surface not being sealed. Overtightening can result in stripped threads, distortion or damage to the component being retained.

Torx key A six-point wrench.

Tracer A stripe of a second colour applied to a wire insulator to distinguish that wire from another one with the same colour insulator. For example, Br/W is often used to denote a brown insulator with a white tracer.

Trail A feature of steering geometry. Distance from the steering head axis to the tyre's central contact point.

Triple clamps The cast components which extend from the steering head and support the fork stanchions or tubes. Often called fork yokes.

Turbocharger A centrifugal device, driven by exhaust gases, that pressurises the intake air. Normally used to increase the power output from a given engine displacement.

TWI Abbreviation for Tyre Wear Indicator. Indicates the location of the tread depth indicator bars on tyres.

U

Universal joint or U-joint (UJ) A double-pivoted connection for transmitting power from a driving to a driven shaft through an angle. Typically found in shaft drive assemblies.

Unsprung weight Anything not supported by the bike's suspension (ie the wheel, tyres, brakes, final drive and bottom (moving) part of the suspension).

V

Vacuum gauges Clock-type gauges for measuring intake tract vacuum. Used for carburettor synchronisation on multi-cylinder engines.

Valve A device through which the flow of liquid, gas or vacuum may be stopped, started or regulated by a moveable part that opens, shuts or partially obstructs one or more ports or passageways. The intake and exhaust valves in the cylinder head are of the poppet type.

Valve clearance The clearance between the valve tip (the end of the valve stem) and the rocker arm or tappet/follower. The valve clearance is measured when the valve is closed. The correct clearance is important - if too small the valve won't close fully and will burn out, whereas if too large noisy operation will result.

Valve lift The amount a valve is lifted off its seat by the camshaft lobe.

Valve timing The exact setting for the opening and closing of the valves in relation to piston position.

Vernier caliper A precision measuring instrument that measures inside and outside dimensions. Not quite as accurate as a micrometer, but more convenient.

VIN Vehicle Identification Number. Term for the bike's engine and frame numbers.

Viscosity The thickness of a liquid or its resistance to flow.

Volt A unit for expressing electrical "pressure" in a circuit. Volts = current x ohms.

W

Water pump A mechanically-driven device for moving coolant around the engine.

Watt A unit for expressing electrical power. Watts = volts x current.

Wear limit see **Service limit**

Wet liner A liquid-cooled engine design where the pistons run in liners which are directly surrounded by coolant **(see illustration).**

Wheelbase Distance from the centre of the front wheel to the centre of the rear wheel.

Wiring harness or loom Describes the electrical wires running the length of the motorcycle and enclosed in tape or plastic sheathing. Wiring coming off the main harness is usually referred to as a sub harness.

Woodruff key A key of semi-circular or square section used to locate a gear to a shaft. Often used to locate the alternator rotor on the crankshaft.

Wrist pin Another name for gudgeon or piston pin.

Note: *References throughout this index relate to Chapter•page number*

Preserving Our Motoring Heritage

< The Model J Duesenberg Derham Tourster. Only eight of these magnificent cars were ever built – this is the only example to be found outside the United States of America

Almost every car you've ever loved, loathed or desired is gathered under one roof at the Haynes Motor Museum. Over 300 immaculately presented cars and motorbikes represent every aspect of our motoring heritage, from elegant reminders of bygone days, such as the superb Model J Duesenberg to curiosities like the bug-eyed BMW Isetta. There are also many old friends and flames. Perhaps you remember the 1959 Ford Popular that you did your courting in? The magnificent 'Red Collection' is a spectacle of classic sports cars including AC, Alfa Romeo, Austin Healey, Ferrari, Lamborghini, Maserati, MG, Riley, Porsche and Triumph.

A Perfect Day Out

Each and every vehicle at the Haynes Motor Museum has played its part in the history and culture of Motoring. Today, they make a wonderful spectacle and a great day out for all the family. Bring the kids, bring Mum and Dad, but above all bring your camera to capture those golden memories for ever. You will also find an impressive array of motoring memorabilia, a comfortable 70 seat video cinema and one of the most extensive transport book shops in Britain. The Pit Stop Cafe serves everything from a cup of tea to wholesome, home-made meals or, if you prefer, you can enjoy the large picnic area nestled in the beautiful rural surroundings of Somerset.

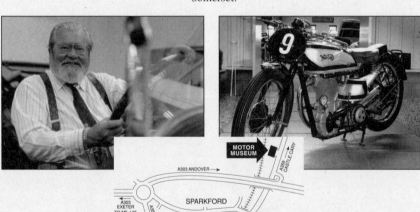

> John Haynes O.B.E., Founder and Chairman of the museum at the wheel of a Haynes Light 12.

< The 1936 490cc sohc-engined International Norton – well known for its racing success

The Museum is situated on the A359 Yeovil to Frome road at Sparkford, just off the A303 in Somerset. It is about 40 miles south of Bristol, and 25 minutes drive from the M5 intersection at Taunton.
Open 9.30am - 5.30pm (10.00am - 4.00pm Winter) 7 days a week, *except Christmas Day, Boxing Day and New Years Day*
Special rates available for schools, coach parties and outings Charitable Trust No. 292048